Catch the Jew!

Tuvia Tenenbom

gefen
publishing house בית הוצאה לאור
JERUSALEM ◆ NEW YORK
Est. 1981

Cover drawing: Shay Charka
Typesetting: Raphaël Freeman, Renana Typesetting
Photographs in book taken by: Florian Krauss, Jan Sulzer, and Isi Tenenbom

ISBN: 978-965-229-798-3

5 7 9 8 6 4

Gefen Publishing House Ltd.
6 Hatzvi Street
Jerusalem 94386, Israel
972-2-538-0247
orders@gefenpublishing.com

Gefen Books
11 Edison Place
Springfield, NJ 07081
516-593-1234
orders@gefenpublishing.com

www.gefenpublishing.com

Printed in Israel

Send for our free catalog

Library of Congress Control Number: 2014954970

*This book is dedicated to my wife and partner,
Isi Tenenbom, who never feared joining me wherever the
wind blew, safe or not, ever sharing with me the brightest
of ideas and offering me the loveliest of smiles.*

Praise for Catch the Jew!

REVIEWS OF THE HEBREW EDITION OF *CATCH THE JEW!*

"A literary sensation." *Haaretz*

"A brilliant book." *Maariv*

"The most important book I have read in the last five years."
Channel 2

"The best book in the bookstore!" *Galei Zahal*

"The humor in Catch the Jew! is razor sharp, it is highly intellectual and it's so funny that it will bring tears to your eyes.... Tuvia is curious as a cat, sly as a fox, friendly as a Labrador, and is also a man with seismographic sensitivities." *Mida*

"One of the funniest books I've read in years – and one of the most heartbreaking. Here is the Middle East conflict as you have never experienced it before. Tuvia Tenenbom is a brilliant satirist and an extraordinary reporter. Beware: This book is like a pungent French cheese – for connoisseurs of truth only."
Yossi Klein Halevi, senior fellow, Shalom Hartman Institute

"A fascinating, picturesque book by a picturesque author."
Yedioth Ahronoth

"Funny, shocking, depressing documentation of anti-Semitism and self-hatred." *Makor Rishon*

"Run to your nearest bookstore and pick up a copy.... I haven't laughed this hard out loud in a long time.... This book is a must for anyone who wants to formulate an independent opinion on the reality in this region." *Israel Hayom*

"It's been a long time since a book affected me so deeply." *Walla*

Tuvia Tenenbom is a political dramatist and journalist. His articles and essays have been published in newspapers including *Die Zeit* of Germany, *Corriere della Sera* of Italy, and *Yedioth Ahronoth* of Israel as well as on various internet sites. In addition, Tuvia is a columnist for *Zeit Online* and *Forward*. Tuvia, who holds advanced degrees in both fine arts and science, is also the founder and artistic director of The Jewish Theater of New York.

,

Contents

Acknowledgments and Thanks

MY THANKS TO ALL THOSE WHO OPENED FOR ME THE DOORS TO THE HIDDEN rooms of their hearts and minds, helping me navigate the Holy Land's maze of never-ending paths and roads: spiritual leaders and prostitutes, professors and miracle makers, warriors and storytellers, talkers and doers, racists and lovers, peace activists of every kind and politicians of every sort, people of faith and people of doubt, seekers of truth and merchants of lies, women of many minds and men of many colors, young and old, rich and poor.

They include the stray cats in my garden, Jibril Rajoub and Moshe Feiglin, David Batsri and Lars Faaborg-Andersen, Brother Josef and Amos Oz, Ahmad Tibi and Ayelet Shaked, Zeev Elkin and Gideon Levy, Hanan Ashrawi and Nir Barkat, Michael Ben Ari and Aluf Benn, Shlomo Sand and Meir Porush.

I also thank my dedicated video crew – Debbie Meininger, Jan Sulzer, and Florian Krauss – who followed me with their lenses any hour day or night; and Dr. Illa Sanger, who spent many days going over the text and graciously offered her comments as well as to David Mills for his enlightening comments. Special thanks to the best mother-in-law one can dream of, the amazing Isa Lowy, who is always here to help and lavishes kindness on all present.

Introduction

MY NAME IS TUVIA. I WAS BORN AND RAISED IN ISRAEL TO AN ULTRA-ORTHODOX, anti-Zionist family, and grew up in the most elitist neighborhood of ultra-Orthodoxy at the time. My father was a rabbi, as were many of our neighbors, and we were the ones who represented God to the rest of humanity. My grandfather refused to come to Israel because he did not want to live with Zionists, and the Nazis rewarded him and most of his family with on-the-spot burials. My other grandfather fled his homeland just before the Nazis arrived, but those who were left behind never showed up again.

My mother was a Holocaust survivor, my father was a refugee, and if not for Adolf Hitler I wouldn't exist. I come from a long line of European rabbis, and I was groomed to become a rabbi as well. This Master Plan worked for a few years, when I excelled in every act imaginable against non-believers, spending day and night studying God's laws and jealously protecting Him from all His earthly enemies.

But then, as my former co-believers assert, Satan got hold of me and I decided that God was strong enough to take care of Himself without my help. Thirty-three years ago I left Israel for the United States, hoping to dedicate my life to the pursuit of science and the arts, both of which had been totally forbidden to me in my former neighborhood. In the fifteen years that followed, I attended various universities and studied various disciplines, ranging from mathematics

1

and computer science to theater and literature. Two decades ago I founded the Jewish Theater of New York, which I direct and manage with my wife, Isi.

In addition to being a dramatist, I'm also a journalist and columnist for various media in the USA and in Germany.

In 2012 Suhrkamp Verlag published my book *Allein unter Deutschen*, which went on to become a *Spiegel* bestseller for four months. *Allein unter Deutschen* is a six-month walking study of Germany today, its people and their most intimate thoughts. It was published in the United States as *I Sleep in Hitler's Room*.

My very dedicated editor at Suhrkamp, Winfried Hörning, asked me last year if I would like to do a similar study of Israel and its people. To spend six months in Israel, a country I left so many years ago and only sporadically have visited for extremely short durations, was both a frightening challenge and an exciting opportunity. I asked Winfried how much Suhrkamp would pay me to do this job and he gave a figure I didn't like; then he gave me another figure that I did like.

I am going to Israel.

With the exception of finding a home that would serve as my base, I haven't planned anything. Let the winds carry me to wherever they blow. I will do my best to let the facts and realities reveal themselves to me and to be objective about what I find. If I like what I see or not, I will report what I see, not what I like. But I will share with you, my reader, what I think and feel at various turns.

My name, as I stated before, is Tuvia – but this is between you and me. Tuvia is a Hebrew name meaning "Goodness of God," and is not always safe. To protect myself, I might at times give interviewees a different accent, let's say, or a dialect version of my name, but they will always know that I'm an author and journalist and that what they say might one day appear in space and freeze in time.

Before going to Israel, a land internationally known as that of an occupying force, I decided to spend a few days in another occupied land, so that I'll have an entity with which I can compare later on. I love mountains – their sheer size makes me be humble – and I go to South Tyrol, a parcel of land occupied by Italy in 1918 and never given back. Like the rest of Tyrol, it is one of the most gorgeous places on Earth, and its Italian occupation is letter-perfect: nobody knows it's occupied. The Italians have signed treaties and agreements left and right and have cleared every legal issue there ever was. They even gave residents some extra rights so they shut up, and before long the German-speaking South Tyroleans started calling themselves Italian. Which is all nice, fine and dandy.

Could this work for Israel too?

I take my time to eat and drink with some Tyrolean natives and after three "milk with water" (beer) and two of the most delicious portions of "Hitlerschmarrn," they start screaming that they've been cheated by the damned Italians.

I guess occupation doesn't work.

I take my Lederhosen, put them in my suitcase in case I'd need a reminder, and now I'm ready to go.

Join me for the ride, *bitte*, and let us all hope that it will be exciting and enlightening indeed.

Istanbul Airport. I love the place!

Look here: ten ladies with niqabs beat the heat of their clothes by licking delicious-looking Turkish ice cream. This is delightfully sensual, believe you me. The men, crazy creatures of nature, go to a small area called Terrace to drag on their cigarettes in ecstatic body motions. Nonsmokers, with or without niqab, sip coffee at $5 a pop, as never-ending waves of women, with hijabs of every color, get busy shopping for merchandise they never knew they needed.

It's boarding time to Tel Aviv, but only about ten people are sitting at the lounge. I think I read about this situation in Israeli papers: Israeli citizens boycott Turkish Airlines because for the last few years the Turkish leader, Erdoğan, has constantly criticized Israel. I would never have believed Israelis would ever boycott anything Turkish, but now I see it. Israeli media, I can tell, are awesomely accurate.

Ahead of me I see three guys engaged in a lively conversation and I sit next to them. I figure these guys know each other, why shouldn't I know them too?

What's the first thing I should do once in Israel? I ask them.

Michel, a Catholic architect married to a Jewish Israeli woman, is very excited to share his thoughts with me: "You want to know what's the first thing you should do once you land in Israel? Get a plane ticket out!"

Thank you, but I have to be there. What should I expect to see? "Heat!"

And then there is Zaki, a Bahá'í, and he tells me that his family has lived in Israel longer than Israel has existed. One hundred fifty years, to be exact. Bahá'ís, he teaches me, are not allowed to live in Israel – it's against their religion – but his family does. His great-great grandfather was Bahá'í's cook! What an honor.

With them is Hamudi, which in Hebrew means "sweetie," who is an Arab Israeli and a Muslim. "Hamudi," he corrects me, does not mean sweet. "It's short for Muhammad." Maybe I should also find a short nickname for myself. How does Tobi sound?

There's a loud announcement now that the gate is about to close. I walk over to the gate, but the three men here don't move. At the gate, how strange, a zillion people are queuing. How did all these Jews sneak in here? And what are they doing in Istanbul to start with? Weren't they boycotting this city? Maybe Israeli media are not awesomely accurate, after all.

As I board the aircraft it appears to me that this plane is about to explode from all those Chosen People inside it. I never knew that so many Jews even existed.

The aircraft is packed but for a couple of seats, and as its doors are just about to close the Three Musketeers from the lounge schlep themselves in. There's one empty seat next to me, one behind me, and one in front of me. Guess where these three are going to sit? They look at me, with bewildered eyes, as if I were a CIA agent who all along has known the seating arrangement of this plane.

Hamudi speaks unto me, important man that I am: "Israel doesn't treat Muslims and Jews equally at the airport. Muslims are stopped and interrogated when they land in Israel." I guess he's preparing himself to be taken to the side upon landing.

The plane lands shortly after 3:00 a.m., and the Israeli security personnel stop only one passenger for an interrogation. No, it's not the brown Hamudi but a young blond lady.

Hamudi and I exchange looks, and I can tell he's quite disappointed. He has prepared for every possible question the security people could ask him, and all they care about is a young blonde.

I walk out of the airport and it's cool outside. The heat I was expecting went the way of the blond lady: disappeared.

It's quite a strange feeling to land in the country of your birth. I hear Hebrew, no German or English, and I can hear the sounds of my childhood. In an instant I transform into a baby, and see my life as in a short YouTube clip. Baby, boy, teenager: the person I once was and the years that have passed are now playing back.

Slowly I wake up to reality and go to look for a cab that will take

me to my abode for the next six months. My destination: a Templar house in the German Colony of Jerusalem.

I learned about this house while in New York. It's an old house, built by German Templars who long ago came to the Holy Land in the hope of personally greeting Jesus Christ. I like stories like this, and I took the house.

From Germany to the German Colony. Sounds a bit strange, I know.

As I reach my new home, I drop my suitcases, take a short rest, and then go out to walk the ground I left so many years ago.

On a wall on a nearby street I see this note: "Excuse me: Is God satisfied with your clothes?" How should I know? And then I see this poster: "Merciful nation of Israel, please pray for my father that he gets rid of his iPhone and Internet so that our family remains whole."

I take my iPhone and capture this poster with it.

This is not Hamburg, nor Istanbul; this is a Holy City. Yes, this is Jerusalem. "Yerushalayim" is how Jews call it in Hebrew, "Al-Quds" is how the Arabs call it in Arabic, and "Jerusalem" is how most others do.

When I left Israel over three decades ago, my first stop was Amsterdam's Red Light District. Now back here, I go to the Old City.

Gate One

*What happens when the feminine side of God, the son
of God, and the messenger of God meet a sexy German
girl who helps the Arabs because she loves the Jews?*

"DON'T WORRY, BE JEWISH" AND "FREE PALESTINE" ARE TWO OF MANY CONTRA-
dicting T-shirts I see in a souvenir and clothing shop once I'm on the
other side of the Old City's walls built by Suleiman the Magnificent,
the Ottoman sultan, over the ruined walls of earlier periods.

Inside the walls, as I walk, is the souk. What's a souk? Most English
dictionaries translate this word as market, but this is because English
translators don't have a healthy, vivid imagination. A better translation,
if you're an English speaker, is this: "an ancient shopping mall." Yeah.
But, please, don't come here if you're looking for a pink bikini or an
iPhone, as this is not the best place to get these items. You should
come here if you're looking for the Virgin Mary made of virgin olive
wood (don't ask me what this means) or if you're in the mood to smell
spices usually available only in heaven.

The architecture of this souk will capture your eyes and make you
believe in legends and myths, which could be very beneficial to you.
This souk is darkish, made of ancient holy stones, arches everywhere,
and if the traders didn't charge you imaginative prices for everything
that meets your eye, you'd think you were in paradise.

Come think of it, a Red Light District would fit here very nicely. I can vividly imagine it. Really.

A few steps ahead of me I see a group of men and women who don't move. They seem to be tourists with cameras and maps, and I join them. I have no idea where they're planning to go but assume that since they paid for this tour, it's probably worth something and I blend in.

Soon their plan becomes clear to me. They want to go on a tour of the tunnels adjacent to the Western Wall, a remnant of the holiest Jewish shrine in history. Also known as the Wailing Wall, this is the place where the Shkhina, the Holy Presence, has resided for the past two thousand years. What is the Holy Presence? This is not totally clear, though it is usually referred to as the Feminine Side of God. Some mystics go a step further and say this is the Wife of God.

A man, the tour guide I guess, takes us to archeological paths around the Wall, way beneath the ground.

We are in Har Habayit (Temple Mount), where the Jewish Temple once stood on top of this mountain. Enemies of the Jews twice destroyed the Temple, the man says to us, but first he would like to tell us the history of the mountain itself, a history that precedes the Temple period by thousands of years.

*   *   *

Genius that I am, I immediately realize: this is not Times Square. I'm in a different world. Totally and absolutely different, for the "show" I'm about to see is not a Broadway musical.

The man speaks: "Everything was created from here. The universe was formed from a rock on this mountain, and it is here that God tested Abraham, when he asked him to sacrifice his only son." The biblical Garden of Eden is here, and it is here that the first human being, Adam, was roaming aimlessly until God made him fall asleep and created a woman out of one of his bones. And it is here that Adam and Eve walked around naked, made love all day and all night and started humanity. It is on this Holy Mountain that the sexual hormones started being active. If you think of this in depth, here's where the first Red Light District of history started.

On a more serious side, it's here that your culture and mine first started. No matter if you or I believe in God or do not, it is here that the foundation of our mutual culture started. If not for this very mountain and if not for this very land, there would be no Judaism, no Christianity, no Islam, no European culture, no American culture, no Western culture as we know it, and no Eastern culture as it is now practiced. If not for this mountain, and what's on it and underneath it, Buddha still might have come into existence, and cannibals might still have existed, but today you and I could be fanatic worshippers of the elephant, the stone, the wind, or the sun.

We are at the beginning of the tunnel and the man, who is a guide indeed, is using small pieces of wood in front of him and is aided by video animations behind him. He explains everything to us as images of the destroyed Temple show up on a screen and on a table with a model version of same. He speaks to us about the Second Temple, destroyed by the Romans in 70 CE, which was built on the ruins of the First Temple (destroyed by the Babylonians in 586 BCE):

"The Temple, right here, was destroyed, burned to the ground."

The screen shows fires consuming the Second Temple.

"The Temple was built by King Herod, who employed an untold number of skilled workers to create a massive, magnificent, colossal structure."

The Temple slowly disappears on the video, crumbling to pieces – except for one wall. The guide takes a little wooden structure, a mosque, and puts it on top of the ruins.

"Many years later the Muslims built a mosque right above the ruined Temple."

Yes, this is not Broadway. This is, if anything, an off-off-off-Broadway presentation. But this is not a show. The little images this guide is playing with have caused millions upon millions of people to lose their lives in the past, and many more millions are most likely to continue this tradition in the future.

A man dressed in a "Peace" T-shirt is listening intensely. A teenage tourist is yawning; he's probably missing his Facebook friends.

"Any questions?" the guide asks.

When I was a religious kid, I wondered about two biblical statues, the cherubs, stationed in a section of the Temple known as the Holy of Holies. Statues are totally forbidden in Judaism; why then did they exist in the Temple, God's own house?

I ask the guide, who's now using wooden pieces resembling structures that existed two thousand years ago, if he also happened to have miniature models of the cherubs.

The "Peace" tourist likes my question.

"Where are you from?" he asks, as if he has just discovered the most amazing man in the world.

Germany, I say.

Yes, I have this strange habit: I enjoy playing with nationalities. By a chance of nature, I have an unidentifiable accent and miraculously people believe me when I tell them that I'm Austrian, Bulgarian, Chinese, or whatever country I happen to fancy at the moment. Recently I saw an international poll claiming that the majority of people interviewed believe Germany to be the greatest country on earth. Why shouldn't I be a German these days?

But Mr. Peace looks at me, totally disappointed. He doesn't like Germany, I can tell, and I'm really offended.

And you, where are you from?

"Britain," he says with pride as he moves away from this ugly German.

Too bad we Germans lost World War II.

Well, I'm not from Germany, I'm from Israel, and I'm into cherubs. But the guide doesn't have cherubs. Sorry. Maybe the cherubs, which according to the biblical account are some kind of creature with wings, have just flown away.

* * *

The guide leads us on a walk through tunnels that never end and he keeps on talking about the amazing skills with which King Herod built the place. He talks about Herod as if Herod still existed. "King Herod decides" and "King Herod builds" and "King Herod wants" – in present tense. King Herod, he also tells us, is a genius of geometry and a megalomaniac: he wants to build the most spectacular temple there ever was.

As the tunnels get more freakish – no sun here and no place to stop for a Starbucks or Jacobs coffee – we're told that Herod is also a very mean man. He kills almost all the rabbis around. "Almost" means that he leaves one rabbi alive, but not before he gouges his eyes out.

A nice guy, no doubt.

We pass by a portion of the Wall that is made of a huge stone, 13.3 meters long and weighing 580 tons. In those days there were no cranes, and I can't even fathom how King Herod pulled this off.

The length of the Western Wall, including the parts that you can see only from here: half a kilometer. Just amazing. Why did King Herod, a non-Jew, bother to build such a huge thing?

"He was a Jew."

Is that why he killed all the rabbis, except for the one he blinded?

"King Herod converted to Judaism!"

This is an important answer: born Jews don't gouge out the eyes of others, only gentiles do.

Why would a rabbi killer and an eye gouger build a temple?

"This is a long story."

Tell me!

The guide gladly obliges.

After King Herod had done what he did to the rabbis, he disguised himself as a simple man and walked past the rabbi he had joyfully blinded and asked him a question: Would the rabbi agree with him, this simpleton, that King Herod was a terrible man and therefore should not be obeyed? The blind rabbi answered: King Herod is our king and we have to obey him.

Impressed and touched, he asked the rabbi what King Herod should do to absolve himself for the horrible things he had done to the rabbis. The rabbi answered that if the king were to rebuild the Temple he would be forgiven.

King Herod immediately moved into action. (King Herod reconstructed the Second Temple, which was in place as of 516 BCE.)

Good story, I must admit.

As the tour ends I speak with Osnat, one of the tourists.

Tell me, in one sentence: What is "Israel"?

"Oh, this is not a simple question. I have to think about it."

Don't think. Just shoot!

"Israelis care for each other."

Other nations, let's say Germans, don't?

"No."

Only the Jews have this quality?

"Yes."

Before I left Germany, a famous German gave me this tip: "Israelis," he told me, "are the only people on Earth who don't care for other people. When you are there, try to find out why." He and this woman, I think, would make for a perfect match.

Outside the tunnel is the Western Wall that we all know, the one you see in so many pictures: a wall where Jews pray. They stand here, awed by the Shkhina, and pray to God: "May You build the Temple soon, in our lifetime. Amen." Hopefully, nobody will have to go blind for it to happen.

Other people, more sophisticated, also write notes and stick them between the stones of the Wall. If you want to send a letter to God, this is better than FedEx because His Shkhina gets your letter directly.

On the Western Wall plaza, a group of American Jews is passing me by. They love to speak Hebrew, their kind of Hebrew. Take a listen to this one, talking to his friend: "Let's meet yesterday night. Okay?"

* * *

The Western Wall is only a tiny part of the huge compound now known as al-Aqsa, named for al-Aqsa Mosque in al-Haram as-Sharif (what the Jews call "Temple Mount") that was first built in roughly 679 CE, as the third-holiest place in Islam and where I go to pay my respects on the following day. It is from this place that the Messenger of God, the Prophet Muhammad, flew to heaven, after he had arrived there with a heavenly animal from Mecca. I arrive there by taxi.

The cabbie tries speaking with me in Hebrew, thinking I'm a Jew, but I let him know he can't be any further from the truth. Immediately he switches to Arabic and asks if I want to get off at "the gate." I have no clue what gate he has in mind but I ask no questions and just say yes.

Within minutes we reach a road in east Jerusalem and he tells me we've arrived. Where's the gate? Allah surely knows, but I don't. I walk up the road and somehow find a gate, or something like it.

Why did the cabbie drop me before the gate? I don't know. What I do know is this: at the gate there are cops, Israeli cops.

"Are you a Muslim?" one of them asks.

I am! I answer without hesitation.

"Know the Quran?"

Of course!

"Show me."

How in the world am I supposed to show him? And why should I? But he has a gun and I don't. So I say: *Ashahdu al-la Allah illallah uAshahdu an Muhammad-ar rasulallah* (I testify that there is no God but Allah and Muhammad is His prophet). This is a declaration of faith and according to Islamic law, if a man says this, he becomes a Muslim – in case he isn't yet.

This should satisfy the gun holder but the problem is that cops are no imams and religious law is not their domain. "Say the Fatiha," he barks at me, as if I were a Jewish dog.

It's been a long time since I studied Islam and I don't exactly remember it beyond the very beginning.

I try nevertheless. I say: *Bismillah ar-rahman ar-rahim, al-hamdu lillahi rabil alameen* (in the name of Allah, the compassionate and merciful, praise be to Allah lord of the worlds).

Should be good enough, I think. But the cop says: "Continue!"

Who does he think he is, Allah? Why should I pray to him?

I don't and he talks to his colleague, discussing why I behave so strangely. They talk and talk and finally they decide: "You're Christian. No entry."

But I want to pray to Allah!

Well, they say, if I want to pray that much I should enter the mosque via the Jew and Christian entrance. But the Infidels' entrance, I protest, closes at 11:00 a.m., in fifty-five minutes.

The cops are not impressed. The walk is only twenty-nine minutes from here, one of them says, and he points at the road I should take.

I look at the name of the road. Via Dolorosa.

I am to walk the way of that old Jew, Christ.

I walk and walk and walk. Twenty-nine minutes are soon over and no infidels' entry in sight.

I spot another entrance, for Muslims only, some feet away. I swear my alliance to the Prophet, loud enough for the Israeli prime minister in west Jerusalem to hear me, but the cop at the entrance is obviously deaf, yelling at me: "Fatiha!"

Again!

I try once more, citing the beginning of the Fatiha quickly, the way some Hasidic Jews in synagogues cite prayers when they loudly recite just the beginning of prayers, only this new cop doesn't know Hasidic Jews. He says: "Don't stop, continue!"

I stare at him, as if he had just offended my most precious religious feelings.

He looks at me, not sure what kind of creature I am, and goes to discuss the matter with his colleague in Hebrew. They discuss between themselves who I could be and decide: half Muslim, half Christian. They point the way for me. The Via Dolorosa.

But I am a Muslim, on both sides of the family! I protest, pleading for my life the way Jesus must have pleaded for his life to the Roman rulers.

"Show me your passport," the cop softens up.

I have no passport.

"Via Dolorosa!"

Having no choice, I continue the way of the old Jew until I reach the gate of the infidels, and finally I enter.

I take a short breath to think a little.

This is not South Tyrol, I say to myself. The Israelis are no Italians and the Arabs are no Tyroleans. Here the ones occupied, the Arabs, dictate to the occupiers, the Jews, that they, the Jews, must protect them, the Arabs, from their brethren, the other Jews, and from the Christians.

I'm in the plaza. To my right is a silver building and to my left is the golden-domed building. I approach a Muslim man and ask him in Arabic which of the two is al-Aqsa. He asks me if I'm a Muslim and I say that of course I am! Russian? He asks. No, German. His eyes light up. Welcome! Al-Aqsa, he says, is the silver building and the golden one is the Dome of the Rock. The rock under the dome, I now think of what the Jewish guide told us yesterday, is where the world started.

I keep on going and walking, around the square and the surrounding areas. Looks like paradise here. Every few steps there's a sign, in Arabic only, reminding believers that it's forbidden to spit here. I'm not sure why there is a need for so many signs forbidding the act of spitting but I guess the locals like to spit. I don't know. Eleven o'clock soon passes and I successfully evade the Israeli police, who by this time have cleared the area of non-believers. Slowly I make my way to pray a little – for the Arabs, the Christians and the Jews. As I reach the Dome, an Arab catches me. "Your time is over!" he yells. "Out of here!"

And just before this guy too tells me to recite the Fatiha, I decide I've had enough and make a U-turn.

I walk out, crossing pathways that are magnificent in their beauty. I realize I'm unwittingly approaching another entry to the mosque. An Arab kid, maybe six years old, stops me. "Are you Muslim?" he demands. Yep. Now I have to recite the Fatiha to a kid.

Go get busy with Facebook, I curse him in my heart but say nothing. This is a holy city, and this kid may be a prophet. That's the last thing I need in life, to get into a fight with a prophet.

I keep walking till I spot a coffee shop frequented by local Muslims. I'm local too, a German Templar in the Holy City waiting for the Messiah, and until He comes I need coffee to keep my energies up.

I drink one cup of coffee after another. Arabic coffee, let me share with you, is much better than any Starbucks, Jacobs, or any of the Italian varieties I have ever tasted.

I drink so much coffee that, naturally, nature calls. I ask the waiter for the men's room. "Are you Muslim?" he asks.

Yes, I am, by Allah!

I'm declaring my Islamic faith today more than the most devoted of Taliban in Afghanistan.

"Go to al-Aqsa."

I was there but the Jewish police think that I'm only half a Muslim. They get on my nerves!

"Show them your passport."

I don't have it on me.

"Then you have to go to the Jewish Wall."

I walk out of the coffee house in the direction of the Jewish Wall and I see Arabic graffiti on an Arab wall outside the coffee shop: "Soon Al-Quds will be free!"

"Al-Quds" (meaning the holy) is Jerusalem. "Free" means free of Jews.

And I wonder: Who's going to protect the mosques from people like me once the Jews are out? Allah knows.

Three little girls, maybe five years old, pass by. They're beautiful, like little angels, and all three are dressed in a hijab. Such an early age and they are already considered a sexual temptation.

I need a toilet and I would rather not go to churches, Jewish Walls or Arab Walls. There must be a toilet here somewhere; not all the people of this city urinate in their God's abode.

I'm determined to find a toilet in a non-religious place. I keep on walking till I pass a house with a man sitting outside and it looks to me as though he's guarding it. If he's guarding the place, I assume, it must be a nice place with a nice toilet inside.

Simple logic, isn't it?

I follow a man who's friendly to the guard, as if the man and I are of the same family, and I enter.

* * *

No toilet yet, but a class. A sign on the wall says this is Al-Quds University. A university must have a toilet, I think, but there's nobody I can ask about the toilet since everybody is attending a lecture.

Well, I'll have to sit through the lecture and I sit down. The lecture, part of a series financed by Europeans, is quite interesting. Here I get to hear about the intifada, about the occupation, about dignity, about the Palestinian "experience of denials of their basic rights," enthusiastically taught by Palestinian experts from Europe. During a short break in the lecture one of the teachers, a Brit, tells me that he's actually a Palestinian, born in the Galilee. This would make you an Israeli, right? I ask. No, he says. A Brit? Neither. He lives in Britain, paid by the Europeans, and his mission is to free Palestine. But before he frees Palestine, I need a toilet.

Have you got a toilet here, Professor?

"Yes, go upstairs and you'll see it."

Great. I go up there.

The toilet is clean and I can use it without being asked to recite the Fatiha or put a skullcap over my head. Once done, I return to the class. There are a few professors here, plus food and drink – as much as anybody would want, all lovingly paid for by generous Europeans.

Number of Palestinians participating in the class: two. This is the only class in the world where each student gets a number of professors just for himself.

A painting of an olive tree is hanging on the wall, with the line: "We won't leave."

A laptop and projector are used. The lecturer speaks in Arabic as slides come up in English. As with the guide to the Western Wall, technology is very important in telling a good story. There's also a video camera here, which looks quite expensive but is not in use today. Maybe tomorrow.

There's no human being on the seat next me, just a book, a law book by Raja Shehadeh, which was published by the Institute for Palestine Studies in Washington, DC. The book's title is *Occupier's Law: Israel and the West Bank.*

I open this American book. It was edited, it says, by the International Commission of Jurists in Geneva, Switzerland. This is not a dry law book, as I had expected, but a really juicy book about Israeli brutality toward Palestinians, the maltreatment of Arab prisoners, the harassment of Palestinian students, about house demolitions and all kinds of other things that don't go very well with coffee and baked goods.

On the next empty chair there's another book: *The Cambridge Companion to Hannah Arendt.* How did she get in here?

With there being hardly any students, a lively discussion flares up between the guest professors, talking to each other because the two students present are not into anything, about occupation and suffering. They don't seem very suffering to me, but what do I know. I just came in to urinate and by chance found these learned men and women.

To add visuals to the discussion the professors have been engaged in, a projected image of ladies in hijab, plus a man, shines on the wall.

If I understand correctly the intellectual talk here, the hijab-covered ladies are flaming feminists.

And I am Mormon.

Why the European Commission, the sponsor of this event, would fly European professors into Jerusalem to talk to each other instead of hosting them, let's say, in South Tyrol is a big mystery to me.

I go to the office nearby to figure out what kind of university this really is, with two students to a class. A man sits by his desk and gladly answers my questions. "The Occupation," he says, talking of the Israelis, "is throwing Muslim residents out of their houses in east Jerusalem and putting Jews in instead."

When? Now?

"All the time!"

How many houses?

"Many!"

How many?

"Everywhere."

How many?

"Thirty!"

Thirty?

"Thirty."

How long have they, the occupiers, been around here? I mean, if we count from 1967, then –

"No, from 1948!"

He's talking about the establishment of the State of Israel.

Okay, 1948. Thirty houses since 1948: that's less than half a house per year –

"We cannot fix our own houses here, they won't let us!"

This place looks quite nice, and quite fixed.

"Look up! You see the paint coming off?"

I see. That's the size of a half a page. Can't you paint it over?

"No! The Occupiers won't let us!"

At this point a blond girl walks in and the man loses interest in me. Immediately.

The young beauty from Switzerland tells me she came to the area to help both Israelis and Palestinians. She is part of a Christian human rights organization, EAPPI (Ecumenical Accompaniment Programme in Palestine and Israel), and is volunteering to be here for the next five months of her life to help Jews and Arabs.

What are you planning to do for five months?

"Study Arabic."

This lovely lady's name is Anna Maria and she's paying eight hundred US dollars for an intensive course in Arabic. Not only does she help Jews, but she's also spending money on them. It might not make sense to you, but not all Swiss always make sense to the rest of us.

I'm hungry and Professor Asma, the coordinator of the lecture series, is willing to take me to the best restaurant in the area and introduce me to authentic Palestinian food.

On the way out I notice a PR sheet, dated yesterday, announcing

that a contribution from the EU and the UN has been made to this very building in the amount of €2.4 million to "preserve Palestinian cultural heritage" and to "safeguard cultural heritage in the Old City of Jerusalem." It adds: "The program will contribute to the development and protection of Palestinian cultural heritage," which includes "Hammam al-Ayn and Hammam al-Shifa."

What is the exact nature of all these wonderful phrasings, I wonder? Asma says she'll show me later the exact nature.

* * *

We go to eat at a restaurant called al-Buraq. Professor Asma, as everybody can see, is not wearing a hijab. How come?

"In the time of the Prophet women were taken advantage of by men, girls were killed, and that's why the Quran advised women to wear the hijab 'for your protection.' But look at what's happening today: If I wear the hijab over my head when I cross an Israeli checkpoint they'll harass me. When I go like this, they won't."

We look at the menu, and she tells me: "My husband, he wanted to marry another wife in addition to me. I said, 'No!' And now I'm divorced."

The menu looks good, and the professor talks a bit more:

"At the time I thought that Israeli intellectuals of the Left accepted us, the Palestinians, but I realize now that they don't. When I was in Germany I felt that the Germans were passionate about us, that they care about us."

Why do you think the Europeans help you?

"When the Europeans come here we take them to the places where Jesus lived and where the Israelis crucified him and that's why they support us."

The "Israelis" crucified Jesus? How did the Israelis get in there, two thousand years ago?

I write down what she's said and read it back to her, to make sure I got it right. She approves.

We have some great kebab and Arabic coffee, and when we've

finished she takes me to the place where the 2.4 million euros are going to be spent.

A *hamam*. A Turkish bath.

Yes.

Earlier I was told that the Israelis don't allow Al-Quds University to paint over a little spot on the ceiling, yet they allow them to reconstruct a *hamam* for millions of euros. Either the Israelis are stupid or the Arabs are liars.

Whatever either of them is, the more interesting question is the Europeans' motivation here. Why is it so important for the Europeans to prove that Arabs lived here, so much that they're willing to spend millions on a *hamam*? Hopefully, at some point during the coming six months I'll have an answer. Maybe, just maybe, Europeans dream of naked Arabs and so they pay for a Muslim spa.

Meantime, the professor and I walk around and about, in a maze of beautiful rooms of the *hamam* that is to be reconstructed, and then she takes me to the roof of it and from there she shows me houses not far from al-Aqsa that she says have been confiscated by the Israeli government.

I ask her to tell me about al-Aqsa. She does: "From Kubet as-Sakhra [the Dome of the Rock] in front of us, Prophet Muhammad flew to heaven, where he met God and where God taught him what Muslim people should do, and what to pray."

That's the famous Night Journey of Prophet Muhammad, how he flew from Mecca to "Masjid al-Aqsa" on a heavenly animal known as al-Buraq, and then, from there flew up to heaven to meet Allah.

Listening to her, it all comes back to me. The Western Wall used to be called Het al-Mabka, the Weeping, or Wailing, Wall, by the local Arabs, in deference to the Jews who were crying at the sight of their destroyed Temple. With the advent of Zionism, however, the Arabs changed the wall's name to Het al-Buraq, al-Buraq's Wall. The story of weeping Jews was deleted from the collective memory and another story replaced it: when Muhammad flew to heaven he tied his heavenly animal to this very wall to make sure it didn't run away.

* * *

Another professor, Omar, shows up. Omar is a nice guy, full of warmth, very social and very personable. He's excited today, he tells me, because a reporter of the *Süddeutsche Zeitung* is coming to interview him. He is sure that the German reporter will write very nicely about him, and he can't wait for the interview to take place. He's going to tell the German the truth, for the benefit of the German readers who are interested in the issues here.

What is the truth? He shares it with me: the Israelis make sure that he, being a Palestinian, can't own a house. I tell him that this is indeed horrible and I ask him to tell me more about himself. He takes a liking to me and he tells me. First and foremost, he proudly shares with me, he is not a man only of the mind but also a man of means: he owns a house in east Jerusalem, and he also owns another one in a place called Shuaffat.

There are people who are alcoholics and there are people who are recovering alcoholics, meaning they've stopped drinking. I happen to be a recovering intellectual and I draw from my former self to understand this intellectual. Logically it's impossible for a man who owns nothing also to own two houses. But "intellectually," you can explain away everything.

Professor Omar likes the fact that I accept everything he tells me and don't question him. He asks me if I would like to see a very interesting film about to be shown in the EU-renovating *hamam* of Al-Quds University.

I would love to.

The professor and I walk back to the *hamam* and I find a stone to sit on. Next to me sit a couple of German girls. They are here, they tell me, because they want to help the Palestinian people.

I chat with one of the German volunteers.

What made you volunteer for the Palestinians?

"Three years ago I volunteered for Israel and I fell in love with the Jewish people."

And that's why you decided to come again?

"Yes."

Three years ago you fell in love with the Jews and that's why you are now helping the Palestinians?

She looks at me in disbelief, very upset: "What are you trying to say?"

I should have drawn from my intellectual years before I made this beauty upset. Thank God the movie starts. Name of movie: *The Land Speaks Arabic.*

Using images from various sources, stills and films coupled with never-ending voiceovers by yet another professor, the movie asserts that "Zionists" came over to this part of the world for no obvious reason and committed countless massacres of innocent Palestinians, such as slaughtering thousands of sleeping civilians in the middle of the night. Those they didn't kill, they expelled.

Thusly the Jewish state was created in the year 1948.

When the movie ends a professor explains to us, in case the movie wasn't clear enough, the essence of Zionism: "Zionism is a colonial, racist ideology. No other way to explain this."

Thanks to the generous funding of the EU, who sponsor almost everything here, I have learned two things today: the Israelis crucified Jesus and the Jews are brutal creatures.

Tomorrow, I decide on the spot, I'll go to see the Christians of the Holy City, the spiritual ancestors of today's European funders.

*   *   *

The Holy Sepulcher. Here the Son of God, Jesus Christ, was buried, and here is where he rose from the dead.

There are fourteen stations that Jesus went through in the Via Dolorosa, the Way of Suffering, and I'm now at the last few of them; the others I passed through on my al-Aqsa journey.

Books have been written about this Holy Sepulcher, widely known as the Church of the Holy Sepulcher, many of them discussing the various denominations that continuously fight over control of the area. The members of the various denominations, some of them monks, wear different clothes, but I can't really tell the difference between them, except for the fashionable design of these habits.

I walk around, up and down, and fairly soon get lost. I see a door, behind which a man with a holy costume sits, and I enter.

"This is an office," a bearded man who looks like a bishop tells me in broken English. In other words: Get out! But I am a dumb boy and I don't get what he is saying. Do you speak Hebrew? I ask him.

"No."

Do you speak Arabic?

"No."

Do you speak Spanish?

"No."

Lucky me, I don't speak one word of Spanish either. Do you speak –

"Speak Greek. Only."

I speak Greek as well as I speak Spanish, and so I try English and Arabic in a Greek accent. Maybe he will understand something.

I want to do an interview for the paper, big paper. In Germany.

He smiles.

Shu esmak (What's your name)?

"Asimo." he says.

Picture of you?

"No."

Picture of you and I handshake, a la Rabin and Arafat?

"Okay. But only one picture!"

*   *   *

I walk down a floor and sit at a corner, only to soon be disturbed by priests walking by with burning incense. One comes, then leaves quietly. Another comes with little bells, stopping at certain spots where he shakes the bells. I calculate, though I am not sure, that those certain spots have some sort of wireless connection to certain heavenly entities. This priest leaves, and another comes. This new guy makes a bit more noise with some other bells.

If I don't get it wrong, this place is where cell phones were originally invented, and each one of these priests is using a different app.

I go back up. To Golgotha, where Jesus was crucified. The New Testament says that Jesus was crucified outside the city's walls, but if Professor Omar can make up stories, why not the Christians?

I go to see Jesus' tomb.

A long line of people, which I estimate to be between one and six million, are in a queue to enter the tomb, perhaps hoping that they will rise to life after their deaths as well. There's an entry point at one side of the tomb and a little room on the other.

In the little room they sell paper for those who want to write personal letters to Jesus, which many here do. Writing done, they drop their notes at the tomb for Jesus to read. I'm not sure why they are doing it, especially since Jesus got out of the tomb alive long ago and

only God knows where he is today. The Jews who write letters to God are a bit smarter: they deposit their letters with His Wife, not at the empty tomb of His Son.

Some of the letter writers also attach money to their letters, obviously thinking that Jesus is in need of some cash. I'm not completely certain how the cash finally reaches Jesus but I can see the Greek monks faithfully collecting it for him.

There are other sacred things happening here besides cash.

An older monk approaches an attractive lady and, touching his head and his torso when he says this, tells her that he's very happy because Jesus is in his mind and in his heart. He adds, speaking to the lady: "I can see that Jesus is also in your head and in your heart." He gets closer to the lady, puts his lips on her face and her torso, exactly where Jesus resides, and kisses both with passion.

It is at this very moment of Holy Porno that I feel the need to butt in. This monk is more interesting than the man who looked like a bishop I met before.

Do you see Jesus in my mind and heart as well? I ask the monk.

"Yes."

You sure?

"Yes!"

Would you mind kissing me too? On my head and over my heart, where Jesus is?

The monk gives me a spiteful look, but I insist that he kiss Jesus. He refuses. I raise my voice at him, for the Lord's honor, and swear to him that I won't leave the place unless he kisses my body with passion, "like you did the lady's."

The lady hears our exchange and promptly demands that he kiss me.

He does. Monks obey ladies.

The woman, who says her name is Olga, laughs loudly. I demand hotter kisses, as Olga looks at him with stern eyes.

As the monk brings his lips close to my head, ready to give me a hot kiss, a blond young girl passes by. The monk moves his head toward the new female in town while he's kissing me. I can only imagine what this monk would do to the blonde if he were not busy kissing me by orders of Olga.

The sexual desires of monks standing guard at a tomb is a very interesting topic and I'd like to explore it in more depth. I write a note in my brain to meet more monks during my journey to this holy land. But for now, I just schmooze with some people around me. Interestingly, one of them tells me that this very place does not really contain the tomb of Jesus. The real tomb, I'm now told, is in a place called "Garden Tomb."

I leave the Old City and walk over to the Garden Tomb. What a nice place! A real garden with trees and spotlessly clean pathways welcomes me as I enter. No monks here, only Anne, who is in charge of the place. Anne is a lovely lady whose husband, who lost his faith in Jesus, gave her a choice: him or Jesus. She chose Jesus.

Is Jesus buried here?

"Jesus has arisen and he's with the Father."

Was he buried here?

"Some say he was buried in the Holy Sepulcher, others say it all happened here."

And what do you say?

"I say: What's the difference? Jesus is alive, and that's all that matters. He got up alive from his grave, he is alive, and he is in heaven with God. Nothing else matters."

*   *   *

I go out of the garden and take a look at the Old City facing me. The Christians have their Son of God, Muslims their Messenger of God, Jews their Wife/Presence of God. The Son was buried here, the Messenger flew up from here, and the Wife is still here. Any wonder that the three monotheistic religions fight each other to the death for this parcel of land? Their very spiritual life depends on a few stones in the Holy City, and each wants the whole pie.

But is this just a religious fight? Judging by the Europeans, many of whom are atheists and who are so excited to renovate a *hamam* here, it stands to reason that Jerusalem is also the capital of the Godless. Why else would their leaders spend a penny on a *hamam* thousands of miles away from their own homes?

To understand the secular mind better, I decide to meet some atheists, agnostics, and whoever is in between. Luckily, the Jerusalem Film Festival (JFF) is opening tonight. Israeli actors, directors, and producers are not known to be big followers of God; I shall join them.

But before I go and join them, I get myself some Israeli food and go to my Templar home to eat it. Have you ever tried Israeli food? If you are one of those people who eat not just to survive but also to enjoy, get onto a plane and fly over here. What wonderful food! Start with labane cheese, the one made of goats' milk, but be careful when you put a spoon of it into your mouth, for your soul might melt with extreme pleasure. Cottage cheese, have you heard of it? It is only here, in the Holy Land, that you can get the real thing. Forget any other cheese that you have ever had; those are all fake.

Gate Two

Did you ever try Islamic beer? Would you like to be blessed by the rabbi of Auschwitz? Would you like to date a Jewish Taliban lady? How would a rabbi know that his wife is menstruating?

IN THE BACKYARD OF MY HOUSE, A REAL NICE BACKYARD WITH A VARIETY OF trees in multiple colors, I notice stray cats staring at me from behind the trunks. I think they are afraid of me. Somehow they smell I'm not a local. Stray cats of the Holy Land don't like Europeans and

Americans, I think. But it pains me to look at them, for they seem to be starving. What should I give them? I don't have any bones, only cheese and milk. Kosher goats' milk. You think they would go for it?

Look how I spend my time in the Holy Land: with graves and with cats. But the cheeses, and the milk, let me tell you, are already worth the trip!

* * *

Opening Night at the Jerusalem Film Festival entails listening to long speeches before any film is shown.

I sit in my chair and try to listen.

What can I say? If this can serve as any proof, secular people are quite dumb.

When the lights finally go down the opening movie starts. It's about a group of aging grandpas planning to rob a bank.

It is an interesting concept, but when the plot thickens I can tell that the real robbers are the filmmakers: they are robbing my time.

Is this the extent of secular people's imagination?

The Festival is produced by the Cinematheque of Jerusalem, located above the valley of Gai bin Inom, where in the old days people sacrificed their children to some gods, not far from the Hill of Evil Council, where the decision was taken to arrest Jesus Christ. Across the valley is Mount Zion, where King David's Tomb is located, plus the Church of the Dormition, from which the Mother of God ascended to heaven.

I hope that the JFF will offer a film or two that are at least as half as fascinating as this city's landscape.

I go to see another film: *10% – What Makes a Hero*, a documentary by Yoav Shamir. Lights go off once more, images come up on the screen in the dark hall and I see Hamburg.

No. Not the Hamburg I left just days before with its beautiful Turkish Airlines lady. No. The Hamburg we are shown here is Hamburg of 1936. A different Hamburg. Instead of the smiling Turkish fan of an actor named Mehmet, what we see here are mobs of Germans giving the Hitler Salute. Soon the camera zooms in on the saluters and there, smack in the middle of the mobs, is one man who won't salute.

This very man, a voice tells us, has triggered the mind of the director of this film, who is also its leading character, to wonder what drives a single man in a huge crowd not to follow the crowd and take such a risk. In short: What makes a man a hero?

The film goes on and, as you might expect, Germans feature in it again. We see for example the daughters of Georg Alexander Hansen, a man killed by the Nazis for his involvement in the attempt to assassinate Adolf Hitler. They are Dagmar and Frauke, one blond, the other not. They try to speak English, which is a bit broken, but the story they tell on the screen with tears rolling down their cheeks needs no words in whatever language.

The film drags on, but at the end we get to see the conclusion: Who is the heroic anti-Hitler of our day and who is today's Nazi-equivalent.

The hero is Jonathan Shapira, a person I don't have any clue about but this film explains. Jonathan comes from a distinguished Israeli family, was a celebrated pilot in the Israeli Air Force, beloved by all, but at some point in his successful life he decided to give it all up. These days he thinks the worst of Israel and declares that Israel commits crimes against humanity. And since this is a film, where mere words do not suffice, we are shown the Israeli army throwing tear gas canisters on what seems to be peaceful demonstrators near the West Bank town of Bil'in. The gas effect, especially in close ups, is not pretty. To Jonathan, this tear gas display squeezes out of him the "last drop of Zionism" he still had in his heart.

Guess who's today's Hitler? Obviously enough, our generation's Chief Nazi is no other than the Israeli army, the IDF (Israel Defense Forces).

Had this film been produced outside of Israel, many would have said the filmmaker was an anti-Semite, but this film is the creation of an Israeli, of a Jew.

As the credit lines roll on the screen I notice that this film was given funding by companies from countries such as Germany and Switzerland. The face of a Jew, the pocket of the German: Who creates whom?

To get a better picture of the film and its people I go to meet Yoav.

Why did the Germans and Swiss fund this film?

"We live in a global world and international entities collaborate. You do movies here [in Israel] and you try to get partners. HBO partners sometimes."

HBO is American, and Yoav is evidently trying to tell me it's not the "Germans" alone doing these things, the American are doing this too. And Americans, as we all know, are Jew lovers.

Did you get financing from HBO in your career?

"I didn't, others did. But in other movies that I did we partnered with international companies such as ZDF."

ZDF. Also German. This man, the Germans, and the Swiss go well together, I guess.

Your movie starts with Nazis and ends with IDF.

"Those were soldiers, and these are soldiers. Those obeyed, and these obey."

The picture you make of Israel makes me think that this country had reached bottom. Correct?

"Lower than bottom."

I tell Yoav that I would like to interview Jonathan and that I'd also like to go to Bil'in. Could he help me? Yoav replies that he would be glad to help.

Great.

Interview done, I again go to the Cinematheque.

As customary at festivals, artists come to meet other artists and network. Standing near me is a director who is struggling to get funding for his next movie. I ask him why he doesn't approach German or Swiss funders. Well, he says, this is not so easy. "If you want German or Swiss financing for your movie, you have to be critical of Israel and then they will sponsor you."

Is this, by the way, what this festival is going to be about, political criticism of Israel? If so, I would rather spend the time I allotted for the JFF and go out to meet some real-life anti-Zionists, and perhaps of the non-secular kind. The most famous of them live not far from here, in the Haredi (ultra-Orthodox) neighborhood of Meah Shearim, right off the ancient Old City.

*   *   *

As I walk in this Haredi neighborhood I notice the "Yeshiva of the rabbi of Auschwitz," a rabbinical seminary of the rabbi of Auschwitz. Auschwitz? I ask Hasidic people standing at the entrance to the seminary. "Yes," they say. "Why not? Auschwitz used to be a Jewish town." I can come inside, they suggest, and the Rabbi of Auschwitz, who is in heaven together with King David, would send a blessing my way. I burst out laughing, for some reason thinking this is the coolest joke I have ever heard, and they immediately join me in the laughter.

We pose for pictures together, just for the fun of it, and think up a scheme how to send these pictures to Adolf Hitler in Hell. He should have a laugh too.

I keep walking the streets of Meah Shearim and a thought creeps into my brain: How come these people are so funny and the secular filmmakers so boring?

Whatever the reason for this little difference, I have a more burning need at the moment: Diet Coke with ice. There's life after the ovens of Auschwitz and I want to live. Problem is, I don't know where to find a Coke here, a neighborhood with many religious establishments but no visible Coke-selling stands. I spot two workers, non-residents, and talk to them.

What's your name?

"Yekhezkiel," says one.

And you? I ask the other.

"Israel."

They don't strike me as Yekhezkiel and Israel, two very Jewish names.

You don't have to play games with me. What are your real names?

"Muhammad."

And you?

"Also Muhammad."

Nice to meet you. My name is Tobi and I'm a German.

You got to see the light shining up in the eyes of Yekhezkiel and Israel! They love this German and happily point to him the store that sells the black ice magic known as Coke.

My thirst quenched, I go to meet the two biggest rabbis of the neighborhood. Not an easy task, let me tell you.

The first rabbi I want to meet is not around. Where is he? "In America, in a hotel," his followers tell me. The second rabbi, what a surprise, is also not around. Where is he? "In an Austrian hotel."

The holy men are vacationing. They don't make movies, their life is a movie: gorgeous landscapes and delicious meals. The people of this neighborhood, who are forbidden to study anything but sacred books, don't have professional jobs and most of them are very poor. How come the rabbis can afford expensive hotels overseas? I ask one of the followers, who points to heaven in reply: "He who created heaven and earth knows how to get a hotel for the righteous!"

If Yoav had any sense of humor he would have made a film about these people.

When holy men are vacationing at places such as Interalpen-Tyrol, the little children of their community stay behind in Meah Shearim to study the alphabet and I go to join them. In their eyes, if I remember from my childhood years in the Haredi world, a man dressed like I am these days must be a creature from the local zoo, a damned Zionist, a cursed goy, a gentile, or a fugitive on the run from a mental hospital.

A bunch of kids, between twenty and thirty, congregate around this stranger the moment he walks in and shower him with love. They chose the zoo option, I can tell; they think I'm a lovely bear.

"Who are you?" they ask.

I respond in Yiddish, a language they never imagined creatures like me speak: And who are you? They love this bear. I must come from a kosher zoo.

Their teacher chats with me and tells me that he's an anti-Zionist "just like you."

How did you find this out about me so fast?

"You wouldn't come to visit us if you were a Zionist!"

We laugh. And the children laugh too. They all try to touch me, a lovely bear on two legs, while shouting with pleasure.

The teacher and the kids communicate with each other in Yiddish, a language that is 80 percent German, and he teaches them the Holy Tongue, Hebrew.

I sit with them and watch how they learn to recognize letters. It takes me back many years, to the foundations of my knowledge, and I close my eyes.

Alef. Beis. Gimmel. (A. B. C.)

Letters are images; A looks like this, B looks like that. Letters are strange creatures, and they lack any esthetics. Why can't letters be more picturesque? Letters are cold, rough, old-fashioned creatures that somehow survived the concentration camps. Letters are powerful, cruel, manipulative, and very smart. I want to control them; I don't want them to control me.

Alef! Beis! Gimmel!

The teacher wakes me up from my daydream. Would I like to see his angelic creatures play? he asks.

It is a marvel to the eye and ear. As they play I ask them to sing. I don't know how they will respond to my request, but the kids and their teacher think this is a hilarious idea and promptly start with songs. They look, and sound, like angels. So inspiring!

What will become of these sweet creatures when they grow up? I ask myself. A clue to the answer I can see on the street outside.

"To the women passing through our neighborhood," a big sign on the street outside says, "please do not pass in our neighborhood in immodest clothes." The parts of a woman's flesh that are not required to be covered are: face and fingers. Some women here, I see and cannot believe my eyes, take "modesty" one step further: they are showing not one iota of flesh, not even their eyes, and when they walk on the street they look like huge black trash bags in movement. Are they the Jewish Taliban?

In my day women like these did not exist. Jerusalem has gotten holier, I think.

Should I try the JFF again, just in case? Maybe later; now I need beer.

I walk out of Meah Shearim and go to settle in Uganda.

* * *

The Uganda bar.

I have been told about this Uganda before, and more than I really cared to know, but today it shall be my refuge from the walking trash bags, the Jewish Nazis, and the aging bank robbers.

It is in this Uganda, people in the know say, that you can get Palestinian beer and the best hummus. I want both.

One of the first items I see upon walking into Uganda is not a beer bottle with an "Allah" logo on it, which I had hoped for, but the German soft drink Bionade. I ask Jula, the bartender, why they import this particular brand.

People around me immediately recognize that I'm a first-timer and so they explain the basics to me: most foreigners who frequent this place, which is named in honor of Theodor Herzl's acceptance of the British proposal to settle European Jews in Africa, are from Germany, primarily Berliners.

Besides Bionade, there are two other images that capture my eyes: a picture of Theodor Herzl on the left side and the Taybeh fountain on the right.

"You have to try the Taybeh," an older man advises me. "It's a Palestinian beer!"

What does it mean Palestinian – was it made by a Palestinian or sold by a Palestinian?

"Made! Made!"

What kind of Palestinian – Muslim?

"Yes! What else?"

Sure?

"One hundred percent!"

Aren't Muslims forbidden to drink alcohol?

"Ah. Maybe he's Christian."

I sit down to have a Taybeh, and Alon, a friend of the owner's and a frequent guest here, starts talking to me. "I'm not a Jew, I'm a Hebrew," he declares while still sober.

He is also "a musician, and I have a band that's called 'Mujahideen,'" meaning people engaged in Jihad. "I am a post-Zionist. No, take that back. I am a post-post-Zionist. I see myself as an Israelite; I like the Bible. A Hebrew, not a Jew. You have to understand: Judaism, as we now know it, only developed about four hundred years ago, and I'm against it. There are maybe ten people on earth who think like me, but this doesn't matter. To me, today's Judaism is like Islam and Christianity, none of which I care about."

There are people Alon likes in particular, he tells me. Who are they? The Germans. Why? "The Germans are the nicest people in Europe." I tell him I'm a German from Berlin and he falls in love with me on the spot.

How easy it is to make people happy.

I drink more beer – after all, I'm German – and enjoy all the mess in this country. With beer in my mouth and belly, I look at them all with a certain distance: they are Jews, I am German, and, sorry for saying this, I am the better of the two.

I get up and the German in me decides to conquer this land with real German pride. No, I'm not from the Germany of old, those who were into conquering other peoples' lands with tanks; I'm a new German, the good German, a contemporary German who is a do-gooder. I'll conquer this land by teaching its residents a better way. Who knows, maybe I will even revive the Uganda scheme and free the Palestinians of their eternal suffering by explaining to the Jews that Uganda would be better for them. I have learned much from history – my own history – and the moral sense that I have acquired will force a new order in this part of the world. I'll be the messenger of peace and change, peace and love.

As I start my conquest outside Uganda, I get a message from the Cinematheque people. Would you like to go to Yad Vashem tomorrow? This invitation, sent to other festivalgoers as well, strikes my newly found German soul very deeply and very personally. Yad Vashem is Israel's Holocaust Museum, and it doesn't take a genius to figure out what I might find there: my grandparents. "Germany of old" is remote; grandparents is personal.

It takes this one little message from the Cinematheque for my moral superiority to sink to the deepest bottom of my being. Being German, how sad, is not fun.

I respond that I'll attend. My conquest of the land has just ended.

Back home, the stray cats in my backyard garden stare at me with spiteful eyes. They don't like me. I don't know if they think that I'm a German, an Arab, a Jew, or whatever. Bottom line: they hate me. But I'm determined not to let any of the mess I have been through today get to me and I walk out to get some sweets. In Israel they have these *rugelakh,* and I buy four of them. *Rugelakh* are little cakes, and when I eat them I know that I'm a religious person too: a Rugaleh (singular of *rugelakh*) Follower. I believe in *rugelakh* and will kill anybody who does not let me worship them.

* * *

Yad Vashem.

A representative of the museum greets the festival people, sharing some statistics with us. Before WWII there were 18 million Jews in the world, now there are 13.5 million.

Yad Vashem is shaped like a triangle representing one half of the

Star of David. The other half, the missing half, represents the Jews that were killed. They are no longer, nor the second triangle.

We walk by the horrible pictures of dead Jews and all I can think of is this: some of the people here are – were – my own relatives and this is how they ended their lives.

I don't want to see this. I would rather see a movie at the Cinematheque.

* * *

Minutes later I'm at the JFF at the Cinematheque. Films offered today: *Hitler's Madman. The Longest Journey: The Last Days of the Jews of Rhodes. Bureau 06* (the bureau that handled the case against Adolf Eichmann).

Damn. Don't they have anything else? Hey, you: the War is Over! But oh, here's one non-Holocaust film: *The Gardener*, a film that takes place at the Baháʼí Gardens in Haifa. I go to see it.

The film starts with a young, white, beautiful lady performing rituals. She's walking about, hopping between green trees and red and yellow flowers, fresh grass and white stones, and she mumbles prayers of love and peace. Then, after the white, pale-skinned female, it's time for the black man, the African gardener. He is dressed not in the soft, flowing garments of the white lady, but in worker's garb. He's rough and dirty, yet his mouth is full of peace and his hands lovingly caress flowers.

The film is extremely boring, having no plot whatsoever. But the people around me, secular folks, are wet with pleasure. If this film represents the essence of the secular, I quietly say to myself, I'm happy I'm a religious Rugaleh.

In an adjacent room, the Cinematheque offers a press conference with the film's director, Mohsen Makhmalbaf, who tries to instill love for Iran in the heart of the Jews. "Iranian people love the Israelis," he says, among some other similar treasures. His country, at least according to Western accounts, is soon to have the capacity to manufacture glowing atomic bombs, and the people here, many of whom are German journalists, enthusiastically applaud this director. God knows why they do.

When the press conference ends, I meet Alesia Weston, executive director of this festival. This is a good opportunity for me to solve a puzzle I have no clue how to decipher on my own.

Tell me, Alesia, how many of the films at the festival were produced with German cooperation?

She takes her time, thinks of it, and finally says: "This is an interesting question. I promise I'll get back to you on this."

What's the film you like most in this festival?

"*The Gardener.*"

What's in it that makes you like it?

"Its incredibly playful way to treat some of the most serious questions we have. I have never thought of the interaction between nature, humans, and religion through a prism quite so gentle, forceful at the same time, and the way they reflect and impact one another."

Give me a moment in the film that best describes what you say.

"One line in it."

Give me the line!

"I will paraphrase, if you don't mind."

Go ahead.

"The flower can judge and respond to a man's character."

Wow.

I again need religious people to offer me a break from the heady, humorless secular high class. I hear that in another part of this city rabbinical graduates are having their final exams today. Maybe I should hook up with one or two future rabbis. Could be nice.

I go out and stop a taxi.

* * *

Mahmoud, the driver, tells me to put on the safety belt. I tell him belts are against my religion. He gives up and we talk religion, this and that, and then I tell him I want to know everything there is to know about the Prophet's heavenly horse, al-Buraq.

Mahmoud: "No, no. Al-Buraq was no horse."

No horse?

"No. No horse."

What was it?

"Camel."

Normal camel?

"Heavenly camel!"

Good. I accept. So, the Prophet arrived here, in Al-Quds, with the camel and then, just before he flew up –

"With angel Jibril!"

Yes, of course. I was trying to find out about the camel. As I remember, the Prophet tied the camel to that wall, the al-Buraq Wall, the same wall that the Jews claim is part of their holy –

"The Jews dug deep and deep in the earth, for years, for many years, to prove they were here before and they found nothing!"

The Jews were never here, but the camel was?

"Yes."

Other than that, is everything okay?

"Where?"

In Jerusalem. How do you, the Arabs and the Jews, get along with each other?

"Just now, today, just before, two hundred settlers stormed into al-Aqsa, desecrating the holy mosque!"

What are you talking about?

"It's all over the news. On the radio."

Today? Now?

"Yes, yes! The Israeli government sent them!"

I check the news on my iPad – American, Israeli and European sites – but find nothing about al-Aqsa. This man must be dreaming. Having no alcohol can make a man hallucinate.

I get off his taxi and I think of the camel story. The truth is, according to the authorized Hadith, *Sahih al-Bukhari*, al-Buraq is no horse and no camel. When Prophet Muhammad was lying down the other day, he is quoted as saying, "suddenly" someone came to him and cut his body from his throat to his penis, took out his heart and washed it, put his heart back into his body "and a white animal, smaller than a mule and bigger than a donkey was brought to me."

Bingo.

In Islamic visual art, notwithstanding, and as author Timothy Insoll notes in *The Archeology of Islam*: "The established representation of al-Buraq comprises a crowned head, often of a young woman, attached to a winged horse."

*   *   *

Ahead of me, right before the entrance door to a huge convention center, there's a bunch of Jewish sacred books lying on tables. The books deal with menstruating women. I read: "It is the tradition of the Daughters of Israel that they check their vagina, using two witnesses, one for him and one for her. The modest of the Jewish women use a third witness. Should a woman check herself if she is menstruating with her husband? No. He might incredibly playful get afraid and then not sleep with her."

Honestly, this material is too deep for a recovering intellectual like me, especially coming off the story of the camel and the penis.

I ask the man who seems to be in charge here: Are we going to have naked women coming over soon to better illustrate the issue?

"Where are you from?"

USA, Germany, and Saudi Arabia.

I really don't know how it happened that my lips uttered these words but this guy likes what he hears, for whatever reason, and he teaches me about women, menstruation, blood, sex, and vaginas. Not exactly in this order, but almost. Women are forbidden to have sexual relations with their spouses during menstruation and these books deal with the big question: What is menstruation? How do you check it? How do you know it?

I get confused. These particular religious Jews start reminding me of the heady secular people and soon enough the images and experiences I have had so far in this land mix up in my head and I ask myself: What will happen if a menstruating woman rides a camel into the Bahá'í Garden, where two hundred settlers, five Greek monks, and three German Taybeh drinkers wait for her? Will King Herod build for her a nice castle made of one huge stone?

The best way to answer this question, most likely, is by becoming a rabbi myself. I walk to the exam room, determined to take the test and become a big rabbi of a huge menstruating community.

A security man blocks my way. No one can take the exam unless he has the right papers; he wants me to show him my papers. I have no papers, just an iPad, and I leave.

I walk around the city of Jerusalem to find a learned person to discuss with me lofty issues such as rabbinical men and menstruating women and I wander into a local bookstore, where I assume I'll find learned people. I see Tirtsa, the store manager.

"I think," she tells me when I just open my mouth, "that all people are fascists: right-wingers, left-wingers, everybody."

What's going on with her? Is she menstruating?

Tirtsa is a secular lady and I can't ask her this question. Instead, I tell her that two hundred settlers, obviously all fascists, stormed into al-Aqsa a few hours ago. She looks at me in amazement. "I listened to the news earlier and I heard nothing about this. If something like this happened, every news media would be talking about it."

This sounds quite reasonable and so I check once more on my iPhone. I get on the Al-Jazeera website, the one in Arabic, and sure enough I see it right there. Top of the news. Dozens of settlers, it says without giving an exact number, stormed into al-Aqsa earlier in the day. They even have a photo of al-Aqsa with about five seemingly non-Muslim men in the foreground. I show it to Tirtsa, but she is totally unimpressed. "That's five people," she counts. "Where are the hundreds?"

This land is too intense for me. So far I've only been to Jerusalem but it's more intense than all of the US of A. I need something to eat, before I fall.

Following a tip in some tourist guide I go to the Makhne Yehudah market to a restaurant called Makhneyidah. Very creative. I sit down and check the menu.

Here's an item called Shikshukit. What is it? I ask the waiter.

"Minced meat with tahini and yogurt. It is good for your health, good for salvation, cures cancer, good for having male children, and it comes with roasted tomatoes."

I think Al-Jazeera should hire this person as their chief correspondent. I try the Shikshukit. It's not as promising as I had hoped, but it beats flying camels, menstruating rabbis, and Iranian love.

What a country. What characters!

Jerusalem.

Here it is where the Bible was formed, a city that the God of Israel called home, and here it is where Judaism took shape. Here it is where Jesus died and rose back to life, and where Christianity was born. From here Muhammad flew up to Allah's House, directly above, where Allah instructed him that Muslims must pray five times a day. And here it is where secular filmmakers try to spin a story with German and Swiss funding but fail miserably.

Vacillating between the holy and the sacred, I get a huge headache. I'm going home to sleep. I hope the cats won't bite me.

Gate Three

Would you like to join thousands of dead Jews
guarded by a German convert?

WHEN I WAKE UP THE NEXT DAY I MAKE UP MY MIND NOT TO SEE ANY MORE movies. No tall tales and people on a screen for me, just the real world and live people. My only dilemma is this: Where do I find the liveliest of people? This being Jerusalem, not New York nor Hamburg, I go to a cemetery to find the liveliest of all people.

Mount of Olives.

Frankly, today is not the best day to go to the Mount of Olives. Today is the first Friday of Ramadan, which in Jerusalem translates into Day of Anger: disturbances, stone throwing, bullets flying, and a long list of other possible goodies. But I go anyway, reasoning that nobody will be shooting in a cemetery; it's too late for that.

It ain't easy to get there.

The Mount of Olives overlooks al-Aqsa, and access to it proves a bit difficult.

For one full month people fast during the day and gorge themselves to death at night, and their highlight is going to pray in al-Aqsa. Anywhere I look I see police and border guard personnel. They are out on the streets in the hundreds, if not in the thousands. Many streets are blocked to traffic, about a million-plus Muslims are on the streets, up in the sky a zeppelin is flying and watching, helicopters too, and every Jewish cop around is tense. As I see it, I can't ask for a more perfect timing: When the Muslims go to pray where Muhammad flew to heaven I go to a place where souls from heaven are soon to fly down to earth to reunite with their dead bodies in the graves.

You might think I have lost my mind, but I haven't.

When the Messiah arrives he will first come here, to the Mount of Olives. He will walk on the mountain, where an untold number of dead are interned, and resurrect them all, one by one by one. He will resurrect all the dead, at least the Jewish ones, in whatever cemetery they are buried anywhere on the planet, but it is at the Mount of Olives that he is going to start.

Did you not know?

This is why a burial plot there costs more than a mansion in many other parts of the world. Let's face it: if you know there is a place out there where you are guaranteed to be the first to get out of your grave, wouldn't you want to be buried there? This is why the richest and most famous Jews are buried there. This is the most expensive Jewish cemetery of history, a five-star cemetery.

Yet, while being buried in this holy place is reserved for the rich and famous, living in it is a different story. And, yes, there are people who live amongst the dead. Two families, to be precise.

I show up in their abode.

*　*　*

One of these families is that of Tziporah and Rechavia Piltz, whose backyard is populated with the dead. My backyard is populated by cats, theirs by the dead. This family, quite alive, likes to have the dead as their neighbors. The only problem they have is with the living. Across the street from the cemetery there is a neighborhood of living people who happen to be Muslims, and the Muslims strongly feel that only dead Jews should be allowed in this area. To keep the Piltzes alive, the Israeli government spends enormous sums of money. In addition to state-provided security, the Israeli government hires private security to make sure that the Piltz family doesn't end up under a tombstone.

The Piltzes have nine children, whom they named in accordance with their belief. These include: Bat Zion (Daughter of Zion), Sar Shalom (Minister of Peace), Tiferet (Glory), Geulah (Redemption).

Outside of her window, Tziporah says, is "the southern eastern wall of the Temple Mount. You can pray here just as you pray at the Western Wall. This wall is from the Second Temple period."

You live in midst of a cemetery, graves touching your house. You are amongst the dead. Isn't it scary?

"I just heard someone saying something this week, which I really liked: 'We should not be scared of the dead, we should be scared of the living.'"

Very nice, but isn't it scary to live here?

She takes me to another window, this time her bedroom window.

"Look! Can you see that grave over there? That's Menachem Begin (former prime minister). And here's Eliezer Ben Yeudah (originator of modern Hebrew). Shai Agnon (a Nobel laureate). Rabbi Zonenfeld (Jerusalem's chief rabbi)."

Tziporah, why here?

"I always wanted it, I wanted to live in east Jerusalem."

Why?

"Jerusalem is the holiest city in the world, and I can't accept the fact that the holiest city is divided, half inhabited by Jews and half by Arabs."

Why here?

"Arieh King, who works for Irving Moskowitz [an American tycoon], told me about this place. Irving buys Arab properties and sells them to Jews, and Arieh told me that they were looking for people to move into this house."

Why here?

"Before us, an Arab family lived here. They uprooted tombstones from Jewish graves in the cemetery and put them on the floor here. Whenever something broke in the house, they went out, uprooted some tombstones and put them here."

Are you happy living here?

"Very much. It's a privilege to live here. Any other place, if I move out of here, will be a step down."

Tziporah is going to the kitchen to cook. The Sabbath starts in a few hours and the food must be ready by then (Orthodox Jews don't cook or bake on the Sabbath). She has eleven mouths to feed, and preparing the food is quite an assignment.

Eight-year-old Tiferet, a beauty by any standard, is talking with me in the front yard, the only place Tziporah's children are allowed to be by themselves outside of the home, for obvious security reasons. I ask Tiferet if she likes living among the dead Jews and the living Arabs. "I would like to live in another place," she tells me, "with more place to roam."

What would you like to be when you grow up?

"An actress."

The sound of applause fits this girl more than the sound of the muezzin that is now loudly being heard, probably even by the dead.

I try to imagine Tiferet as an actress in *The Gardener*: a settler in an Iranian director's film. Would the German journalists still applaud?

Outside the cemetery thousands of Muslims, who have just finished praying in al-Aqsa, walk the streets back to their homes. To take a little break from the dead, I mingle with the fasting Arabs and stop twenty minutes later at Gat Shmanim (which in English got corrupted into "Gethsemane," the place where Jesus prayed before he was crucified). I take a little sip of cold water and a man immediately screams at me: "Ramadan! Don't drink!"

What's his problem?

"Here you never know," an Israeli policeman standing by tells me. "One person says something, or throws a little stone, and the whole area will get inflamed. That's how things work here."

I keep on walking, walking and smoking. I might have left the cemetery but thousands of graves line the road I'm walking on, many of which have only partial tombstones on top of them, containing a line, a word, a letter. The rest were broken for the sake of desecration, or stolen for the sake of a better wall or floor. I look at the broken graves and ask myself: How much hate would you need inside your heart, or how poor must you be, to do this to the dead?

I walk back to Tziporah's. She suggests I meet her neighbors, her only living neighbors, and together we go to the Gans family.

Gilad, father of six children, is happy to meet new souls.

Drinking his German Jacobs coffee, the man talks unto me. While his mother tongue is German, which goes well with the Jacobs, he speaks English and Hebrew as well. Growing up in Hamburg, one of the richer cities in Germany, he felt something was missing in his life: people to trust. "Deep down," he tells me, "the average German didn't get over anti-Semitism. It is rooted very deeply." Having a Jewish father and a non-Jewish mother, this feeling he had didn't make his life in Germany easy, and one day he made his way to Israel.

Gilad and his family love Israel and love this cemetery. As they see it, this cemetery is much nicer than Hamburg. I don't agree, but

you can't argue taste. They offer me a cake, made of only natural ingredients, they assure me, and I take a slice. Then another slice. And another. And another. I don't know why, but eating cakes in a cemetery is really special.

*   *   *

Outside the cemetery, only a few minutes' walk away, is the Palestinian neighborhood of Ras al-Amud. And right there, in the heart of a Muslim community, Irving Moskowitz has bought land from the Arabs and a Jewish foundation has arranged for the construction of housing complexes for Jews: Maale Zeitim and Maalot David.

It is in Maale Zeitim that Arieh King lives. I like his name. In English it would be "Lion King." Have you seen *Lion King: The Musical*? I saw it in, of all places, Hamburg.

Arieh King deals with Jewish tycoons who can't buy what they want on their own. Namely, Arab-owned properties. Irving Moskowitz is one of his clients and he has a number of others.

Despite his young age, Arieh King is quite known in this land, especially in certain circles, and there are many people who wish him the worst.

I am sitting in his living room, and we chat.

Arieh, what would you like the world to know about you?

"The least possible."

Brilliant answer! But I keep plugging: What would you like the world to know about what you're doing?

Arieh gets serious: "I do everything I can do for Jerusalem, because the future of Jerusalem will affect Jewish survival."

Why is that?

"From the time the Jews were expelled from Jerusalem we are not what we used to be."

What do you mean?

"We don't have the capacity to worship God as we once had."

You mean the slaughtering of animals in the Temple? Is that what you want?

Arieh doesn't like the word "slaughtering" and he corrects me: "'Offerings' to God, as is written in the Torah. We also don't have the Sanhedrin." (The Sanhedrin was the Jews' highest religious court in the Temple's time).

Israel has a Supreme Court; isn't it good enough for you?

"This *is* our problem! The Supreme Court is based on British law."

In the old days of the Sanhedrin, a woman betraying her husband would be stoned. Is that what you want?

"The Sanhedrin will decide, and whatever it decides I will accept."

In the old days, the justice system of the Sanhedrin worked in unison with the Temple system. Are you planning for the Temple to be rebuilt?

"I'm doing my best."

What are you doing?

"I try to convince people, as many as I can, that the Temple is very important. It's the only way to make peace. When our enemies see the good that will come from the Temple, they will end up liking it. The Third Temple will give them the opportunity to worship God, since the Third Temple will be a place of worship for all nations as it says in Isaiah 56:7: 'For my house will be called a house of prayer for all nations.' And before that God says, 'I'll bring them to my holy mountain and give them joy in my house of prayer and their burned offerings and sacrifices will be accepted on my altar.'"

This man, the most secretive real estate broker in the world, a man whose life is at risk at any given moment, can't stop talking.

"Do you know any other religion which does something like this? You don't have to convert to my religion, you can keep yours, and still your prayers will be accepted by *my* God! Something like this, the message of the Temple, is that happiness and wealth will be shared by all people."

I have enough of his biblical scholarship; I want the broker in him to come out. How do you buy Arab properties?

"Almost every day between one to three proposals from Arabs, in Jerusalem and other places, come to my desk."

What's the story with buying properties from Arabs, why is it so complex?

"Twenty years ago Israeli-Arab religious leaders issued a fatwa: 'An Arab found selling land to Jews will be killed.'"

How many deaths so far?

"In the last seventeen years nobody has been killed."

How come?

"We use certain procedures to hide the identity of the real seller, or we give the seller a good cover story: that he sold to another Arab and not to a Jew. Sometimes we bribe Palestinian Authority officials, at all levels of government, to make no issue out of it. Other times we have to wait, three or five years, to give the seller enough time to make up stories of what happened with the land."

So far, how many properties have you been engaged in?

"In Jerusalem: dozens. Rest of Israel: hundreds."

When did you start doing this?

"In 1997. Ras al-Amud was my first."

Arieh has a cozy home, a huge apartment in a residential building that is guarded around the clock by men toting machine guns and by army jeeps patrolling the area. An impressively big balcony overlooks the Temple Mount, which the Muslims call Haram al-Sharif, and the al-Aqsa Mosque, among other Jerusalem treasures. The man lives comfortably. God takes care of His brokers and provides for them well.

How much does your apartment cost?

"Million and a half shekels. In 2003 it was 800,000."

What's your official title?

"Founder and director of Israel Land Fund."

Do you also initiate some of the deals?

"Yes! Yes!"

Deals, his kind of deals, means having enemies. His most bitter of enemies, he tells me, is none other than the Israeli prime minister, Benjamin Netanyahu ("Bibi").

"The Israeli government today is implementing an anti-Semitic policy in the capital of the Jewish nation. Jews are not allowed to build in Jerusalem for the past four-and-a-half years. Arabs, Muslim and Christian, are allowed. This is a policy of Prime Minister Benjamin Netanyahu."

Other than this, is everything going well?

Not really.

"I can enter the Vatican while carrying my Jewish holy books, but in my own holy place I'm not allowed to do this. Jews have only one holy place in the world, the Temple Mount, and when you pass through Israeli security, they check if you carry Jewish holy books. If you do, they will take them away from you."

Who is the bigger of your enemies, Bibi or Abu Mazen [Palestinian President Mahmoud Abbas]?

"What kind of question is this? Of course Bibi!"

In fact, Arieh tells me, he gets along with his Arab neighbors better than he gets along with Bibi.

"The Arabs here like me, they love me. They call me 'Assad' [lion]."

Arieh has stories, and I can never tell what's real and what's not. And before I leave him, he says he wants to share another one with me.

Please!

"A German, son of a Righteous among the Nations [a non-Jew who helped shelter Jews from the Nazis], came here a few years ago and decided to help us. He founded a church, legally (on paper) but not in reality, through which he buys properties from Arabs. The Arabs like the Germans and when a German church approaches them they are comfortable in selling them real estate."

Do the properties belong to the church, or –

"We pay the lawyers of the church."

What do you mean?

"The church lawyers are actually our lawyers."

Israeli filmmakers have their Germans and Arieh has his.

Peace activists spend a lifetime attempting to talk with Arabs and Arieh lives with them.

I leave Arieh and move on, walking about the Arab residents of Ras al-Amud.

Across the mountain from where I am now, two young Palestinians have stabbed an Orthodox Jew on his way home from the Western Wall. From my location I can't see it, but I read about it on my iPad. Haaretz reports that the Jew, with medium to severe injuries, was taken to a hospital. The article also mentions another stabbing that took place last year right where I am: Ras al-Amud.

Elsewhere, I read this report by the *New York Times*: "The European Union issued guidelines this week that for the first time ban the financing of and cooperation with Israeli institutions in territory seized during the 1967 War." This was almost fifty years ago. What has happened now that is making the EU get busy with this story? I

don't know. I keep reading the article: "Hanan Ashrawi, a member of the Palestine Liberation Organization's (PLO) executive committee, welcomed the decision."

Hanan Ashrawi. I want to see this lady. She will be a fine complement to Arieh King.

It is time to leave Jerusalem, seat of the Israeli government, and enter Ramallah, seat of the Palestinian government.

Gate Four

Facts: No Jewish state ever existed here. Jews must pay Arabs for five years of music training. Palestine was founded fourteen thousand years ago.

HANAN IS THE "HUMAN FACE" OF THE PLO AND HAS BEEN THE "HUMAN FACE" of the Palestinians for many a year. Her business card reads: Hanan Ashrawi, PhD, PLO Executive Committee Member, Department of Culture and Information.

When I arrive at her office, the PLO HQ building in Ramallah, she isn't there yet but her secretary, Maggie, a beautiful blond Palestinian lady, is. Maggie tells me that her German husband, who is "so straight, precise," works for the German GIZ (Deutsche Gesellschaft für Internationale Zusammenarbeit) and that Germany invests huge amounts of money into building the Palestinian state.

Sitting at her desk, a map of "Palestine 1948" (meaning one with no Israel) behind her, she is full of smiles and energy. She asks if I want Arabic coffee.

This is not the cemetery and no Jacobs coffee is anywhere in sight, just pure Arabic coffee of heavenly quality and taste.

Good that Maggie is Christian. Otherwise, in this Ramadan month, I'd be welcomed with only a smile and a map.

The TV at the PLO HQ is on. Playing now: a variant of *Sesame Street*.

"Oh, this is for the little child here. His mother brought her baby with her," Maggie says, referring to another employee.

As this Sesame is playing, Al-Jazeera TV, the most powerful Arab TV, is calling Hanan's office. Could they come, they ask, for a few minutes to interview Hanan? "It will be only five minutes," Maggie promises me.

Waiting for Hanan, I look at Maggie's Kharta.

Kharta means a map in Arabic, and in Hebrew slang *kharta* means fake or imagined. The Hebrew slang originates, I think, from this very map, where even the city of Tel Aviv doesn't exist. I say "I think" because not many Israelis speak Arabic and there are not many to ask. A few months ago, for example, Benjamin Netanyahu made a speech in which he spoke about the uniqueness of Israel. He mentioned the word "dugri," meaning something like "straight," and said that no other culture has such a word, only Hebrew. The Israelis, he was pointing out to the world, are the straightest people of the world and that's why they have an additional word for straight. If he, or his

listeners, only knew that *dugri* comes from the Arabic *durgri*, which means, what a surprise, straight.

I need a cigarette. I was attempting to smoke before I arrived at the PLO HQ but people on the streets of Ramallah wouldn't let me. Over and again I was told by passersby to immediately extinguish my cigarettes. "It's Ramadan!" they yelled at me. I share my problem with Maggie and she shows me where I can sneak a smoke. I go there, swallow three cigarettes, one after the other, until Hanan shows up and I go to join her.

Hanan's office is nicely and cleanly decorated. She has a plate of cut fruit and vegetables, with many colors of the rainbow, at the center of her desk. There are some pictures hanging on the wall, all with good taste, but I can't locate the ubiquitous al-Aqsa Mosque, the symbol of Palestine, in any of them. Hanan is Christian, and perhaps that's why she doesn't want a mosque in her office.

We shake hands, I sit down, and the Al-Jazeera team enters just as I get ready to open my mouth.

This Al-Jazeera team is the most professional I've seen in the longest time. It takes them less than a minute to set up their expensive set, and they are ready and in action in a snap. They know what Hanan thinks but what they want is a "sound bite." Everybody interviews Hanan, why not Al-Jazeera? The correspondent laughs, chuckles, and smiles. And so does Hanan. They seem to know and like each other.

Smiles end just before the interview starts, when faces change to serious. They remind me of actors in dressing rooms before show time. Gotta be serious now. Then, with a sad face in addition to the serious appearance, Hanan talks about how bad Israel is and the interview is quickly over.

At the speed of light the Al-Jazeera team disembarks and exits.

* * *

It's now Hanan and me. How would you like to present the Palestinian people, and yourself, to the rest of the world?

"As a people, we are probably like every other people in the world.

We have the same aspirations; we want to live in peace and in dignity and respect for human rights. The problem is that as a people we have been historically prevented from that. So, even though we have been living in a context that is darkly seen, and is actually a tragic context of either dispossession and dispersion and exile or living under the boot of a military occupation, so to speak.

"We also like to live; we love life. We like to create. We love to write, to read poetry and to paint and to dance, and to have festivals in Palestine. There's a constant pull and push that you have to resist the occupation, you have to deal with issues of exile and dispersion, but at the same time you have to maintain your humanity and maintain your commitment to a larger goal as well, the fact that we are part of the human community.

"So, this has been a sense of exclusion, constantly for us as Palestinians. We have been excluded from the human community, because we have been labeled, we have been stereotyped, and we have been described by our adversaries, rather than by our own selves. So, I

believe, we are also a people like the ancient mariner, you know, we have a tale to tell, we have a narrative that we want to present. That narrative has been absent from human discourse, and we are trying to make it recognizable. It's authentic, it's our narrative, and we don't want the rest of the world to deal with us through the perception and the discourse and diction, let's say, of political control like this, the Israeli occupation."

Hanan surprises me. Watching her on TV, or reading about her, I always had the impression that she was a harsh lady, a person who lives at a distance and a woman of cold personality. But sitting opposite her, feeling the warmth in her voice, I cannot but be touched by her and respect her. She is smart and well spoken. Unlike Arieh King, she speaks long sentences and has a rich vocabulary and, it occurs to me, she is no broker. If she tried to sell me a house while answering every question I had with her long sentences, most likely I'd invite her for coffee and cake and stay in my old house another few years.

Maybe I should be more precise in my questioning and see if she can give me shorter answers.

But before I have a chance to butt in, Hanan has more ideas to share.

"To me, the startling fact is that the Palestinians have been living on their land historically for hundreds and thousands of years and suddenly they are told that they have to give up most of their land and that another state will be created."

Hundreds and thousands of years is quite big news to me, and I'm happy that she tells me.

"Israel has been victim – not Israel itself, the Jews in Europe have been victims of one of the worst chapters in human history. I mean we talk about the Holocaust; that's the worst the human mind can come up with in terms of cruelty. So in a sense we have become victims of those who have been victims of European anti-Semitism."

She talks and talks and talks, as if giving a lecture to hundreds of students.

"We are a people of the land. We are a victim of a myth, the myth of a land without a people for a people without land, so all ours lives we try to prove that we exist, that we are the people of the land."

I butt in.

You were talking about a culture of hundreds and thousands of years, long before Israel. Give me a sense of Palestine before –

"Palestine has always been pluralistic, and has never been exclusive. I, as a Christian, see myself as the expression of the longest standing Christian tradition in the world. So I don't need to prove myself to anybody."

Hanan is an educated, erudite person, and I must view her from this angle. This brings me back to my university days, and I try to evaluate Hanan's argument according to academic standards. She is trying to prove to me Palestinian rights to this land by claiming that they are a people of the "longest Christian tradition in the world." This would be a nice argument had this been a reality, meaning if Christians were the majority of the Palestinian people. But this is not the case. When Israeli forces moved out of Ramallah, I read somewhere, Christians made for 20 percent of the inhabitants. I bring this to her attention.

How many Christians are here, 20 percent?

"It went down from 20 percent to 1.5 or 2 percent for a variety of reasons."

Oops. This means that after Israel's withdrawal it was the Muslims who kicked out the Christians, the truest Palestinians. The argument she has built against Israel is collapsing with one fell swoop. Yes, she spoke of a "variety of reasons," but she did not elaborate. I start pushing.

Why?

"I don't want to disc – "

She stops in mid-word. My professor is getting lost. "Is this the subject?" she mumbles, obviously irritated that I brought up this issue. This doesn't look good, and she knows it, but quickly she regains her composure: "First of all, the occupation. Second of all, the low birth rate. Third of all, connections with families outside."

But most of them left, right?

"I guess so. In Ramallah you can say that."

Twenty percent to one and a half. In how many years?

Hanan pauses. A worried expression shows on her face. She would prefer to talk about other issues, not this one. But being the pro she is, she regains composure, maneuvers a bit here and a bit there, and tries hard to regain my trust.

"We are the result of so many cultures and tribes. Probably in my background there are Jews."

And then she gives me this line:

"Palestine is open, is accommodating."

So accommodating, I point out to her, that when I smoked on the street today I was yelled at.

"Really?"

*   *   *

Hanan the Erudite knows what happened here thousands of years ago, but not what's happening today, at least this is what she is conveying, and so I try discussing history with her. Could she point out to me the exact date for the creation of Palestine, not just "hundreds or thousands" of years ago?

"People say we were here when the Jews came (in biblical times) and killed the Palestinians."

Then, quickly enough, she softens on this her assertion before anybody can accuse her of accepting any Jewish historical claim to this land. "Jewish tribes have been here," she tells me, "but there was not, you know, a state."

Was there a Jewish Temple here?

"I have no idea. I'm not an archeologist."

Did you ever think about it?

"I don't pass judgment. If an archeologist tells me there was, fine. If an archeologist tells me there wasn't, fine. This land is not an onion;

this land has so many layers. When you peel an onion, you reach the core and there's nothing left."

I actually love onions and I think I get her. Finally. Many thousands of years ago, though she does not supply the exact date, there existed a pluralistic state by the name of Palestine, and Jewish tribes came in and slaughtered its cultured residents. Biblical Israel never existed, no matter what her Christian Bible says, and nobody has ever proved that a Jewish Temple existed here either. Too bad for Arieh King, who speaks in terms of a Third Temple, as if the First and the Second indeed existed.

She then tells me: "I say: if your God tells you that you are chosen, our God didn't tell us this."

Hanan was one of the chief architects of various peace negotiations between the Israelis and the Palestinians, and I bring up this issue.

Will there be peace here at any point in our lifetime?

"I don't know. I promised my daughter, when we started the peace process, and my young daughter said: 'I lent my mother to peace, the peace process, the negotiations, so she could make peace and spend more time with me,' and not only didn't we make peace, she lost her childhood, her teenage years, and now in adulthood, as a woman, and a mother, they [Israel] took away her ID card so I cannot have my grandchildren."

She is choking, fighting back tears.

"All my life I've been struggling for peace. I made promises that I couldn't keep. So I can't tell you. But I think eventually there will have to be peace."

And now Hanan is crying, covering her face with both her hands.

Where is your daughter living now?

"In the States."

Which part of the States, New York?

"No."

Strangely, Hanan adamantly refuses to tell me in which state her daughter lives.

Well, if I can't get any info about the Daughter of Hanan I try to get some about the Son of God.

Do you believe in Jesus?

"Do I believe he existed? Yes, I believe he existed."

As a deity, as a God?

"No."

Do you believe in God?

"I don't think much about it, frankly."

Are you an atheist?

"Haaaa. I...I don't label myself."

Are you an atheist?

"I really don't know. I really don't know. Why do you want to label me?"

I don't want to label her. It was she who asserted Palestinian rights to this land by saying that Palestinians are of the "longest Christian tradition in the world," yet she does not believe in the one thing Christianity is about: the deity of Jesus. In addition, she who blames Israel for all the ills in her society would not point one single accusing finger at the Muslims who chase away the Christians from this land. Hanan has this intellectual capacity to avoid facts, just like Professor Omar of Al-Quds University, only she's more poetic in her language than he is.

As I bid her farewell, she orders her staff to connect me with other Palestinians of interest. I assume that her office will introduce me to people who would make her proud and not to extremist Palestinians, and I'm very grateful. Before leaving, an official at Hanan's office asks if I would like to visit the Mausoleum of Rais [President] Yasser Arafat, the first Palestinian president, buried at the Muqataa compound not far from here, and I respond that it would be my honor.

I guess that so far I'm doing very well in this part of the world, going from one dead to another: from the Mount of Olives to Arafat's Tomb.

A man arrives and takes me from Sesame to Rais Arafat, where I pay my respects.

I wonder what the soldiers standing at attention here would say, think, or do, if they knew who I am. For my part, I tell them I'm German. "Welcome to Palestine," they say to this German and take a few photos with me.

*　*　*

Photos done, I walk the streets of Ramallah, a gorgeously beautiful and rich city, when my eyes catch an interesting house: Dar Zahran Heritage Building.

I enter. Zahran, who is the founder and owner of this private museum, avails himself to guide me through an exhibition of Palestinian life in the last two hundred years. He pours me a cup of coffee and tells me the history.

"Somebody wanted to empty the Middle East of all Christians in order to show that the Arab world is a closed community, so that the Western world wouldn't support Palestine."

Who is that somebody?

"The occupation."

Who are they?

"Israel."

How did Israel do it?

"They made propaganda, spreading the story that locals were being killed by the government. The people heard this, got afraid, and left."

Makes a lot of sense. But why did the Christians leave and the Muslims stay? The Muslims stayed, didn't they?

Zahran gets very upset with me for asking this question. A radio journalist interviewed him the other day, he tells me, and that journalist didn't ask him this kind of question.

Where was the journalist from?

"Germany. ARD."

I don't know this reporter but perhaps he's one of the German journalists who applauded at *The Gardener* press conference. The questions I ask Zahran are questions that every journalist, using basic standards of journalism, should ask. Yet they don't.

It's getting late and I have to go back to Jerusalem. Ramallah is pretty close to Jerusalem but I'll have to cross the checkpoint into Israel first and, according to many media news reports, this can last hours.

As I get to the checkpoint I check the time on my iPhone, so I can determine the precise number of hours. It takes exactly two minutes and fourteen seconds.

I get home, ignore the cats, and go to sleep.

*　　*　　*

Thanks to Hanan's office, I'm to meet the "Spokesperson of the Government" this coming Friday, and one or two other people. I happily oblige.

Going from Jerusalem to Ramallah on a Friday of Ramadan is an experience. When I arrive at the Arab central bus station in an area Arabs call Bab al-Amud, Jews call Sha'ar Shkhem, and most others call Damascus Gate, no bus is at the station.

Where are the buses? I ask people walking by.

"Straight up."

The central bus station has moved up the road for Ramadan.

I walk up the road, walk and walk. A kid and his papa pass by. The kid carries a huge plastic rifle. Gift from papa, I guess.

I keep on walking.

Another kid, carried on his papa's back, holds a plastic bag. Sticking out of the bag is a shotgun, also of plastic. At least this is what I hope.

I keep on walking and see a big stand where a man is selling unique holiday items: tons of plastic guns, rifles, shotguns, and pistols.

Moments later, navigating my body around an endless stream of people, I mount a bus to Ramallah.

With Allah's help I reach Ramallah and safely arrive at the office of Dr. Ehab Bessaiso, "Spokesperson of the Government," at the Ministry of Information, State of Palestine. Following a UN General

Assembly vote in 2012 which recognized Palestinian statehood, the "Palestinian Authority" officially changed to "State of Palestine," Dr. Ehab explains to me.

Dr. Ehab has tons of other information he'd like to share with me.

Palestinians are like any other nation of the world, he tells me. They have thousands of years of history.

When was Palestine founded?

During the Canaanite period, he answers.

When did his people develop from Canaanites to Palestinians?

"You have to check this with historians, specialists in ancient history."

Do you have a historian here?

"Not on a Friday."

Ehab might not know about history, but he knows about "Information." And on this fast day this Spokesperson of the Government has food on his mind.

"The Israelis have taken falafel and humus as their food. Does humus exist in Poland? The Israelis have taken our food and call it Israeli food!"

Falafel reminds me of culture, I don't know why. I ask Dr. Ehab, who used to be a professor before joining this ministry, to define for me Palestinian culture.

"Tolerance and coherence define Palestinian culture."

In this tolerant environment, I ask him, how come Christians like me can't smoke during Ramadan?

"This is about respect."

Did this respect exist in Ramallah ten, twenty years ago?

"Yes."

Dr. Hanan Ashrawi, I tell him, who knows Ramallah better than both of us, was very surprised to hear that I couldn't smoke on the street.

This shakes him, for it implies that either he or Hanan is a liar.

He has no clue how to walk out of this little problem and he gets lost. He gets testy. He gets aggressive. He's upset, very upset. He goes into long monologues about totally unrelated issues, not allowing me to interrupt him, and by the end he lets me know that I know nothing and that the West is nothing but a bunch of arrogant people.

* * *

Thank God that Hanan's office arranged for me to meet yet another person, for otherwise this would be a total loss of a day. Moments later, in a café next to the ministry, I get to meet a famous Palestinian singer, whom I'll call here Nadia. She sits at a table with her good friend, a man named Khaled, a poet from Gaza who is presently staying in Ramallah.

During Ramadan there are a couple of restaurants open for unbelievers in Ramallah, mostly tourists, of course, on the condition that they are served their food away from the public's eye and that the front entrance of the restaurant looks as if they were closed. It is in a café like this that we sit. And Khaled speaks to me.

"The history of Palestine dates from fourteen thousand years

ago, in a place called Tulelat al-Rasul, a place between Jerusalem and Jericho. If you say that Moses came here in 1200 BCE, you have eleven thousand years before Moses. Who was here in those eleven thousand years? Palestinians! Joshua bin Nun occupied Jericho in 1200 BCE, who was there at that time? Palestinians. Of course! In the Torah itself it tells about wars between Israelis and Palestinians and it says, letter by letter, the word Palestinians. The BBC, before 1948, and in every news broadcast, they called this land Palestine and the people they called Palestinians."

I'm happy somebody is finally able to pinpoint exact dates of Palestinian history. But here's an entry from the *Encyclopædia Britannica* on the subject: "In 132 the emperor Hadrian decided to build a Roman colony, Aelia Capitolina, on the site of Jerusalem. . . . The province of Judaea was renamed Syria Palaestina (later simply called Palaestina), and, according to Eusebius of Caeseria (*Ecclesiastical History*, book IV, chapter 6), no Jew was thenceforth allowed to set foot in Jerusalem or the surrounding district."

Khaled has written the lyrics for Nadia's CD. She plays them on her smartphone and I ask her to sing along. The lyrics are in Arabic, and she translates them into English thusly:

The night carries me,
And the Northern Star.
I am stronger and far away,
And I'm not coming back.
I see skies and moons in fire,
And the light coming out of pain.
The night carries me.

"Formally, by passport, I'm an Israeli Palestinian, but I call myself 'a Palestinian from the occupied lands of 1948.'"

In the eyes of the Israeli government you are an Arab-Israeli, correct?

"Yes."

Nadia, according to her own words, studied social work at the

Hebrew University in Jerusalem for two and a half years. She didn't finish; she took a break, and then "studied music for five years at the Jerusalem Academy of Music and Dance, where I got a degree in music, specializing in voice." She tells me that her music teacher, a German-Jewish woman, was "my mother," but that after graduating from school she is no longer in touch with her.

Why?

"She is an occupier."

Nadia's capacity to throw away a woman she had called "mother" for five years at the very moment she didn't need her anymore is striking.

I ask her the most important question anybody has ever asked here or ever will: Did you ever fall in love with an Israeli man?

"No. I couldn't."

Why not?

"I am a Palestinian. It is the same as a Jew falling in love with a German Nazi officer."

Would you like for Palestinians and Israelis to solve their conflict by dividing the land into two states, Palestine and Israel?

"No. Zionism is racism. As simple as stealing my country, my land, and daring to find excuses for it, trying their best to erase me. Israel has stolen my mother's dress; they call this dress 'Israeli.' They have stolen my food; they call my food 'Israeli.'"

What on earth is going on today with this falafel thing!

Nadia, who lives in Jerusalem, is an Israeli citizen and carries an Israeli passport, tells me that "life under occupation" is awfully bad and that the Jews "almost killed my daughter."

What happened?

Well, this is what happened. Nadia was coming back from the West Bank the other day and the occupiers had put a roadblock before the entry into Israel. She was in the first in a line of cars, she recalls, on a very hot August day. She had her baby daughter with her and the baby wanted to be fed, breast-fed that is. Nadia begged the soldiers to allow her to just drive on but they said, "No, it's a roadblock." The baby was crying, and she had no choice but to feed the baby in the car.

How this translates into murder, or almost murder, is beyond my capacity to comprehend.

Wait a second: You got free higher education for God knows how many years, right? You, as an Israeli citizen, get medical care, free or for a token payment, you are a famous singer –

"Occupiers have to pay a price for their occupation: they must pay for the occupied's medical expenses, food, and higher education," she cuts me off.

I'm not sure which law book decrees that a state, of whatever nature, must pay for five years of music classes, in addition to over two years of social studies to its citizens who are not Jewish (Jews don't get free university education in Israel), but if this is called Occupation, I'd like to be occupied for the rest of my life.

Nadia, who is a Christian and married to a Muslim, blames the Israelis for another thing. Her children, she tells me, are being brought up Muslim because this is the Israeli law. The Occupiers have dictated that a Christian woman married to a Muslim must raise her kids as Muslim.

Knowing that I'm a German tourist, she feeds me everything she imagines a German like me would have the stomach to digest on this fast day. But I was born here, not in Germany. What she claims to be an Israeli law is actually Islamic law, yet I don't challenge her. She has spoken to Western journalists before, and if I challenge her she might doubt my Aryan roots.

Her hatred for Israelis is immense, like that of Dr. Ehab. Why Hanan Ashrawi's office would introduce me to these two is a mystery to me. My guess is that this couple is regarded as "moderate" in the Palestinian society. If these are the moderates, I ask myself, who could the extremists be?

* * *

Evening soon falls and eating is permitted. I ask Nadia for a nice

Palestinian restaurant and she drives me to central Ramallah in her Opel. She points to a building across the street from us and tells me that on the fifth floor there is a restaurant I should try.

I do.

It is an all you can eat place. Price? Eighty-nine shekels, the waiter tells me. It's a great price but I tell him that this is way too expensive for a man like me. He immediately realizes that I'm actually a Palestinian and he lowers the price to forty-five.

I sit down, starting with a delicious cold chicken soup – this is the first time I realize you can have cold chicken soup – and move on to the rest of the food. Like every good Muslim I've been fasting all day and I need all the food there is on the planet.

I'm getting it all here.

Men, women, and children are packing this place. People, including old ladies in hijab, smoke shisha and cigarettes, as a singer performs wonderful Arabic music. When he reaches high notes, a frequent occurrence, the dining smokers let out huge sounds of approval. They clap, they sing along, and they shout. O they shout!

This is just beautiful.

And if this is Palestinian culture, they should be damn proud of themselves.

*   *   *

After having consumed some elaborate food, I go back to Jerusalem.

In the van to Jerusalem, there are more people than seats, but no one says a thing. The price is nevertheless the same.

Two Palestinian ladies with the most gorgeous hijabs are on this van as well. I look at them and wonder how this piece of clothing can make people look so attractive. Yes, I mean it: these ladies are plain beauties.

This makes me think: I like the Palestinians. No, this is not exact. I love the Palestinians. Damn it, it's true. I might not agree with what they say but as people I just love them. I see them in this van and I realize how close they are to each other, even if this is the first time that they have met. There's a brotherhood here, warmth, friendship, sense of togetherness. And, oh by God, the Palestinian hijab is plain gorgeous. Really. Turkish women should learn from the Palestinians how to make hijabs.

It is Friday, which means it is Sabbath (in the Jewish calendar the day starts in the evening). Public transportation is not working and the stores are closed.

It takes but minutes to ride from the de facto capital of Palestine to the de facto capital of Israel, and they are two worlds apart. You sense it immediately when you cross from one to the other. Different atmosphere. Different spirit. Different culture. In one country God doesn't like you to consume food, in the other country He doesn't like you to buy food. And if you think this difference is not a question of life and death, you better take the first plane out of here.

There is a white guy out there by the name of John Kerry, husband to Teresa Heinz of the world-famous ketchup-maker H. J. Heinz Company, and he is the current American Secretary of State. He has just announced that the Israelis and the Palestinians are to resume peace talks a week later in Washington. After Washington he's going to come here again and move back and forth between the two neighbors, stay in a posh hotel here and in a posh hotel there, never lacking the capacity to buy or eat on certain days or at certain times, and he's never going to learn that the Middle East is made of Arieh and Nadia, not of ketchup and mayonnaise.

Kerry, of course, is not the only peace seeker of humanity. Jews who live in the States do this as well. Some are like Irving Moskowitz, while others are on the opposite side. It's time I get to meet them.

Gate Five

An American Jew loves his old mama so much
that he wants to see her homeless.

TOBY, A NICE AMERICAN-RAISED GRANDMA NOW LIVING IN THE GERMAN COL-ony, invites me to her home to eat the Sabbath meal with her. I never say no to food and I go.

Toby is the mama of an American Jew who is very busy raising money for Adalah ("justice"), a pro-Palestinian human rights organization. I would like him to raise money for me, but I don't think it's going to happen. He raises money only for worthy causes, I learn, and Adalah is a worthy cause. What the heck is Adalah? I never heard of Adalah and I'd like to know. If they are that good, maybe I should get myself a seat on their board.

I try to get Toby to explain to me what Adalah is, but Toby doesn't tell me much. Is it a secret organization? Just the idea that this might be a secret organization makes me very curious to learn more about them. Thank God there was Steve Jobs and he invented the magic iPad, which I have with me.

I check Adalah on Steve's tablet and I find some intriguing articles about them. According to *Haaretz*, the most left-leaning daily Israeli paper, Adalah's legal initiatives include abolishing the Jewish identity of the State of Israel, the abolishment of the Law of Return (which enables diaspora Jews to immigrate to Israel), and the institutionalization of the Right of Return (which will allow "diaspora Palestinians" to immigrate and to claim lands).

In short: millions of Jews out, millions of Palestinians in.

Not bad for an American Jew who has nothing better to do. The only problem is this: if he is successful, his beloved mama will become homeless.

Should I raise this issue with Toby? I don't know yet. Let me first see how the meal progresses.

Renee, Toby's good friend, is also sitting at the table. Both observe the Sabbath, eat only kosher, go to the synagogue, and pray daily.

The food at Toby's table is of the "healthy" variety: natural and tasteless. Usually, for me this is a sign that my host is an intellectual. Is she? Time will tell. Meantime, I try hard to swallow the stuff. The stray cats in my backyard garden, I can guarantee, would bite the hell out of me if I tried to give them this food.

As I struggle with the food, Toby starts a conversation. She asks me which people I have met so far. Should I tell her about Arieh? About Tziporah? Nope. Her baby loves the Palestinians and I tell her of two Palestinians whom I have just met: Nadia and Khaled.

She asks me to tell her what they told me. I tell her.

"Perhaps you met fanatic Muslims with no education."

I tell her that Nadia is no Muslim, not to mention fanatic Muslim, and that she has quite a few years of higher education.

"This cannot be the truth. They don't talk like this in Ramallah."

Should I tell her that Nadia is actually from Jerusalem, and an Israeli citizen? Toby would have a heart attack, and so I add no details.

As another portion of food is brought in I learn that both these ladies are of high academic achievements, and it appears to me that they are not used to having their opinions challenged. When I tell Toby what Dr. Ehab said to me, and she again says that "This cannot be the truth," I snap.

Toby, I say, intellectuals who refuse to acknowledge facts are worse than idiots.

I can't believe my lips have just uttered these words. Toby can't believe it either and reminds me that I'm just a guest here.

I should get the hint and shut up. But I don't.

I'm a recovering intellectual, Toby. I come from where you come from, the university, and I think no idea or evidence should be abandoned before it is expressed and examined. That's what we have been taught in academia, haven't we?

What's a "recovering intellectual"?

Toby doesn't get it, but Renee is laughing, hard. She has never heard this phrase either, she tells me, but she thinks it's really, really great.

Toby still doesn't get it.

Renee tries to explain to her: "It is like 'recovering alcoholic.'"

Toby: "In Ramallah people don't talk like this! What you say is a generalization. You are generalizing!"

Why "In Ramallah people don't talk like this!" is not a generalization, I don't know. It's a waste of time to argue with her, but I can't resist asking her one more question.

Toby, when is the last time you visited Ramallah?

"Never."

As I leave Toby's home I think to myself: Did people like her exist in the Israel of my time? How come I don't remember them?

Gate Six

An Israeli soldier detains President Barack Obama.

THE OFFICE OF THE PRESIDENT OF ISRAEL, MY IPAD TELLS ME, HAS JUST ISSUED an exciting announcement. "President Shimon Peres," it says, will host at his residence "an Iftar dinner to break the Ramadan fast. The dinner will be attended by leading Muslim figures from within Israel, including imams, community leaders, ambassadors, heads of municipalities, national service volunteers and social activists.

"President Peres will deliver a speech at the dinner during which he will convey a greeting for Ramadan to Muslims in Israel and across the world. During his speech President Peres will address the resumption of peace talks between Israel and the Palestinians."

Naturally, a man like me must mingle with leading Muslim figures and foreign ambassadors.

I get to the president's residence as soon as I can.

As you walk into the president's residence and pass into the security check-in room, just below the air-conditioning unit, there are pictures of Obama and Peres hanging on the wall. You can see them walking together, looking up at something together, or standing next to a car together. I wonder if Obama hangs the same pictures on the walls of the White House.

I pass through this room and go to join the leading Muslim figures in attendance. The end of fast for today, an official says to members of the press, is 7:41 p.m. This reminds me of Orthodox Jews counting the moments till the end of the fast on Yom Kippur. Of course, this is the residence of Israel's president and we are talking Ramadan here, not Yom Kippur.

Press people have seats designated to them. All others are welcomed to sit at tables to be served a presidential dinner.

I look around and wonder which table I should sneak to, without anybody telling me to get up. To my left is a table with old people; to my right is a table with army commanders – or at least this is what I think they are: a group of healthy-looking men wearing uniforms with pieces of shiny metal on their shoulders.

Should I sit with the muscled men or with the wise?

A huge dilemma.

Nope. Don't ask me why I think old men are wise; this is something I was taught when I was a baby and somehow it has never left my brain.

Interfering with my thought process is a sudden, new development: a Qadi decrees, we are told, that Iftar in Jerusalem is at 7:49 p.m. Wow.

This Qadi must be from Meah Shearim. They like it holier.

At 7:49, the time permitted to eat, I make up my mind to sit with the commanders. Wise is good, but mighty is better.

Peres speaks, in Hebrew. "This house is also yours," he says. He is cute, this ninety-year-old man, I think to myself. Never tiring, always smiling.

And then he talks of the peace talks:

"I know there are people who say nothing will come out of it, but I say it will. The terrorists who want to hurt us, hurt themselves. I want to praise the two leaders who decided to renew talks. My friend Mahmoud Abbas... and the prime minister of Israel."

Interesting that he uses the "friend" term only for the Palestinian.

"We are all adults here, and I know that there will be times of hardships... but we have no other alternative to peace."

Not adults; commanders!

"All of us were created in the image of *Elokim* [sic]." Interestingly, Peres is using the Orthodox way of referring to God. The mention of God to them is forbidden. Whereas God in Hebrew is *Elohim*, the Orthodox change the H to K. Why? God knows.

Peres keeps on talking. Here's one of his great lines: "There is no other truth than the truth of peace."

* * *

People all around me are eating. This is a presidential meal, after all. I talk to the big shots sitting at my table. To my left, I find out, is a doctor in the security jail of Megido. Next to him is a "mayor" of a small village. The others are pretty much the same and, with one exception, everybody at this table is Circassian, not Arab. The one Arab here, a man dressed in civilian clothes, is a computer security specialist.

I exchange a few words with him. Are Arabs and Jews getting along in this country?

"No way."

He must be kidding. There are "leading Muslim figures" here, though not at this table, and if Arabs and Jews don't get along, why are they here?

Shamefully enough, I can't recognize the important leaders here and I ask people to point out to me the leading Muslims and the ambassadors. They can't. If there are any leading Muslim figures here, I soon conclude, they are the Circassians at my table.

The people at this gathering, many of whom know each other, lead communities the size of Tziporah's house at the cemetery. And even with such a community size, not all the tables here are taken.

I mingle with the crowd. There must be more to what my eyes see, I say to myself. I approach a young man wearing a suit and start talking to him.

What's your name?

"Obama."

Excuse me?

"I came to make peace," he admonishes me, "but got stopped at a checkpoint."

Who is President Peres inviting to his party? This guy must be either a self-deluding man or a stand-up comedian, though he might be both. When asked, he tells me he is "the only Arab comedian" there is.

Back at my table, I again talk to the Arab.

Is life really so bad here?

"I don't want to talk, but yes."

Would you like to leave this country?

"No way! They [the Jews] want to force me out, but I won't leave!"

And if they wanted you to stay?

"I'd leave on the first plane going out!"

He tells me he wants to have freedom, like the Europeans have, and move from country to country just like the Europeans do. I ask him if he studied history, and if he remembers how many rivers of blood have been flowing there just in the last century.

I tell him: If you, people in this area, had spilled as much blood as Europe so recently has, not one human being would exist in the Middle East by now. He looks at me, in huge amazement, as the other Muslims all stare at me. Do you remember, I ask him, that just before 1989 civilians could not cross from one side of Berlin to the other?

There's silence at the table.

After seeming hesitation, the computer specialist breaks the silence.

"I never thought of this, but you're right."

I walk up to Shimon Peres to shake hands with him and tell him he spoke well. What else could I say?

"How did you get such good Hebrew?" he asks me.

As I start making my way out, I think: even during this particular week, with peace talks taking place, not even this internationally admired Jew could get bigger Arab leaders than "Obama" to attend his dinner.

In the president's garden there is a fragment of decorated stone from the "southern entrance to the Temple Mount" on display, dated "first century BCE."

Dr. Hanan is not here to see it, neither is Ehab or Khaled. Only Obama.

What happened to this country while I was away? Even its president is a deluded man.

I have an idea: collect bones from the tables for the stray cats. I walk back to check for bones, but the tables have been cleaned.

Gate Seven

Little white Jew doesn't want to marry little black Jew. German teenagers wouldn't mind watching Jews being stoned. A soldier drives nine hours to meet his dead comrade.

NOW THAT I GOT A LITTLE TASTE OF ISRAELI POLITICS, I MOVE NORTHWARD, TO Haifa and vicinity. I first stop at a youth village for orphans, Yemin Orde, near Haifa. They must be less deluded than the Israeli president, I hope.

First off, I meet Chaim Peri, the president and founder of Yemin Orde Educational Initiative. Chaim's father and mother were German Jews, "Yekkes." His mother was picking apples in the fields of Palestine during WWII, in 1941, and only after Chaim was born did she become aware of what was happening to her family in Germany. This caused her a mental breakdown, from which she never recovered.

If you wonder what a Yekke is, here's an example: "My grand-mother, on my father's side, who was from Berlin and was called '*die blonde schikse mit die lange fiss*,' used German to remember Hebrew words. For example, *toda rabba*, which is Hebrew for 'thank you,' my grandmother memorized as *toter Araber*." *Toter Araber* means "dead Arabs."

Yemin Orde is a non-traditional boarding school; it looks more like a village than a school, but it is a boarding school. They don't call it boarding school, he says, as that name that implies a closed world.

It emulates real life, non-institutionalized life, where one part is the school and the other is the home. Kids study at the school and then they go "home" like kids with parents do, and at home they can talk about school, even complain about the school. For the most part, the kids here are Ethiopian and Russian, Israel's newest immigrant communities.

Chaim is a religious person, but as you might expect from a son of Yekkes, he has his own ways of looking at things. According to him, "The most God-fearing people are the atheists." Go figure.

This village is a great idea, I tell him. Question to you: if you were not a Yekkes' son, would you have the same great ideas and frame of mind that you have today?

"Let me say this: Anything that started in this society, started with German Jews."

Rakheli, a young Ethiopian who is part of the staff here, is a vivacious and smart young woman who loves to talk *dugri* (straight). Asked if there's racism in Israeli society, she says: "Yes, there is. It is not the same racism as the one America has been dealing with – no blacks are being killed here – but racism definitely exists in our society."

How do you deal with this?

"I tell my students: Our black color will not change. Their white color will not change. Physically we look different. No matter what you do to cause a change in society, the colors will not change. Live with it."

This little speech helps?

"I say to my students: There are twenty-four hours in a day. Nobody will give you more hours in a day, and nobody will take any of them away from you. These twenty-four hours belong to you, do with them what you can. If you want to spend them complaining, you will pay the price. You can make anything you want out of yourself, but you have to do it."

I meet a young kid, a grandson to one of the white volunteers here, and I play with him. We get to like each other, and joke together. Then, after a while, I ask him some stupid questions. One of them is this: When you grow older, would you like to marry an Ethiopian woman? I could arrange one for you, would you like me to do it?

"No."

Why not?

"No."

Why?

"Because."

What do you think, black people are good?

"No."

What makes them bad?

The child catches sight of his older brother who is gesturing him to shut up and he does.

It always amazes me how hard it is for one people not to discriminate another.

*   *   *

Time to move on, to Haifa. *The Gardener* film, a PC film, as PC as you'll ever get, plays to the same discriminating concept as I have just encountered: white and black. There you have the softy white woman and the roughish black man, in a film shot by an Iranian lover of Israel. *The Gardener* was shot in the Bahá'í Gardens in Haifa, which is my first stop in the city.

Bahá'í Gardens.

I walk through the enchanting gardens and make my way up the steps leading to the shrine. It is closed at the moment, and four young people are seated on the steps by its gate. They are Mo, Selina, Birte, and Marvin. Two of them have just finished high school, two have graduated from college, and all are German.

They are on a two-week trip to Israel, have been to Tel Aviv and Jerusalem and are now in Haifa. In Jerusalem they saw Arabs throwing stones at Jews in the Old City for about two hours, they recall, and then Israeli police came "with guns and horses." This is a brutal behavior of the Israelis, they say, because the police should have "talked with them" instead of coming in with force. Interestingly, they don't have a single word of criticism against the stone throwers.

Did any of you change his or her mind about Israel, now that you are here?

Mo tells me that he saw "more aggressiveness on the Jewish side" than he had thought.

What do you mean?

"Jewish soldiers with guns in worship places!"

What would have happened to the Jews if no police had shown up with guns?

"I don't know."

No matter what could have happened to the Jews, getting hurt or killed, he says, the Jews should accept the stones.

At least he's honest.

Selina used to think that the conflict between Arabs and Jews was easier to solve, it was black and white for her, but being here she realizes it's not that simple.

Birte thinks that "you can't just come into a country and throw the people out," which is what the Jews did, and she felt it while here. I guess she's talking about 1948, when the Jewish state was founded, long before she was born, and most likely before her parents were born. How does she manage to "feel" it?

"I had a good teacher at school and she taught us all about it."

I came to see black and white and I got Germans.

* * *

Haifa University is a cab ride away, and I go there.

Fania Oz-Salzberger, the daughter of the famous Israeli author Amos Oz, is a professor of history at the Haifa University School of Law.

Fania, a lady of proper manners, orders cold drinks for her guest at the university's cafeteria, and as soon as we both light up and inhale the smoke into our lungs, we start discussing extremely important issues. For example: Who's a Jew?

Israeli lawmakers have been trying to solve this question for decades but still have no clue. Fania has.

"Ours, meaning the Jews, is not a blood line but a text line."

Is this the most important definition of being Jewish?

"Yes."

How do the Palestinians figure in this equation? I have no idea why I'm asking this question. The word *Palestinian* has been hammered into my brain so many times since I've arrived here that I must release it on somebody. Surprisingly, Fania answers my question as if it were the most logical in existence.

"They don't, they are like any other nation."

Fania is proud of her people and her culture. "Israel is the greatest exporter of meaning in the world, and we have done this since the time of Jesus. This land proves that size doesn't matter."

Fania doesn't stop here, she keeps on: "This place works like a magnet and is also radioactive, spreading out. Call it mystical. I don't know what it is. Think of the Crusaders: why did knights mount horses and come here? Why did prophet Muhammad come here to fly to heaven from Jerusalem? Why did the Jews come here again? There are forces at work here, call them magnetism and radioactivity. This place draws energy in and it spreads it out."

Fania has a fresh voice, whether you agree with her or not, and I listen. "This place is the densest in the world in terms of words. Ten kilometers from here is Armageddon. Every place in this country has an in-built library. This crowdedness of textuality is the meaning of this place.

"Jews and Arabs are killing one another. Arabs and Arabs are killing one another. But Jews and Jews don't kill each other, they scream at each other. This is because Jews are made of words, words that are in books and have been in books for twenty-five hundred years."

This is not exactly true. Former prime minister Yitzhak Rabin died by a bullet of a Jewish assassin. The Zionist leader Haim Arlozorov was most likely killed at the hands of Jewish assassins. The journalist

Rabbi Jacob Israël de Haan was murdered by the Haganah (a pre-state paramilitary Jewish organization that eventually became the IDF), probably by order of David Ben-Gurion, Israel's first prime minister. And of course there's the Altalena Affair, in which nineteen Jews were killed by other Jews.

Yet, these numbers are minute in comparison to other nations.

And Fania keeps charting her course.

"I like some Greek books, from the ancient era, more than most Jewish books. But no other nation, except the Jews, 'forced its children to go to school at the age of three.'

I never thought of this, though I should have. When Fania says it, she magically brings me back to my baby years. I started studying Judaism at the tender age of three.

I leave Fania, one of the few intellectuals I met who actually made me think, and walk the streets of Haifa, a city peacefully populated by both Arabs and Jews. Haifa impresses me as a laid-back city, a nice and calm city, but way too hot. I miss Jerusalem weather. No, not miss; need. I board a bus to the capital, of the Jews or of the Arabs, and sit down on the single seat available, next to a soldier with a submachine gun.

*　　*　　*

I introduce myself to him as a man named Tuvia. He likes the name and he opens up.

He was allowed to leave his base for a day and a half and is now on his way home to Jerusalem, where his mama and papa can't wait to see him and spoil him. He's stationed on the Lebanese border and has been on the road for some time now. To be exact: nine hours. His day and a half, if you deduct his rides back and forth and add sleeping time, is in reality just a few hours.

Before coming to the Lebanese border he was stationed in Hebron.

I ask him if any of his political views were changed after being in Hebron or on the Lebanese border.

"Yes. I've become more of a rightist. Standing at a checkpoint is not easy. You don't know what will happen next. Every day, almost every day, they [Palestinians] push their ten-year-old children, sometimes even younger, to come near the checkpoint and throw stones at us. What can you do to a child? You can't fight children. The parents teach their children – and sometimes I could hear the lessons in the nearby school – to hate Jews. It's not the children's fault, but it's the children who throw the stones. I heard and I saw, and now I've moved to the right. When you stand at a checkpoint, sooner or later you'll change your views, if you were a leftist. You experience the hate and you know there's no chance for peace."

I assume you are a proud Zionist –

"I'm not a Zionist. When I finish my army service, I think of leaving Israel and going to Brooklyn. I have family in America."

Why then are you serving in the army?

"When I was a kid growing up in Israel, someone out there protected me. Now it's my turn to protect the kids."

How's life on the border?

"Boring. Dangerous."

Do you sleep in tents?

"Tents?? If we lived in tents we would be dead."

Describe your living conditions –

"We live in a fortress, with no windows anywhere. It is hot. Hot. Hot. I have three fans running, just to have a little air."

What do you do when you're not in the fortress?

"I don't know if I'm allowed to speak to you."

Yes, you are allowed!

He pauses. He thinks. I smile to him and he goes on:

"At the border. We look at them, they look at us, and nothing happens. Sometimes I miss Hebron, because there something was happening, always, even if it wasn't a nice experience. The Arab kids with the stones, or the adult leftists. They come too, and they curse the soldiers. Some are Jews and some are not. But at least we didn't hide in the dark, like on the Lebanese border, not knowing what will happen and if anything will happen.

"Yes, true; this is also an experience. People from all walks of life share the same fortress, and the same rooms. I made friends in the army that I wouldn't have made otherwise. Ethiopians, Russians, everybody. Rich and poor, educated and not. We learn to know each other in very difficult circumstances and we become brothers. Being in the army teaches us that we are all the same. For this I'm very happy."

How much money do you earn in the army?

"I'm in a combat unit, and we make more than others."

He earns, all told, €150 a month.

This "more than others" huge pay he spends on cigarettes and alcohol. "When I get a day off, I go out and I drink. Just to clear my head. It's very difficult otherwise."

As the bus reaches Jerusalem I hear him on his cellphone, speaking to a friend or a family member: "I'll be in the cemetery in the morning." When he gets off the phone I ask him who died. A fellow soldier from his unit, he answers. He pauses for a minute, takes a straight look at me, and says: "I don't really know if I'll leave this country. I don't think I will."

He was talking to me about a drink, and if it had not been for the phone call I wouldn't have known about the dead. He drove all the way to meet his dead friend. His name is Ariel. And Ariel will never leave his dead soldier friend behind. You can't take a cemetery with you.

Gate Eight

*An American Jewish lady finds the Jewish libido and an
Israeli biblical expert can't recall the Book of Isaiah.*

NOW THAT I'VE VENTURED OUT OF THE DE FACTO CAPITALS OF BOTH ISRAEL
and Palestine, by going to Haifa, it is time that I brave into Tel Aviv,
Israel's cultural capital.

Outside my hotel room is the beach. I look out and see huge signs
proclaiming that there is no lifeguard on site and that swimming or
bathing are prohibited. I marvel at what I see on the beach: Hundreds
of people, all ignoring the signs.

As for me, I go to meet Ran Rahav, Israel's best-known PR person,
who represents the richest and most famous of Israel and who, in
addition, is a very famous TV persona in his own right. He has a wonderful office, walls covered by expensive paintings and floors covered
by invaluable works of arts, and we have a chat. Ran tells me that the
engine driving the Israeli people is this: "Survival."

Ran, who is the "Honorary Consul of the Marshal Islands in
Israel" – don't ask me how he got himself this title – knows his people
much better than many.

Survival.

With this one objective in mind, the Jews of this country planted
trees in the desert, erected skyscrapers on swamps, and built one
of the strongest armies in the world from scratch. This place, call it

Israel or Palestine, was a mix between desert and swamps before the Musulmänner of Auschwitz-Birkenau showed up on its shores. Israel's Jews, whose home was a concentration camp, have managed to move to the forty-ninth floor of luxury apartments in Tel Aviv. These people, who stayed alive by drinking one dirty cup of water a day in Treblinka, are now licking the most delicious ice cream at sunsets. These people, who authored the Bible, are now the authors of the most advanced technology there is.

Sitting down for dinner with an American Jewish lady, she tells me that she has just found the hidden meaning of Israel. What is it? Sex. Yep. She noticed, she says, that wherever she goes in Israel she encounters "sexual tension" in the air. I'm not sure, but I think an Israeli man has flirted with her and she's all hot.

I go out to check Tel Aviv's sexy creatures.

I walk to Rothschild Street, where the Ashkenazi liberal rich dine, entertain, and work. Here one can find restaurants offering healthy drinks that fit the taste and philosophy of Jewish peace lovers, usually at exuberant prices. It is interesting for me to see, as I walk, that the leftists of this land are also its richest. How does this work, and why, is a puzzle to me.

*   *   *

When I lived in this land, Professor Yeshayahu Leibowitz, an Orthodox Jew who studied at Berlin and Basel universities and taught at the Hebrew University, was the leftist I knew and to whose lectures I went to listen. He had the sharpest of tongues and the most brilliant of minds I knew of, and I wonder if today's Israel's leftists are the same.

The next evening I sit down with a number of leftist intellectuals, university professors and such, for dinner in quite an expensive restaurant, and talk with the nicest-looking of the bunch who holds the title of "political psychologist." The first thing she says to me is this: "I am a liberal, super liberal, and I'm an atheist." When the waiter comes she orders café latte, but being an intellectual that she is, she can't just order latte without making it tasteless. Her latte, she tells the waiter, should contain coffee without caffeine and milk without fat, and be served in a clear glass.

Her specialty, she informs me, is religious extremists, mainly settlers. The settlers, she declares with authority and certainty, are idiots. And when I ask her if she read any of their literature, just to make sure that they are "certified nuts," she tells me that she doesn't have to do so since she has read many of their detractors who quote them, and this is more than enough.

In addition to her settler expertise, she tells me that she's also an expert on Judaism, which she classifies as a "pagan religion." I ask her if she has ever studied Judaism, a question that makes her raise her voice in anger. For years and years and years, she yells at this offender of her high stature, she has been studying Judaism over and over and over. I light up a cigarette, inhale and exhale, look at her and ask her: Could you tell me, please, what the "Vision of Isaiah" is? That's the most basic question one could ask and any student of Bible 101 could have answered this question in his sleep, but this learned lady has no clue. What vision? What Isaiah?

I am befuddled by her lack of knowledge but everybody at this table asserts beyond doubt that I lack the mental capacity to understand higher concepts. They pound me with super brainy words of no meaning, and as I sip my Chivas Regal I reminisce about one of my favorite rabbis from the days of old, a genius by any standards: "He who cannot explain his thesis in simple words is he who has no thesis."

Yeah. These professors are no Yeshayahu Leibowitz; they are not worthy to even be his servants.

Gate Nine

A man who invented three words, Na Nakh Nakhman,
changes a country.

THERE ARE PEOPLE IN THIS LAND WHO KNOW THE BOOK OF ISAIAH, AND MANY other books as well, and in the morning of the next day I decide to spend some hours with them. They are the ultra-Orthodox people of a city called Bet Shemesh who, I am told, are the most righteous of the Chosen Couples. The women are also known as "Taliban,"

because they wear more "modest" clothes than the most pious of Saudi ladies. The "trash bag" ladies I saw in Meah Shearim actually live there, I'm told.

I get there faster than an eagle.

On what seems to me to be Bet Shemesh's main street I meet a bunch of Hasidim, all of whom look quite bored.

Are you married? I ask one of them.

"Yes."

Is your wife a great woman?

"Oh, yes."

Can you share with me two bad things in her character that you really don't like?

"My wife has only virtues."

How about your wife? I ask another man, as if this were my business.

"She has only one bad quality: she possesses not one good quality."

I laugh out loud.

How come these Jews have such a great sense of humor, while the rest of Israeli society is, in comparison, humorless?

I walk further and I meet Yoel, member of a sect known as the Reb Ahrelakh (followers of Rabbi Aharon) dressed in his community's unique silver coat, and chat with him about current politics.

What do you think of the peace talks (between Arabs and Jews)?

"You have to ask the rabbis, I have no opinion."

I'm not asking you for a religious ruling, I'm asking you what you think.

"What I think? What is there to think? According to Jewish law, Jews are not supposed to fight the Gentiles. We shouldn't fight the Arabs! But, peace? There will never be peace. The Gentiles don't like us, and they never will. What peace? Peace is a dream."

Let me ask you another question. I came here to see the Jewish Taliban but I don't see them. Do they live here or not?

"Here we have only about twenty of them. They don't live in the same place but they meet together and they do what they want. The rabbis have ruled against them."

Because of the burqa/niqab?

"No, no. If they want to dress in black all over, let them; this is not the problem. The problem with them is that they decide for themselves what is permitted to do and what is forbidden, and they don't follow their husbands. A husband for them means just a 'thing,' and this is against Judaism. Wives should follow their husbands."

This guy, though he tried to play humble with me, is actually a teacher in the community.

Maybe I can get him to teach me a thing or two, I think to myself. There is something I have been wondering about, something unique to Israel, a peculiarity that I've not seen in other countries, nor in the Israel of my past. All over Israel, and I mean all over, there is this sign in Hebrew displayed on almost every available wall: *Na Nakh Nakhma Nakhman Me'Uman*, which refers to Rabbi Nakhman of Breslev, who passed away about two hundred years ago.

"The Nanakhs are not real Hasidim, they are just *meshugehners*. They are lazy people who don't like to study. Instead they spend their days and nights telling people to be happy all the time and dance all day. This is not normal, this is not real."

Nanakhs is a word I am hearing for the first time; *meshugehners* means idiots in Hebrew/Yiddish.

How did this Nanakh movement start?

"You don't know?"

No.

"This started many years ago, maybe thirty, by a good guy, not like the Nanakhs. He had a problem: he was a sick man, sad all the time, and nobody could help him. One day one of his friends decided to do something about it. He took a piece of paper and wrote on it: 'He who says these words, *Na Nakh Nakhma Nakhman Me'Uman*, will be happy and healthy.' Then he added a line next to it: 'This paper has dropped from heaven.' He put the paper inside a book he knew the sick man was reading and left.

"When later the sad, sick man opened the book and saw the paper, he believed that it was really sent to him from heaven. He followed what heaven suggested, said this Nanakh all day and it helped him to be happy and healthy ever after. That's the story."

Americans came up with McDonald's and Coca Cola, Israelis come up with computer chips and Nanakhs. Any wonder these two countries are getting along?

* * *

Normally, when I arrive in a new place I try to taste the food its people eat, which is exactly what I want to do now, only here I encounter a big problem: no restaurants. The Haredi of Bet Shemesh don't go to restaurants because they believe that restaurants are from the devil. In restaurants, after all, men and women can meet and then the men, God forbid, might get an erection when biting into a chicken's leg while looking at a Taliban.

In addition to the No Restaurant policy, these people have their own buses, where men sit in the front of the bus and women in the back. It is by this sectional division, God has obviously revealed to them, men won't be staring at the tempting creatures known as women and won't entertain sinful thoughts.

Egged, the public transportation system in most of Israel, also operates in this city but does not divide its buses into sections.

I walk around in search of a cookie, instead of a restaurant meal, when I spot on the road ahead a police car, blocking the traffic.

What happened? I ask a Hasid walking by.

"Oh, that? An Egged bus was stoned on the other side of the road."

Why?

"Was stoned. It happens sometimes."

By a Palestinian?

"No. In Bet Shemesh we don't have Arabs. Here it's only Jews."

Why was the bus stoned?

"Because the bus, which is not our kosher bus, belongs to the Zionist government," he answers, as if this makes a perfect sense. It sounds strange to me and I walk over to the police car, inside which the cops sit, drinking coffee and playing with their smartphones. They order me to go away and I show them my press card. A cop by the name of Liran is not impressed: "I owe you nothing, I'm not going to tell you anything. Get the fuck out."

Is this the way you're supposed to talk to the press?

"What? What did I say? I said nothing."

This is rude, I think, and a Hasidic woman passing by tells me: "Write this! People should know how Zionist cops talk and behave. People don't know. They humiliate us all the time. There will be no buses in the neighborhood for hours. They punish us for the act of one crazy person. Write this!"

I call Chief Inspector Micky Rosenfeld, the police spokesman, and ask him if this is normal behavior. The man, professional that he is, raises his voice at me in anger: "You don't let anybody talk. You listen only to yourself! Why can't you listen to others?!"

I can't even guess what's the source of his anger, but he goes on: "Where are you from?"

I was born in this country, if you really want to know.

"No, no, no. Where are you from?"

Obviously he wants me to say another country, and so I do.

Germany.

"It shows!"

I check on my iPad, as maybe it might know better than me what's happening right under my nose. Steve's machine tells me: in the Egged bus a religious man approached a lady who sat in the front and asked her to move to the back. She refused. And a fight started. It became violent, spread out, and three other buses were soon stoned by the devout.

Horny Jews, I guess. They see a woman who's not a Taliban, smell her tempting flesh, and get violent.

Crazy tribe.

Luckily, there are cultured people in this land, too, with fourteen thousand years of culture, and they are not fanatic, they are tolerant. Provided, of course, you don't light up on Ramadan.

It is hot today, as I should expect it to be in the middle of summer. I ask a Hasidic Jew wearing a fur hat, a heavy black coat and woolen *tsitsis* (a garment with fringes) how he can tolerate his clothes on this particular day of blistering heat. He looks at me, notices my wet face, and answers: "You are sweating, I can see, and you have no coat and no hat. What are *you* going to do about it, are you going to get rid of your face? No. Same with me. My clothes are a Jewish uniform and I'm very used to them, they are part of my body. Summer is always hot, for you and for me. You are not going to replace your face, are you? My clothes, this uniform, save me from committing sins. With these clothes no girl would want me. This is good, because it's easier to fight temptation when the women don't want you. Do you understand?"

Very well said, my good man. But if you knew history, or read ancient Jewish texts, you would know that your clothes have nothing to do with anything Jewish. Moses didn't wear them. King David didn't wear them. No Talmudic rabbi ever wore them. They are European, of old Europe, and your obsession with tempting females is not Jewish, either. It is Catholic, my man. Are you, too, going to glorify the Virgin Mary?

And as for your "Jewish" uniform: it is a combination of clothes that Austrians, Cossacks, Hungarians, Poles, and others of the sort wore at the time when you, Jews, lived amongst them and under them. When they came to your communities, to kill you because you were Jewish, you saw their clothes and you got jealous. By the time they left, if you were one of the lucky to survive, you copied their ways and their taste.

I say this to him inside my heart, not using my lips. There's no point in arguing with a fanatic man, as there would be no point in arguing with an intellectual, *intellectual* just being a nicer word than *fanatic*.

Gate Ten

God is naked and gay.

NOT EVERYBODY LIKES FURS IN SUMMER. GAYS, FOR EXAMPLE, ARE NOT INTO wearing more and more clothes.

In just a few hours' time they plan to march in the streets of Jerusalem. They gather in the Garden of Independence, in Jerusalem, for a Pride Parade, and I want to join them. Pride Parades have a tendency to feature half-naked flaming mono-sexists, and after spending time with Jews showing no skin I deserve to see some naked Jews.

Once Liran and his band have cleared the traffic, I ride to the Nude Jews.

Gay pride is not exactly what Jerusalem is known for, but a man I stop to chat with tells me that the former chief rabbi of Israel "is homo."

How do you know?

"Are you kidding me? Everybody knows! There are many gays in the Haredi community. You didn't know?"

Wouldn't be funny if it turned out that the man who tried to force a woman to the back of the bus in Bet Shemesh was actually gay and was pissed off because the woman in the bus was blocking his view of other men.

I stick around in the garden for some time, listening to speeches about the problems of homos, this or that, and then the paraders, about four thousand people, start their march. No real nudists here, but naked posters are aplenty. At the front of the parade, there is this big poster in Hebrew, Arabic, and English: "Jerusalem march for pride and tolerance." There are American and Israeli gays here, but I can't locate one single Arab.

Though they are not naked, they do show some flesh. And most strike me as atheists. Which is refreshing after Bet Shemesh.

About thirty minutes into the parade, someone from the roof of a building we are passing by throws stink bombs on us. It really stinks. A Hasidic homo, I believe, got horny and didn't know how to fight his desires.

For the most part the path of the parade, as approved by the local authorities, is on roads without buildings. The residents of this Holy City would be offended, or get too horny, if a gay passed through. Many of the marchers come in male and female units. Some are couples who identify with the gay cause, and some are actually gays who have a friend from the other gender; to them it probably feels like walking a dog, which is an interesting concept.

Jerusalem is not Tel Aviv, which has recently been voted to be the best gay city in the world. This is at least what a couple, gay and hetero who live together, tell me. They also say that 30 percent of Tel Aviv residents are gay.

The interesting feature in this parade is a group of Orthodox gays, happily singing: "Ay ya ya, the King Messiah, ya, ya, ya" and "God in heaven, we love you!" If I understand them correctly, they believe that God is a naked male. Gay, of course, and that's why He has no son.

They are loud.

Would be nice if some Taliban lesbians showed up here as well.

* * *

This is Israel, a land of opposites where, by some strange force of nature, no two are allowed to unite in thought. Yes, there are followers and herds here aplenty, but even they are split into so many sections that it's impossible to count anymore. Who are these people, the Jews?

How did they come into being? Perhaps it is time I visit the First Jew, who for centuries is resting inside an ancient cave and waiting for his lost son, me, to pay him respect.

When the sun rises on the Holy Land on the morrow, I go to Hebron.

Gate Eleven

What's a German minister doing among stray dogs? Why are Israeli soldiers scared when Arab kids throw stones at young Jewish ladies? Why is Catalonia spending millions on an old lady?

YES, HEBRON. OF COURSE, AS IS CUSTOMARY IN THIS PART OF THE UNIVERSE, Hebron is what we call it in English. It's *Hevron* in Hebrew and *al-Halil* in Arabic.

Hebron, the city that a billion journalists and authors have written and spoken about; the famous Hebron where a couple of Jewish settlers live amidst half a million Arabs and rule terror over the whole city. It is there in Hebron where a structure, second holiest to Jews and fourth holiest to Muslims, stands. And, yes, just like its famous sister in Jerusalem, the structure was first sanctified by Jews, then Christians came and made a mess, and Muslims built a sacred place on top of it. As might be expected, not everybody agrees with this short summary; what is day for one is night for the other.

I land in Hebron in the heat of day and the moment I arrive I feel the power of hallucination. Maybe it's the unforgiving sun cooking my brains, maybe it's the multitude of soldiers constantly on the move here, maybe it's the quietness of the streets, maybe it's the deafening sounds of various prayers and, yes, maybe it's just me in an urgent need of the liquid known as Coke.

Hebron is a biblical city. Here the creators of Judaism and their spouses are buried: Abraham, Isaac, Jacob, Sarah, Leah, and Rebecca. The Jews call the burial site Me'arat Ha-Makhpelah (Cave of the Patriarchs), the Muslims call it al-Haram al-Ibrahimi (Sanctuary of Abraham). The Jews claim the dead are theirs, the Muslims say the dead are theirs. European and American leftists, who don't believe that Abraham and the others even existed, take the Muslims' side. The rightists of those countries, who believe all Jews who don't follow Jesus are doomed to die when Christ arrives, staunchly protect the Jewish side.

Hebron also is a place of two massacres. In 1929 the Arabs went on a rage against the Jews and slaughtered sixty-seven of them. Just because. In 1994 a Jewish physician by the name of Baruch Goldstein entered the holy site and massacred twenty-nine Muslims. Just because.

A happy place, no doubt. Not exactly Norway, but Norway is strongly interested in this place.

It's a Norwegian, Christine Fossen, who heads an interesting international observers mission here called TIPH (Temporary International Presence in Hebron), whose cars can be spotted patrolling the Jewish part of Hebron in obvious search of misbehaving Jews.

Jews may live only in one section of Hebron, as has been decided by the politicians a long time ago. How big is this section? Very small, 3 percent of the city. I know this, because there are signs on the streets providing info to the visitors. The three percent is an important figure, for a very simple reason: By order of the Israeli army, Jews are not allowed to walk out of their allocated space. For the Why and How in this city one would need a doctorate in politics and psychology, a process that will take you years of hard studies.

For those of you who are not willing to spend ten years in academia just to understand the complex formulas governing this place, here is what you can learn just by walking around: At some point a few years ago, when everybody could move anywhere they wished and no fences were around, Arab residents got into the habit of shooting the Jews, aka settlers, living here. The Israeli army, probably as a result of its inability to calm the situation, shut down Arab-owned stores in the area, causing most of their owners to relocate their stores into the other 97 percent of the city, and erected fences around the Jews.

The division into Arab and Jewish areas requires multiple doctorates in mysticism, philosophy, engineering, and maybe Hinduism too, just in order to comprehend. It is a maze. Cement fences, wire fences, and whatever kind of barriers divide the two sides. Sometimes, if I see correctly, a house is divided into two, part here, part there.

Around and by these complex borders, one governed by Israel and the other by the Palestinians, a huge mass of trash and destruction can be seen. Some of the trash was left by Arabs, some by Jews. The Israeli army evicted both Arab and Jew from different locations and those who departed didn't care, and still don't, for the look of the place.

I am in Hebron to spend the Shabbat (Sabbath) with the Jews.

The first soul I meet is a man by the name of Eldad, and he speaks unto me: "We are a microcosm of the Israeli society. Five hundred Jews amongst 170,000 Arabs. Just like Israel itself: a few million Jews surrounded by billions of Muslims."

I go on a tour of the local museum, an old house with old pictures, where Jewish life in Hebron before Zionism is depicted. By sheer coincidence, a Jerusalem resident named Hana, an eighty-nine-year old lady who lived in Hebron long before Israel was born, is also touring the small museum. She looks at the photos displayed in the museum from that period and points to a little girl in one of them. That's her, in the year 1927.

She remembers the story of 1929, when she was five years of age.

The Arabs were yelling her father's name: "'Haskel, Haskel'! But Haskel wasn't home at the time, he was in Jerusalem, and they tried to break the door to the house, which was locked, and then the British soldiers came and took the family out of the house. They sent us to Jerusalem."

She might not have known it at the time, but she was one lucky girl. If her family had been in Europe in those years, soon enough she would have been like the ashes of my cigarette in no time.

* * *

I walk over to a checkpoint, one of many in this area.

The border police manning the checkpoint, a security apparatus that is made of both police and army personnel, ask me if I'm an Israeli, in which case they would not let me pass. I say that I'm not. They ask if I'm Jewish. I ask them if they are planning to demand that I drop my pants for them, just to show them. They repeat their question: Are you Jewish? No, I say; I'm a faithful Christian follower of the Messiah. Do you understand Hebrew? they ask. I tell them: And Arabic too.

They demand to see my passport. I tell them I don't have it on me. They decide I'm a Jew. I get very, very nasty with them. I am German, I scream at them. Can't you see, for God's sake?! Oh, they now decide, I am from B'Tselem, a pro-Palestinian Israeli NGO. That's so stupid, I tell them: How could a German like me be a Jewish-Israeli leftist?

Pretty convincing German logic, and so a border police man contacts command to help him in this dilemma: here is a guy, he tells them, who doesn't look Jewish, carries a press card but no passport, and he seems to understand Hebrew. Is the creature a Jew or not? I listen to this bizarre conversation and tell the young man that he is too *shater* for me. He shoots back: You *do* understand Hebrew, you just called me *shoter* (cop)! An Arab passing by tells the young man: No, he didn't say *shoter*, he said *shater* (smart in Arabic).

How comforting: an Arab is defending me, a Jew is accusing me. Which side should I choose? I don't know. What I do know is this: an absurd discussion goes on between the security people on the radio, all in an attempt to figure out what kind of a creature I am: Jew or German?

Maybe Fania Oz should come here to help them.

This goes on for some time. Palestinian residents of this Jewish ghetto, who come and go as they please, look on in amazement and can't stop laughing. But finally a decision is made: I am no Jew and I can go to Palestine. "But if the Arabs kill you," a Russian-born soldier tells me as I cross, "don't come back to complain that we let you cross." He is one of the million-plus Russians who immigrated to Israel after the Iron Curtain fell and he knows a thing or two about borders.

Idriss, an Arab who minutes before laughed and smiled with the Israeli soldiers as if he were their best friend, crosses with me and immediately starts singing totally different tunes once we are on the Palestinian side. He opens his mouth, takes out his bottom dentures and says: "This is what the Jews did to me. They beat me up inside my home, they wanted me to leave my home. I didn't want to leave, I'll never leave my home."

I light up and Idriss tells me not to walk in the street with a cigarette on Ramadan. "Hebron is not Ramallah. If you smoke here the police will arrest you and put you in jail."

Hebron, on the Arab side, is full of life. Stores all over, captivating landscapes and buildings, and people of all ages are roaming the streets.

I try to compare it to the Jewish side, the one I have just come from. No comparison. The Jewish side is not just small and tiny, but it is also lacking life. So much trash, so much destruction, and then those deserted buildings.

*   *   *

Am I on the same planet? I cross back to the Jewish side, just to make sure I was not dreaming that part up. No. I was not.

The Jews here not only live in the midst of destruction, but the worst part is this: they live in a ghetto. They can't move out of this eyesore of a place. They are buried in it. No way out unless they take their cars, or a bus, and drive out of this area altogether. But what surrounds them, the nearby that encircles them, is forbidden to them. I stop people walking by, those few who will stop, asking them to explain to me this ghost town they call home. "This used to be a very nice place," they tell me. "We could go in and out, walk anywhere we wanted. We used to shop in the Arab stores, and they used to come here. It was one city, and we loved it. But then it all ended, one day and it was all over."

What happened?

"Peace broke out."

What?

"Oslo Accords, the peace process, destroyed our life together, destroyed the city."

Never before have I heard this expression, "peace broke out." War breaks out, but peace??

In Hebron it has.

*   *   *

I am invited to a Jewish family, religious like all of them here, for a Shabbat meal, the first of three meals in the next twenty-four hours that religious families celebrate together every Sabbath.

And we talk. Parents, children, and friends of children. I want them to explain to me what it means to be Jewish. I ask it because I changed from a Jew to a non-Jew, or vice-versa, in a matter of minutes just moments ago.

They respond by saying that a Jew is a unique being, a preferred being, a chosen being, a being born with a "Jewish soul."

Isn't this, more or less, in line with Adolf Hitler's idea of a German? You don't tell a Jew, whatever "Jew" means, that he or she is a Hitlerite and expect them to agree with you. The people sitting at this Shabbat table think that I have lost my mind or, better yet, that I'm a psychotic leftist.

Truth is, and I must admit, there's one huge difference between them and Adolf. If I told Adolf Hitler that he's just like the settlers of Hebron, a right-wing Jew, I don't think he would have continued to feed me. Adolf would have fed me to the animals, but here I get fed some animals: excellent chicken, for example. I eat the chicken as I keep pushing my hosts to the edge and they tell me to eat more.

That's a difference. Yes.

But I stick to my guns and keep on asking for answers. The Jew, they finally react to my earlier question, doesn't have different blood, as Hitler said about his Aryan friends, but a different soul.

What the heck are you talking about?

"Every human being has a soul. Don't you know that?"

Jewish and non-Jewish?

"Yes, of course."

And the non-Jewish soul is like that of animals, let's say dogs, but the Jewish soul is Godly. Right?

"We didn't say that. We said that the Jews, by God's design, have a different soul."

Sorry. What does this mean?

"If you don't know what a soul is, there's nothing to talk about."

Well, maybe you could explain to me.

"A soul, you don't know what it is?"

Honestly, I don't.

This creates a new discussion, esoteric in language, absurd in thought, and totally incomprehensible to me. I hear words flying around the table and I have no clue of their meaning. In short: I'm lost.

I tell them: Could you please stop hovering above reality and start communicating with me via the use of human communication?

"Try the chocolate cake," they suggest.

I do. It's delicious.

"This is the best Shabbat meal we ever had," my hosts' son announces to the assembly, and profusely thanks me for challenging them. "We will not forget this evening and it will make us think," he declares, gratefully shaking hands with me.

* * *

This is a face of Hebron I learn of by being with these people. Eating with them instead of talking about them with a tour guide. When you walk the streets here you can see the guides and you can hear them. For the most part, they are leftist activists whose purpose it is to show the world that the Jews living here are ruthless occupiers. They must have, using the lingo of the people here, a leftist soul.

By living with the Jews here, albeit for just one day, I realize that theirs is a life of the doomed, much more so than I had ever thought before. No new houses within the 3 percent zone are permitted for them, and existing ones are not allowed to be expanded. Arabs, and there are Arabs within this 3 percent, can build or expand as much as they desire.

I walk over to these Arab houses and see something strange: The Arab houses that are being renovated and built, evidently to the tune of multi-million euros, are not built by the Arabs themselves. Nope. Arabs, meaning Palestinians, don't put a penny down. It is all given to them. I know this because I can read. There are plaques on the walls of mansions, yes, mansions, denoting who made them come into being, who created them.

Who are the good uncles and aunts who build the mansions here?

Europeans. A gorgeous house I'm passing by right now, for example, was built by the Catalonians. I knock on its door, wondering who lives inside it.

"I live here," says an old Arab lady, inviting me inside her beautiful abode. "My daughter, she is in Germany."

Where in Germany?

"I don't know. She is in Germany, that's all I know." It makes her feel good, she tells me, because her daughter is with friends. Yep.

I hear a loud noise down the road, near an old cemetery, and I walk there to see.

SCENE: Jewish girls walk in the street. Two Arab kids throw stones at them.

Soldiers and police arrive.

A bunch of Arab kids, in the cemetery, are arrested.

Soldier in a watchtower across the street is asked to identify the stone throwers amongst them.

Soldier identifies two, one in a green T-shirt, one in a red.

An Arab man shows up, claiming he is the father of the kids and denies his children did anything wrong.

A woman shows up claiming she's the mother of the kids. She, too, denies her children did anything wrong.

Soldier from the watchtower is called to come over and identify in person.

Soldier enters.

By now, about fifteen soldiers and border police officers are on location.

Soldier identifies the kids in person.

Father slaps the children on their faces, pretty hard.

A soldier asks him to stop. Another soldier tells the first soldier that it's better the father slap his children than any of the soldiers.

From somewhere inside the cemetery a man and a woman show up with a video camera.

Soldier informs other soldiers of the camera's presence.

Soldiers move, with kids, to edge of cemetery.

Soldiers and parents talk and argue in two different languages, Arabic and Hebrew, and it transpires that no one understands what the other is saying.

Video camera holder comes closer. Soldiers, with the kids, move out of cemetery to the Jewish area, where the video takers cannot enter.

More police are called in.

Another man, an Arab from outside the Jewish ghetto, shows up in the cemetery. He stands at the edge of a stone fence, then jumps out – permitted or not. He claims he is the father.

A police top brass shows up, gestures to me that I should leave and says, "*Shalom, chaver*" (the words President Bill Clinton uttered in his eulogy of Prime Minister Rabin, which soon became a recognizable phrase of the Left). He views me as a leftist troublemaker and wants me to go.

I stay.

Soldiers and police are ordered to release the kids and move away.

The cemetery and its vicinity are cleared of Arabs and Jews.

Only the dead and the dogs, many stray dogs, stick around.

* * *

When I think of the man and the woman who appeared from a cemetery with a video camera and walked between graves while taking pictures I start believing that Jesus indeed rose from the dead and that Muhammad indeed flew to heaven. Everything is possible in this land.

Sorry, but so far the Jews have proven nothing about their faith.

Army jeeps and a great deal of soldiers armed to the teeth constantly move and drive about in an impressive show of force in this part of Hebron. But it is just a show, I now see; an impressive show of nothingness. It takes but one video camera to defeat them all.

The two people with the video camera, at least judging by the hijab the lady was wearing, are Arabs. I don't remember Palestinians carrying video cameras in my time. When did they start doing this? Somebody out there, I start suspecting, could be behind them. Who are those people?

I will have to find out.

Now that the humans have gone, more dogs show up. They go wild, and oh boy they bark! I have not seen so many dogs in one place ever before and don't know what they're waiting for. Maybe some wounded girls or fresh graves.

I think of the stray cats in my backyard garden. They are much nicer. I should be nice to them.

As I write this, I see one of the real powers of the place here: A TIPH car, which is patrolling the area. They seem to be the real kings here. They drive here as if they owned the place.

I check on my iPad and read more about TIPH. "German Federal Minister [Dirk Niebel, Federal Minister for Economic Cooperation and Development] Visits Hebron," TIPH proudly announces. I often see Germans in the Holy Land, not knowing much about them, but at least now I know about one of them.

I get on a bus, saying my goodbye to this holy city. Allah is the greatest, the muezzin shouts at me as I leave, and Muhammad is His true messenger.

The non-believing Europeans invest millions to keep the message of Prophet Muhammad alive in this city. I pay the bus driver ten shekels to get out of it.

* * *

I have pity on the Jews of Hebron, prisoners of their own making and the making of their state. Yet, I know I have only heard one side and it would be only fair if I met their opponents, perhaps even their biggest opponent. Who could that be? A name comes to my head: Gideon Levy. Gideon is a columnist for *Haaretz* who for years has dedicated his time and writing in defense of the Palestinians and attacking the Right, the Israeli government, the Israeli army, and, his most bitter enemies, the settlers.

Allah is the greatest and Gideon is my man.

Gate Twelve

A Jew finds the "Jewish racist DNA."

I HAVE TO GET USED TO TEL AVIV, A CITY THAT HAS GROWN MUCH FASTER THAN I. Whereas in the old days there were quite a number of synagogues, and the Great Synagogue with its five hundred seats was a desired place of the believers, today the Great Synagogue packs in fifteen souls, and the houses of prayers have been replaced by houses of fashion, art, and luxury goods. Tel Aviv was never a really religious city, only today it is even less so. Some streets in Tel Aviv have more clothing, shoe, and various other fashion stores than humans. Not exactly, but almost. Not to mention the cafés, the restaurants, and all the other varieties of food and beverage selling points.

Gideon is in his newspaper's office in Tel Aviv, where I have just arrived to meet him.

His father, he tells me, is from Sudetenland and he spoke German as a child.

But Gideon doesn't care about Sudetenland, what he cares about is The Occupation. He wasn't always like this, but when he started working for this paper "the more I understood that the occupation is brutal, criminal, and the more radical I became."

Do you think that the nation of Israel is brutal by nature?

"No, totally not. Others are the same. But there is one thing that's different from other nations, which is a DNA in the Israeli mentality, the belief that they are the Chosen People, which is a racist view, and this is something very deep in the DNA of the Israeli, of the Jew, that we are better than anybody, that we deserve everything, the kind of belief that Prime Minister Golda Meir had, that Jews can do anything they want, and this is in addition to the thought that we are the greatest victims of history. These are the very thoughts that make us believe that we have rights that others don't have, and that therefore we can do anything. Out of these comes the demonization of Palestinians."

Could we say that the Israelis and the Nazis are one and the same?

"No."

Why not?

"You could make a comparison to the Nazis in the thirties. But that's the most you can do, not more. Here there are no plans to annihilate other nations, no plans to rule over the world, no concentration camps. I prefer comparing Israel with South Africa during Apartheid."

Is it ever going to change?

"Only if Israel pays for it. Only under pressure on the Israelis, economically or, God forbid, by bloodshed."

Do you think Jews have always been like this, with this racist DNA?

"Certainly."

In this kind of environment, I ask him, why doesn't he just pack his suitcases, jump onto a plane, and simply leave this country?

"I'm an Israeli patriot," he answers. Israel is very important for him, this is his place and, besides, he asks rhetorically: "What will I do in other places, write about tourism?"

Europe, as a rule, sides more with the Palestinians, while the United States sides more with the Israelis. What do you think is the reason for this?

"Europe is much more ideological, complex, intellectual. America is shallow, everything in black and white, and brainwashed."

Under the intellectuals' Rule of Generalization, Gideon should be stripped of his right to speak in public. This is never going to happen, of course, because Gideon Levy is practically the best source of information for all intellectuals with even the slightest interest in Israel.

Why, do you think, are the Europeans so interested in this land?

"Very complex. For one thing, you can't ignore the past. In some European countries, I'm sure, and I'm talking about feelings they have in their sub-subconscious, there is this thinking: 'if our victims are engaged in horrible acts perhaps it's not that bad what we have done to them.' It makes the Europeans feel better and it compensates for their guilty feelings. But it's also true that Europe is more sensitive than America to human rights violations in general."

We keep on talking, and Gideon tells me that he doesn't speak Arabic. I ask him how can he write about the horrible things Israel is doing to the Palestinians, which he constantly does, if he doesn't understand the language of his interviewees.

Gideon replies that his team includes Arabic speakers for those interviewees who don't speak English or Hebrew. I mention to him that the people here speak in two languages, one amongst themselves and one with foreigners, and that if you don't know their mother tongue they will sell you tall tales. Even Al-Jazeera is doing this, giving two very different viewpoints: One for the "brothers," in Arabic, and one for Westerners, in English. But Gideon, who does not understand Arabic at all, claims that this is not the case. And when I ask him if he also reports on Palestinian human rights violations, he replies that what the Palestinians do is none of his business.

I have no clue how he can report on abuses of one side if he doesn't even bother about the abuses of the other side. Violence, after all, many a time comes in circles: one shoots and the other shoots back, but if you fail to mention the first bullet and only report about the second, the second shooter turns into a plain murderer by the strokes of your pen, not because he really is.

What does he think of the settlers in Hebron?

"They are the worst. No doubt."

His issue is not just the settlers.

"I think," he says to me, "that the average Palestinian wants peace more than the average Israeli. I have no doubt about this." Yet, despite his love for the Palestinians he doesn't really know them. And he admits it: "All my friends are Israelis. I don't have one Palestinian friend."

This is sad. For so many years Gideon has championed the Palestinian cause, but not one Palestinian has befriended him, or he one of them. Obviously, despite what his articles may suggest, he really doesn't care about the Palestinians, only about the Jews. He's an Israeli patriot, as he says to me. He wants his Israel, his Jews, to be super-humans and reply to a bullet with a kiss. In short: he wants all the Jews to be Jesus and die on the cross.

There can be only one reason why he would want them to be a Jesus: Inside of this man's heart, in its darkest corners, this Gideon is the biggest kind of Jewish racist that has ever existed. Jews must behave like super-humans because they are. And as long as they do

not behave as a master Jesus race, he hates them. He is the strangest self-hating Jew you can find.

We talk more and more, about this and that, and as the interview is drawing to a close I ask him one final question: Would you mind if I join you on your next excursion to Palestine?

That's fine with him, he says, and suggests we keep in touch for the details.

I'm looking forward to next week. Gideon goes out to meet Suffering Arabs once a week, has for years now, and I'll get to see a born German-speaker, a super racist Jew, communicating with Arabs in Hebrew. If this is not great theater, I don't know what is.

* * *

While still in Tel Aviv, the Left Wing City of Israel, I go to meet Udi Aloni.

Udi introduces himself to me as a filmmaker and a writer with a Berlinale prize in his pocket, awarded to him by the German Minister for Economic Cooperation and Development, Dirk Niebel. Dirk again, the man busy in Development.

Udi is very proud of his Berlinale prize, and he does not share with me that the prize he got is not the normal Berlinale prize, but I don't raise this issue with him.

Udi is the son of former Member of the Knesset Shulamit Aloni, the matriarch of the Left in Israel, and Udi's movie, *Art/Violence*, is soon to appear on multiple screens in Germany, he tells me with pride. Shulamit, who is now in dementia and is cared for by her son, was a forceful leader I still clearly remember. "She was the best," Udi says of her, and I concur.

As we sit for coffee in one of Tel Aviv's myriad cafés, Udi nostalgically recalls another place. "I lived in Jenin for one year, and in Ramallah for two." A light shines in his eyes, as if he had just mentioned two women of his dreams.

Udi is a shining example of the new Left of Israel: the extremist Left. This is a Left that I don't know, a Left as far as one's left hand can reach. Gideon is not alone. He, Gideon, and the "political psychologist" I met earlier on, are members of a new club. "People in Tel Aviv don't believe in God, but they believe that God promised them the land," is how Udi describes the non-radical Left. His Left is different. He is on the forefront of the campaign to boycott Israel and Israeli products, he shares with me with ecstatic pleasure.

If his boycott campaign succeeds, he, as an Israeli, would suffer greatly. If Israel cannot sell its products overseas and no other nation were to sell any product to her, Israel would go under and people would die of starvation. Is this what he is after?

In a way, yes.

"At the end there should be one state here, with one man one vote," is how he puts it.

In such a case, and since the Palestinians are likely to be the majority of this one state, the Jewish state would cease to exist, correct?

"I dream of it!"

In addition to this dream, he also has nightmares.

"For me, the thought that one day I'd wake up and there would be no Palestinians around me, is a nightmare."

Do you speak Arabic?

"No."

It is mind-boggling to me how people who say they love Palestinians so much and dedicate their lives for preserving Palestinian identity and culture, don't even entertain the thought of studying this culture. They know Kant, they know Nietzsche, they know Sartre, they know Aristotle, but they know no Quran, no Hadith, and no Arabic.

I studied the Quran, I studied the Hadith, and I studied Arabic. Udi is an Arab lover. What am I?

Udi doesn't strike me as being the self-hating Jew of the Gideon Levy variety. Udi is not a "patriot" Israeli; he doesn't want a "Jesus" Israel, he wants no Israel. Udi is the normal self-hating person. He loves the Palestinians not for what they are, since he doesn't really know them, but for what they are not: they are not Jews, they are the Jews' enemies, and this makes them fantastic people.

*   *   *

A few hours later I go to a Georgian restaurant and sit at the table with an Israeli scholar. She is left-wing through and through and she loves Palestinians. So much so that she keeps mentioning to me – in case I didn't hear it ten times already in less than an hour – that for years she had slept with a Palestinian. They weren't going out together, not really, but they were having sex. An intellectual leftist sitting with us is very pleased and he gives her this remark: "I'm happy to hear this; now I know you're okay." She knows a big zero about the Palestinians' culture, but she's been sharing her bed with one. That's respect, isn't it?

Honestly, these Jews make me miss the Palestinians. Maybe I should go visit them, just to clear my head.

Bethlehem, birthplace of Jesus, would be nice. I haven't been there in decades. Let's go!

Gate Thirteen

Palestinians discover "Our Lady of Palestine"
plus 368,000 Zionist colonialists.

I DO HAVE ONE PROBLEM. WHO, OR WHAT, AM I GOING TO VISIT IN BETHLEHEM, a city in which I know no one?

Well, I could meet the Palestinian tourism and antiquities minister, Rula Ma'ayah; she would know people, places, treasures, and many stories.

I go to her.

On the door to the ministry, just as in Dr. Ehab's, it reads: "State of Palestine."

"I was born in Jerusalem, lived in Ramallah all my life, and after my marriage I moved to Bethlehem," she tells me as I sit down in her office. Rula, a very charming lady, is a Christian. I can tell she is because there's a painting on her wall of "Our Lady of Palestine." I never knew there was a Lady of Palestine, but I don't know many other Christian ladies and saints.

How many Christians live in this city?

"Total Christian population in Palestine: 1.5 percent."

Why so little?

"The Christians left in the year 2000."

Why?

"I think the reason is because most Christians are middle class and they left because of the occupation."

How many souls reside in this city and in the surrounding areas?

"Some 180,000 people live in the Bethlehem area, out of which 3,500 are Christians."

I'm not in the mood to go into the Christian exodus from Palestine again, I went through this with Hanan Ashrawi and I know that no matter what the facts are, the "occupation" will always be blamed. I change the topic.

What would you feel if Gideon Levy were here? A man who fights for Palestinian rights?

"I think that he doesn't love us. He is a leftist who fights against his government, not for us."

Is the peace now being negotiated between the Israelis and the Palestinians a good one?

"My grandmother lived in Jaffa, she built her house there. I don't

think that it's fair that you would be forced to leave your country. And even if we have an agreement with Israel, it's not fair."

She is talking about 1948. She is talking about the injustice, as she sees it, of having Jews live anywhere here. I try to get her to be more precise in her statement.

Are you suggesting that the Jews fly out of here?

She avoids this mine. "We are negotiating peace now," she says dryly.

But would you prefer that the Jews leave?

"We are negotiating peace."

Would you prefer that the Jews living here disappear?

She wouldn't directly answer this, other than to repeat her previous statements.

I move closer to her and I knock on her forehead, like one would knock on a door, while whispering words of wisdom into her ears: I am an angel. You're asleep in bed. And I come to you, knock on your forehead, and say: Rula, Rula, Rula: What would you like me to do with the Israelis? Tell me your wish and I will exercise it. Whatever you want, I'll do. Talk to me, speak to your angel. Tell me: Would you like me to send all the Jews back to Europe?

Rula can't control herself and is laughing really hard.

And once she calms down, she says: "You're not a journalist, you're a politician."

No, I'm an angel! A real angel. Talk to me, Rula, and I'll grant you your wish!

She laughs again. She looks at me, her lips about to move, but then no sound comes out.

What's the matter, Rula?

"I'm a minister, I cannot answer this."

Ask your angel what you want, and say it in your own words.

"What I can say is this: there is no fair solution." She gives me a smile, a knowing smile with eyes smiling as well, and adds: "You know how to interpret this, you know what I think."

Yes, I do. She wants all the Jews out, including Gideon and Udi. She might indeed get her wish, and Jaffa would be cleansed of Jews, but nobody can predict whether she, a Christian, would be given a house.

*   *   *

We are having a good time together, Rula and I, and we laugh a lot. She likes Germans like me, Mr. Tobias, and I like her. Here I settled on Tobias, not Tobi, because I thought it might be sexier for the ladies, and I think it is working out really fine. But time moves fast and I have to leave. I want to see the city. Rula appoints a lady named Sakhar to accompany me on a tour of Bethlehem.

First we drive to the center of town. There, between the Church of the Nativity and the Omar Mosque, around the Manger Square, is a building called Bethlehem Peace Center. I walk in. I love peace. Inside, as you might imagine, there is "peace information." For example, this: Israelis, or the way they're being called here, "Ashkenazi Jews," are not real Jews. They are rather some kind of creatures who went through a mass conversion to Judaism a few hundred years ago. This piece of information, to make sure no one misses it, is provided in different languages.

Just in case you missed this important info provided to you free of charge by the State of Palestine, there's more info about the Israelis outside.

Yes. Outside, at the center of the square, there is a big "Tourist Guide to the Occupation" section. I picked up a printed copy of the guide in the Peace Center and I now sit down to have a look at it because Sakhar wants me to know everything. The guide states that by the end of WWII, "368,000 Zionist colonists had immigrated to Palestine," massacred Palestinians, and "planted fast growing pine trees" to cover up their crimes.

There is even a list of sources provided here, some of the most outstanding of which are either fully Jewish or financed by Jews.

It's worthy to note that those Jews, grandchildren of Musulmänner, choose to describe their grandparents who ran away from the ovens of European racism as a bunch of wild beasts.

I can't get caught up in this; I must keep on walking.

On the walls around the square I spot posters praising and celebrating *shahids*. The *shahids*, martyrs, are pictured with assault rifles. Usually, *shahids* are people who got killed after killing "planters of pine trees."

* * *

I'm going to pray to Jesus.

At the entrance to the Nativity Church I see the Tourism Police. I'm not sure of their exact nature and mission, but I notice that they carry paper and pen instead of rifle and bullet.

A group of tourists is about to enter the church, but a tourism cop stops them.

The tourism police, Sakhar tells me, are here to gather statistics.

"Where are you from and how many are you?" a cop asks.

"We're from Japan, and we are seven people," one of them answers.

"Ok. Markhaban, Welcome."

A man from this group goes to the cop, to talk to him.

"I am with the Japanese," he says, "but I am Swiss. Is that ok?"

I look at him and I think. This is the biggest proof that God exists: Who else could create such an idiot as this Swiss? No Big Bang ever could.

The cop, for whom this is not the first Swiss he has encountered, winks at me and smiles.

The Nativity Church, in case you need to know, is divided into Greek Orthodox, Armenian, and Catholic sections.

Like a good Christian, I go down and into a cave to bow at the exact place Jesus was born. Two feet back is the manger. These two tiny sections, I learn, belong to two different denominations. Oy to you, and the curse of the Lord be on your head if you, as a member of one of the two denominations, try to pray at the other's.

This is this land. Intense in every square foot of it.

Talk of the conflict between the Arabs and Jews…here two Christians fight over a space two feet wide, a fight that at times turns violent, yet there's a Kerry out there who thinks he can make peace between nations.

A monk walks quickly past me, holding a tray with dollar notes. Lucky for him Jesus is dead. If Jesus were alive, this monk and his church would be dollarless.

* * *

After prayer, Sakhar takes me to the Milk Grotto church, a white rock church. Today, I guess, the Palestinian government wants me to pray. The Milk church is where the Mother of God took her baby Jesus to feed and a drop of milk from her breasts fell on the ground. That's why the rocks here are white.

A statue of King David stands at the church's entrance. "King David was a Palestinian," Sakhar tells me, as she poses next to the king to show me the similarities. "He was born in my village. King David was my great-great-grandfather."

They look like Siamese twins, same height same age.

Is there anything else special about this church?

"Mothers who want to have children come here, even Muslims. They mix part of the stones with water and drink it, which helps fertility."

I thought for such a purpose you would need to eat Shikshukit at the Makhneyidah restaurant in Jerusalem. I guess I was wrong.

* * *

We walk back to the Bethlehem Peace Center. Now that we have prayed, we can have true peace.

There we meet Maryiam, who works at the center. Kindly, she allows me to smoke in her office.

"You can't smoke outside, the Muslims won't let you. Until the year 2000 the Christians made up 95 percent of the population in Bethlehem, but now they are 1.5."

Why did the Christians leave?

"The Christians left because there is no money here."

Why didn't the Muslims leave?

"They get money from the Saudis."

Christians don't?

"Saudis only give to Muslims."

After my cigarette, two or three of them, I'm going for a walk on the streets of Bethlehem.

Here is a store where they sell, among other things, Jesus and Mary made of holy wood. Jack, the owner of the store, says of his little wooden gods: "Americans care about size, not quality. Germans care about quality, not size. Palestinians like color."

The Old City of Bethlehem, a miracle of beauty and a feast to the eyes, is being washed by development funds. Almost every house here, I notice as I walk, is being renovated by nice and loving countries from overseas. Norway, Italy, Belgium, and Sweden, for example, are just a few of the countries that catch the walker's attention when passing through.

In between the gorgeous houses there are tens of stores on the marvelous streets of this Old City, but almost none is open. I ask Sakhar why, and she tells me it's the fault of the Israelis. "Occupation," "Israelis," and "Jews" are automatic responses to anything bad. Israel left Bethlehem decades ago, but why not blame them?

I get a different answer when I ask a local lady why the stores of her neighborhood are closed. "The [Palestinian] Tourism Ministry doesn't want the tourist buses to stop at the stores in the road. If the buses stopped there, tourists would walk in these streets on their way to the Church and the stores would be packed. But government officials don't want this."

Why?

"I don't know."

I enter one of the houses. It has five rooms, two bathrooms, a living room, a kitchen, all made of rock and marble. A palace made possible by European generosity.

Do the Europeans fund Jewish projects as well?

In order to find an answer to this question I drive to Jerusalem and hook up with Irene Pollak-Rein of the Jerusalem Foundation, one of the most prosperous foundations in Israel. Irene is the Director of the German-Speaking Countries section within the foundation. Irene tells me that she is worried about the various European-initiated boycotts of Israel, the BDS (Boycott, Divestment and Sanctions) movement. "BDS is the result of many, many years of work done against Israel. In the German-speaking lands the ones who push for it the most are the Germans. In general, German foundations and German government funders will donate only for projects that are geared for Jews and Arabs together or projects that are only for Arabs. Germans will not fund any project that is geared only for the Jewish community."

*   *   *

I don't want to hear about Germans anymore and I'm also starving. I go to a nice café in Jerusalem. As I enter I see a bunch of German journalists. Only God knows how all these Germans have landed here, I don't.

Well, no point running away from the Germans. If you can't beat them, join them, the English saying goes. I sit down and order myself food fit for angels, and swallow it all in one sitting. This country, what can I say, is packed with the most delicious food there is.

Outside, I see this sticker on a car: "I am a Yekke driver." I go out and take a picture of it. Two young Palestinians approach me. They wonder why I was taking a photo of an old car. Do you know this Yekke Jew? I ask them. They laugh loudly. The car, they tell me, belongs to their friend who works in the restaurant kitchen.

The old German Jewish banker I imagined is in reality a teenage Palestinian dishwasher.

What a country.

Somehow I'm reminded of "my" German, Gideon Levy, and shoot

him an e-mail about our common trip to Palestine. He replies quite fast: "Dear Tuvia, We will do it after I get back from abroad. Gideon."

No problem.

Gate Fourteen

Germans in the Holy Land: dead and alive.

A COUPLE OF BLOCKS FROM MY HOUSE IN THE GERMAN COLONY THERE IS THE cemetery of the neighborhood's former residents, the German Templars. The Templerfriedhof is usually locked, but today it's open. Should I go in? One of the dead here, a thought comes to me, built the house where I am staying. Perhaps I should pay my respects. Looking in, I see that these graves are intact, unlike those on the Mount of Olives.

I enter.

It's a strange feeling, kind of a meeting with history, with a place and with a people once alive. Here goes one of the lines on a tombstone: "Hier ruht Gottlob Bäuerle, geb. den 17. April 1881. Gest. den 12. Juni 1881. Auf Wiedersehen!"

What a short life! And what a sweet, touching end to a tombstone: See you again!

Christoph Paulus, who lived for eighty-two years, has this engraved on his tombstone: "Ja, ich komme bald!"

Religious, romantic people who loved their families and Adolf Hitler. They came to the Holy Land in the late nineteenth century, hoping to welcome Jesus when he arrived for his Second Coming. Jesus didn't come, but Hitler came in the twentieth century and so they waited for him. The Brits, who then ruled the land, arrested them and later deported them.

They lived here, sweated here, built here, and died here.

They are gone, but today other Germans are in the Holy Land taking their place. I see a bunch of them at the King David Hotel, which is not very far from the cemetery. Who are they?

* * *

They are German journalists, who have gathered here to take part in a conversation that the German Federal Foreign Minister, Guido Westerwelle, has offered to have with them. Yes, it's not exactly a press conference, instead it's more of an attempt by the Foreign Minister to endear himself to the media, a gesture the meaning of which is: I will be kind to you and spend my time with you, and you'll be kind to me.

"The talks with Livni were very good," he says, referring to Minister

Tzipi Livni, head of the Israeli team to the peace negotiations with the Palestinians. Guido talks about the political issues in this part of the world as if they were his own. He wants the two troublemakers, the Arab and the Jew, to shake hands and be good friends.

Orange juice, hazelnuts, and chocolate cookies are offered to the assembly here, and I try some. I'd prefer falafel balls, but I'm not complaining. Sweet stuff goes well with a Guido speech, to be honest. Once Guido said what he did, a Q&A starts.

Given the obvious history between Germany and Jews, I ask him, how does he feel the Jews and the Arabs view him? Also: Is that history part of his motivation for getting involved in a conflict that is not his?

In a longwinded answer he asserts that nearly all German teenagers view Israel as the only democracy in the region. It will take more than hazelnuts and chocolate cookies to convince me of this absurdity, and when I just open my mouth in a follow-up question he asks me if I'm recording him. I say that, yes, I am. He tells me that this meeting is not to be recorded.

Oops. This means that I cannot quote him directly, but I can write "in general" what he says.

What does His Honor want to share with us, which, however, is not directly to be quoted?

He tells us, for example, of a trip he made to Gaza and the little kids he met there. They were so sweet, and he was touched so very deeply. Whatever he is doing in this area, he gives us the impression, he does it for the sake of those kids.

He also talks about Iran's nuclear program, which he thinks is dangerous not just for Israel but also for the rest of the world. If Iran is to have nuclear weapons, he says, six other countries will get the same as well.

I have not been following all his public pronouncements, and he may actually have said these same things in public as well and before, but it looks good when it's "us together" sitting here talking.

Auf Wiedersehen.

The German ambassador, sitting at Guido's right, looks a bit bored. At one point he even takes out his smartphone and gets busy with it.

* * *

The German Foreign Minister is not the only German working for peace in this land. The Konrad Adenauer Stiftung (KAS), a German foundation, is hard at work at peacemaking as well and they want to implant peace in the hearts of both Arab and Jew. The Arabs and Jews they have in mind are not journalists but teachers, people who are more into children than hazelnuts. The question is how to get this done, and they have come up with a magic idea: Make the two antagonists meet, have them fall in love with each other, or at least befriend one another, and they will, in turn, instill their newly found love or understanding in the hearts of the children they teach.

Since the people KAS has in mind are both Arab and Jew, the reconciliation they are planning for them cannot take place on territory that is being fought over by both sides. Some neutral territory will have to be found, a country none of the teachers will claim as their own and a place where KAS can organize a multi-day Peace Conference to host them. Thank God there is Jordan, and KAS rents a Jordanian hotel for this purpose.

It will be interesting to see what happens when the two meet.

Gate Fifteen

You are heartily invited to attend three days of romantic
German-inspired dances in Jordan performed by
Germans who are in love with peace and Arabs.

KAS IS IN JERUSALEM (THE ISRAEL BRANCH) AND THE WAY TO JORDAN IS ABOUT
thirty minutes of a joyful ride if one crosses the Allenby/King Hussein Bridge. This would make things easy, but the Middle East is not
known for making anything easy. The Jordanians, long story, don't
allow Israelis to cross this bridge into Jordan. Instead, they make them
use another bridge way up in the north. This means that we must
go all the way up to the north of Israel, enter Jordan there, and then
come all the way back south on the Jordanian side. Trip duration:
nine hours, instead of thirty minutes.

KAS has hired a nice bus for the ride and I'm happy. I talk with
this and that fellow participant when the phone of the KAS person
in charge rings. One of the participants, actually the key speaker of
this peace event, is calling to say that she is not coming. Her Palestinian Catholic school has ordered her not to come; they don't want
her to meet Jews and they don't care for the German peace effort. I
eavesdrop on this conversation and wonder if the rest of us will be
informed of the lovely reason for this cancellation? No.

On one of our rest stops I hook up with an Israeli teacher, a smoker
like me, and ask him why he is here and what is driving him. He tells

me, how stupid I am not to have figured it out on my own, that the Palestinians are right in claiming that this is their land, since they lived here before the Jews, and he wants to meet them and tell them his thoughts. He's also very excited to visit an Arab country such as Jordan, something he has never done before.

This guy already likes the Palestinians, and I wonder what the purpose of having him here is. I share my wondering with him, and he wonders at my wondering.

"All of the Israelis here are like me. Why would we come if we didn't think as we do?"

He's right, when I come to think of it, only now I don't understand what the point of the conference is.

Perhaps the idea is to get Palestinians to like Jews.

Could be, could it not?

The person in charge of this event is a German who first heard about Israel from an Israeli friend of her parents who suggested to her to come to Israel when she was a young girl. She didn't have anything better to do and she came to the Jewish State; fell in love with it and with a nice Arab man as well. They live in a neighborhood where no Jews live, and where no Arab will sell or rent to a Jew. This is such a touching love story that I'm sure Eugène Ionesco would have appreciated very much if he had lived to hear it.

Time moves and at long last we arrive at the Jordanian side of the border.

One of the Israelis in our group, I notice, has a Hungarian passport in addition to his Israeli one. There's not a single stamp in his passport, and he doesn't really use it. He got it just in case. If Israel disappears from the map he wants to have a place to live. Many Israelis, he tells me, acquire European passports just in case.

Peace is this man's god, but I think he's an atheist.

We wait for hours at the border. It must be a very busy crossing, I say to myself, and I look out to see how many cars are crossing in and out of Jordan and count them, one by one. Total number coming out of Jordan: Two. And now I count the number of buses going into Jordan. One. Asian tourists. Wow.

In the waiting room a border official looks at the list of the KAS people who have come to this Kingdom to make peace and he crosses out every Jewish name with a blue pen. He counts the Jews, and his face is quite serious. He goes out, he comes back and the visas are given. The Israelis, the Jews of them, get a group visa, meaning none of them can walk anywhere on their own. I get a normal visa; I'm no Jew.

And just before we enter the bus that is going to take us back us south on the Jordanian side, we are told that there will be no stops on the way, unlike what we had on the Israeli side. No ice creams, no colas, and no toilets. Go to the toilet now, we are advised, as it will be some time before you'll see a toilet again. Nobody tells us why, and nobody asks for an explanation. The reason is simple: Jews in an Arab land are not safe, but nobody wants to hear this, least of all the Jews themselves. We're on a peace mission, not a urinating mission.

It is interesting to see the people on this bus, great teachers of tomorrow's leaders: the Arabs stick to Arabs, the Jews stick to Jews.

It is the first step in making peace, German style.

But I shouldn't belittle them. The truth is that KAS has pulled off something very big: the Germans are paying for this trip, the travel agent who has been contracted for this journey is Jewish, the travel manager and the bus driver are Palestinian, the toilets are empty and the hotel we soon to arrive at is Jordanian.

To date, even American president Barack Obama hasn't pulled off such a miracle.

We drive through Jordanian cities and villages. Through most of the ride I see half-constructed houses, an untold number of King Abdallah's face on posters, and a poverty that screams in horrifying pain. Most of the people here are Palestinians, and I ask myself why Catalonia is not erecting gorgeous white mansions here as well. Would be a really great help.

We arrive late at the Jordanian Dead Sea Spa Hotel, and the

opening session is taking place the next morning. The real peace talks between Arab and Jew, which Secretary of State John Kerry is organizing, and of course unrelated to our efforts here, will start tomorrow. As an introduction to Kerry's peace talks, a rocket was fired into the city of Eilat; it was intercepted by the "Iron Dome" anti-missile system.

*   *   *

When time has arrived for our proceedings to start, we meet again. On our chairs there we find a printed schedule, on which it says that this project is funded by the European Union.

The proceedings are in English. A Jewish speaker stutters in bad English, an Arab speaks clearly in both English and Arabic, and a guest from Norway speaks the clearest English and tells us that he's here of his own will, which means that he is not paid by anyone. A righteous man, and it's great that he makes it public. Since he's already here, by the way, and he's so great, he will be stepping in as our key speaker, to replace the one that cancelled.

There is one problem, of course: most of the people here don't understand English. When I approach them in English, asking for example, "Where are you from?" I get an answer, not in English, whose meaning is: "Good morning." KAS, I guess, wants to be "international," and so English is great. Kidding aside, it's probably a great idea to collect people who don't understand one another and make sure they can't talk to each other. It's a deep concept and I'm going to discuss it in a multi-volume book I plan to write about this.

Speeches done – that is, for now – the session starts.

An Israeli peace activist tells us to move the chairs away and stand and form a circle. We are not to touch hands, she says. Arabic music starts and we are to think that we are in a kitchen cooking.

Next step, after we have "prepared" our mutual food, we are to face each other and talk. I offer my hand to a Jordanian lady with a hijab next to me, in clear violation of the rules, but she doesn't shake the hands of a man, she says. A Jordanian man, who does shake my hand, asks me if I'm a "Jew." I tell him that I don't remember who I am, but that if I'm not mistaken I'm neither Jew nor Arab. He counters this and says that I must be one or the other. I say I'm German. Welcome to His Excellency King Abdallah's land.

Next step: Western music comes up on the speakers and we are told to dance. I look at the dancers, none of whom can move in any graceful manner, and for a moment I think that I have just been dropped into a mental institution. It's really bizarre, but the people here seem to have a good time. It's kind of a sport for them, I guess. Burning calories in the gym doesn't need rhythm, does it?

It's a big mess, and a German lady suggests that we break for coffee. The lack of leg coordination must have been torture for her.

* * *

In the coffee break I meet some Jordanians from the city of Zarka and some Palestinians from Jerusalem, but I can't locate any Palestinians from the West Bank. There's a delegation here from Ramallah, I'm told. Where are they? A man volunteers to show me to the Ramallah delegation. He finds none. But this does not mean they are not here; they are. Where? In the toilet, he says. All Ramallah people are urinating at the same time.

Time passes and he locates one of the pee-makers. Right there, he says, is the Ramallah group. I approach the person shown to me. He's from Ramallah. He says, that's true. What school in Ramallah does he teach at? Oh, no, he teaches in Jerusalem. And where are his friends, the other Ramallah people? They are in Ramallah, naturally. Not here? No, not here. In Ramallah.

Ramallah is better, cooler.

There's a big difference between having people from Ramallah and having people from Jerusalem in this hotel. Jerusalem is governed by Israel, and its Arabs don't need to come to Jordan to meet Jews. But there are no Jews in Ramallah, home to the Palestinian government, and if its Arabs are to meet Jews, KAS would be able to claim to be a great matchmaker. But the Ramallah delegation is either urinating in some Jordanian toilet or joyfully eating falafel in Ramallah.

What does KAS really think?

This German peace event costs about 200,000 shekels (around 45,000 euro), I'm told by an official. At least it's cheaper than the *hamam* in Al-Quds University

I look at the people and notice a striking difference between Arabs and Jews. The Jews are overeager to please, while the Arabs walk with their heads up and with pride. And as much as the Jews try to hide their culture, with not one of them wearing or showing any distinguishing Israeli or Jewish symbols, the Arabs show theirs with great self-esteem.

After coffee break the groups are divided into three, each assigned a different room: Palestinians, Jordanians, and Israelis. I guess that's how you make people love each other, by separating them. There's one interesting rule: the groups are not supposed to talk politics.

I go to check the Palestinian group, but I'm not allowed in. So I wait till they are done to find out who they are. A blond, a brunette, another brunette, and a few Jerusalemites come out, all talking to one another in English. This "Palestinian" group is composed of foreign nationals who teach in Palestinian schools, plus the Jerusalemites.

*   *   *

I take my time to chat with a Brit named Warwick, general manager of the Dead Sea Spa Hotel. His wife, he tells me, is a Palestinian from Bethlehem.

Muslim?

"Christian. Church of England."

When did she leave Bethlehem?

"In the 1950s, when the Israelis occupied the city."

Wait a sec: Were there Israelis in Bethlehem in the 50s?

"Let me check."

He takes his smartphone and checks. "Oh, nineteen-sixty-seven," he corrects himself.

Good that he knows how to use Google to find out when his wife left Bethlehem. I love Brits like him.

*   *   *

I go back to the KAS event.

As I enter I offer my hand to one of the Arab men. He responds by asking: "Are you a Jew?" No, I say: I'm half American and half German. He shakes my hand.

Evening comes. Dinner is done and we sit outside listening to loud Arab music by a local band. I offer one of the Israelis, for whom this is his first time in an Arab land, to show him Amman. Amman is nice, I say to him, and I wouldn't mind driving to the capital with you. He is dying to see Amman, he tells me, but he's not allowed to leave the hotel.

Why?

He was told by KAS that "I cannot leave the hotel. All of us were told this. It's not safe for Jews in Jordan. Just a few days ago a Jordanian parliament member called for the kidnapping of Israelis in Jordan, if there were any, and to hold them hostage."

In between musical beats I sit down to talk to a Jordanian lady, "I'm a Hashemite Jordanian," as she puts it, who is doing her PhD at the moment. She's vivacious, independent, and still not married. No man has yet been found who is good enough for her, her mom says, and in her traditional society, Mom decides issues like marriage.

This is not the first time she has taken part in a German peace initiative. She loves the Germans, and has strong opinions about Jews.

"To be honest with you, I always believed that the Jews were some kind of animals."

And what do you think now?

"I was taken to Jerusalem, to see al-Aqsa and the Holy Sepulcher, and when I was there I saw the country around and what the Jews built. I didn't know they were building cities, but when I saw what they had built I realized that they were not going to leave the area."

Who are the Jews, what do you think of them?

"Invaders. I have no problem; I tell you the truth."

Would you mind if some of them came to live here, in Jordan?

"No, they shouldn't come here. No!"

How about Americans?

"What kind of Americans?"

Normal Americans, good Christians.

"They can come here to live with us. No problem."

How about American Jews?

"No, no. They should not be allowed to live here. No."

No Jews in Jordan?

"Sorry. No Jews here."

Are you a believing Christian?

"I am!"

Was Jesus Christ a Jew?

"No. He was killed by Jews!"

Does this mean he couldn't have been a Jew?

"If he was a Jew, the Jews wouldn't have killed him!"

Who killed Saddam Hussein?

"Why do you ask?"

Who killed Muammar Qadafi?

"What are you trying to say?"

You tell me. You want to get a PhD, you should be able to answer these questions.

"They were Arabs, both of them, and Arabs killed them."

What does this mean, my dear PhD?

"Okay, I got you. If the Jews killed Christ it is no proof that he was not a Jew. Right. I never thought of it but now I will have to think about it."

By the way: How do you know that the Jews killed Jesus?

"Everybody knows."

What does the Holy Book say?

"In Jordan they teach that the Jews killed him. They all teach this: the Romans, the Protestants."

But what does the Holy Book say?

"I don't know. I have to think about it."

Why think? Why not look at the Holy Book, open it and read it?

"Not the Jews?"

The Holy Book says the Romans killed him.

"This is new to me."

Maybe today, or tomorrow, you will open the Holy Book and look.

"Tomorrow I want to take a picture with you. Is it okay?"

Anytime.

We bid each other goodbye and good night.

*   *   *

Ramzi Nazzal, the owner of the Dead Sea Spa Hotel, tells me how his hotel came into existence: A German tourist agency was for years bringing German psoriasis patients to the Dead Sea in Israel. In 1986 company executives came to Ramzi with an idea: they would divert their patients to Jordan if he built a hotel on the Jordanian side of the Sea.

Some people would go quite far just to make sure Jews make less money.

*   *   *

As KAS participants are busy with more dance-like maneuvers, I take my time to speak with the Norwegian "Conflict Resolution" man, the leading expert of our KAS gathering.

Since he was not getting paid, I ask him to explain to me why he was here, why he even bothered, and what exactly motivated him. In short: How does a do-gooder man like him get created?

What makes a hero?

He's befuddled by my question. Didn't I know, he muses, that the essence of Norwegian culture is to care for people?! No, I didn't. Do they? Does he? Does he, for instance, care about other conflicts: the Hutus and the Tutsis, the Kurds and the Tibetans, the Chechens and the Albanians, the Iraqis and the Copts, the Afghans and the gypsies, to mention but a few?

He looks at me with nervous eyes and he wants to know on which side I am. Are you a J— he starts asking, but stops right before the "e" sound.

It is a weird moment. I let it stand there for a minute, feeling it. But then I have mercy on him and I tell him that I'm German.

He is relieved. Germans are good, and we continue to talk.

What do your country's people think of the Arab-Israeli conflict? I ask him. On which side are they? This is easy for him to answer, he's an intellectual and he knows his stuff. Ninety percent of Norwegians side with the Palestinians, he tells me, because they think that Israel is racist and that Israel is an Apartheid state. And what do you think? I ask him. Well, he thinks his countrymen are right. Norwegians, he tells me, are attuned to the sufferings of weak minorities. Always have been, are, and always will be. This is the history of Norway and this will be its future as well. Good people.

I ask him if he can tell me how the Norwegians acted during WWII.

He wants to know why I'm snooping around his country's history.

I'm German, I remind him, and Germans talk of WWII. Strange habit of ours.

He looks at me with some unease, but no Norwegian like him will lie to a German like me.

We don't like to admit it, he says in a low voice, but we collaborated with the Nazis.

I push a little harder and ask if this included sending the Jews to some ovens.

Yes, he says, his hands shaking a bit and a nervous tick showing on his face.

But isn't it a bit strange, I share an observation with this scholar, that people who are attuned to the sufferings of minorities as the

Norwegians have always been, would send the weak minority of Jews to the ovens?

He does not answer.

Lucky for me he believes I'm German. If he thought I were a Jew he would probably tell me to stop complaining about "that WWII thing" again and again.

Lucky for him, KAS switches course and decides to pay him nevertheless. His services to the organization, a man who thinks that Jews are racist and Palestinians are pure souls, are too dear as to not be paid.

*   *   *

The KAS conference is over and I cross back into Israel on my own, taking the shorter route. I board a "Special," a taxi for more than one party, into Jerusalem, sitting next to an intellectual-looking lady.

We talk.

She is from Bethlehem, and she works for an environment-conscious Non-Governmental Organization.

How many NGOs are there in this land? I ask her.

"Thousands. In Bethlehem alone we have about one hundred."

Her name is Nur, and she's indeed an intellectual. She has studied much and she practices what she knows. She's paid well, she says, and lives very comfortably, thanks to the Americans, Germans, and the rest of the EU, who are paying her salary.

"In Palestine the economy is NGO. Palestine is an NGO country. We call it 'NGO Palestine.' Who pays our government leaders? NGOs. Almost nothing is manufactured here, nothing grows here or is produced here except for NGOs. That's it."

Are you happy about it?

"In the short run, yes. But in the long run, this will kill us. One day the NGOs will go and we'll have nothing. It's not healthy for a country to live on handouts. We have a weak government, and one day we'll pay for it. This is not real."

Do you know of other countries that live like this?

"Only Palestine."

The Western world cares only about you?

"No. The Jew tells them to do this!"

What?

"They throw all their money here into Palestine because they know that if they didn't give the money to the Palestinians the Jews would have to do it, because Israel is an occupying power and occupiers must pay the people they occupy."

Is that so? I mean, the Europeans and the Americans want to save the Jews money?

"Why else would they do it?"

Where in Jordan have you been with your NGO?

"Aqaba."

What did you do there?

"We had a three-day teachers' seminar, to help them teach their students about the environment and about water resources."

Another teachers' seminar, by another NGO, also in Jordan. It'd be great to know how many NGOs are having seminars in Jordan at any given time.

Before I left the hotel, Warwick the Brit told me: "Here anything can happen. If somebody came to me and said, 'There are goats flying over the hotel,' I'd ask him, 'How many?'"

* * *

Back at home I sit down to read what's new in the world, and here it is:

1. Over five hundred Egyptian supporters of the Muslim Brotherhood movement were killed by the Egyptian government security forces; Brotherhood activists set forty Coptic churches and buildings on fire.

2. The United Nations Secretary General is presently in the Middle East urging peace and stability.

Sounds great, doesn't it? Well, there's one catch. The UN man is not in Egypt; he's in Israel. Thousands upon thousands die these days in the Middle East, but the UN is busy with Israel. You have to be a Norwegian or a German NGO to think that this makes perfect sense.

Gate Sixteen

Cats, the UN *and the Chosen Golden.*

WHEN HUMANS FAIL ME, I THINK IT'S TIME I MAKE FURTHER ACQUAINTANCE with my cats.

I go to my garden, but when they see me they run away. They don't want me, I figure, and I think of a scheme to get KAS to make them love me. I think of a KAS dance but then I would need an infusion of 200,000 shekels. Perhaps I should call Suhrkamp in Berlin; they are my publishers and they should wire-transfer the money for such a great cause. But then I think: Why not try treating the cats with the same respect with which I treated the Hashemite lady?

I wish I had some bones here, but I don't.

Milk. That's what I have. I go inside the house, take a soup plate, pour milk into it and put it outside.

It's kosher milk, and I hope the cats will be okay with it.

I walk back inside the house and watch.

One cat comes to drink, and she finishes the milk in a minute.

Must have been starving, thirsty, or both.

I give her more.

Another cat wanders in. This one is bigger and stronger.

The first cat, still hungry or thirsty, waits for the stronger one to let her have more, but the stronger doesn't.

The plate is clean again.

I fill the plate once more.

The strong cat gets the first shot, then moves a step back and the first cat tries her luck. She succeeds for four or five licks, until the stronger cat approaches the plate.

The plate is empty again and I fill it up again.

The stronger cat now lets the first cat drink together with her.

They go on like this for another minute and then the stronger cat takes away permission and the weaker cat moves away.

The stronger cat enjoys the plate by herself but then moves away a bit.

Weaker cat comes back.

I watch the cats, creatures I'm just getting to know, and think: cats are street smart, especially these stray cats, and they know the rules of nature better than I. The rule they have here, as far I can see, is this: Might makes Right. Are humans the same or are they different? The UN Secretary General, who is now in this land, represents a collective human body that decides, at times, to enforce sanctions against a country of their choice or even authorize an invasion of such a country. Practically, such decisions are voted on in the UN's Security Council, which means the members who make up this council. Who are they? Well, the members of this council change, except for the most important of them, the permanent members who have veto power. They are China, France, Russia, the UK, and the USA. How did they get there? They are the victors of WWII. So what? Well, Might makes Right. As with the cats outside.

Many a time, when I walk the streets of this land I see UN cars, usually parking where mere humans like me can't, because they have immunity and I don't. Might makes Right. The UN also operates a special agency called UNRWA (United Nations Relief and Works Agency for Palestine Refugees) which, according to their literature, helps some five million Palestinian refugees. How they got this huge number I don't really know, but maybe I should visit a UNRWA camp during my current journey.

By now the cats have gone, probably busying themselves with various social activities on the sidewalks and under parked cars, and I have one little problem. It is Friday night and I'm in Jerusalem, where everything is closed. What can I do with my time?

Well, the Haredi people who made sure businesses are closed today are not sitting home doing nothing. They entertain themselves with holy activities; why shouldn't I join them?

*   *   *

I pack my *zekel beiner* ("sack of bones," oneself) and go to the most extreme of them, the Toldos Aharon group, the ones whose little children I visited a few weeks ago. I put on a white shirt and black pants, hide my iPhone and cigarettes, both of which are forbidden for use on the Sabbath, and put on a black skullcap. Life is a little theater.

The Rebbe (grand rabbi) must be back from his summer vacation in Austria, and on this night, at 11:00 p.m., I'm told, he will conduct a *tish* (table). This means that he will eat his Friday night meal in public, engulfed and encircled by his followers, as holy angels circle around him.

I enter Toldos Aharon.

The place is empty.

What has happened to the *tish*?

Well, how could I forget! I used to live in this neighborhood and I should know better. Yes, it starts at 11:00 p.m., and it is 11:00, but it's not really 11:00! It's 11:00 in the rest of Israel, but the people here have their own clock, Heaven Time, and according to their clock it's only 10:00 p.m. now.

The good thing is that there's another *tish* going on in the neighborhood. The Rebbe's father, a famous miracle maker, had two children and when he died the Hasidic dynasty split into two. The other Rebbe starts his *tish* at 10:00 p.m. Heaven Time which is exactly now, 11:00.

I go to him. And *tish* he does.

On the Sabbath, or as pronounced here Shabbes, the followers dress in holiday clothes, which here means donning a bigger than average Hasidic fur hat, called a *shtreimel*, and golden gowns with thin blue stripes, plus a special white-and-gold belt, the *gartel*.

They look utterly beautiful and amazingy handsome. These men, let me tell you, are the only human males who know how to dress. A picture. They look, in a word, gorgeous. How come, I really want to know now, all other men on the planet dress themselves with the most horrible clothes known to the human mind? Not to mention most of my gay friends, who think human clothes mean T-shirts. Come here, O you gay men, and see how beautiful men can really look!

A striking image.

It takes these beautiful men mere minutes and they transform their synagogue into an arena, complete with bleachers for them to stand on to watch their Rebbe eat and drink. Men watching a man eat.

Is this a gay show, or what?

No, no. God forbid. Rebbes are holy and watching them eat and drink is the best cure to all diseases, of body and soul.

The Rebbe stands in front of his kingly armchair, as the multitudes of gold stare at him and sing unto him. "Ai ai ai, na, na, na, la, la, la, da, da, da, ai, ai ai, oy, oy, oy, ai, ai, ai." Over and over, louder and louder.

Two bread loaves, khallahs, are in front of him. Each the size of an average missile, huge, covered with highly decorated pieces of cloth. Around him are gold and silver pitchers and cups, brilliantly shining, of the style and kind the richest of kings own. Six servants, here called *shamashim*, are standing ready to serve him.

He blows his nose.

All look how a holy man blows his nose.

It is important to know.

A servant pours the wine.

All start singing.

And as soon as they start, they stop.

The Rebbe picks up his wine cup.

All sing, again. Loudly.

The Rebbe opens his mouth. Quietly, with unrecognizable diction, and I can hardly hear a syllable. All are quiet. Then he screams something, in a very unclear voice, but his followers don't care. He is a holy man, directly connected to God, and whatever he says, God understands. God understands the language of cats, dogs, lions, and birds, and He surely understands the language of this Holy Rebbe.

Time moves on. It's midnight soon, meaning 11:00 p.m. Heaven Time, and I'd like to see the other Rebbe too.

I go there.

The Rebbe is not yet there, only his followers, who are waiting for him.

They, too, are golden people.

Quite a number of them, by the way, are blond. This is the highest concentration of blond Jews that I've seen so far in this land. Blond Jews dressed in gold. Excellent combo.

Until he comes, I check out what the Golden study in this place.

I read: "On Friday, in preparation for the holy Shabbes, a Jew must cut his fingernails. How to cut the nails? Thusly: First cut the nail of the fourth finger of the left hand, then of the second finger, then of the fifth, then of the third, then of the first. Switch hands and start cutting the nail of the second finger, then of the fourth, then of the first, third and fifth. Do this and you'll be safe."

Bingo.

The Rebbe enters and about a thousand followers cheer him on with "ai, ai, ai" that hardly ends. This Rebbe looks as if he has more energy than his brother, which might explain why he has more followers.

The Rebbe emits some painful sounds, and they listen. I'm not sure, but the pain could signify his longing for the hotel in Austria. He makes an attempt at singing, and they loudly respond back: "Oy, oy, oy."

A non-religious outsider coming in would probably think that these people are total nuts, brainwashed cultists who get a high by staring at their leader sneezing. This outsider would be right, indeed, and it reminds me what I felt when I saw educated people in the States and in Europe screaming with excitement when they watched President Barack Obama raise a hand or move his nose.

Are these Golden People in any way similar to the secular intellectual Jews of Tel Aviv? Not in one iota. These Jews here, though as anti-Zionist as their brethren in Tel Aviv, are proud people and they're dressed a million times better than the others. They are The Chosen Golden, the Hot and the Beautiful.

*　*　*

I leave the Hot Boys and walk back to my stray cats. I don't see them. I put a big portion of milk out for them, just in case. In seconds they fly in from God knows where, the whole family, plus a new relative I have never met before, and they drink, together. And two of them, having no shame and doing it right in front of my eyes, start making love in my Holy Garden for all to see. If the Chosen Golden saw this, they would be shouting their "Oy, oy, oy" so loud that all the dead in the Mount of Olives would jump out of their graves in ecstatic dances.

In Egypt men fall like flies, in the German Colony cats make love. I go to sleep.

Gate Seventeen

Sponsored by the European Commission, Italian teenagers come to the Holy Land to take pictures of homeless Palestinians.

TIME GOES BY AND I MEET ALL KINDS OF PEOPLE AND DOWNLOAD ALL KINDS of apps. For example this one, which is capable of telling me which bus in the city is closest to me. Amazing how things work, real life on a chip. No printed schedules at any bus stop around, just your iPhone. Why can't they do this in New York? My iPhone connects with the GPS of buses all around and I can tell where a bus is at any given moment. Is it accurate? Let's see: Which buses are moving around? It says here that bus number 18 is approaching. Is it? Yes, right there ahead I see it coming.

I let it pass and check my surroundings. Here I see a bunch of IDF Bedouin soldiers, who seem to feel pretty comfy in army uniform. Here's a bunch of Russians. And here's a bunch of American religious Jews, speaking in Los Angeles accent. Funny. And here's a German guy who greets me. Here is a bunch of French people, and here a couple of Ethiopians. And then some more Germans, and then a few Brits. This street looks very much like the United Nations, only without a Security Council; nobody here has a veto power.

I take the next bus. Today I'm going to join an Israeli tour guide and a bunch of Italian teenagers, on an educational trip arranged by an Italian institution in Milano.

*　*　*

We meet at Damascus Gate/Bab al-Amud/Shaar Shkhem, and we are heading to an "Arab village destroyed by the Jews in 1948."

Good.

Itamar Shapira, the guide hired by the Italians, will be leading the tour.

"Welcome to Israel, Palestine," he greets us on the bus, belonging to an Arab company and driven by an Arab. Itamar is the only Jew here.

We are going to be treated today to a research tour that will teach us about Israeli occupation and annexation of Arab lands in Israel, Palestine.

"Jerusalem has 900,000 residents: 36 percent Arab, 20 percent ultra-Orthodox, 10 percent secular, who are the Israeli elite of European background, and the rest are the monster creatures, the settlers." So says Itamar, as the bus is moving to its destination. A police van is

driving by us, and Itamar explains: "This is the 'skunk,' a vehicle used by the police to disperse demonstrators." The impression we all get, and I guess this is what Itamar is driving at: Israel is a police state.

We keep moving, until we reach our first destination, at the main entrance of Jerusalem. The "village," a bunch of deserted houses called Lifta. We get off and start walking down the hill. Itamar spots a shaded area and we pause our walk for a short lecture by him. The Jews "seized this village in 1952," after passing a new law, when they also seized "92–94 percent of the rest of Israel," within what's called the Green Line. It is via this law, he adds, that the "Jews expropriated Arab-owned lands all over."

The young Italians stand or sit around Itamar and listen. They take pictures, some write down everything he says, and all are intimately involved, as if this piece of land belonged to their grandparents. They look at the deserted structures of the old houses, as one would look at his or her childhood favorite place, and they are pissed off that grandpa and grandma ain't here anymore. No human walking by and observing them would in a million years guess that these kids landed at Ben-Gurion Airport only yesterday, and that for the first time.

Itamar has maps that he uses to teach us history, and he loves to talk about "Jews." How many Jews are there in the world? One asks. Itamar says this is hard to tell. "Some say there are fifty-five million Jews in the world, some say twenty million, others say twelve million."

Is he Jewish?

"I don't consider myself Jewish, I consider myself an ex-Jew."

They laugh. And then one asks: Can Christians become citizens of Israel?

"You can convert to Judaism, become a Jew and become a citizen. But I wouldn't advise you to become a Jew."

The Italians now laugh louder.

I take a moment to speak with the organizer of the Italian group, a young lady named Alice. I ask her which organization is behind this trip and how much it all costs.

"This trip is organized by Casa per la Pace Milano, a peace organization, to provide peace education training. Each person pays around one thousand euros for two weeks in Israel and the Occupied Territories."

Alice is visiting the Occupiers' land for the fourth time. It all started a few years ago when she spent three months in Nablus and fell in love with the Palestinian people.

How many other countries is Casa per la Pace Milano interested in?

"Israel is defying and breaking international law, does not keep agreements it signed, does not respect human rights, and is an occupying force."

Got it. But how many other countries does Casa per la Pace Milano organize trips to? Or, maybe, Israel is the only country in the world that does not respect human rights?

"There are other countries, yes, there are."

And is Casa per la Pace Milano organizing trips to those countries as well?

"No, no. Only here."

A thousand euros, including flights, tours, hotel, food, and whatever else?

"Yes, a thousand euros. But don't publish the article before next month, okay?"

Why not?

"The Israelis would expel me if they knew – "

A thousand euros is very little. Who is paying the rest?

"The organization."

Who gives them the money to do this?

"The European Commission."

So, the European Commission is funding this trip. Right?

"Yes."

We take a photo together. Next month, when back in Italy, Alice would love to see her picture published.

I ask Alice if, for the sake of looking at all sides, she and her friends also go to the other side, the Jews, and hear what they have to say.

Well, she says to me, the group is with the Jews today and tomorrow, meaning with Itamar, and later they will be with the Palestinians. This way they will see both sides.

No wonder Silvio Berlusconi was the longest-serving postwar prime minister of Italy. It takes the Italians ages before they figure out they make no sense.

I take a moment to think of what has just transpired: The European Commission, meaning the EU, is funding trips of young Europeans to Israel, educational trips of course. These EU-funded NGOs know exactly which tour guides they want to use, ones like Itamar. In other words: The NGOs search the land for the "best" Jews, the ex-Jews, who are guaranteed to speak the worst about Israel and its Jews. Why, in God's name, is the EU funding them?

The trip continues. The Italians want to eat, and they are taken to Damascus Gate to eat in Arab restaurants. From there they are going

to continue the trip and see more evidence of Israeli illegal and brutal treatment of Palestinians.

* * *

While they are to have their lunch I take the time to meet Gerald M. Steinberg, who founded the right-leaning NGO Monitor, which is supposed to be "observing the observers."

I reach his office by taxi. His office, which is quite simple, is made up of fifteen employees who are "monitoring around 150 international NGOs" operating in Israel and Palestine, or those that are dedicated to this issue.

Of those 150, he tells me, "at least 50 NGOs are funded by Germany or German foundations."

And they are on which side?

"All of them are pro-Palestinian."

The German Protestant Brot für die Welt, he tells me, "is one of the worst." They fund social groups that try to "convince Israeli youngsters not to join the army."

How do you explain that Germans are so pro-Palestinian?

"They follow the crowds. NGOs started in Scandinavia, and Germany was the last to enter into the world of NGOs and the world of anti-Semitism and anti-Zionism activities."

I ask Gerald if he also knows how much money is flowing from the German TV and film industry into Israeli movies.

Gerald gives me a look of total shock. Somehow, he never thought about this little genie. He doesn't even know how to check it, but he'll try.

Which reminds me that Alesia Weston of the Cinematheque promised to get back to me on this but still hasn't. I shoot her an e-mail.

* * *

Time flies fast and I am to re-hook up with the Italians. I call Itamar, just to make sure the group is still at the Gate, but he doesn't pick up.

I walk the streets and see an advertisement on a wall about a rabbi named David Batsri who is "repairing sins" of people in the yeshiva that he heads. Sounds interesting, right?

This is better, much better, than any app ever invented by any Israeli high-tech genius!

Gate Eighteen

Ordained by God and the angels, a rabbi will
save you from turning into a she-ass.

AS HIS NAME IMPLIES, DAVID BATSRI IS OF THE SEPHARDI COMMUNITY, AND reading the ad it appears that he is part of the Sephardi Haredi world, politically known as Shas. This part of society is huge in numbers and quite powerful. They are Jews who originated in Arab lands, but who have come under the influence of Ashkenazic fanatic rabbis. As a result, they study like a German and imagine like an Arab. This can be a great mix, but can also result in a huge mess.

Let's see how Shas people mix.

Rabbi Batsri is not in attendance when I enter his Yeshiva, but other rabbis are, and at least one of them, I think, is Batsri's son.

All present, by the way, have been told to fast the whole day, as part of erasing their sins. Sin erasure is very important, by the way. For, be it known to all: if you spill your seed, even only once in your life, you will be sent to burn in hell for the rest of eternity.

Of course, according to Rabbi Batsri, who enters a few minutes later, and the others here, who themselves follow Batsri, God is merciful, especially to his Chosen People. It is therefore that God is offering a solution to the seed spiller: if he fasts 420 days, Batsri says, the spillage sin will be forgiven.

Just so no one confuses reality here, the rabbi is offering everyone in attendance a printed sheet of fast days for different sins. Murder: 1,199 days of fasting will get you off the hook. Sleeping with a married woman: 325. Masturbation: 4,000. Yes, this is not a typo; playing with your penis is worse than murder. You will have this sin forgiven and forgotten only, *only*, if you fast 4,000 days. In other words: eleven years.

In general, the rabbi says, each individual present should be fasting for 26,249 days if he or she wants to be purified of all sins. In other words: seventy-two years.

How could we, the Chosen, survive a lifetime without food?

Ramadan suddenly looks really, really cool. Could I still convert to Islam?

Rabbi Batsri is not impressed by my worries. In accompanying pages handed out to us, he lists the following: "A man who has sex with his wife during menstruation will be reincarnated as a gentile woman. A man who has sex with a married woman will be reincarnated as a donkey. A man who has sex with his own mother will be reincarnated as a she-ass. A man who has sex with his father's wife will be reincarnated as a camel. A man who has sex with a gentile woman will be reincarnated as a Jewish whore."

And then he clarifies: We don't have to do any of the above listed acts to be reincarnated as a she-ass or a Jewish whore. No. God, he says, will bring us back to life as a donkey if we merely imagine sleeping with a married woman, or as a camel if we just dream about a little romantic affair with our father's woman.

Of course and of course, Rabbi Batsri is not going to spend his time on us, horrible sinners, just because he likes to scare us. He has better things to do in life than spend his time with eventual donkeys like the rest of us.

The reason the rabbi is here is that he is a man of good news. Knowing how terrible it is to be in our shoes, the rabbi has had an audience with God and the angels, Gabriel and Rafael, and the three of them came up with a brilliant plan: a fasting payment. Yep. You can pay instead of fasting. And this is the way it works: one shekel will subtract one day of fasting. Quite cheep, right? The rabbi is in a good mood today and he is willing to go an extra mile for us, which he calls payments: 101 shekels a month for twenty-six months and we will be cleansed of the sins we are presently burdened with. Of course, if we sin again, we will need to add. But for now, it's very simple: twenty-six months for only 101 shekels a month. God is merciful.

There are other sin-cleansing plans available, according to the rabbi's agreement with God and the angels: Pay per Sin. This works really, really simply. Assuming, for example, that you murdered your neighbor. Send in 1,199 shekels and you'll be as white as snow. Masturbated? No problem. Heaven takes Visa. Give in your Visa number, we'll deduct 4,000 shekels from your account and you'll be doing just great and fine, clean of this sin. Of course, if you masturbated twice, that's only 8,000 shekels. Every time you touch your penis, just remember, that's 4,000 shekels less in your bank account. The more you do, the more you pay. The less you do, the less you pay. And, please, don't think of sex with your neighbor's wife, or Visa will work extra hours subtracting figures from your bank account.

The people around me, believe it or not, take out their credit cards.

This is not all. The people, who otherwise look normal, are commanded by the rabbi's clerks walking around. "Not yet," they yell at those who submit their credit cards too fast.

What follows is a ceremony. The about-to-be-cleaned of their bank and Visa accounts are told to tie their feet with special chords they are given. This is to purify the soul, because God won't take the money of those who are not humble.

Frighteningly, the people follow the orders. I leave the place dismayed and shocked.

Who said that Jews were smart?

I think of the stray cats in my garden, and how happy they were making love in public. Most likely they will be reincarnated as Jewish whores. That will be fun.

Gate Nineteen

The European Commission heartily invites you to a fact-finding mission led by an ex-Jew who will take you to the Holocaust Museum in Jerusalem and unveil the true face of lying, brutal, murderous, syphilis-ridden Jews, dead and alive.

ON THE NEXT DAY I AGAIN JOIN THE EX-JEW ITAMAR AND THE ITALIANS. TODAY they go to Yad Vashem, not another Lifta, and I wonder how they'll feel at the Dead Jews' Museum.

Itamar is leading the tour but he's not just a tour guide, he's also an educator and as we walk from section to section in this museum Itamar does his best to turn the WWII story into a contemporary one. He achieves this admired goal by making comparisons between then and now. If you are perplexed and don't know what this means, let me be clearer: between yesterday's Nazis and today's Israelis.

"In Israel today, Africans are being put into concentration camps," Itamar says, referring to illegal Sudanese and Eritrean immigrants.

I've heard about various problems and issues with those Africans, though I have never heard about them being put into concentration camps. But, to be fair, I write a note for myself to meet these Africans and to also check whether there is forced labor or crematoriums operating in Israel.

We move to another section of other dead Jews, where a normal visitor to this museum learns about the most potent phase in the mass extermination of millions of Jews, but our ex-Jew has other things on his mind. He says:

"With the beginning of the loss in 1942, what is called 'extermination of the Jews' starts. What you see here is all from the eye of Jewish victims, this is after all a Jewish museum. But what you see here, with the Nazis and the Jews, is also happening today, in Palestine. What happens here in Israel is Holocaust. Today, the Israeli army is doing the same thing, and the American army too."

We move to the Łódź Ghetto section, where the infamous Chaim Rumkowski's "Give me your children" speech is played out on a screen. Rumkowski was the Nazis' appointed leader of Łódź Ghetto and in September of 1942 they demanded that twenty thousand Jewish children be given to them, for the purpose of burning them. Rumkowski was ordered to deliver the children and on September 4, 1942, he made this speech to his fellow Jews: "A grievous blow has struck the ghetto. They are asking us to give up the best we possess – the children and the elderly. I never imagined I would be forced to deliver this sacrifice to the altar with my own hands. In my old age, I must stretch out my hands and beg. Brothers and sisters: Hand them over to me! Fathers and mothers: Give me your children!"

These chilling words are interrupted by Itamar's voice, as he continues comparing Jews and Nazis: "The Palestinian Authority today executes many people at the command of Israel."

We get to the section of the mass killing of Jews, with Jews digging their own graves in various countries conquered by the German army. And Itamar, self-certified historian, notes: "Eighty percent of the killing was not done by the Nazis but by the local people."

The Nazis, like Israel, were commanding others to kill.

Brilliant.

Time to talk about the Final Solution of the Jewish Question, the infamous Nazi masterful job of Jew killing. Itamar speaks.

"We don't have any order from Hitler that says, 'Kill all the Jews in Europe.' Today we know that the killing of Jews was not something that started from above but something that came from the ground, by soldiers who were experiencing death around them – from partisans, for example – and had to find ways to deal with it. Then one thing led to the other and people killed more and more. I can give you an example from my experience, serving in the Israeli army. I arrested two hundred, three hundred Palestinians, sometimes little children, and sometimes I beat them up and then put them on a truck. Without asking any questions. Having this experience myself, I can imagine myself doing the same thing that the Germans did."

It is interesting to see what the EU people are busy with these days: using Yad Vashem, the monument for millions of Jews slaughtered at their hands, as a platform for poisonous propaganda against the survivors of their butchery. When you walk here with Itamar, seeing the dead of Auschwitz but hearing the name of Palestine, watching a Nazi officer on a video but hearing the name Israel, you can't deny how hugely effective Itamar's propaganda is. When you leave Yad Vashem after touring it as a gift of European generosity, what remains in you is this: the Poles arrested six million Palestinians, who were then gassed by Jews in Tel Aviv, and later burnt at Treblinka crematoriums operated by Palestinians at Israel's command.

Oh, another very important info that Itamar gives us as a bonus before we leave is this: Theodor Herzl, the man whose vision made for the foundation of the State of Israel, died of a "sexual disease." When I ask him what sexual disease this was, he tells me it was syphilis. Obviously Itamar is worried that he didn't paint the Jews badly enough, so he comes up with this new detail.

(This syphilis story became the "scientific" cause of Herzl's death by some bloggers of interest, following an Internet article written by a bored journalist a hundred years after Herzl's death stating that Herzl visited a prostitute in his early years, contracted gonorrhea from her, and that this "possibly" caused his death twenty-four years later.)

As an ex-Jew, this Itamar excels in his new identity.

These days I learn more than I have ever wanted to know about

Europe. The more I walk in this land the more I see them: NGO here, NGO there. I find it painful to witness young Europeans travelling to this country just so that they can suck into their system a little more hatred toward Jews than they already have.

It is also today that I learn things about Israel I didn't know before. Yes, I already met some "good" self-hating Israelis in the last few days, but I would never have dreamt that it could reach to such a degree as I see now.

I have been out of this country long enough to not feel comfortable with so much self-hatred around me. I need, for my mental well-being, to be surrounded with normal people.

Thank God Palestine is near. Hallo, Ramallah: I'm coming!

Gate Twenty

Meet the most charismatic man in Palestine, a genius spymaster,
a raging, kind, serious, funny, ruthless leader, and find out
how a Jew, Tobi the German, became a Saudi prince.

GENERAL JIBRIL RAJOUB, FEARED AS WELL AS ADMIRED BY MANY, IS MY MAN today.

Jibril speaks unto me: "I hope I could deliver what I believe in. For me Germany and Germany's people are very important. Your people are one of those who suffered last century, you were the scapegoat to fundamentalism and extremism, but later on Germans proved that they are great and that they could rebuild their country, and now Germany is an important player in the international community. I think that my people should learn a lot from you and I think that we have a lot of common ethics and values. Ethics and values are the only way to convince the world that the Palestinian people deserve self-determination."

It is a special occasion for me to meet Jibril. I have written about this man. Kind of. Over a decade ago, in a play that I authored about the Israeli-Palestinian conflict ("The Last Virgin"), one of the four characters on the stage was based on Jibril. His stage name was, as you might guess, Jibril Rajoub. To see my character, my creation, in the flesh and in the real is a feeling few will understand. This man I know intimately, though we have never met before.

Tell the world what Palestine means to you, what being Palestinian means to you –

"For me Palestine is my mother's land. I was born here, my father and my grandfather, and I am committed to my people's cause. I joined the resistance when I was young. I was arrested six times by the Israelis. All in all I spent seventeen years in Israeli jails. I fought against the Israeli occupation and I'm proud of that."

Jibril is a living legend. To the Israelis he is a terrorist, convicted once and again, arrested once and again, and his list of offenses is quite impressive. At present he is heading the Palestinian Football Federation and the Palestine Olympic Committee, but don't kid yourself. Among his list of previous jobs is being the leader of the Palestinian Preventive Security Force, a fearsome intelligence and security apparatus. This man is a master fighter, a master spy, and a master manipulator.

My kind of man.

Why would a commander of his country's biggest secrets get involved in soccer? Good question, but nothing Jibril does is simple.

His life experience has taught him that "resistance does not mean only military resistance," he tells me, and one day "I started to understand that our aspirations could be achieved through other tools." One of those tools, what a shocking surprise, is sport. Sport, he teaches me, "is an effective tool to achieve our national aspirations."

Jibril gets excited when he talks about Palestine. "Palestine is everything for me," he tells me, enjoying every syllable he utters.

"I was and will remain devoted to the cause of the Palestinian people," he says in the clearest of language, adding: "Equal rights for women is for me a commitment. I am trying. I hope that the other side [Israel] understands the dimension of what we're doing and opens a bridge" for both of them to walk on.

Bullshit. I know it, he knows it, but he has to say this. How did we get into equal rights for women here? Part of the bullshit. German journalists love this stuff, and so he feeds it to me.

France is perfume. Germany is Mercedes. The USA is McDonald's. What is Palestine?

"It's enough that Christ was born here in Palestine, it's enough that we have al-Aqsa, it's enough that Palestine is sacred for three religions: Judaism, Christianity, and Islam."

Jibril, enjoying his game, keeps at it. There were many wars in Europe, he says, but in this place Christ was born, and he "spread love and peace."

More bullshit. Jibril is no Christian, and to Muslims Jesus was a prophet, no Christ, but Jibril knows that a good European Christian like me would be impressed by it, and so he says it.

He, the Master of Masters, really believes me that I'm a German Christian. I'm good!

For the fun of it, and to see how he will respond, I remind Jibril that the Palestinian president, Mahmoud Abbas, did not mention the word "Judaism" when he gave his most important speech to the UN General Assembly in New York just a couple of years ago, making it

clear to the world that Palestine was home to just two major religions, Islam and Christianity. How come Mahmoud "forgot" Judaism and Jibril remembers it so well?

"I don't want to defend Abu Mazen. I think Abu Mazen can defend himself, and I am even ready to arrange a meeting, an interview between you and him."

Jibril asks me to write my name down, and also write an official request for Abu Mazen and he'll take care of it. How in the world am I going to write "Tobi the German"? It's one thing saying Tobi the German but totally another thing writing it down. "Official Request from Tobi the German."

Of course, I tell him I'd do it at the first opportunity I have.

The Palestinians are ready to divide Jerusalem, Jibril goes on to tell me, selling me another one of his sound bites, and that they also agree that the Jewish side will have jurisdiction over the Jewish holy places. But the Israelis don't want this.

*   *   *

I think that by now I have heard enough sound bites, and so I ask him for his thinking about the EU's decision about boycotting Israeli goods made in the West Bank and east Jerusalem.

"For the first time in their life Israelis became isolated all over Europe," he declares, immensely happy.

"They [the Israelis] have no right to keep leading the whole world by their nose because of the Holocaust that was committed by other people, not the Palestinian people."

Raising his voice, screaming: "Israel is racist, fascist, expansionist!"

Calming down: "I think the international community all over is fed up!"

Good.

You were in Israeli jails for seventeen years. You lived with Israelis, you tried to kill them, they tried to kill you. What have you learned from the Israelis?

"I think I've learned a lot."

What?

"First of all, you should know, I learned their language.... Second, I studied the whole history of the Jews, the Zionist movement, and I think that I know more about them than they know about themselves."

Jibril, does Zionism equal racism, yes or no?

"I think that Zionism, according to the current Israeli behavior, is the worst kind of racism."

Remembering the man who died of a "sexual disease," which an ex-Jew taught me, I ask Jibril if he is talking about the Zionism as envisioned by Theodor Herzl.

"Excuse me! They can call themselves what they want." And lest I forget, Jibril reminds me that years back even the UN equated Zionism with racism.

I like it now. I succeeded in getting him to stop his sound bites. Some good stuff might come out now.

Why is there so much NGO money here? Is it because they love the Palestinians so much? Is it because they hate the Israelis very much...? Why!

The Middle East conflict between Israelis and Palestinians, he answers, is the "source of fundamentalism and extremism" worldwide, is a "threat to global peace," and that's why "the whole world is investing money, time, energy in this region."

I don't get it. Why would a country like Norway even care what's going on here?

Jibril is surprised by my surprise. It is obvious, he argues, why Europe is getting involved; Europe wants to protect itself and its citizens. What, don't I read the news? He elaborates: "How many terror attacks happened in Europe, even in Germany, as a result of this conflict? How many? How many planes were hijacked? How many people were killed? Excuse me!" It is because of Europe's involvement in the Middle East, he teaches me, that "blood shedding is no longer used to assure my national aspirations."

In short: Palestinians now know that the world is not against them and so they don't blow up planes in mid-flight.

To make sure I got him right, I ask him whether he has just told me that terror would engulf Europe if it did not give money to the NGOs supporting Palestinians.

He realizes that he might have gone too far and he tries to correct himself:

"I think," he switches mode, "that they are sympathizing with the suffering of Palestinians."

I got news for you, I say to him, we don't fucking care about anybody. We, the Europeans, really don't care. Period. We would bomb every walking soul, just like we did in Iraq not so very long ago, if we perceive that our bank accounts are endangered. We have a rich history of killing even each other, for no real reason; why in the world does he think that we sympathize with anything or anybody?

Jibril, I say to him, we are a bunch of killers and we have no sympathies with anything or anybody! I got news for you, Jibril: we are not ethical, and we are not moral.

He laughs: "This question, I think, you should pose to the chancellor of Germany."

*　*　*

I like the guy. Agree with him or not, this man has pride. He has no shame. He loves his people. And he is happy as hell being who he is, unlike many Jews.

To know Israel, I realize, you must come to Palestine. It is through this contrast that you understand Israel better, and Palestine as well.

It is at this point that I try to move away from politics, and have the man talk to me as Jibril, Jibril the man and not Jibril the master.

What does Jibril Rajoub do in the mornings when he wakes up? What's the first thing he does in the morning? Does he, for example, kiss his wife?

"When I get up in the morning I read the newspapers. I have to know exactly what's going on, because I always expect surprises."

Tell me, how do you spend time with your wife?

"I dedicate 100 percent" to the Palestinian Cause. Since I joined Fatah (the PLO) I never, never, never had a vacation. I never had a personal or a private life. What else do you want to know?"

How much sport do you do?

"I walk twice or three times a week. Minimum twenty-five kilometers, non-stop. You can join me on Thursday and you'll see. I walk from here to Jericho. Last time I walked with Fayyad [the previous prime minister] twenty-one kilometers in three and a half hours."

It is at this very moment that the Israeli TV's most-watched news broadcast starts and, like many Israelis, Jibril turns on his TV. I try to move my head away from the TV, since I'm not supposed to understand Hebrew. Occasionally, I do look and ask him to translate for me. Jibril does.

Jibril and I feel good together. We connect. And he shows it. He tells me he would like to go off record from now on, and just talk man to man.

I can't stop laughing hearing what he says off record, on politics and other subjects. Obviously, I can't share what he says off record, except to say this: at this point of our talk there's not even one "sound bite" uttered.

Smart man, this Jibril, the way I envisioned him in my play.

When everything is done, he asks me what I'm doing this evening. I tell him I'm his and he invites me to join him at one of Ramallah's luxurious hotels for a party, at the Mövenpick.

It is at the party that he delivers the keynote speech in which he thanks this German, me, on national TV, for joining him today. How could a man like him, master of espionage, not see that I'm not Aryan? I guess, if I may say so, that I did a good job. If the Israeli Secret Service were to get wind of this, they would pay me a very fat salary to join them.

Jibril is an excellent orator, he's passionate; he's the most charismatic man in Palestine. He calls Israel racist and fascist, and says that if Hitler woke up from his grave and saw Israel's brutality, he would be shocked.

As I'm about to depart, Jibril gives me his business card. This is not your average card. In size it is, but that's where the similarities end. The card is a gold-plated slab of impressive weight, protected by a nylon covering. It reads: Jibril M. Rajoub. Major General. Member of the Central Committee of the Fateh [sic] Movement, Deputy Secretary of Committee, President of the Palestinian Olympic Committee, President of the Palestinian Football Federation. Palestine, West Bank, Ramallah.

Man of power.

We get along so well that Jibril wants me to come back the next day.

I don't know if I should. How long will I be able to play the Aryan?

I don't let fear and doubt overtake me and I say that I'd love to come.

And I do.

* * *

After I leave the party, a van on the Palestinian side of the crossing picks me up. Lina, a lady of eastern beauty, sits in front, and a man sits in back. She and the driver are the guides, the man in the back has some function though I'm not clear what. Lina is from Saudi Arabia, previously married to a Palestinian and now divorced; she works for Jibril.

We are going to Hebron.

We drive, in a white Chevrolet van, on roads that never end. It would take half an hour between Ramallah and Hebron, Lina says, if not for the Israelis. Again blaming the Israelis, only in this case she's right. The short cut would require passing through Jerusalem, and for this she would need a permit, hence driving around and about, on mountain roads and wadis. But this van does the detour fast, flying on Palestinian roads, allowing me to marvel at the beauty and secrets of mountains revealing themselves to us, kilometer by kilometer. Naked mountains, picturesque and cruel, dry and tall, each in striking different shape – just like the people of this land.

Why we're going to Hebron I don't know. I'm flowing with the currents, wherever they lead me.

We pass a National Park called Herodium. What is it? Lina doesn't know. We see a bunch of ancient-looking pillars standing in front of us. We check a tourist brochure and read that these are pillars from two thousand years ago. Next to the pillars is a small house, with an old Arab couple sitting outside, making sure that the sun is moving well from east to west. Lina approaches them and asks what the pillars are; nobody in Saudi Arabia ever told her. The man answers: these pillars are here since about twenty years ago.

Who put them here?

"The Jews."

In front of us there's a mountain going up, way up, perhaps the abode of heavenly angels.

What's on the top of the mountain?

"Jews from very long time ago."

Up there, I slowly find out, is the Israel Nature and Parks Authority. What are they doing here? Well, this is a site from thousands of years ago, a palace that some archeologists assume is also the burial place of King Herod, a Jew "from a very long time ago."

Yo. That King Herod. From the Temple Mount.

This place doesn't square all too well with the Palestinian narrative, but I say nothing. I'm a dumb German.

We get back to the van. We drive further and further, and in no time this flying van reaches Hebron. As we get out I look at the van's license plate. This is not a normal plate. Nope. This van belongs to the Palestinian government.

Good to know.

We walk the streets of Hebron, on its Palestinian side. Last time

I was in Hebron, I chiefly stayed in the 3 percent section of the Jews, and only a few minutes on the other side, at the beginning of it. Now I'm at the center of the city. What a nice city. Alive and kicking, teeming with people and activity, and quite big. "33 percent of West Bank Palestinians," Lina tells me, "live here." On the streets I see USAID signs, which denote projects funded by the US government. They too are in Palestine.

It is here that I see much clearer the difference between Hebron's Arab and Jewish sections. No desolation here, no ugly trash, and no ghetto. Much ink has been spilled by foreign media journalists describing the hardships caused to Hebron Arabs by the Jewish settlers, habitually neglecting to mention the riches of this city and the comfort of its residents. Why don't the various foreign tourist guides do tours in this part of Hebron, in the captivating 97 percent of it?

Lina, probably on orders from Jibril, wants me to visit the Ibrahimi Mosque, the "Cave of the Patriarchs" that I visited when I was in the Jewish part of the city, a holy place to both Muslims and Jews that is divided between them with two separate entrances, and I say that I'd be delighted. Once we get there, I am delighted indeed. The place is spotless, magnificent, and inspiring. Lina is praying, I walk around, trying to sneak a glimpse into the Jewish part, and then Lina says we have to go.

We go to see a youth soccer match, where Jibril is also waiting for us, in which the Palestinian team loses. Game over and another one starts: Jibril wants me to attend a protest tent, where he says a demonstration is taking place, somewhere in town.

We get there fast, to a tent on the ground. Many posters. Plastic chairs. People sit next to a sad-looking old man, with red eyes and hardly a spark of life, and they mumble words into his ears. The old man stares at a distant place, as if he can see his son who is miles and miles away. He can't. His son, Mahmoud Abu Salakh, is a prisoner in an Israeli jail, sentenced to many years behind bars for terrorist acts.

What did he do? I ask Lina. "Nothing," she says, and adds that he's suffering from incurable cancer. These days, as Israelis and Palestinians are negotiating peace, Israel is releasing a number of Palestinian prisoners, but it won't release Abu Salakh. In minutes Jibril shows up and gives a short speech, asserting that Israel's "fascist occupation will not succeed." This demonstration seems to have been hastily organized and I think Jibril is behind it, performing a little show for Tobi the German.

*   *   *

As it turns out, there's a wedding not far from here and Lina says that Jibril wants me to go there.

Gently, and fast, I'm pushed into the van again, by the man from the back of the van. We drive. Faster than fast. The van stops. Right by a huge crowd in the open air, with blaring music and hundreds of people all around. The people here have obviously been waiting for me and I am accompanied out of the van into the center of the happy event, as if I were a Saudi prince. Did I say prince? No way. King would be a much better word. People are standing in line to greet me, to shake my holy hands. King. Yes. If you watch Saudi TV and see the crowds greeting the king, which is what Saudi TV shows millions of times a day because they won't show anything else, you would recognize my honor in a second.

I feel great. I own oil fields.

People look at me, smile at me.

As I keep walking, it occurs to me that some of the people don't know who my honor is, but since they saw their friends shake my holy hands they do as well. They are as curious as I am to know who I am. Yeah. And between you and me, I have no clue what's going on. A horrible mistake must have occurred, but only Prophet Muhammad knows. He is in Heaven with Allah and he knows all. I know nothing.

Though, I must admit, I quickly get used to my new status. It takes no time to get used to being worshipped; it feels natural in seconds. King Tobi the First. The speed at which I get used to power, to being a prince and a ruler, to being worshipped and admired, mixed with the knowledge that these worshippers are under my full control and I can do with them whatever I want, that I am the real King Herod, is amazing and shocking.

I'm shown to my chair, a plastic chair at the center of honor.

And just then, as I'm about to sit down on my throne, Lina says we must leave.

What!

From a powerful King Herod I turn back into just another German, a Tobi. What a fall!

What happened? Nobody tells me. Nobody shakes my hands on the way out. Easy come, easy go.

We speedily drive away from the wedding. Did somebody discover my real identity? I really hope not.

The van stops. Tomorrow, Lina says, General Rajoub will do his famous walk, from Ramallah to Bethlehem. Would I like to come?

Yes, I say, happy that my suspicion has proved wrong.

I guess I don't need Gideon Levy to show me around Palestine. I'm managing on my own.

Lina drops me by a checkpoint near Jerusalem. I can cross into the Jews, she can't. We shall meet tomorrow.

I cross. In minutes, Lina sends me an e-mail. No walk tomorrow, she writes. What has happened? I don't know. And maybe never will.

I go back to Jerusalem, to see how the stray cats are doing, and I feed them kosher milk.

Gate Twenty-One

Homeless Palestinians park their Range
Rovers in front of their gated villas.

WHAT SHOULD A JEW DO WHEN HIS WALK WITH A PALESTINIAN IS CANCELLED?

Become a Palestinian himself.

Which is exactly what I do on the next day. But not just a Palestinian. I prefer a Palestinian with a special touch, something that will show my appreciation and thanks to the EU.

How could I achieve such a feat? Lederhosen. I have a pair, and I put them on.

I don't know if anybody will notice my Lederhosen, as I don't know how many people recognize this special piece of clothing, but it's worth the try. I look at myself in the mirror and for a second there I'm reminded why I initially brought my Lederhosen with me. I wanted to compare two occupied lands, but as soon as I think of it I forget it. Sorry, Tyrol, but you are just a little fly facing a lion, Jerusalem.

I walk leisurely through the souk of the Old City, somewhere between Bab al-Amud and al-Aqsa, and stop by a man selling Arab headdresses. How much? I ask. "One hundred twenty shekels," he says.

This rate, let me enlighten you here, is the opening shot between two learned, hardened men. None is willing to move a penny toward the other. A perfect opportunity for the EU and the USA to get involved, not to mention host an NGO conference in Jordan to solve the issue via dance.

Sadly, none of them cares about a little Arab head covering.

And so, having no allies, we negotiate.

"Twenty," say I, "One-hundred," says he. We go on and on, each enlisting Allah's help in the matter, and Allah finally declares this heavenly ruling: forty-four shekels.

Deal done, I walk my way to the Western Wall.

It will be interesting, I amuse my heart, to see how the Jews will react to Sheikh Tobi of Austria in their midst. After all, I don't remember ever seeing an Arab, at least an Arab dressed like one, at the Western Wall.

I get a first inkling for my strange appearance at the security gate before the Wall. This gate is manned 24/7, as nobody takes this holy area lightly. Two cops who stand by an x-ray machine can't believe their eyes when they see me walking in, as if I had just dropped from a mental institution in the sky. They stare at each other. Evidently, they have never been taught what to do under such circumstances.

But then, one of them has this great idea: he takes out his smartphone and tells his friend to snap a photo of himself and me standing next to each other. Sheikh Tobi likes all people who like him and I immediately stretch out my hands in a warm embrace. You want to take a picture of me? You can take twenty! We stand next to each other, like two lovebirds, and Mr. Security takes a pic of the Sheikh. Then another one. And another one. And another one. They are so excited, these security people, that they neglect to check me and they let me pass. I, Salah ad-Din with Lederhosen, gleefully walk on to capture the Holy Mount.

I enter the area, continuing to the Wall or, more precisely, al-Buraq, as if I were the owner of the place. Jews look at me. They have no clue how I landed in their Holiest Shrine, but they say nothing. I walk and walk and walk, like the king I really am, but no one comes to kiss my hands or bow to my kingship. This area, which is guarded by the best of Israel's security apparatus to make sure no Arab terrorist shows up to make some trouble, strangely and weirdly accepts me, albeit with no words. There are security cameras all around, must be a thousand eyes looking at every single move anybody is doing here, but none reacts to mine.

The Saudi-Tyrolean King that I am, I get offended that nobody notices me. And so, in order to get some attention, I pass near a group of Sephardi religious teenagers, separated into males and females, and slowly walk to the females, as if I want to pluck one or two of them for me. The male guardians of female purity notice me and some yell, "Death to the Arabs." Not only them. A New York Jew then approaches me with the greeting, "Fuck you!" Hearing these two words coming out of his mouth, I transform from a king to an imam in a split second. This is a holy land, I tell him. Here we don't use such words. Go back to New York, Jew, for you don't deserve this holy ground!

What can I tell you? Honestly, I think I was born to be an imam.

As I leave the area, one of the teenagers approaches me. "I think that you are a leftist Israeli and you tried to provoke us into saying something ugly," he says to me.

How dare he talk like this to an imam like me!

*   *   *

Night falls and I go to have dinner with an American friend who's in Israel these days. After dinner he takes me around his neighborhood, not far from the Hebrew University. We pass a number of magnificent houses in what seem to be gated communities, with Range Rovers and Audis waiting to serve their lords.

Who lives there? I ask.

"These villas belong to the Lifta people."

My friend, who happens to be a leftist activist, knows the history of the place much better than I do. There are no poor Lifta refugees, he tells me, an impression I also had after visiting the deserted village of Lifta with Itamar. Lifta, located at the entrance of Jerusalem, used to be a pirates' village in the old days, and the villagers made their living by forcing pilgrims to the holy city to part with their earthly goods.

Historically, those villagers owned much land all around, and to this day their descendants are some of the richest of Arab clans, and they own these beautiful houses.

Who knows, maybe the EU will soon donate another €2.4 million to "preserve Palestinian cultural heritage" here.

I go back to my stray cats, which by this time I have a colony of, and I sit down to read the free paper of Israel, *Israel Hayom*. The most-read paper of Israel is this right-wingers' daily funded by Sheldon Adelson, an American tycoon whose reported net worth reaches $35 billion. To get the pulse of this paper's readers, I look at the ads section. Here is a sample of goods highly desired by the Israeli public: German, Austrian, and Polish passports, plus natural Viagra.

Sheldon Adelson, by the way, is only putting in the money. It is *Haaretz*, the most-left daily paper in Israel, that has been physically printing *Israel Hayom* for quite some years, making it one of *Haaretz*'s biggest financial backers.

I try to explain this to my cats, with whom I start developing a cautiously friendly relationship, but they give me this strange look, as in: Did you lose your mind?

They are smart, my cats.

Gate Twenty-Two

A Jewish pilot with a mission: Catch the Jews!

I HAVE BEEN WALKING HOURS ON END, ALMOST EVERY DAY SINCE I ARRIVED in this country, going where the people are and trying to reconnect with the land I left so long ago. Perhaps it's time I sit down and have people come to me, just like a native. I choose to do this in Tel Aviv, the cultural center of Israel.

Right by Rabin Square in the center of Tel Aviv there is a bookstore-slash-coffee shop called Tolaat Sfarim (Book Worm). I take a table, order boiling "opposite coffee" (café latte), and get ready to meet some Jews.

I start the day with Jonathan Shapira, the hero of the *10% – What Makes a Hero* film I saw at the Cinematheque. Jonathan is also the brother of Itamar (of Lifta and Yad Vashem), and I hope he'll enlighten me today.

"I was the model Zionist kid, he who read aloud names of the fallen in Israel's wars or of those who died in the Holocaust. My dream was to be in the Air Force, just like all the good kids of Israel. I finished my army training and became a pilot in 1993, and luckily I was in a rescue helicopter squadron. I risked my life to bring injured soldiers to hospitals. I felt I was doing a clean and good job."

These days Jonathan is no longer an Israeli army pilot. "Now I'm working occasionally in the USA, as a helicopter pilot on special flights for post-storm clean-up. I wish I could do the same thing here, in Israel, but here they wouldn't give me such a job."

Jonathan has an MA in conflict resolution, a degree he earned at a university in Austria. For a second I entertain the thought of talking to him about Tyrol, but immediately give it up. Talking about Tyrol in a bookstore somehow doesn't look right.

I look at his figure and wonder how he'd look in Lederhosen, but I don't think he'd go to the Western Wall. The man has changed. How did a man who risked his life for the Zionist cause turn into an Austrian conflict resolution person?

"I still risk my life here, but on the side of the oppressed and not of the oppressors."

Jonathan uses harsh words when talking about Israel: "Everything I was taught was based on deception and self-deception."

What made you change? What was the critical moment that turned you around?

Jonathan speaks softly, quietly, in measured tones and with comforting warmth. His change took place, go figure, during a peace initiative geared to spread love between Arab and Jew, when this Jew started to hate other Jews.

The initiative, taking place at the peace-chasing Arab-Jewish village of Neve Shalom, featured a Palestinian man talking about his sister being paralyzed from the neck downward, victims of the Israeli-Palestinian conflict. Deeply touched by this man's speech, Jonathan started to reevaluate everything he had believed in. Up to that moment, he tells me cynically, he was like the average leftist, "shooting and crying," holding a gun in his hand while talking peace with his mouth, but at that moment he changed.

How a story of a paralyzed Palestinian girl could touch him so deeply, he who has flown many Jews to hospitals with severed limbs or lifeless, is not clear to me. But according to him, the notion of his army causing that Palestinian's injuries "drove me crazy."

If luck had had it that the Palestinians had won the war, how do you think they would have treated your children? Jonathan doesn't like this question and immediately goes on the offensive: "This is a classic right-wing argument!"

I tell him that this is not an answer. Does he have a better one?

Well, he goes on at length talking to me about history this and history that. Not good enough for me, and I try to bring him to the present, to be pragmatic with me.

What would have happened if Israel had lost in 1967? How do you think the Arabs would have treated the Jews?

"I have no idea."

What do you imagine would have happened?

"I don't know."

Of course he knows. He has seen many enlightening samples from his cockpit.

Jonathan spends his energies criticizing Israel, not other countries. Is Israel really the only devil in the world? I remind him that

Switzerland has just recently passed a law against building mosques with minarets on Swiss soil. Why isn't he fighting the Swiss as well?

"I will join you if you open a BDS campaign against Switzerland for their outlawing the building of mosques in their own country."

Yes, I have nothing better to do with my life than fight the holy Swiss.

How about the other righteous European nations?

"If you open a BDS campaign against Sweden for jailing Sudanese refugees in their country, I'll join you."

His sharpest comments he reserves for Israel: "If you ask me, hundreds of thousands of Sudanese should be allowed to enter this land. Such an eventuality will save Israel from its racist behavior and conduct."

Jonathan and Itamar, the Royal Shapiras, are being serenaded by various critics of Israel, but it is Jonathan who has earned a song, titled "Jonathan Shapira," in which the Israeli pop singer Aya Korem sings of her wish to have children by him. She is like the Israeli scholar from the Georgian restaurant. One is proud for having slept with an Arab, the other dreams of sleeping with a Jonathan.

Of course, not all Israelis have such a bad view of the Jews and of Israel.

*   *   *

Say hello to the new "Book Worm" comer, Mickey Steiner, who is the managing director of the German-held company SAP Labs, Israel.

Are you a *Yekke potz*?

"Not me, my dad."

Mickey is a positive person who marvels at Israel's high-tech achievements. "International companies come to Israel because of the technological inventions that are made here. Innovations made here are not made there."

Why is that so?

"The character of Israelis is to find solutions to seemingly insolvable situations. It started with German Jews who came here to establish a state, long before the Holocaust, when there was no infrastructure here beyond the very basic, and they had to build things from scratch."

How come Israel is so good at high tech?

"It is in our genes, already from the days of the destruction of the Second Temple."

I should have used this answer years back when I studied mathematics and computer science and my Haredi family, which did not condone any studies other than rabbinical, was furious at me. Too bad I didn't know Mickey in those days.

In today's technology, what's made in Israel?

"Seventy percent of Intel's revenue is based on inventions made in Israel."

Give me some examples of inventions made here.

"USB stick is an Israeli invention. Voicemail is an Israeli invention. SMS. Computer chips that run laptops. Medical scanning devices, such as MRI. VOIP. Data security for cellphones. Flash memory."

In other words, if not for Israel there would be no cellphones today, assuming, of course, that others wouldn't have found this technology too.

"Yes."

Do you really believe that there are Jewish genes?

"Yes, in the sense of the culture which influences those who are part of it, in this case Jews."

So, do you think that the Jewish nation is the smartest, most innovative?

"Yes."

How come the Jews have so many fucking problems everywhere they show up?

"Because they are too fucking smart and people are afraid of the Jews, suspicious of the Jews, and jealous of the Jews."

I am God, and I'm offering you this: I'll make you less smart, less innovative, and in return you'll be like the rest of the world and you'll be loved. Take my offer?

"No."

Why not?

"I'd rather stay in my heritage and my roots even at the price of hatred."

How come smart, innovative people with such genes follow Rabbi Batsri and Rabbi Yosef (a famous and divisive rabbi, Ovadia Yosef, who loves to curse anyone opposing him)?

"I don't know. You have to ask a sociologist."

* * *

Avi Primor, Israel ambassador to Germany from 1993 to 1999, is no sociologist, but he has come over to this book worm for a little schmooze. Avi has founded, and is the head of, the Center for European Studies at Tel Aviv University, which is in association with Al-Quds University and the Royal Scientific Society of Jordan.

Maybe Al-Quds U could teach Tel Aviv U how to get funding for a *hamam*.

Avi, and others, teach MA studies at all three universities, where after one year of studies students from the three U's go for another year at Heinrich Heine U in Düsseldorf.

Who is paying for all this?

"I am. I raise funds, mainly in Germany. It costs over one million euros a year."

How many students are there in total?

"Sixty. Twenty from each side (Israeli, Jordanian, and Palestinian)."

Avi's mother is from Frankfurt. She came to Tel Aviv in 1932, "met my father, fell in love and stayed here. None of her family who stayed in Germany survived the Holocaust."

Would you like to have been born a Palestinian?

How the heck did I come up with such a question, I don't know. I think I have drunk too much whiskey today, and maybe Avi has done the same because he is seriously answering my question. No, he says, he wouldn't like this because the Palestinians are a "luckless nation" and because "I don't appreciate their culture."

How can you work with them if you don't appreciate them?

"I'd be very happy if our neighbors were the Swiss and the Norwegians…"

I like Tel Aviv. It's not as beautiful as Jerusalem – actually it's quite ugly – but Tel Aviv has something special, an inner beauty, a certain atmosphere. Maybe it is its people, who for the most part are young and horny. Tel Aviv has another thing that Jerusalem doesn't have: a beach. Why not go there? I pack up my iPad and do just that.

There's nothing more comforting than the sound of the waves. Would Jerusalem be as tense as it is if it had a beach? Imagine that instead of its holy places there were a beach there, smack right in the middle of it. No Shkhinah, no holy tomb, no special airport to heaven; no wife of God, no son of God, no messenger of God; just water and bikini.

Somewhere along the way between Tel Aviv and Jerusalem there is a famous village, not a holy village and no bikinis. The name of the village is Abu Ghosh, and I go to see it.

Gate Twenty-Three

Gun-toting men in search of sweets and Germans.

FOUAD ABU GHOSH, OF ABU GHOSH, IS MY MAN TODAY AND HE IS WILLING TO show me around his village.

Abu Ghosh is a peculiar Arab village near Jerusalem whose residents have been friendly to Jews since the first days of the state. This village is a thorn in the behind of those who argue that Arabs and Jews can't live happily with each other in a Jewish land.

"We, in Abu Ghosh," Fouad tells me, "are Arabs. We get along with the Jews, but Israelis on the Left have a problem with us."

I thought rightists wouldn't like Abu Ghosh, but I guess I was wrong. I learn for the hundredth time today: When it comes to "Arab & Jew," I must move logic off the table and reformat my brain.

Abu Ghosh is famous not because some leftists don't like Arabs who get along with Jews, but for another reason: its restaurants. I ask Fouad to take me to his favorite restaurant in Abu Ghosh. In front of us, as we drive ahead, is a car with this sticker on its bumper: "Jews love Jews." Must be a right-winger, though it could also be an Arab Yekke, like the one I saw the other day. You never know anything in this land.

When we get to the restaurant, Fouad introduces me to Jawdat Ibrahim, owner of this quite expensive Abu Ghosh restaurant, who says to me: "In 1948 all Arab villages around Abu Ghosh were destroyed, except for Abu Ghosh, because the Mukhtar [community leader] made peace with the [Jewish] government." Jawdat likes to surprise his German listener: "Abu Ghosh is sister city with Bad Gastein in Austria. You know the name of the mayor of Bad Gastein? Abu Yussef."

Bad Gastein is a place I know, and where I have stayed on occasion. I have never heard about Bad Gastein being a sister city to Abu Gosh, nor have I ever heard of Abu Yussef. But Jawdat knows better than me.

Jawdat is a smart man, not just when it comes to politics. "My chef, in this restaurant, is a dentist." Dentists, he explains to me, understand best about chewing and about eating, a process achieved by the teeth.

Before I get to chew the dentist's delicacies, I have to listen to Fouad: "I cannot blame only the Jews for what happened here in 1948. I spoke to the people of Abu Ghosh and they told me that the Arab armies had told villagers to leave their homes. 'Give us two weeks and we will wipe out the Jews for you,' they told them. Arabs in other villages left, but not Arabs of our village. They told me: 'Egyptian soldiers came in. They didn't have maps and they pointed their canons at us.' No, I cannot put the blame only on the Jews. Facts are facts, and you cannot change the facts."

The food arrives. It is good, but you can get similar food anywhere else for a fraction of the price charged here. In general, the food in Israel, and in Palestine, makes me happy to be here. There's no day I don't think – or talk – about this. I don't know how they do it. I have been to many countries, and God knows how much I have eaten in each, but nowhere is the food as delicious as it is here. Maybe it's the ingredients grown only here, or a know-how gained in endless wars fought here. I don't know. All I know is this: "Facts are facts."

Abu Ghosh is an interesting place. The EU and European NGOs are not investing here, maybe because this place is a thorn in their behind as well, but this doesn't mean that there's no outside financial intervention here. Who gets involved here? Chechnya. Yep. The leader of Chechnya, Ramzan Kadiro, is building a huge mosque in

Abu Ghosh with a gorgeous golden dome. Price tag of new mosque: ten million dollars, for which Ramzan donates six million.

How big is the mosque going to be?

"The second-largest mosque in the region, after al-Aqsa."

Wow!

But this is not all.

Later on Fouad takes me on a ride to the soon-to-be-completed mosque. The street leading to the mosque, about a mile long, is also being fixed and shaped by the good Chechen uncle. New green fences with shiny white stones are right now being constructed, and the street will be renamed after this leader.

And then Fouad asks if I'd like to see soldiers who frequent a local café.

Yes, I say. I would love to witness this miracle of love between Arab and Jew, soldier and resident. And so Fouad takes me to the café. The "soldiers" he was talking about are mostly young Israeli girls, noshing sweets. I look at them and notice that there are no others to look at. In other words: no local people eating here.

How come?

"Locals don't go to cafés and restaurants at this time."

Will I see the locals later in the evening, if I stick around?

"No. They eat at home."

Forget this café. How about other cafés or restaurants? I notice a sudden change in Fouad's facial expression.

"Israelis, they are the ones who come to eat here. They come here to be served."

Are there places where Arabs and Jews go together? Let's say, are they playing ball together?

"This doesn't happen."

The two sides never meet – ?

"Yes. That's the way it is. It all looks nice, yes, but when you look at the details there you see a different picture."

Arabs love Arabs.

When I lived in Israel I knew of Abu Ghosh, every Jew did, and it comforted all of us. It was the proof, the one solid proof, that Arab and Jew could live together in friendship and harmony. I never went to Abu Ghosh, but I knew everything about it.

I thought I knew. What I knew was a myth; reality is very different.

I stare at Fouad, my host, and share a thought with him. You guys got it all: a beautiful country, best food on the planet, sweetest of fruits, tastiest of vegetables, and best spices available. But you kill each other. Why?!

"Adam and Eve were in Paradise, had everything, but then 'had' to do what God told them not to do. They had everything and they had to destroy everything. That's what we do in this land."

A myth is good until you touch it, and if you do hell breaks loose.

This is Abu Ghosh, a village of the affluent, making its profit from restaurants catering for and eateries catered to myth-loving Jewish visitors. On the weekends, locals tell me, you can't walk in this town because there is traffic bumper to bumper, full of Israelis who come from all over to eat in Abu Ghosh. "I like Arab food and atmosphere," an Israeli I meet in a café tells me. "It's not safe for Jews to be in Arab places except for here, in Abu Ghosh. That's why we come here."

The brave, gun-toting Israelis you see on your local TV screens, the ones you read about in your local papers or watch on your tablets are nothing but little kids wanting to be loved and accepted.

Two music bands from Berlin are coming to perform here soon, I read on a poster next to me. I guess, just a guess, that some German foundations are sponsoring the event. But to better understand the flow of German money I go to meet Mark Sofer, president of the Jerusalem Foundation.

*   *   *

I let my feet rest in Mark's comfortable office in Jerusalem and my lips start to move.

Who are you?

"One of my least favorite things to do is talk about myself."

Please!

"I joined the Foreign Service in 1982, and since then was stationed in Peru, Norway, in New York, Ireland...I was also the foreign affairs adviser to Shimon Peres."

Are you that smart?

"If you place a broomstick in the Venezuelan army, in forty years it will become a colonel."

Are you a broomstick?

"No."

What's the budget for your foundation?

"Last year we raised over $30 million."

Can you name German government money given exclusively for the Jewish community?

"To the best of my knowledge we don't get any money from the German government, only from German states."

Can you name funds given by German states for Jews only?

"I don't want to get involved with this issue, and I would rather not go down that path."

Mark is made visibly uncomfortable by my question. We keep on talking, most of which is off record, and I leave.

As I leave, Lina of Jibril Rajoub's office calls. The man is going for a walk this afternoon, by foot from Ramallah to Jericho, and he wants company. Would I come?

Well, why not?

But before I meet the famous Arab walking by the mountains and the hills, let me first meet a famous Jew sitting in his living room in the Tel Aviv bourgeois neighborhood of Ramat Aviv.

He is Amos Oz, arguably Israel's most famous author.

Gate Twenty-Four

The Bus Stop University is alive and well in the land of Israel.

AMOS OZ LIVES ON THE TOP FLOOR OF HIS BUILDING, THE TWELFTH, AND AT the entrance of his apartment on your left there is a big bookcase with Amos's own books, the ones he has written, lying side by side. More bookcases, quite a number of them, adorn the living room, where Amos welcomes me to sit down with him.

About thirty years ago he wrote a book about his encounters with Israelis, *In The Land of Israel*. Should I expect to find, I ask him, the same land and people that he did?

"Yes and no. There are things that have changed, and there are things that haven't changed in the last thirty years. First, Israeli society is still a multifaceted society. This society is composed of religious and secular, rightists and leftists, people of peace and settlers, Arabs and Jews."

Interesting phrasing: "Settlers" is to be self-understood as people of war.

And what has changed?

"First off, during this period a million Russians have immigrated to this country. Second, we now have hundreds of thousands of settlers in the territories [captured by Israel in 1967], that hardly existed thirty years ago."

The doorbell rings. A huge bouquet of flowers is brought in. Somebody loves Amos, or maybe he has bought it for himself.

Tell me, did the new Russians and the settlers make Israeli society worse than it was before?

"Society is not made of slices of cheese that I can tell you it's better or worse. What I can say is: it is a different society."

Well, this says a lot, doesn't it?

Amos speaks in a low voice, mostly keeping the same tone. He hardly smiles and he never raises his voice. I think he went through some medical procedure lately, though I'm not sure.

"Israeli society turned right within the years, but at the same period of time the rightists have greatly changed as well. Today the right-wingers also speak about peace and compromise with the Palestinians."

Left-leaning Israelis will have the word *Palestinians* or its sister word *settlers* come out of their lips within the first twenty-one to thirty-four seconds of your meeting with them. Amos is no different. He speaks of Palestinians as if they were living next to him and as though he were encountering them a million times a day. But where Amos lives, if I may be direct here, is where people with lofty bank accounts live. The ones who cannot live here are not the Arabs but the poor, of whatever religion. Yet in Amos's mind this little fact doesn't seem to register, for he is obsessed with Jew/Arab division only.

Of course, Amos Oz is not unique in this regard. Many in the Israeli elite cannot stop talking about the poor Palestinians, while hardly mentioning the poor Jews. According to social political studies done in Israel this year, over 20 percent of Israelis live below poverty line, and more than 35 percent are in financial distress. Social justice, I believe, should not be dedicated to only one segment of the population, and if we really care about those doing less well than us, we should not be consumed with just a part of them. The Israeli left is ever consumed with the Muhammads of their world and rarely with their Yehudas. It's a pity.

That said, I don't want to open a discussion about this and I simply swim along with Amos. It's his ship here, after all. Will peace prevail? I ask him.

"There is no other option."

Will two states be here, living side by side?

"Yes. There's no other possibility."

Why?

"If the two states are not becoming a reality, we will end up with one state and that state will be Arab. I don't want this to happen."

Amos does not observe either the Sabbath or Ramadan, but he wants a Jewish state. And like his daughter, Fania, he knows what a "Jew" is. "Other nations built pyramids," he tells me, while the Jews wrote books. "The Jews never had a pope who told them what to do. Every Jew is a pope."

And so is Israel, he says of the little country of eight million. "Eight million opinions, eight million prime ministers, eight million prophets and eight million messiahs. Every Jew here sees himself as a

leader, a prophet, a guide. This society is actually one huge seminary. You can stand at the bus stop and you see Jews who don't even know each other and still they argue about religion, politics, security. The bus stop is at times a seminar. This is what Israel is, what Jews are."

Amos shares his thinking not only about the Israelis but also about the Europeans.

"Europeans very often tend to wake up in the morning, read the paper, sign a petition in favor of the good guys, launch a demonstration against the bad guys, and go to sleep feeling good about themselves. Except that Israel and Palestine is not about good guys and bad guys, it is a clash between two perfectly valid claims over the same country."

Gate Twenty-Five

*Walking with the lions of Palestine and licking ice cream
in solidarity with Adolf Hitler of blessed memory.*

A CLASH IT IS, INDEED.

An attempt by a special unit of the Israeli army to arrest a suspect in the refugee camp Qalandiya, near the checkpoint between Jerusalem and Ramallah, has failed and three Palestinians were killed.

Jibril would like to talk to me about this incident, Lina tells me when we talk on the phone right after I get out of Amos's house. I thought he wanted to walk, I mention to her. Oh, yeah, she says, he wants to walk and talk. "Come to the checkpoint in Qalandiya and we'll have a car waiting to pick you up."

That's fine with me. Tobi the German always likes to be driven around and listen to Palestinian sufferings, just like the rest of his German brethren.

I take a taxi from Tel Aviv to Qalandiya, and the driver drops me at the checkpoint, as he is not allowed to cross into Palestine. I look around and I can tell something is wrong here, because the checkpoint is almost empty.

Lina calls. Would I mind to take a taxi to the Mövenpick Hotel and she will pick me up from there?

What has happened to the car that was supposed to pick me up?

"It's hard to send a car to you because the traffic in Qalandiya is overwhelming."

What is she talking about? A cemetery is busier. But go argue with Lina, a Saudi Palestinian, and you'll never win.

I walk around to look for a taxi and suddenly, in the blink of an eye, the place turns into a war zone. Teenagers, faces covered, burn tires on the road and throw stones at the Israeli soldiers near the checkpoint. Some of the stones are heavier than I am, flying over my head and at my sides.

I should run away from here, but my curiosity is more powerful than any stone. I want to see the response from the other side, maybe live shots, but the Israeli soldiers choose not to react. Psychologically, I notice, this is the worst that can happen to these teenagers, and indeed they get exhausted pretty quickly. I hope they don't turn their attention on me. If any of them finds out who I am, I'll be thrown into the fire and a big party will take place here – without me.

No wonder Lina doesn't want to send a car over. If anything is to explode here, it had better not be a Palestinian government car.

* * *

After some failed attempts I find a cab and drive to the Mövenpick.

What gorgeous riches! The flags of Palestine and Switzerland stand high in front of the hotel, water is profusely sprayed on the greenery next to the flags, shiny German cars move in and out, and servants dressed in high fashion are at the ready to fulfill my innermost desires.

This too, like it or not, is Palestine. Not the horrible images so frequently associated with it, the desolation and destruction brought upon it by the Jews. No. Sorry, iPad: you don't supply me with the truth.

Lina arrives and we drive to Jibril's office, where a government car is waiting for us.

"We cannot smile today, three of us have just been murdered by them," says a guy in the office.

This serious, sad welcome takes about a minute. Tobi the German is here, a man whose family has seen death as a result of the Allied Forces' bombings in WWII, yet he still laughs, and so laughter immediately takes over.

Welcome, brother.

The car soon takes us to The Walk.

The former Security Chief of the Palestinian Nation today is the Sportsman of Palestine. A man feared by many, a man in whom all the secrets of this nation lie as in a safe, a man whose middle name is Trickery, a man of iron will and mind, of a stone heart and soft soul, a man who can make you cry and laugh in the very same minute, a man who will shoot you at his will and pamper you if he so wishes, a man made of these sands, a man who will betray you at a moment's notice and will kill you at the speed of light, a man compared to whom the heroes of legends are pale by comparison, a man with feet of flesh but nerves of steel walks the hills and mountains, high roads and low valleys, for the sake of Palestinian sports.

You may laugh, you may cry, but inside of you the knowledge brews: there is no other like this man. The American president plays golf, the German chancellor sits listening to Wagner, the Israeli president eats Iftar with Obama wannabes, and the Russian boss goes for a swim with the fish. All of them do these things with tens or hundreds of security personnel watching over them, with limited or no public eye viewing them, or if so, for a relatively short duration of time.

Not Jibril.

He walks and everybody can see.

There is security around him. Kind of. A car behind and a car in front, and he walks with about ten people or so. This security entourage doesn't flaunt assault rifles and other impressive metals. Nope. What they have is of another kind and sort: water, ice cream, bananas, dates, yogurt, and other such smart weapons. Whenever they feel like it, in a wadi below or on a mount above, they open a bottle, lick a sweet, or bite into a fruit.

So does Jibril. The feared man of the East is licking an ice cream.

And whenever Jibril licks or bites into anything he makes sure I lick and bite as well. Him and me by now, as everybody can see, are Siamese twins.

Jibril started the walk at around five or six in the late afternoon and has now been on the road for about three hours. I am with him for the second part of his delightful walk.

As we walk, Jibril rages against Hamas. He really doesn't like them. A few years ago he ran for a PLC (Palestinian Legislative Council) slot against his brother, Nayef, and Nayef won. Nayef is with Hamas, Jibril with Fatah. Fatah lost big in that election, and eventually lost Gaza. Jibril has much to tell me about those days, but he asks that this may remain private.

We walk. Walk and walk.

Human fingers could not paint the view surrounding us, not even the most talented of artists. The roads go in circles in and amidst massive displays of white-brown sand, narrow and wide roads hidden between hills and mountains as the wind blows softly on our wet faces. You walk and you walk, but the road never ends. Parts of the walk are

inside Israel, parts inside Palestine, and parts in shared areas, but it is hard to tell when we enter one country and when we leave the other. I always thought that heavily guarded checkpoints separated these countries, but boy, was I wrong.

For many people on the planet, those who for ages have read and heard about the Israeli-Palestinian conflict, the area in dispute must sound like a huge area, bigger than Canada, but as you walk with Jibril you realize not only how small the land is, both Israel and Palestine, but also how interrelated the two are. The only way you can tell which country is which is by the road signs: here they are in Arabic, here in Hebrew – some warning Israelis that entry is legally forbidden to them. And in between a car passes. Not an armored vehicle, not a tank, not a plane. Just a car. And a cat. Yeah, the cats don't care about politics, they just want a little ice cream. My cats get kosher milk, this cat gets halal ice cream.

We are walking on the road, the main road: cars and us, machines and Licking Sportsmen.

We walk and we talk, talk and walk. Side by side, and at times hand in hand. We are: Number One security agent of Palestine, posing as a sportsman, and Tobi the German, a non-posing kosher Aryan.

* * *

Then, at one particular section of our walk, and for no particular reason, Tobi decides to leave the guidance of Jibril of Arabia and examine the Holy Land on his own.

"Don't go there on your own," Jibril of Arabia warns Tobi of Germania. "They will see your blond hair; they will slaughter you!"

Who are they? I better not ask.

"Did you visit our refugee camps?" the Olympic Walker asks his Aryan soul mate, as if refugee camps were Disney, a tourist sight not to be missed.

No, not yet. But I'd love to.

"Nidal!" Jibril calls one of the lickers, who immediately comes to serve the master. "You arrange for the German to see a refugee camp!"

Nidal nods in obedience, and then offers me a banana.

Palestinian bananas, let me tell you, are sweeter than honey. They are not the bananas I know in the States, tasteless and imported. Not at all. These are Holy Bananas, fresh and sacred.

I bite into the banana, spiritually elated, and Jibril asks: "We have a good German doctor living in Jericho. Good German. Would you like to meet him?"

This is the last thing I need. Meet a German that Jibril personally knows. God in heaven: I won't be able to fool a real German with my pure German accent.

How do I get out of this certain death sentence?

This Jibril, I think to myself, ain't no dummy. He is laying a mine under my feet.

I will need to know how to dance on his soon-to-explode mine.

How should I handle this?

Well, like a real Aryan. Tobi the German, an original Aryan, loves German people and will do everything he can to meet them. Yes, I say to Jibril. It would be my honor and pleasure to meet a German doctor who donates his time and expertise to help the Palestinian people.

At once Jibril tells Nidal to arrange a lunch that will include: Jibril, Tobi, the German doctor plus three more German friends.

Oh Lord: How many Germans does this Jibril have in store?

How will I be able to fool four Germans? Allah is great and he will send an angel my way to keep me from the probing eyes of my fellow Germans.

We reach an intersection, and Jibril asks: "Would you like to turn right, into Jericho, or would you like to keep going for a few more hours?"

How many hours?

"Until midnight or, if you prefer, two o'clock in the morning. Whatever you want is okay with me."

I think it's time we see Jericho. It's the oldest city in the world, I heard people say. Is it true?

"People say that. Yes."

How old is it?

"Ten thousand years."

We should see it!

"As you want."

We turn toward Jericho.

It's dark and I can't see much, but Jibril has a house here, and people there are preparing dinner for us.

We have been walking for an hour or two, and still have a long way before we reach Jibril's home.

A police car passes by and the officer driving it stops to bless Jibril with all the blessings of Allah. Jibril asks him what's new. The officer gets out of the car and stands next to Jibril. I can only hear a few of the words they exchange, something to do with "the Jews," but I don't know in what context.

Only after the officer has left I ask Jibril what has happened.

"The Jews asked him why I was walking tonight."

We share a laugh about the stupid Jews who don't understand sports, and keep walking.

I light up a cigarette.

Jibril says that I shouldn't, walking and smoking ain't the perfect combination. I tell him that I'm addicted, that there's no chance he could convince me to stop. This is who I am, a Smoking German.

Standing next to Jibril is a young man, also named Jibril. Jibril the older puts his hand on the arms of Jibril the younger, and they walk together, step by step.

"His mother named him after me," Jibril tells me in pride.

And then General Jibril has an idea, a brilliant one:

"Your name, from now on, is Abu Ali."

I gleefully accept.

For too long I've been playing with names, and I get tired of it. I want to be what I am, live openly with my real name. Abu Ali. It fits me. It's the perfect name for me. Finally I don't have to change names any longer. Abu Ali.

* * *

Jibril and his closest and newest friend, me, Abu Ali, finally reach Jibril's home – one of Jibril's homes, to be more exact. Dinner is served. Everything is delicious. Humus, hot peppers, fresh tomatoes, fresh bread, scrambled eggs, tea, coffee, apples, and a host of other goodies.

"Eat, Abu Ali, eat," Jibril orders me.

I do.

Everything.

Jibril, on the other hand, eats only vegetables. Tomatoes, cucumbers, onion. The healthy stuff. And halva. Yep. "I need some sweet, Abu Ali," he says.

An older man approaches me. "Do you know what 'Abu Ali' means?"

You tell me.

"The Brave. The Hero."

Fits me perfectly!

All agree.

What they don't tell me, and maybe they assume I already know, is which other white man the Palestinians have honored with this very name.

Adolf Hitler.

Maybe I should go back to Amos Oz and introduce myself to him by my real name. But not now. Now I eat, and eat and eat. Another pita, and another pita and yet another pita. Abu Ali likes to eat, but Jibril has had enough with his flat food and tries to occupy himself with something tastier. He has a phone and he does what every man and woman without pitas do: he calls somebody. Who? The German doctor. They talk for a minute and Jibril hands me his phone. Jibril wants to hear Abu Ali speak perfect German.

You must admit: this could be great entertainment.

"Abu Ali," Jibril says, "the German wants to talk to you."

All present focus their eyes on me. Most of them have walked for hours, and now it's perfect time to relax while listening to the romantic sound of the German language.

I take the phone.

How, oh dear Jesus, do I avoid your fate on the cross?

I put the phone closer to my mouth and I go on a religious fervor. "Allahu Akbar! Allahu Akbar! Allahu Akbar!" I scream from the top of my lungs and throat over and over, and when I'm done I start singing it.

No German worth his name would protest against a brave Abu Ali when he feels the need to pray to Allah.

If Jesus doesn't help, Muhammad will.

The people present are elated. "Your Arabic accent, Abu Ali, is excellent!"

Thank you. Thank you.

"You know," adds another, "it would have been very good if Rommel had succeeded." He is referring to Nazi Germany's attempt in WWII to enter Palestine. "We would have had all the land," he says, since no Jew would have survived.

"My blood is German," another says to me. "All of us, all Palestinians, are German."

There is a swimming pool steps from our dining table, and some of the walkers decide to jump into the water, inviting me to join them. I respectfully decline. I will only swim with Eva.

What a world. I started the day as a Jew, continued as a German, and now I'm an Austrian.

When I arrive in Jerusalem I give the cats some meat and they laugh at my Austrian jokes.

Gate Twenty-Six

Lawmakers: from the granddaughter of a Zionist leader
accused of collaborating with the Nazis to the granddaughter
of a persecuted model who survived the Nazis.

IT WAS GOOD YESTERDAY, WHEN THIS AUSTRIAN VERY MUCH ENJOYED WALKING
in the corridors of power. What powerful grounds will this Austrian
walk on today?

The Knesset, Israel's parliament, could make for a good choice. I'll
have to hide my Austrian identity from those Jews, but this is a small
price to pay for the pleasures of power. The only problem is this: Jibril
Rajoub is not in the Knesset, sadly, and I'll need to get myself a friend
there who will walk me around. The question is: Who?

I must devise a plan. Perhaps I should corner the MKs. Yeah. As
simple as that: When I see people of power, MKs that is, I'll stop them.
Brilliant idea, I just hope I won't get arrested.

I get to the Knesset and I ask myself: Whom should I corner first?
Well, whoever walks by me.

*   *   *

My first victim is a lady who answers to the name, MK Merav Michaeli.

I don't know much about her. The little I do know is this: Merav,
MK for the centrist Labor party, has written opinion articles for
Haaretz, the paper Gideon Levy writes for, and is a former talk show
host and anchor on Israeli TV and radio. She is also one of the better

known of Israeli feminists, and is normally identified with the Left, despite her centrist affiliation.

This is not enough material to intelligently engage her in a conversation but, being the famed Austrian that I am, I also know that lack of knowledge has never stopped my people from achieving the highest of positions. Unfortunately, this great piece of wisdom does not help me to know more about this MK, and so I ask her to fill in the dots. I use nicer words to say this, of course. We sit down and have a chat.

MK Michaeli, tell me about yourself, about your country, about your dreams. Share with me what's going in your mind, deep inside.

"This is an open question."

Yes, it is. I want to know who you are. Tell me anything you want. Dream together with me. Think I'm God, or His messenger, who comes to you and says: Let's chat. Share with me, please, your most intimate thoughts!

I have no idea how I came up with such an ingenious line of questioning. But, what the heck? I want to have some fun.

The MK, a bit lost, finally talks: "My thinking, I think, starts with the place called gender. Gender division, dictated by culture, a division between man and woman, this division, I think, is the starting point of all other divisions."

Oh, Lordy Lord! I, Abu Ali, was shooting for some dirty thoughts and what I get instead is a brainy discussion on nothing and nothingness. Who is this lady?

Well, this is who she is and I have to suffer through this interview. Her Intelligence continues: "The system that divides people, starting with gender division – "

God, this is going to be a long lecture!

Her Highness continues: "When I think of a society that is more equal, a society that's better, where everyone can enjoy the best, I think of a world that offers more options."

Brilliant!

"I imagine a world in which you don't have to be a man or a woman – "

She must have an IQ of at least 255. I, with my IQ of only 25, try to understand this glorious dream she's sharing with me, and I ask her: Can you give me an example?

"No, there's no example. Today we have sub-gender, let's say gay and lesbian. But I don't know. It can be that you are a manly man but at the same time you can wear anything you want."

At this point I decide to pour my heart out to her. "I don't understand what you are saying."

She tries to help me. "Male and female is the sex; but then man or woman is what is built around it."

Was she like this on TV? How do you change the channel in real life? The Israelis might have invented an app for this.

As luck would have it, I can't find such an app on my iPad, so I try to use my tablet to summarize what she's been trying to say. I write: "Equality is the name of the game." Did I get it right? No, she says, I got it wrong. What am I missing? One word: *solidarity*. So, I rewrite her thinking: "Equality and solidarity is the name of the game."

She is happy. But a minute later she is worried. "Is it too abstract? Did I go too far?"

I calm her down. What she is saying, I tell her, is understood because it is actually also the thinking of the modern liberal people of Europe and America. I don't know what I'm talking about, but if she can talk gibberish, why not me?

I'm getting good at this, actually. I say things I don't understand myself, and it works!

Getting deeper into my own bullshit, I ask this respected MK when she started to have these great ideas of hers – did she just wake up one morning and the thoughts just dropped into her head?

She takes me seriously, and is even impressed with the depth of my intellectuality.

General Jibril thinks I'm Aryan, MK Merav thinks I'm a Western intellectual.

"It has to do with my history," she continues, "the Kasztner family. My grandfather was murdered here, after being accused of collaborating with the Nazis. The truth is that he saved many tens of thousands of Jews" from certain death by the Nazis.

This is the last thing I expected to hear today: Dr. Rezső Kasztner and the Kasztner Affair. The Kasztner story dates back many years, and is arguably one of the strangest chapters of the Holocaust, if not the strangest of them all. It happened in 1944, when the Nazi leadership realized that soon they would end in defeat, and when some of the Nazi leaders started thinking of the Day After. They had just arrived in Hungary, where hundreds of thousands of Jews were still alive, and the Nazi leaders thought that they could use the Jews as a card to their own survival.

Adolf Eichmann, the man in charge of the Final Solution to the Jewish Question, negotiated with Dr. Kasztner, a Jewish leader in Hungary, a deal known as "Blut für Ware" at the time: spare the lives of one million Jews in exchange for ten thousand trucks packed with goods. To prove that he meant business, Eichmann allowed Kasztner to choose a number of Jews to be sent to safety out of Hungary. The "Kasztner Train," with fewer than two thousand Jews, indeed left Hungary to eventual safety in 1944.

But the Allied Powers, and perhaps the Zionist leadership as well, didn't approve of the ten thousand trucks deal and so the Nazis went back to their original plans. Hundreds of thousands of Jews were promptly ordered to board the trains that would take them to the crematoriums, only the Jews did not know that this was to be their destination. Dr. Kasztner didn't tell them. They burned in the ovens; Dr. Kasztner did not.

In subsequent years Dr. Kasztner was accused by some of collaborating with the Nazis, and the State of Israel brought charges against one of Kasztner's accusers. But the state lost in court and the chief judge asserted in the court's explanation of this ruling that Kasztner had "sold his soul to Satan." An appeal was filed before a higher court, but before the court had the chance to rule on it, something happened. A gunman approached Dr. Kasztner when he was on his way home in Tel Aviv and asked him if his name was Dr. Kasztner. When affirmed, Dr. Kasztner was shot on the spot.

Merav is Dr. Kasztner's granddaughter.

With this information, this Austrian loses steam. I become more respectful.

We talk for a while longer and she shares with me one of her biggest dreams: to become a prime minister. I think there is a bigger chance that Dr. Kasztner would be resurrected than that she will beat Benjamin Netanyahu at the polls, but I don't say it.

I get up and walk around from one hall to the other in the Knesset building. Then, in one of the halls, I spot MK Ayelet Shaked, of the Jewish Home, a far-right party.

*　*　*

What I know about MK Ayelet is more or less on the level of what I knew about MK Merav before talking with her. The only item about MK Ayelet that I have is this: various leftists have mentioned her name as the most compelling example of utter stupidity, brainlessness, and idiocy of the Right.

I approach her. Would the esteemed MK mind sharing her time with me?

Let's go to my office, she suggests, and I gleefully follow her.

Tell me what you want to tell the world!

"I would like to explain our position about the Israeli-Palestinian conflict and why we are against the two-state solution, and why I think the world shows its hypocrisy when dealing with Israel. The Arab world, as can be seen in Arab countries around us such as Egypt and Syria, is collapsing, yet at this very time there are countries outside that try to force us into negotiation with the Arab world and want us to give up part of our country to regimes that are anything but stable.

Our party is against it. Every parcel of land that we gave the Arabs in the past, such as Lebanon and Gaza, is today under the control of fanatics, be it Hamas in Gaza or Hizballlah in Lebanon.

"The way Europe is treating us, enforcing boycotts against us, is in my eyes shameful and hypocritical. The EU and the UN are obsessed, I don't know why. I expected Germany to stand by us, not to be in the camp that is against us, only this is not the case. Germany should adhere to a moral and historical responsibility when dealing with us, and for sure not join any boycott against us. I had hoped that Germany would stop the boycott."

Ayelet doesn't know who I am. This interview was not arranged via her spokesperson, and all she knows is that I'm German. Yes, I forgot that I was supposed to be Austrian today. Ayelet looks me in the eye and asks: "Are you Jewish?"

Yes.

"Is Europe anti-Semitic?"

And then, speaking quietly, almost swallowing her words, she answers her own question: "Most of them."

What's your husband doing?

"He's a pilot."

Commercial or military?

"F-16."

For the record: his name is not Jonathan Shapira. Also for the record: Ayelet graduated from Tel Aviv University, in engineering and computer sciences. Another item for the record: Merav Michaeli's academic achievements: high school. Of course, since Ayelet is a rightist and Merav is a leftist, it is Ayelet who is called stupid, brainless, and an idiot. Why people cannot have political disagreements without name-calling is beyond me.

I leave Ayelet's office and resume wandering in the Knesset zoo. Who shall be my next victim? Maybe I should try hooking up with Haredi MKs. I'll walk around and the first MK I see with a big skullcap I'll capture.

* * *

Hunting takes some time but eventually I spot a Haredi MK standing at the entrance of his office. The sign on his door states that he is part of the Haredi Sephardi party, Shas. He might even be a friend of Rabbi David Batsri, of the masturbators redeeming unit. I open the door, say hallo and sit down. It is just then that I realize: I don't know this MK's name. I walked in too fast. How am I going to call him? Well, what the heck: I don't have to call him, he's already here.

And he speaks: "We have an exemplary state, with respect to almost every category, especially from an ethical and moral view point."

Ethical and moral, really?

"Yes, of course. But this has not started now. This has been a continuation of the history of the Jewish people, from thirty-five hundred years ago. There were powerful empires thirty-five hundred years ago, but they have disappeared. Not so the Jewish nation; we are still here. Same culture, same intellectual capacity – "

Nothing has changed in thirty-five hundred years? You really think that this is the same culture?

"Yes. Even better!"

I really would like to know who this guy is. Two MKs of his party spent years in jail for stealing money, the former Israeli president was found to be a common rapist and is presently serving time, the former chief rabbi is accused of stealing millions, the former prime minister is now in court for a variety of financial misdeeds. And this guy is talking about ethics and morality?! I have to find out more about him. I ask: Where are you from? Where is your family from?

"I was born here, but my family comes from Tripoli, Libya. And where are you from?"

Poland.

God, how I mix up the countries today!

"My grandfather's home in Libya and your grandfather's home in Poland were the same homes. The character, the intimate shine of both of them is the same. Same ethics, same thinking, same Light unto the Nations. Yes, yes."

Wait: What are the Jewish ethics?

"First off, who gave humanity its ethics? Judaism. In the beginning everybody around was a cannibal, with no ethics and no morality, but then the Jews gave the world the Bible. The nations of the world copied it. Our Bible, the Jewish Bible, was translated into more than seventy-two languages."

You know, dear MK, that most Israelis do not follow the Bible. Come with me, I can take you to the beaches of Tel Aviv and show you the Jews –

"Let me explain it to you. Something happened here in this land, something that your grandpa and my grandpa didn't even dream of. Israel, you see, was founded by Russian radicals who were atheists. But that's over. What you see on Tel Aviv's beaches is still a result of what those radicals did here years ago, but there's a movement in the nation toward the roots, to your grandpa's and my grandpa's roots. You can see it – "

I can see what?

"In three years, the majority of kids entering elementary schools in Israel will be Haredi."

Are you serious?

"Yes, yes. Those kids have already been born!"

Are you telling me that in fifty years, let's say, the majority of Israelis will be ultra-Orthodox?

"Like your grandfather and my grandfather."

In fifty years the beaches of Tel Aviv will be empty on the Sabbath?

"Not totally empty. There will still be a few secular Jews, but they will be the minority. Blessed be the Lord, for the secular culture will soon disappear."

At exactly this point the time is 2:00 p.m. Every hour, on the hour, there's a news broadcast on Israeli radio. The MK turns on the radio to listen. He wants to know what's new in Syria, Israel's neighbor. He listens, and listens, and listens.

This is an Israeli thing, a unique habit, and he reminds me of it: listening to the news every hour to make sure, may God help us, that Israel still exists.

This habit is one of the most interesting, most touching, and most frightening realities you would ever encounter in Israel. It contains no words, almost no emotions, just one short move of a finger pressing a button or clicking a screen in order to turn on a news broadcast. But don't think of it, for if you do you might start crying for these people.

"No war," he says after he's heard the news, happy that he can still cling to life. He turns off the radio and talks again.

"The Jewish nation has survived because they kept a unity amongst themselves. Do you know why the nations of the world hate us?"

They do?

"Yes, they do. They are anti-Semites. Do you know why they are anti-Semites? Because they are jealous of us!"

The nations of the world hate you?

"Certainly they do."

The Americans too?

"The Americans I don't know. But there is anti-Semitism all over, let's not speak of individual countries. There's anti-Semitism, the lot. Look, last century the Germans wanted to kill all living Jews. Why? What did we do to the Germans? What kind of fight or argument did we have with them? Why did they kill us? What's the reason? Why? Is there a logic that could explain their hatred? Is there any reasonable explanation for their action?"

He reflects a bit, thinking through what he has just said, and he shares another thought with me. The anti-Semitism of the world is coming from Christian countries, not from Islamic countries. Before Zionism, he tells me, Muslims and Jews went along just fine.

I change the topic.

What do you think of Rabbi Batsri?

"Righteous like the rest."

How is he accepted in the community?

"Like the other rabbis. They are all wise, they are all smart, all are well versed in the Bible."

I want to ask him if he, too, would give Rabbi Batsri 4,000 shekels but fast hold my tongue. I don't even know his name and it would be totally unfair to accuse him of masturbation.

What's your dream?

"Peace."

With whom?

"Between us and the Arabs. There is no reason, believe me, that we will not have peace with them. The problem is this: Ashkenazi Jews, and they are the ones negotiating with the Palestinians, will never reach any peace with them. If Israel sent Sephardi Jews to negotiate with the Palestinians, there would have been peace here already a long time ago. Ashkenazi Jews don't want us, the Sephardi Jews, to talk with the Arabs.

"Listen to me: the Zionist movement, from the start, didn't get it that in order to speak with other people you need to understand the others' culture. If you want to make peace with the Palestinians you must first understand them, their culture, and the nuances of their culture, but the Ashkenazi Jews have not internalized this fact yet."

As I leave his office I check the name on the wall: MK Yitzhak Cohen.

Who is he?

This is the Knesset's official info about him: head of the Knesset's Ethics Committee, former Minister for Religious affairs, former Deputy Finance Minister, father of ten.

*　*　*

Ten children may sound a bit crowded for some people, but not so for MK Meir Porush, in whose office I sit after I have done with MK Cohen. Meir is the father of twelve.

Meir is a leading MK for the Ashkenazi equivalent of Shas, called Torah Judaism, and is dressed in traditional Haredi clothes, which include a long black coat that was initially designed for Siberia. The weather today is very, very hot, but that's okay with Meir. He has his air conditioner set to freezer levels, making it very comfortable for him and his normal guests, not people like me.

Talk to me. Tell me what you want, and I'll tell the world what you are saying.

"I don't know if your readers want to know about us," he replies.

I tell him to go ahead, and he does.

"We represent authentic Judaism, the culture that started three thousand years ago at Mount Sinai."

Sephardi MK Yitzhak was talking of thirty-five hundred years, but this Ashkenazi MK Meir is talking of three thousand. Maybe the Sephardi Jews are older, I don't know.

"Why is it important that we have preserved this old culture?" MK

Meir asks, and immediately answers: "The Jewish nation is the oldest nation in the world."

Some people might dispute this account of history, but Meir is not impressed. "There is no other nation that is so ancient," he emphasizes.

And what is this Jewish culture? Well, there's one thing that it is not, according to MK Meir: "If you like to buy Made in Israel goods and think this makes you a Jew, you're wrong."

MKs, I see, like to talk philosophy, ideology, ethics, and history but I try to bring this MK to earth for a minute or two.

The Knesset is convening today to discuss what it calls "equally sharing the burden." Can you explain to me what this is?

"Nobody knows!"

This man's funny, but he isn't answering my question.

The truth is, "equally sharing the burden" is an explosive issue in Israel at the moment. Haredi Israelis don't serve in the army (don't "share the burden"), but get government help when they need it like

any other, and often even more. Half a century ago it was not a big problem, as there were not that many of them, but now their community is in the hundreds of thousands.

I push him to give me a better answer than "nobody knows" and he responds that this "sharing the burden" is just a tool by secular Jews who have nothing better to do than to attack the Haredi people. "Why is it that male Druze serve in the Israeli army while female Druze don't? Where is the equality?" Of course, having female Druze serve in the Israeli army is the last of MK Meir's worries, but it's a good method to get some people off his case.

For my part, I ask him to be more precise in his reply and he obliges: "I don't view it as 'holy' to have a Jewish government here. Of course it's more comfortable if the government here is Jewish, but if this Jewish government is making it hard for us to observe our traditions, it is not my dream that Jews should govern the state."

Putting it simply, what MK Meir is saying is this: if having a Jewish state means that the Haredi community will have to serve in the army, he and his party would rather have an Islamic state. This is something I had never thought I'd hear, but "facts are facts."

* * *

After having left MK Meir's office I encounter Minister Uri Orbach and ask him if he would like to be interviewed. He responds: "Why? Why should I spend my time doing Israeli PR clichés? No, thanks."

* * *

MK Dr. Aliza Lavie is a member of Israel's newest party, Yesh Atid (There is a Future), created by journalist-turned-politician Yair Lapid. MK Aliza is one of the better known feminists of her country, a religious woman and a university lecturer, as well as an author of books. I ask her to tell me what "Israel" is.

"The State of Israel for me means a home. A home is something you work on, a place you love, a place you repair, preserve, and a place you don't run away from."

Are you proud to be an Israeli?

"Sure. But even more than that, I'm grateful. I was born into a generation that has a home, and I'm very happy about it. My grandma is from Bucharest. She was a model when she was twenty, twenty-one years old. She had a fashion studio, she had everything, but one day they burned her place and everything she had. Some people cared for her, and she was brought here. Slowly, she built herself up again, in this land. I see it as my task to help every Jew anywhere in the world who wants to come here, and help them in whatever they need. This country is the home for Jews, and my job is to keep this place alive."

What is an Israeli?

"A human who wants to live, to get ahead, to survive. The desire to live can be found in every part of the Israeli's being. Why is Israeli high tech so advanced? It's not just the 'Jewish brain,' it's much more than that. It's the desire to live to the fullest. Being Israeli means having a home. And despite all the differences between Jews, despite all the yelling at each other right here in this Knesset, Israelis have some kind of glue that unites them. We all share the same home. I cannot

explain it. This togetherness, this unity, gives me the strength to sit with German media, to give this interview. It gives me strength, and I can forgive the past."

She's talking about me; I am the German she needs special strength to talk to. Good.

Can you give me an image of "this togetherness"?

"If I fall on the street, I hope it happens here [in Israel], for here someone will help me up. I have no other land, no other home."

These are the present leaders of the country I was born in. This country is also blessed with a zillion cats, a few of which are in my garden. I go there.

Gate Twenty-Seven

What do humanist foreign journalists do when a half-dead Syrian civilian is lying next to them?

I DON'T KNOW WHERE THE CATS ARE TODAY. MAYBE THEY WENT TO JORDAN for a KAS conference.

Uncle Sam is threatening to intervene in Syria, where a man kills his neighbor for no reason and where a child goes starving until he no longer is. So far, well over 100,000 lives have been lost in Syria, according to published estimates, and the number of wounded is far greater.

The Middle East being the Middle East, a place where loyalties can form and break at the sound of the wind, some of those wounded in Syria's war have crossed the border to Israel, to be treated in Israeli hospitals. Syria is one of Israel's most bitter enemies, but Israel is the one place that separates the wounded from death.

I safely arrive in Tzfat (Safed), in the north of the country. One hundred forty war-wounded Syrians have somehow crossed into Israel by now, and a number of them have ended up right where I presently am: Ziv Hospital.

On a bed, barely alive, is Khalid: a finger gone, a hole in his torso, face connected to tubes and wires that keep him breathing. He has been here two weeks, and only Allah knows what his future will be. He can't talk clearly, and he gestures with his face and hands.

A bunch of journalists, mostly foreign and also a local Palestinian, are at the scene. Cameras, camera recorders keep on clicking. One asks him: How do you feel in Israel?

He stares, as if saying "good."

Where are you from? I ask him.

He looks at me, gestures that he wants to write his answer; he can do that.

I ask the hospital staff if they could give him pen and paper.

They do.

He writes. It takes ages: Daraa.

Where the war started, two years ago. There, in the center of hell.

He points at his belly and he tries to talk to me, "Belly," he says. May Allah give you health, I say to him. He touches me gently and gestures that he wants to write something else.

A TV crew asks me to move as he starts writing. What's the story? They want to take pictures of him with their reporter, no matter that this wounded man is making so much effort to communicate with me.

To hell with them. I don't move.

Khalid shows me his fingers, five of them. Barely speaking, he says: five children.

He is father to five children, if they are still alive.

And what about your wife? I ask him.

He is moved. He is not used to journalists having a real interest in him.

He moves his wounded hand closer to me, takes my hand in his hand and slowly brings my hand to his lips, and he kisses it.

I want to cry.

I kiss him too.

This simple human gesture has overwhelmed him. He motions to me to send the other journalists away, and then takes my hand again and kisses it again.

This is heart-breaking.

He takes my left hand in his right hand and holds it. I caress his left hand and his head. He can hardly breathe, very heavily he does, and holds on to me as tight as he can. This makes him feel better and again he gestures to the other journalists to leave. I wonder if he wants me to leave as well and I start moving, but he takes my hand again.

I want to cry but instead I caress him.

The staff asks that we all leave. I step back, but Khalid doesn't want me to. I come again and he slowly moves the blanket off his body to show me his wound, a huge hole where a belly should have been.

Will this man survive or am I staring at the cruel face of death?

I want to hug him, to give him comfort. He looks at me, a man he has never met before, with two eyes packed with love.

I will never forget Khalid, face of humanity in a landscape of mercenary journalists.

Outside, at the entry to the hospital, where I now stand to vent my anger with the foreigners by smoking a cigarette, I see an ambulance

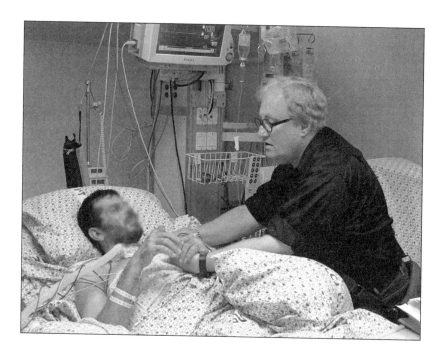

with this writing on it: "In memory of the six million who perished in the Holocaust."

This ambulance was donated by one Victor Cohen of Boca Raton, Florida, USA.

* * *

The mercenary journalists and I keep going north, closer to Syria. Higher and higher toward the Golan Heights, huge mountains welcome us. Am I in Tyrol?

This country, owner of the lowest point on earth at the Dead Sea, here rises to heights one can hardly imagine ever reached in this short and small area. The geography of this land, from what I have seen so far, is as different in locations as it is in its people. Extreme in the belly of its soil as it is in the people living on it.

The road continues up and we arrive in Majdal Shams, a Druze village on the Golan Heights. The Druze, Arabs who are not Muslim, live on both sides of the Israeli Syrian border. Sitting at a local restaurant, a Druze guy gives me his business card, in case I'd like to come again. His address, it reads, is Occupied Golan Heights.

On the other side of the restaurant I get the chance to see and hear how European journalists do interviews geared to extract answers that will fit their worldview. It is fascinating and intriguing to watch.

A British journalist and a Druze villager discuss the likelihood of war with Syria and the possibility of bombs containing chemical poison flying in the area. Here it goes:

J: Do you have gas masks?

D: No.

J: Did the Israeli authorities supply you with gas masks?

D: No.

J: But in general, Israeli authorities supply Israeli citizens with gas masks, right?

D: Yes, I think so.

J: They give masks to their citizens but not to you. Right?

D: I think that they do.

J: The Jews get it but you don't. Interesting.

D: I don't know.

J: They didn't offer you any mask, did they?

D: No. I think they distribute masks only in the big cities, like Tel Aviv or Jerusalem.

J: But do they or don't they distribute them to the locals here, the other people, the Jews?

D: Maybe. I don't know.

J: It is possible that they distribute masks to "them" but not to you.

D: Could be.

J: So they offer the masks to Jews but not to the Druze. Really interesting!

At this point the villager is totally confused, lights up a cigarette, and talks to another villager sitting by him.

As for the journalist, he watches me looking at him and his face turns angry. He gives me a spiteful look and moves away.

God bless the Queen.

*　*　*

Mount Bental is our next stop. Here you stand and you see Syria right in front of your eyes. Syria, where Khalid comes from, where his wife and five children are, if they are still alive.

What a small country Israel! It took three hours, with stops for coffee, cigarette, and toilet, to get here from the center of Israel. And I take into account that this is not America, which means that often enough the ride goes through small, side streets. In other words, you can cross the length of Israel by car in about five hours, south to north. Crossing the width of Israel will take you a fraction of that time, between ten minutes and two hours, depending where you choose to cross.

A teeny-tiny country, yet the world is so hugely interested in it. This has nothing to do with logic; could it be a "spiritual" thing? Perhaps I should find myself a spiritual leader and see if he or she has an explanation.

Gate Twenty-Eight

How do you become an international human rights rabbi? What does a Christian Zionist girl love more, man or grapes?

A RABBI IS A SPIRITUAL LEADER, RIGHT?

Rabbi Arik Ascherman, dressed fashionably and elegantly, with the coolest of sneakers, is the president and senior rabbi of Rabbis for Human Rights, and the man I'm going to see.

Have you heard of the Rabbis for Human Rights? They are apolitical, Rabbi Arik tells me, and by their own by-laws cannot take any political side. Rabbi Arik tells me that he is apolitical to a fault, that he'll never take sides in the Israeli-Palestinian conflict, and that he will never ever make any move that could be interpreted as taking sides.

My kind of rabbi, and now all that's left for me to do is have him tell me what he thinks in his heart and how he turns his thoughts into deeds. He is very glad that I ask him these questions and happily obliges. He believes, he tells me, the following:

Israel is abusing Palestinians inside Israel and out.

Israel practices racism against the Palestinians.

Israel steals Palestinian lands.

Israel imprisons Palestinians illegally.

Israel constantly engages in discriminatory measures and actions against innocent Palestinians.

All settlements are illegal.

Israel regularly breaks international law.

Israel is a brutal occupier.

Israel's army routinely helps and protects settlers' criminal activities against Palestinian villagers.

Israel acts and behaves like any other brutal dictatorship in history.

Israeli archeologists routinely destroy any evidence that might support Palestinian claims to the land.

And so on and so on, but I jot down only part of what this apolitical rabbi tells me. What's amazing about this man, and I can't explain how he pulls it off, is that he doesn't himself break into laughter when he tells me he is apolitical.

In an ever serious mode he moves on to tell me about the deeds part, what he and his associates do: (a) they challenge the Israeli government through the court system, filing one lawsuit after another against the state; (b) they travel to Palestinian villages to serve as human shields against murderous Jewish settlers and soldiers.

None of the above, as has already been mentioned, is supposed to have anything to do with politics and nothing of what has been said so far could possibly be misconstrued as taking sides between the Israelis and the Palestinians.

Rabbi Arik, a biblical scholar by profession, confidently assures me that the Bible prohibits wars of any kind. The fact that the Bible is full of wars, even ordered by the Lord, is unknown to him. Page after page of the Bible speaks of wars, but none of these pages is known to Rabbi Arik.

I get a bit pissed off at him. I take the Bible, which is in his room, and tell him: Look, almost every page here is full of wars. Are you denying this? Start reading with me!

He refuses.

This rabbi is so righteous and scholarly, in addition to his being apolitical, that he has even lived with Palestinians for two years. As he shares this with me, his eyes glow. I saw a pair of eyes similar to his not long ago, I recall, and try to remember whose eyes they were. Oh, yeah, the British journalist. Is there another similarity between the two? Yeah, both are into human rights.

*   *   *

Rabbi Arik, no matter what I think, views himself as a holy man. The Palestinians, His Holiness tells me, live in horrible conditions imposed on them by the Jews. They live in utter poverty in refugee camps and if not for the rabbis' abundance of holy mercy, their fate would have been sealed with a one-way ticket to eternal Hell.

I ask the rabbi when was the last time that he visited the refugee camp known as Palestine, not including olive fields? Well, he doesn't remember, but maybe it was about three years ago or so.

This Palestine resident, it turns out, travels into Ramallah and Nablus at almost the same frequency that I travel to the sun and the moon. He knows Palestine as well as I do outer space.

Why is it, I ask him, that all Do-Gooders have such touching hearts and souls, while the right-wingers are always so mean?

He is offended by my question, because he thinks I make fun of him. But I tell him that I don't; I'm just fascinated by his self-hate. I personally love the Palestinians, I tell him, because the Palestinians have pride in their identity, but I have no respect for self-haters, Jew or black. If I had a beloved daughter, I'd rather she married a proud Hamas activist than a self-hating Jew like him.

Arik's wife looks at me, surprised by this statement, and says just four words: "You can't change them," meaning her husband and his colleagues. I ask her to elaborate, and she does. Being a human rights activist in our time is to be a persona, not a philosophy; it's a fad, it's a fashion. A human rights activist does not look for facts or logic; it's about a certain dress code, "cool" clothing, about language, diction, expressions, and certain manners. "We argue a lot, but I know I will never change him. No facts will persuade him. He *is* a human rights activist, it's his persona, it's who he is. That's all there's to it. You can't ask a person not to be the person he is."

When it comes to complex issues, more often than not women understand much faster than men.

Arik is deeply offended by his wife's remarks. He is engaged in *Tikkun Olam* (repairing the world), he tells me. What the heck is Tikkun Olam? It has to do with Kabbalah (Jewish mysticism), as taught by the mystic Ari of Tzfat, known as the Holy Ari.

Would you like to learn more about it? Bear with me, actually it's quite interesting.

When God created the world He had a big, huge problem with it: He was too big to dwell in the world that by nature was too small for Him. Get it?

God, in case you haven't figured it out by now, is fat. Obese. Huge. So huge, in fact, that even just one eighth of His belly is much bigger that the whole planet. This means – keep bearing with me – that if God's creation of the world were to survive, God would have to move away from the planet, in which case only Satan would stick around with us humans. A horrible thought, as you can surely imagine.

To fix this problem, God came up with an ingenious solution: He made a contraction of Himself and put Holy Sparks of Himself into special containers. Got it? Brilliant, isn't it?

Only there was one more problem, that for some reason God neglected to think of, but the Ari did think of. What is that? Our friend, our old friend, Satan. Satan, being Satan, is constantly busy drilling little holes into the Holy Containers, which make the Holy Sparks disperse.

Holy Arik and his team of 120 rabbis work endlessly and tirelessly to repair and fix the holes in the Holy Containers. How do they do it? Human rights for Palestinians.

I ask the Holy Container Fixer to share with me his rabbinical history. Plainly put: where, when, which, and what congregations did he lead prior to his leading the world at large. And since his credentials, at least as he presents them to me, are in the rabbinate, I would also like to know what the size of his former congregation or congregations were.

Rabbi Arik tries his best at manipulating me to let him off answering that question. But I don't let go, until he gives in. Under his leadership in the rabbinate, which was in the US of A, he attracted "about ten" people, and "sometimes fifty," of his own congregation to listen to his sermons.

What will you do when you reach bottom as a local rabbi? You become an international rabbi. How do you become an international rabbi? You tell people that you, a rabbi, will speak the worst of Israel and of the Jews. Who will fund you? Easy: find other self-hating Jews, and don't forget self-loving Europeans. The New Israel Fund, funded by just such Jews, Jews with an extraordinarily loving heart for the needy, gave (according to their latest available annual report of 2012) Rape Crisis Centers in Israel a total of $6,721 and it gave the Rabbis for Human Rights $328,927. The European Commission, which pays for special trips to the Holocaust Museum and teaches young Europeans about Israeli atrocities, is another donor to these rabbis, in addition to other European donors such as the Swedish, British, and German believers in human rights.

I'm lost here. Is this what Israel has become? Is this what being "Jewish" means?

* * *

I hear that at this very moment, on the hills of Judea and Samaria, foreign people are harvesting grapes at a Jewish settlement. Not all foreigners hate the Jews. There are Christians who love them, and I go to meet those Christians.

Caleb and Candra, a couple, "'Christian Zionists" from the USA, tell me that they are here to fulfill God's prophecies. What prophecies?

Candra reads to me, from the book of Jeremiah, as follows: "You shall yet plant vines upon the mountains of Samaria: the planters shall plant, and eat them as ordinary food. For there shall be a day, that the watchmen upon the mount Ephraim shall cry, Arise ye, and let us go up to Zion to the Lord our God."

Caleb interjects: "We believe that in the latter days the mountains will come back to life."

They come to this vineyard and fields for ten weeks every year, Caleb tells me, and they are volunteering their time to help this settlement. They pay for their flights, they pay for their stay, they pay for their own food, and if they want a bottle of wine or two made here by their sweat they pay for them. In short: they get nothing for free and they spend quite a lot of time and money for the pleasure of working for other people.

Today there are 150 young people here and in the nearby mountains, mostly from the USA, but also one person from Sweden, one person from Switzerland, and zero people from Germany.

Do you have any romantic stories you can share with me that have happened right here on this mountain?

"I got to know my wife here. We actually got married here."

His wife interjects: "We got married in Psagot!" Psagot is a neighboring settlement.

At this point another Christian Zionist intervenes. He tells Caleb to find out my details, where I am from, who I am, and if I am a friend or a foe. "We want to make sure it's all good," the man says, adding a piece of advice to Caleb: "You have to be careful."

Caleb starts an interrogation: "Are you Jewish?"

This is what they say.

"Are you an atheist?"

I am still trying to find out who I am.

He likes my answers, don't ask me why, and he continues from where he stopped, telling me his love story: "I went to bed one night and I had a dream that I was in a vineyard and I was having a picnic. I looked up and a gorgeous girl was sitting across from me. I extended my hands to her and she put her hands in mine. That's how love first started for me."

You dreamt it right here?

"Yes, in this area."

Was she on these mountains only in your dream or also for real?

"She was here for real."

And she entered your dream?

"Kind of, sort of."

He tells me he first came here when he was fourteen years old, and that it was his father who started the program of bringing people here from abroad.

His wife-to-be came here for the first time when she was twenty. "I always had love for Israel when growing up. I inherited it from my parents," the dream-slash-real wife says, adding that she is very happy here, "where the Bible took place, in Judea and Samaria."

In case I didn't get it right, she goes for the details: "Eighty percent of our Bible took place here."

When you first came here, what made you feel more excited, being here or meeting Caleb?

"I think that the restoration of the land is more important than Caleb," she tells me, giggling and serious at the same time.

Caleb has met other Jews in Israel, such as those who live in Tel Aviv, but he gravitates toward the people here, the settlers. "I connect with them more. The people in these mountains, I believe, have a purpose in life and dedicate their lives to achieve a goal. I believe that they have a connection to something that's bigger than what they have a grasp of."

For the record: Christian Candra knows her Bible better than Jewish Rabbi Arik. At least she knows how to quote it.

Gate Twenty-Nine

Will an educated, beautiful Arab lady fall in love with a Jew?

NEARBY THESE AWESOME MOUNTAINS WHERE CANDRA IS TOILING HARD IS THE city of Nablus, a city that no Jew can enter. Judenfrei. Naturally, I'm attracted to the place and go there. If what I have heard from Israelis is right, Nablus is a poor city economically but rich in fundamentalists. I have visited some wonderfully designed and super attractive Palestinian cities; it's time I visit a poor one.

In minutes I'm there, and I can't believe the sight that greets me. The Nablus that I expected is not the Nablus that I find. In short, and to avoid any drama, Nablus is a gorgeous city and one that I immediately fall in love with. With roads engulfed by huge developments shining from bottom to top of two parallel mountain ranges, Nablus welcomes its visitors with warmth, picturesque views of unparalleled beauty, and a constant beat of life that I never imagined to have existed here.

The EU and the USA are building paradise on earth here. It's an all-embracing city, a place where you can find heavenly food and clothes, and not a square meter boring or quiet.

Next to a gorgeously designed new building complex someone has built for himself a stable with one horse in it. It's strange, it's bizarre, but it captures your eye and imagination as it offers you an immense feeling of greatness.

I walk and walk and walk in Nablus, and my eyes dance with sheer pleasure.

What a city!

Only after feeling totally exhausted from walking, I go to the main station and take a taxi out.

Sharing this taxi with me is a young lady with an angelic smile and sharply dressed, who goes by the name of Eternity. Yeah, that's her name. From which part of Heaven has she just appeared to me?

"I live in Ramallah," she shares with me, "and I study in Jerusalem."

One day I'll be able to call you Dr. Eternity?

She laughs. Yes, this is what she hopes for.

What do you study?

"Literature and political science."

What university?

"Hebrew University."

Oh, you study with the Jews –

"Yes."

Could it happen that one day you will fall in love with a Jew?

"Impossible!"

You are a beautiful girl, and maybe one day a very handsome young man will come your way. A very sweet man, very charming, and he will fall in love with you. And he will be really nice, really good for you. A Jew. Couldn't it happen?

"Never!"

Why not?

"I'll never marry a Jew."

Studying at Hebrew University, did you learn anything about the Jews that you didn't know before?

"Yes."

What did you learn about them?

"That they change history."

What do they change?

"They say that they came to Palestine in 1948 because they wanted to help the Palestinians. This is a total lie."

Is this what they teach you?

"Yes."

I don't get it: Why would they say such a thing?

"Ask them."

But it makes no sense. Why would they come all the way here just to help you?

"They say that they came here and that they helped. This is what they teach. They invent history."

So, they didn't say that they came here to help the Palestinians, it just happened that they did... right?

"Yes, this is what they teach."

But then why did they come here? What do they teach you at the university?

"They came here because Ben-Gurion told them to come here."

In 1948?

"Yes, after the British left."

Why didn't they come before?

"Because Ben-Gurion didn't tell them to come before."

Was there any other reason why they came here in 1948?

"No."

No other reason at all?

"Not that I know of."

Why don't you study in a Palestinian university? Why do you go to Hebrew University, a Jewish university?

"Hebrew U is the best university, much better than Bir Zeit or Al-Quds."

Like Nadia, Eternity gets higher education for free. And like her, she studies with the Jews and she spits on them. These two women, I think, are smarter than the Jews who pay for their education.

It is time to go to my cats, organisms far smarter than these ladies.

Gate Thirty

*Heeding the advice of my stray cats, I go on a ride
north to see how people prepare to greet the newest
made-in-the-USA super-killer missiles.*

A UNITED STATES SENATE PANEL HAS APPROVED THE USE OF FORCE AGAINST Syria. The situation in Syria is horrible, and since Rabbi Arik doesn't do anything about it, the American Senate has to get involved. As far as I know about the history of American and European involvement in the Middle East so far, their records show close to a 100 percent failure rate.

The logic of the West is this: If two people of the East shoot each other with a rifle, why not join the party and drop a few super-killer missiles for extra sound effect? I chat with my cats and they suggest, at least as far as I can understand them, that I should drive up north in the direction of the Syrian border, to see if people are prepared for the possibility of missiles flying over their heads.

*   *   *

First stop is Kibbutz Kfar Haruv, a secular kibbutz at the foot of the Golan Heights. The whole of the Golan used to be part of Syria, but was captured by Israel during the 1967 War. Immediately after the war, Israel offered to give the Golan back to Syria in exchange for peace, but the Syrians said no. Years later, in 1981, Israel annexed it, but the world at large does not recognize Israel's sovereignty of it. Israel's offer of citizenship to Druze residents of the Golan was rejected by almost all of them.

The Golan Heights has nothing to do with the Palestinians. Zilch. The enemy here is quite a different one, a neighbor more ancient, and the chance for peace is as likely, about one big zero. But don't tell this to the people living here.

It is the Eve of the Jewish New Year and the Israeli seculars celebrate this holiday their way. In religious congregations the High Holy Days is a period of pondering and a time when the Chosen Children ask the Lord of Lords for health and success and beg Him to forgive them their transgressions. According to tradition, it is on this day that the Heavenly Court is in session and God sits in judgment to decide the fate of man, animal, and all of creation: who will live and who will die, who will be healthy and who will be sick, who wealthy and who poor, who will see success and who will fail.

The Chosen Kibbutzniks of Kfar Haruv have this prayer to offer in song:

May this coming year be a year of
Peace and security,
Peace and tranquility,
Peace and happiness,
Year of peace and not year of war.
Singing done, they proceed with rituals.

In synagogues all over Israel a shofar is blown on this day, to waken the sinners from their sleep. Not here. Here, a cage with many doves is brought in. Children and adults gather by the cage to look at the little creatures. "Fly, doves" is recited with pleasure and the doves are let out.

This is a peace ritual, if I get it right, which is quite so much more colorful than the traditional shofar blowing.

Apples with honey are served, as people wish each other "Happy

New Year." "The service is concluded," comes an announcement. "You are invited. The tables are full with food!"

In Orthodox communities, the songs of the Jewish New Year go like this: "Father in Heaven, forgive us for we have sinned." Here, this is what they sing: "In the New Year, in the New Year, in my garden, a white dove."

Following these rituals we are treated to a speech. A man gets up and talks about values and finances. We have produced more milk this year, he says, 10 percent more, and tourism is great. We hope, he wishes all, that the coming year will be successful as well.

The kibbutz people, in a nod to tradition, are now to pray. A member takes a Jewish prayer book and recites a prayer. Here it goes: "Today is Friday, when creation of the heaven and the earth was done…" There is one little problem with this: Today is not Friday. Few, if any, notice.

We get to hear some figures as well: The kibbutz has 160 adult members, 300 including the children. Value in shekels of agriculture this year: forty million. The kibbutz also owns a company in Dortmund, Germany.

No one mentions Syria, America, or any country in between them.

Kibbutz Kfar Haruv, part of an ideological socialist experiment of the last generation, is now anything but socialist. What has remained from the glory days of the Kibbutz Movement, if one can judge by the service conducted here on this "Friday," is the spectacular incapacity to properly comprehend ancient Jewish texts.

I leave the kibbutz, sad to note how a great movement, one of the most endearing of human experiments I have known of, is no longer.

I hit the road again.

* * *

Majdal Shams (Tower of the Sun), in the north of the Golan Heights, is ahead of me, and I hope the British journalist is not there again.

Maneuvering the roads to Majdal Shams takes time, and when I reach my destination and get out of the car, I step into winter.

I'm freezing. Yet, even if the weather is cold the residents here are warm.

Hamad Awidat, a Druze who produces segments for various European news agencies, welcomes me into his office and offers me delicious hot drinks. He is sure that President Obama is soon to drop shiny new missiles on neighboring Syria, and he's getting ready for it.

"I think that Obama is going to engage in a war with Syria because he wants to show the world that he is a big man, that he has power."

What will happen after Obama has attacked: Who will win and who will lose?

"Muslims can make new kids in one night," he explains, and at the end they will win, no matter what happens in the meantime. People here have faith and they won't lose it. The Arabs will win, because they are connected with the land and will stick by it. Not so the Jews, he shares an important piece of wisdom with me. "The Jews are connected with their bank accounts, not with the land."

He likes to talk about Arabs and about Jews, and I want to talk about the Druze. What is the Druze religion?

"Druze is a group of humans who believe in reincarnation."

What else do you believe in?

"This is our religion, this is our belief."

What is unique about your faith?

"We believe in the mind, not in the body."

What are you going to do with stupid people?

"They are bad."

What's the holy book of the Druze?

"Hikmeh."

Did you read it?

"No."

Aren't you curious?

"No. I have read the Quran, the book of the Christians, the book of the Jews. That's what I'm interested in reading."

Is it true that you're not allowed to read your own holy book?

"The Holy Book, Hikmeh, is a secret book. You can't find it on the Internet. There are no printed versions of it, the Holy Book is written by hand."

Hamad might not know his Hikmeh, but he knows the news and he knows European style and taste. Clouds fill the garden of his house every morning, and from his house, he says, "You can see Syria on the left, and the Occupiers on the right." Hamad has built a special room, with 360-degree glass windows, to serve journalists for the next war.

Hamad shows me a YouTube clip of a movie his company produced, *Apples of the Golan*, which was paid for by Irish, Swiss, and Austrian companies.

"The land always has five of these seeds," the film teaches us, as we see an image of Golan apples cut into two, with five seeds in each. "The Syrian flag stars have five points," the film continues, while the star of the Israeli flag has six points.

What does this all mean? This cannot but mean: the Golan Heights belongs to Syria. The earth has spoken. Period.

Out of 139 Arab villages in the area before 1967, the movie asserts, only five have remained.

Hamad calls Israel "the daughter of America," and accuses it of planting mines all over the Golan during its war with the Syrians. I ask him: Before 1967 this area belonged to the Syrians; could it be that they were the ones to plant the mines?

Instead of giving me a good counter-argument, he offers to take me on a tour of some deserted old houses on the mountains, a la Itamar's tour to Lifta, whenever I want.

But Hamad is not Itamar, definitely not. Hamad is a warm Druze, not a cold ex-Jew. When I ask him to feed me hot food in addition to the hot coffee, he arranges for me to have lunch with a Druze family.

I love it! I've never been to a Druze home before and I can't wait to experience one.

Aqab, a Druze teacher of English and sport in the neighboring Boqata, is the man of the house, and he tells me that the Muslims and the Druze are Arab brothers but that the Jews are occupiers. He prefers, he says, to live in poverty and under a dictatorship, as a part of Syria, to living in riches and in a democracy as a part of Israel. To him, Jews are occupiers not only in the Golan Heights, but also of all the land around.

The Jews, he argues passionately, have no right to have a land of Jewish nationality, because this is racism, but the Arabs have a right to have a land of Arab nationality because this is not racism. I ask him to explain this obvious discrepancy to me but for the life of him he can't. I ask him instead of giving me a reply to my question to give me his beautiful daughter for a wife. In addition, because I'm such a good-hearted do-gooder German, I even offer to pay him for her. We laugh a lot about it, but she is not for sale to a non-Druze. But if I offer a new Mercedes, we might find a way.

His wife is feeding me Druze food. I don't know what it's made of, but it is as delicious as his daughter is beautiful. Paradise.

The Golan: from the height of its Heights to the lowest of its wadis, it is one huge celebration of nature. Nothing I have seen in any mountainous area anywhere, including all of Tyrol, is as beautiful, as gorgeous, as cruel, as naked, and as rich as these mountains here.

*   *   *

There are more cities and towns that might be affected by flying missiles, if they indeed are to come, and I again drive to Tzfat, the picturesque city among these mountains and valleys, the city whose hospital I visited just days before, but I did not walk around the city. Tzfat is a city celebrated for its long line of mystics and traders, a city where the famous Holy Ari lived ages ago and where he first came up with his Tikkun Olam, a term used these days not just by Rabbi Arik but also by President Obama and celebs such as Madonna.

Tzfat reveals itself to me in its most naked form. Its old city and its new, with their mazes of stores and eateries, which are all closed, shut down in observance of the Jewish New Year. Here, as in some other cities in Israel, the Haredim rule with an iron fist. Businesses must be shut on Jewish holy days and only what is holy is to remain open: houses of prayer, ritual baths, graves, and tombs.

Tombs are a big business, as I find out. People from all over the country have come to this most mystic of cities to spend the Holy Days in the presence of Dead Holy Men.

Not just the Ari's grave is here, but his holy ritual bath – the one he bathed in hundreds of years ago when he communicated with angels regularly – is also here. It is a very holy place, I'm told, and if I bathe in it fascinating things will happen to me.

I go to see what is supposed to produce the miracle for myself. At the entrance to the site there's an announcement: This bath is for men only; women who try to bathe here will be bitten by a snake.

Wow. What a holy place.

The bath is much smaller than I imagined it to be. Only one man at a time can bathe in it, and men are waiting in line.

Here is a man, totally naked, immersing his body up and down seven times. This would be a perfect place for gays, I think.

"Are you a Jew?" a naked holy man asks me.

What's the difference?

"If you're not a Jew, bathing here won't do anything to you."

Why not?

"Are you a Jew?"

The most Jewish of all!

"Then go in!"

Why did you ask me if I was Jewish? Are non-Jews not welcome here?

"If you go to Rome and the pope sprinkles over your head what popes sprinkle on the heads of Christians, will it do anything for you? No. But it does for Christians. Right? Here it's the same. Now, you go and immerse your body in the waters and you will feel it. You'll become a changed man. It will affect your soul in the most powerful of ways."

How?

"Try and see."

But can't you explain to me what will happen?

"Not in words. This is spiritual, and the spiritual you cannot explain. Take off your clothes, jump into the bath, and you'll see for yourself. If you need a towel I'll get you one. Want to try?"

Maybe this man is gay. Go figure. Pointing at the water, I ask him: Can you just describe what happens while you are there?

"All your sins disappear, and you become like new."

Just by jumping naked into these waters –

"You must immerse yourself seven times!"

Why seven?

"Mystical secrets. That's the way it works. Try. Try. You'll be a new man!"

Honestly, I'd rather have a Diet Coke now. Sadly, no store is open for miles and miles. These religious people want me to have water around me, not in me. They want it holy, not sweet. They want it natural, not chemical.

I criticize them but I must admit that these kinds of places have a certain aura. Ancient baths. Graves. Tombs. They are a bit like horror movies, and horror sells quite well.

A ten-minute drive from here there is the tomb of the Rashbi, another mystic, in the neighboring city of Meron. I go there. Outside I see this announcement: Whoever owns an iPhone will not enter Paradise.

Bingo.

I guess spirituality as practiced here is not my cup of tea. I take my iPhone with me and I leave.

*   *   *

I head north again, this time to the highest elevation in Israel, right by the Syrian border. To be in sync with Mother Nature of the Golan and its apples I put on my head a baseball cap made in the image of the Syrian flag, as I reach Mount Hermon.

A Druze sees me and gets very excited. "Are you for Assad (Syria's struggling president)"?

Yes, I am.

"Assad with the people," he shouts with pleasure, in what amounts to: Long Live Assad.

There are two daily tours to the Hermon, which take tourists for a walk to the top of Mount Hermon. I missed the last tour but I still want to go. Two Israeli soldiers, stationed at a barrier stop me: "Sorry, you can't continue from here."

Why not?

"You can cross this point only with a tour guide, who knows where civilians can and cannot walk. It's also for your safety because part of this area is mined."

Who mined it?

"Doesn't matter."

You or the Syrians?

The soldiers don't seem to like me that much, and I can't blame them. With my Syrian cap I don't really look my best in Israeli eyes. I try to argue with them that I should be allowed to cross, saying that my tour guide is waiting for me.

"Where is he?"

Up there!

"Where?"

I look up, pick some imaginary point, and say: There!

Well, don't try to outsmart Israeli military. In no time a jeep fast comes my way. In it is the commander of these soldiers.

I want to go up there, I say to him.

"To your country, Syria?"

I realize that my cap is not doing me much good and so this Syrian starts speaking in Hebrew: I'm not Syrian and, between you and me, I don't even know where Syria is!

The tension drops way down, at the speed of an American missile, and he laughs healthily. He rushed here with his jeep thinking a Syrian soldier had penetrated the area, and all I really am is a Jew. We laugh about it more and more until by the end he lets me cross the barrier on my own and walk anywhere I want.

Ain't that hard to sneak into closed military areas. All you need is a good joke.

And so I walk. Anywhere I feel like, dancing on all the mines. I see huge antennas on top and I go to see them up close. I take pictures of every IDF position and base on my way, and nobody stops me. I think of the many years of jail time I would get if I did the same near sensitive American bases.

From time to time I stop walking, taking a deep breath, and watch the winds. The view is so spectacular that at certain points I can't even move, completely hijacked by beauty.

I think I have discovered the real meaning and essence of spirituality: beauty. I was looking for spirituality, and now I met it.

* * *

An hour or two later, I go back to the soldiers I encountered beforehand. They are still there.

They are Aviv and Bar. Aviv is Sephardi – his grandfather immigrated to this land from Syria – and Bar is Ashkenazi. Both are in their early twenties, both carry assault rifles, quite a cache of bullets, and a variety of other military items that are attached to various parts of their young bodies, making them look obese.

Knowing that I'm an important person (after all, I've been allowed to wander here according to my heart's desire), they share with me everything they know regarding the Israeli army's preparation for a possible war with Syria – in case America bombs Syria and Syria bombs Israel in return.

"The number of soldiers at various positions has been doubled. New rules prohibiting soldiers to wander out of their bases at night have been put in place. A tank unit was moved up [to the top of Mount Hermon] last week, and is still in its new position, due to the situation."

Okay. Time to discuss the really important stuff: girls.

Which girls do you dream of?

Aviv: "Israeli girls."

Of what background, Ashkenazi or Sephardi?

"Sephardi."

How dark should her skin be, like yours or darker?

"I don't know – "

What kind of Sephardi girl you want, Yemenite?

"No; they are too dark."

Moroccan?

"Yes."

How about Tunisian?

"Yes, also good."

How do you imagine her: tall or short, skinny or fat, small breasts or big?

"Not taller than me. Skinny, but not too skinny. One must: breasts."

How big?

"Medium to large."

Anything else?

"Hair color I don't care, as long as it's not red. And firm ass."

Bar is less detailed. He is Ashkenazi, after all, more into brains than heart, more rational thinking than sexual imagination, and only after I push him over the psychological edge he shares one detail: his beloved had better be dark-skinned with black hair.

Tunisian…?

Yep. And he starts laughing, feeling relieved and released.

These two soldiers are the eyes of Israel, stationed at its highest point of entry. The Nation of Israel, and all its Jews, are protected by two young men dreaming of a Tunisian girl.

Every night, they tell me, they see the fighting across the border: bombs, fire, smoke. It is the image of a Tunisian woman, with big breasts and firm ass, that helps them fight off their fear.

I get off Mount Hermon and drive on to Metula.

* * *

I like the sound of this town's name: Metula. Try it yourself: say "Metula" ten times and you'll fall in love with it. Of course, once I arrive in Metula I have no clue where exactly I am, beyond just the name Metula. I go to the first restaurant I spot, Louisa, to have dinner. When I hear my belly singing in thanks, I go for a walk. I move north on the road, and in a minute or so I spot an armored vehicle flying the Druze flag.

Druze?? Have I crossed a border into Druzeland? I move closer and I hear them speaking Hebrew. I ask them who they are. "We are Druze," they say.

Like the ones in the Golan Heights?

"We are Israeli Druze, they are Syrians."

Aren't you brothers?

"Cousins."

Like Jews and Arabs?

They laugh. "We are related, but not too related."

What are they doing here? I ask. Well, they serve in the IDF and they are protecting the border.

Where's the border?

"Right here."

Right where we stand?

"No, no. You see the road over there? That's the UN and after it is Lebanon. Hizballah is there, in the villages that you see. If you want to get closer, go down the road and you will be at the border."

Is it a quiet border?

"Now it is. But this is the way it goes: it's quiet, quiet, quiet, and then the explosions come. No end of them. Where are you from?

Germany.

"Welcome!"

So, let me get it: What's the relationship between you and the Druze of the Golan?

"We are related, but some of them like us and some hate us."

How does it work? Some of you serve in the Israeli army and none of them do?

"Not 'some' of us; all of us. Here we all serve in the IDF."

How do you get along with the Jews?

"Blessed be the Lord. We get along with them. Excellent."

These IDF soldiers, Druze sharing their fate with Jews, are eager to talk to strangers. They tell me some interesting stuff. For example: there are Druze all over, including in countries like Saudi Arabia, but those don't tell their neighbors who they are because "they would be killed."

Before I get back into the car, I ask the Druze for the exact location of the closest border point to Lebanon. They position their armored vehicle in front of my car and tell me to follow them.

It is strange to follow an armored vehicle flying the flag of a country that doesn't exist but, hey, why not?

They stop just steps from Lebanon. "Do you see the flags?" one asks me, pointing to flags right close to us. "This one is the flag of Lebanon, and next to it, the yellow flag, that's Hizballah."

Hizballah's flag is at the border, he's right. I am in Druzeland, at the border to Hizballahland.

This is the Middle East. No foreigner will ever comprehend.

On the road between Druzeland and Hizballahland, I see white UN cars driving back and forth. But the eyes, at least in this part of the world, can mislead their owner. The cars might be UN, but they can also belong to somebody else.

I go back to my cats. They are real cats. What a comforting thought.

* * *

I am in Jerusalem and I jump into a cab. Avi, the cabbie, talks to me.

"I picked up a couple the other night, from Har Zion [Mount Zion] Hotel. Young, nice-looking, and they were going to the airport. They were talking nicely with each other, and then they asked me if I feel Chosen. I asked them who they were, because usually it's me who initiates talks in my cab, not the passengers. They told me that they were lawyers who came to Israel to check how the Jews treat the Palestinians. I asked them why they were asking me whether I felt Chosen, and they said, 'We think we understand why the Jews torture the Palestinians: they think they can do everything and get away with it because they are the Chosen People and are above the law.'

"The first thing that came to my mind when I heard them, do you know what it was? I wanted to get my car into an accident, but in a way that only the back part of my car would be smashed. But I didn't do it, I just talked. I moved my front mirror so that I could see them better, and I said: 'Yes, I am Chosen!'"

They were happy to hear it.

I said to them: "I am Chosen not because any God chose me. I chose Him. Do you understand? I chose Him because of His teaching:

treat the orphan and the widow with justice, rest on the seventh day. He started socialism, do you hear me? When everybody was working seven days, God said, 'No!' That's why I chose Him.'"

It's been over thirty years since I left this country. I have taken thousands of cabs since, in whatever country I have been to or lived in, but the cabbies in Israel are different. It makes me think of what Amos Oz told me. In Israel, even a "bus stop is at times a seminar."

As luck would have it, on the very next day Al-Quds University in Abu Dis, where the main campus is located, is going to conduct "The International Human Rights Competition" from 8:00 a.m. to 5:00 p.m.

As my cats were sipping their kosher milk (today I gave them settlement-made goat milk, which you can get in Jerusalem but not in Tel Aviv, where it's boycotted), the cats told me I should attend the competition, provided I left for them a big enough portion.

I've watched how people prepare for the possibility of war; it is now time that I find out how people prepare for peace.

Gate Thirty-One

*Roadmap to peace: paint a swastika and win an
international human rights competition.*

I TAKE A BUS TO ABU DIS. WHAT A WONDERFUL RIDE. WE PASS THROUGH A
great display of mountains weaving into each other, as if protecting
the Holy City in a majestic show of strength. Passing towns on the way
to Al-Quds University I see swastikas here and there, of different sizes
and colors, but to a Syria-loving German like me they look fantastic.

In case I forgot to mention it, today I'm wearing my Syrian flag
baseball cap and the youngsters of Palestine, those who occasionally
get a kick out of throwing stones at Israeli soldiers, cheer me when I
pass by them. "Syria," they call out.

At the entrance to Al-Quds University I'm told that the Israeli
army tried to enter the campus yesterday but the guards and students
wouldn't let them in. A fight ensued and eventually they got in.

I don't know. I wasn't here then, I've just arrived.

All Palestinian female students I encounter are wearing the hijab.
Females without it are foreign students. Al-Quds and the American
Bard college, I learn here, are sister universities. I would've talked
more with the Americans but I don't want to be late for an international human rights competition.

There's one little problem: I can't find the competition. Where is the International Human Rights Competition being held? I ask a fat man passing by me.

"Go there," he points at a group of four men, "they are Human Rights Professors."

I approach them. They know of no competition. Well, I'm here already and I'd love to discuss the subject matter with you. They would be willing to sit down with me and talk, they say, but they are so sorry because the classes they teach start in just minutes. Human rights classes, of course.

I walk to the public relations center of the University, where I meet Rula Jadallah. Where can I find the human rights classes? I ask Rula.

She calls up various departments, checks schedules, but finds no human rights class taking place anywhere on this campus at this time of day.

The professors, sadly to say, sold me a story.

Of course, I'm not upset. This is the Middle East, and in the Middle East it's all about the story. Nothing about reality.

Behind Rula's desk is a USAID letter hanging on the wall, plus an official letter announcing a $2,464,819 grant for the year 2006–2007 by the US government. "This is the only time we have so far gotten money from the US for this program," Rula tells me. But Germany is good. The Nano Technology Lab of this university was sponsored by Germany, Rula tells this German with a smile.

Does Rula know anything about the Human Rights Competition taking place today at the university? No. Or, better said, yes, she knows: there is no competition anywhere near here.

I tell her that I saw on the university's Internet site that a competition was taking place there right now. Rula checks the website of her own university and discovers there is a competition. So, is there or is there not? The answer is yes and no. Yes in cyberspace, No in reality. Why is the university announcing something that doesn't exist? What a stupid question! The competition gets funding, but except for this

Syrian German, no other European bothers to come all the way to Abu Dis to take part in such an event.

Life is a fiction. Period. And Rula is laughing. The best PR, I can see now, is laughter.

I think of the difference between Arabs and Jews. When Arabs make up stuff, they laugh it off once they get caught. Jews, like the atheist Gideon or believing Arik, get very tense.

How do Jews believe, even in their wildest imagination, that they will survive in the cruel, funny landscapes of this Middle East? Maybe that's why Arabs have lived here for so many years, whereas Jews just pop in for a visit once in two thousand years, to rest a while after an Auschwitz.

The south of Israel, I once heard, is different. Maybe I should go there and see how they view war and peace.

* * *

I hop on a bus going south and soon arrive in Ashkelon, where I meet Ofir.

Ofir lives in this city, Ashkelon, which is near Gaza, but he can't go to Gaza. "There used to be a bus here, public bus number 16, and we would go to Gaza whenever we wanted. We were on good terms, the Gazans and the Israelis. We worked with each other, ate with each other, and visited each other. Life was different then. Now Gaza is a world apart. We can't go to them; they can't come to us. But this is the Middle East and things turn around; you need to have patience. I hope that one day my daughter will get to live the life that I had, that she will be able to go to Gaza like I did: get on a bus and be there in minutes. Sadly, she is growing up without this experience."

I ask Ofir to tell me about Ashkelon, and how he got there to start with.

"My grandfather settled in Ashkelon, when it was called Majdal, around 1948. He came from the Ukraine and I don't really know how he started here. He told us that the Arab men of the town left and that he and the other immigrants lived in the same houses with the

Arab women and children who had stayed. My grandmother told me something else. She said that they came to Majdal and entered the Arab houses, you know, after a fight, and moved in. Only some Arabs stayed in the houses together with them, she said, and they took care of the animals and the farming together. This used to be an Arab village, but this city is mentioned in the Bible more than one time."

If this is what has happened here, I think, that Jews just showed up and kicked out the Arabs by force, this would mean that those Jews behaved in a manner compatible with the cultures they came from, the rest of humanity. A tribe comes in, kills those who live in the place and nicely moves in. It's harsh, cruel, and horrible and some Jews indeed didn't like this, like my grandfather; they ended up in Auschwitz and such places.

Not all Jews agreed with this arithmetic, and they said that there are more colors than just black and white. Most of them, in fact, preferred the grey color. They "skipped" or survived Auschwitz and Treblinka but did not act in the manner of their brethren in Ashkelon; they did not force the Arabs out but opted for coexistence instead. Decades later, today, Ashkelon has only Jewish residents and Ashkelon doesn't find itself lambasted by foreign circles for its cruelty to Arabs.

Ofir doesn't think it really matters what happened back then; this is the Middle East and bad things occasionally happen in this region. In fact, something equally bad happened to him as well. "I was evicted from my own house in Gaza. I had built it, I lived in it, we were one big family and then the Israeli government forced everybody out of the town and bulldozed all our houses. There was nothing we could do."

Born in Ashkelon, when he was older he moved to Nisanit on the northern tip of the Gaza Strip, where he built a home for himself and his family. But the house didn't last. Former prime minister Ariel (Arik) Sharon's government evicted all residents of Nisanit in August 2005 and demolished the town. The state offered compensation to the residents, mostly just a fraction of their homes' worth, but the mental and psychological sufferings they endured went uncompensated. Many of Ofir's former neighbors, he tells me, suffer severe depressions to this day and the divorce rate among them is extremely high.

Ofir, who knows that life can at times be turbulent, has come back to Ashkelon and is doing okay. He is a manager at the local Dan Gardens hotel and has his own computer business as well. Two jobs are better than one, because you never know where life will take you.

* * *

My life takes me to Josh, at Ashkelon National Park. Josh, an archeologist from Harvard University who's spending his summers digging in Ashkelon, gives me a better understanding of who lived where and for how long, and which group kicked out the ones who had lived there before.

The history of this place did not start in 1948, Josh tells me, and he gives me a short history lesson:

"Canaanites, early to late Bronze Age, 2850–1175 BCE.

"Philistines, 1175–694 BCE.

"Phoenicians, 550–330 BCE.

"Greeks, 330 to … I don't remember now the exact year.

"After the Greeks, these are the others that came in: The Romans. The Byzantines. The Umayyads. The Abbasids. The Crusaders. The Ottomans. The British. And now Israel."

You didn't mention the Jews. Did they not rule here before?

"Archeologically speaking we have no proof that Jews ever controlled the area of Ashkelon."

So says Josh Walton, lab director and archeologist, Ashkelon National Park.

Is he saying that there's no proof that Jews lived here before?

"I am talking only about this area, about Ashkelon."

Omri, who works at the National Park, prefers to talk about modern times and not about ancient times. He tells me of the rockets from Gaza that used to land here mostly before Operation Cast Lead in Gaza in 2009, though some occasionally still fall today.

Here?

"You want me to show you a Grad missile?"

Yes!

"You're standing right next to one."

What! I look behind, and sure enough there it is.

I pick it up, to feel its weight. Oh, boy, this is heavy!

Why would the Palestinians fire a missile into a park? Well, they tried to kill a few living Jews in the city but ended up shooting some dead Canaanites in the park.

This is an interesting park, an open museum on the sands of the Mediterranean seashore. You walk around and you see statues from three or four thousand years ago, columns and other objects lying around as if they were stones of no value. Here you can even see "the most ancient arched gate in the world," from the Canaanite period. Interestingly, not one tourist can be spotted here. The Israeli government's tourism office should get into the Guinness Book of World Records for the worst job in marketing.

Nir, a man who works for the Israel Antiquities Authority, comes by, and he has a pistol. No, his job is not to kill you but to make sure that real estate developers in the area don't build over ancient ruins, or that the Israeli army doesn't destroy ruins when paving a road to a base. I ask Nir to take me to the Israeli border with Gaza; I want to see how far it is from where I am at the moment.

Six minutes and thirty seconds is the total amount of time it takes him to drive from Ashkelon to the Gaza border at the Erez crossing. Knowing about this crossing only from countless media reports, I expect tough Israeli soldiers with assault rifles and beastly faces to greet me, and no other but them. This picture I had does not materialize. The first thing I see when I get to the border is an Arab ambulance crossing from Gaza into Israel. The sick of Gaza, it turns out, come to be treated in Jewish hospitals in Israel.

I advance toward the point of crossing. A young woman, with a smile bigger than all of Gaza, greets me. The tough males I thought I would see ain't here.

How many people have crossed here today? I ask her. "By this time, about three hundred. Would you like to cross?"

She would like to help, in case I need anything.

I don't think the average Lufthansa stewardess has ever been so eager to serve me.

And a thought crosses my mind: international journalists take courses at Al-Quds University.

Take me to Sderot, I say to Nir.

Sderot is a famous city, upon which and upon whose residents various Palestinian factions have many a time enjoyed firing rockets. In the follow-up of Israel's withdrawal from Gaza, thousands upon thousands of rockets have been fired on Sderot for years and years. In fact, this is the most fired-upon city in the country, and maybe in the world.

Nir takes me to Sderot.

I get off the car and start a conversation with the first person I meet, young Daniel.

How do you like Sderot?

"I love it. Sderot is the safest place in the world."

Did you lose your mind?

"Listen, I was born here, with the bombs. For me, this is still the safest place."

Safest?? Flying bombs don't scare you?

"Weak people are scared. This is not me."

Will you stay here all your life?

"Always and forever. No one will take me out of here. Not even a girl."

I wonder if a beautiful Tunisian girl with a firm ass and a pair of lovely breasts, the one Aviv and Bar are dreaming of, would also not be able to convince Daniel to move out of Sderot.

There is one city in Israel that stands for peace more than all others:

Tel Aviv. I have been there before, but perhaps I have overlooked its "peace potential," and so I go there again.

I bid goodbye to the south and move to the center of Israel, to the City of Peace.

*   *   *

Tel Aviv, the Bauhaus capital of the world known as White City (Tel Aviv is a UNESCO World Heritage Site) is a city that Sharon loves much. Sharon, a Sushi restaurant owner, is about to mount his bike when I approach him. I ask him to explain to me the essence of the average Tel Avivian and, luckily for me, he takes a liking to me, as if I were one of his fish, and he obliges.

"You want to know who we are? We walk, we like to walk, and then we sit in a cafe, drink and eat something, and then walk a bit more, and then we sit to have another drink in another cafe. They say that we live in a bubble, and it is the truth. There are problems in the north and in the south of Israel, Syria and Hamas and Egypt, but we are out of it. We just sit, hope that everything will be okay, and then we have beer. We like beer, but we don't drink it as much as the Germans do; we don't have their capacity of beer consumption.

"We have clubs and, very important, we have the sea. The sea gives us inspiration and offers us the calm of the waves and of the sea winds, and infinity. Every day, when I ride to work, I make a detour and ride along the beach. Sea is very important. Go walk a bit, sit down, have coffee, beer, and just feel good."

I follow Sharon's advice and walk a bit, to experience Tel Aviv-style peace. On the next building on my path of walk I see graffiti on a wall that's quite funny: "'Bibi' is a name of a dog." I walk a bit more and then I sit down at a café and drink a bit. And then I walk a bit. I see another café, and I sit. I have a cup of latte and then I walk a bit. Stop for a Coke Zero, sit, get up, walk, buy a cookie, sit, walk. Walk and walk. No direction.

I walk slowly, leisurely, turn right and left, and straight, and then I meet a man holding a loudspeaker. He speaks into it: "Tonight we take the illegal Sudanese, put them on the fire, and make kebab out of them."

Did I enter some kind of enemy territory?

Maybe.

On the street I'm now walking on there are no liberal Tel Avivians anymore; I've obviously walked too far. The neighborhood I just entered is the habitat of the poor, dead poor. This is a neighborhood in whose residents' names liberals and socialists engage in wars, only they don't live here and don't walk here.

The Supreme Court of Israel has just decided, I fast learn, that illegal Sudanese immigrants, known as Infiltrators, who have been arrested and jailed by the authorities, must be set free within ninety days, a ruling that scares the poor because once the Infiltrators are released, they will come here, where older Infiltrators live. Right next to the poor, in the area where the old central bus station used to be, thousands upon thousands of Sudanese and Eritrean refugees have taken over the old houses and the streets around in the past number of years. Where will the released prisoners go, the poor ask me? Here.

I walk over to see the Infiltrators.

Street after street, house after house, the neighborhood looks like anything but Israel. There are some "Luxurious Show Rooms" establishments right next to dilapidated houses and, if anything, this place looks like Harlem of the old days, where no white person could be spotted.

I try talking with them. A task that's not so easy for a white man to accomplish. They see me and they think I am an immigration officer, coming to arrest them. "No pictures!" are the first words they utter when they see me.

*   *   *

I sit on a street bench, next to a couple of them, but they don't talk to me. They are very busy, extremely busy, doing nothing. They roam around, sit about and sleep wherever they find a shaded corner. I look at them and I say to myself: I can do what they do. My world-famous specialty, after all, is doing nothing. If I were a site and not a living creature, I would no doubt win a UNESCO recognition.

Slowly the Infiltrators, people who got into Israel by trickery, talk to me. They realize, I guess, that I am a UNESCO candidate and not a government inspector. An Eritrean man, who tells me he sneaked into this country by foot via Egypt five years ago, takes a look at my iPhone and asks: "Is it yours?"

No New Yorker has ever asked me this question. This is a different world, I can tell, and in this world you don't get your iPhone at an Apple Store.

Life is hard, he shares with me, but he gets by. Added to the pack of the difficult life of the illegals is another problem: "The Eritrean and the Sudanese don't get along. We are Christian, they are Muslim." Even here, at the bottom of the pit of life, people are strangers to one another and won't mix.

I walk and walk and walk. On the outskirts of this neighborhood, two African kids walk by licking ice cream from cones. One is around

five years of age, the other around six. They speak to each other in Hebrew. They walk by a photographer with a big camera and ask him if he can take a shot of them. As they talk, the younger kid makes a wrong move and his ice cream falls on the sidewalk. He is devastated. The photographer, a white man, gives him five shekels to buy a new one and the kid takes the money, but his older brother does not approve: "Why did you take the money from him? You have enough money and you don't need anybody to hand you gifts. Give him back the money!"

The kid refuses. He got five shekels and he wants them.

"I know why you took the money from him. You want to have more money than me. But you don't need it. If you want ice cream you can buy on your own."

The kid still refuses.

"Here," says the older brother, a kid himself, handing his own ice cream to the younger: "Take my ice cream and give the man back his money!"

I watch and listen to this and I think: I have never seen kids at this age of such ethics. Not to mention adults. General Jibril, MK Cohen: this is ethics. Remember this next time you use the word.

* * *

I resume my peace walk. Slowly I leave Africa, more impressed than I've ever imagined I would be, and I reach Arabia. Back at the adjacent neighborhood of poor Jews, most of whom came here from Arab countries, I see them holding a demonstration. They don't want the Africans next to them. If the Supreme Court says the law requires Israel to have the Africans within Israel's borders, let the esteemed judges find a place for the Africans. A man with a loudspeaker yells: "Don't worry, friends. We'll send them to the Ashkenazi neighborhoods!"

I talk to many of the demonstrators, and the repeating phrases are these:

The white liberal rich are ruthless hypocrites. If they really believe that the Africans should be welcomed in Israel, why don't the liberals put the Africans in the rich sections of Tel Aviv? Who sent the Africans to us? Rich Ashkenazi, who are the politicians and the judges. Why here? We don't have money to go on trips, not even for a day, and now we can't even walk outside of our small neighborhood because in Africa people steal, rape and murder.

To the educated classes of the elite, the African refugees are like the Palestinians. They don't see them, don't know them, yet they fight for them. Like Jonathan and Yoav, and their European sponsors. No Bayerischer Rundfunk producer, enjoying life in the Englischer Garten, is paying the consequence of his love of either Arab or African.

The demonstrators here are not political activists and this demonstration is not political in nature but a collection of people who have gone to the street to vent their pain and their anger in public. Some cry, and others curse. They block traffic and scream at judges who are not anywhere in sight. Of course, as is normally the case in any social upheaval anywhere, there are politicians who show up in order to exploit peoples' anger and translate it into votes.

One of them is former MK Michael Ben Ari of the far-right. Aided by a mobile loudspeaker, he 'sings' with much pleasure a poem he had just composed: "We want a Jewish state! We want a Jewish state! We want a Jewish state! We want a Jewish state! Sudanese, go to Sudan! Sudanese, go to Sudan! Sudanese, go to Sudan! Sudanese, go to Sudan!" A man in the crowd yells back: "Racist! Racist! Racist! I'm also against the government, I understand the people here, but what you are doing is racism. Racist! Racist!"

I take a few moments to talk with Michael. "I say: the court has just decided that this country is not a Jewish country but a multi-national country. The Infiltrators are border thieves. They are thieves and their place is in jail! The court, instead of sending them to jail is arranging for them a hotel here. I want to see the Chief Judge of the Supreme Court taking ten of the thieves to his home, I'm not even asking that he takes home the thousands of them that he had sent to live here. Ten!"

What do you say to the people who yell "racist" at you?

"It was just one person, the rest of the people here hug me and kiss me. We are not racists, we are Jews. In Europe, I was told, the refugees say to their hosts: 'You are not racists but, by God, you are idiots! Real idiots!' If the Europeans want to be idiots, let them be. Those idiots, the European idiots, will pay the price, for soon Europe will cease to exist. But this country is not Europe!"

I'm losing perspective here. The more I get to dislike the hypocritical leftists, the more I get to dislike the honest conservatives. The centrists, experts in adopting the worst of both their political rivals, are today quiet as fish.

*   *   *

I came to Tel Aviv to experience peace, but what I'm experiencing here is liberal hypocrisy and conservative hatred.

There are places in Tel Aviv, of course, where the rich and the poor meet: on the stage. Should I take a look? Why not!

Tel Aviv's Cameri Theater, located away from the people here, is playing *Kazablan*, a musical about the early days of the state and the tensions between Ashkenazi and Sephardi Jews at the time.

The plot of the musical unravels in a slum, and the first character we see is a Sephardi street cleaner. He says: "God loves the poor and helps the rich." This almost sounds like *Fiddler on the Roof*, but in an Israeli version.

Love or help, both the Ashkenazi and the Sephardi poor in this musical live together in the same slum and occasionally curse each other, yet the Ashkenazi poor still feel they are the superior class. An Ashkenazi girl, now parading on stage, would not lower herself to say good morning to a Sephardi guy she passes by. His name is Kaza and he is hurt and he is upset. I'm good enough to serve in the army, he bellows, why shouldn't I be good enough to be greeted? "I have honor!" he yells.

The street cleaner, the poorest of humanity that rich playwrights like to portray as the wisest of men, proclaims that Kaza's love for this Ashkenazi girl will never work out. These young people are of very different cultures, he says, and east will never meet west. "Blue eyes say: Love me or I'll die. Black eyes say: Love me or I'll kill you," is how he puts it.

When another character says, "We are a young country only, only ten years old. Give it thirty, forty years and it will change, and no discrimination will still be there," the liberal audience, people who believe Israel to be a corrupted occupying state, is hugely entertained by this line and laughs mightily.

That the people in this audience, who encounter the "other" only on stage, view themselves as peace lovers and peacemakers is a comedy better than any actor would be capable of depicting on stage.

Gate Thirty-Two

Roadmap to peace 2: become a European
diplomat and beat up Israeli soldiers.

JERICHO, AS I HAVE BEEN TOLD, IS THE "OLDEST CITY IN THE WORLD." WOULD be interesting to see how ancient people lived together – and perhaps I'll learn a chapter or two about living in peace and tranquility.

According to the biblical account, the Jews entered this land via Jericho (*Arikha*, in Arabic). It wasn't easy to break through the walls of Jericho but a lovely prostitute by the name of Rahav made it possible for them. In other words, if not for a whore, the Jews wouldn't be here but would have stayed in Egypt and the president of Egypt today would be Benjamin Netanyahu. Imagine that!

*   *   *

Jericho.

The first thing I notice when I enter Jericho (I walked here with Jibril, but that was at night) is that this "ten-thousand-year-old city" looks ancient even now, at least in terms of tall buildings, which almost don't exist here. The second thing I notice: this is quite a small city. Third: Oh, God, this city is boiling hot, with no wind blowing anywhere. Fourth: there are two tourists here besides me. Two more than in Ashkelon's National Park.

I walk to the tourist information office, which I find while sweating on the street, and ask them for some great suggestions on what to see. There's no line of people waiting to be served and I get the best attention anyone could expect of any tourist office anywhere.

First off, I get a map. Nice map. Really. I look at it. "The map publication was funded by Japan International Cooperation Agency for Jericho Heritage Tourism Committee," it says on its back. Yes. Japan printed this map, to help the Palestinian cause.

This stupendous love for the Palestinians from so many nations that I keep seeing in this region is quite interesting. Some years ago I was in a Palestinian refugee camp called al-Wahdat, in Jordan, where people live worse than the average cockroach. No foreign government was helping them in any way, no NGOs around, and the Jordanian government was doing its best to make the life of these people a bit less intolerable. It doesn't take a genius to know why the world "loves" only certain Palestinians. I don't want to think about it.

There is a Sycamore Tree, a lady at the Jericho tourist information tells me, that I should see. A Sycamore tree? I was dreaming of a tempting prostitute and they tell me to go see a tree. Well, this is a special sycamore tree, from the times of Jesus. I forgot that I'm a German Christian and should be excited by anything Jesus. I have to adjust, and that fast. Yes, Jesus Christ! I can't stop showing some excitement.

And this is the story: When Jesus entered the city some two thousand years ago a short tax collector couldn't see him because of the crowd and he climbed on this very tree to take a look at the Son of God. Yep, this very tree. Would I like to see it? Yes! There's nothing else I'd like to see more, I tell the lady. Hopefully, I think in my heart but do not utter it, I will be able to steal a glimpse of Rahav of some one thousand years earlier than Jesus when I climb that tree.

I walk toward the tree. I walk and I walk and I walk, and now I am on Dmitry Medvedev Street. Wait a second: Am I reading this correctly? This is the name of the Russian prime minister. What is he doing here? Could it be that he got lost while following a Japanese map? I take a closer look at my surroundings, just to verify that I'm not suffering from hallucination, and see that right next to where I'm standing is the Russian Park, a gift from Russia.

I keep on walking, in the direction of either a tall tree or Vladimir Putin Road. And as I walk, an old man stops me. Did you see the ancient tree? He asks me. Where? He points to a small tree, and I have no idea what he wants from my life. So, I check my Japanese map. Yes, of course: this *is* the tree, with a fence around it. No point trying to climb this tree, I immediately conclude.

Where should I go next?

Well, there is a place in this city, the Japanese have pointed out, named Mount of Temptation; that's where Satan tempted Jesus Christ. Only this would require a cable car, at the cost of fifty-five shekels. A bit expensive, but I need to be tempted by something or I'll keep thinking of the Jordanian refugee camp al-Wahdat.

The cable car, for reasons that only the Son of Allah knows, stops midway, hanging between heaven and earth. Under me, as the car is shaking from the sudden stop, is the ancient city of Jericho. No sign whatsoever, sorry, of Rahav. She must have gone somewhere, maybe urinating with a Ramallah delegation at a KAS peace conference. I try to find some traces, a yellow sock or a blazing piece of red underwear, but then the cable car starts to move again. What bad timing.

But at least, and at long last, I reach the Mount of Temptation. And there, built into the mountain and looking every part of it, which is a magnificent sight to behold, is a monastery. Inside this monastery is the Stone of Temptation, exactly where Jesus was tempted by Satan. You should come and see it. This stone has the shape of the tip of an uncircumcised penis, and good monks pray by it. Plain gorgeous. Olga, who was kissed by a monk at the Holy Sepulcher and told him to kiss me, would have a blast if she saw this.

This is, more or less, Jericho. A small city with Japanese and Russians.

* * *

I hook up with Raed, a man born to drive a car, and he takes me to

Bethlehem. Raed likes to talk, and talk he does: "Here it is hot, but in twenty minutes' time, as we approach Bethlehem, it's cold. Here hot, there cold. This country has many different climates. This country has everything."

No other country on earth has such change of climates?

"No, here is special."

How come?

"Because this is a holy land."

Are you happy to be in this land?

"There is an occupation here."

Where? Are there Jews around? Show me!

"I would like to live in my birth city."

Isn't it Jericho?

"No. I am a refugee here."

Where are you from?

He points at mountains away, in Israel's direction: "Over there."

There? When were you there last?

"In 1948."

You said "there" was your birth city. You look like a thirty-year-old. How long ago was 1948?

"My grandfather lived there!"

I see. And you feel under occupation because of that?

"I want to go to the sea, pick up fish from the waters, like the Germans do in their country, but I can't do it because of the Israelis."

Fish? Will you starve without fish? Let me tell you something: You, Palestinians, have better food here than we have in the whole of Germany! Show me in Germany olive oil like the Palestinian olive oil!

"That's true. If you have a cold, you know what you do? You spread warm olive oil on your torso and on your neck and in two days you'll be healthy. It's in the Quran, and Prophet Mohammad said it."

But you don't have fish...

"I don't!"

You have humus here that no German will ever have! And you have some other food too. You have –

"We have dates here. If you eat seven dates in the morning, no bad eye will hurt you. On the Internet, in 'Genius,' they checked it and found that the seven dates create x-rays around you to protect you."

So, what's your problem? Fish, that's it? Why are you complaining?

"I'll tell you the problem: We, Muslims, call our children after Christian and Jewish prophets. We have Musa, Isa, and I'm going to call my daughter, the next one I'll have, I'll call her Maryam. But Christians and Jews don't call their children after Muslim prophets, like Muhammad, May Allah pray for him and offer him peace. Why? Show me a Christian or a Jew calling their sons 'Muhammad'!"

I must agree with you. I don't know even one Jew or Christian by the name of Muhammad. This is a real problem!

Raed drives and I consult my iPad.

Gideon Levy, who gave me his word to have me join him on his frequent forays into Palestine, is responding to a message I sent him some days ago: "Dear Tuvia, I was yesterday in the Jordan Valley and Jenin, but could not be joined. I don't know what will be the next opportunity, but I will let you know. Not always it is possible. Gideon." Funny.

The Israeli media reports that an Israeli man, driving with a Palestinian coworker to his town in Palestine, was murdered in cold blood and that his body was thrown into a pit. Not funny.

It's an awful reminder of what can happen to Israeli-born people crossing into Palestine. How long will I be able to play this game of Tobi the German before somebody catches me?

I get off at Bethlehem and start walking. Hopefully I won't end in a pit.

"This shop will be open during the Bet Lahem Live Festival, 13–16 June 2013," a piece of paper on a locked shop door reads. ("Bet Lehem" means House of Bread in Hebrew, which conflicts with the Palestinian narrative of the ancient Palestinian state. Since Beth Lehem – or Beth-lehem – plays a major role in the New Testament, its very name could prove that the Jews lived here and not the Palestinians in Christ's time. To solve this problem, a little correction was introduced, by changing a vowel. "Bet Lahem," with an 'a' instead of an 'e,' is giving a new meaning to the city's name in Arabic: House of Meat.)

This shop, in a beautiful street with an endless rows of closed shops, is open four days a year only.

I walk and I think: How do the people here make a living? Doing what? Oh, here's a beautiful house, must have cost a fortune. No, not really. It's a gift from Italy. Italians love the ex-Jew, Itamar, and the Palestinians. Every second building on this street, if not every building, is funded by righteous Europeans. I'm also righteous, I fund my stray cats. I miss them and go back to Jerusalem to see them.

*   *   *

And there was night and there was day, as the Bible says, and I go to join an event organized by the International Christian Embassy Jerusalem (ICEJ). No kidding, they exist. Perhaps, what do you know, they will bring peace to this land.

The ICEJ is an organization that advertises itself as Christian Zionist, and this evening it is celebrating the biblical Feast of Tabernacles at the Dead Sea. Don't ask for more info, I don't know. This organization, "the world's largest Christian Zionist organization," as its brochure says, "was founded in 1980 to represent Christians from all over the world who share a love and concern for Israel and the Jewish people."

I love "love" and I'm here to see love and to feel love.

Many people are on the scene, five thousand of them as I'm told by the embassy spokesperson, or thirty-six hundred as I'm told by the bus operators who actually bring the people here.

And the loudspeakers proclaim, as loud as can be: "Jesus you are the light, Jesus you are the reason. There is no one like you, Jesus."

Good, at least these people love one Jew.

The gathering is very American in style, with a black singer and a blond dancer amongst others, which by itself creates a happy shmappy feel. The crowd, made of people from Hong Kong and Switzerland, amongst many other nations, all go for it. There are other visual impressions in addition to the black singer and the blond dancer: there are brown mountains behind us, a bluish Dead Sea in front of us, plus big screens on the right and the left and quite a spacious stage to accommodate the big choir.

The volume coming from the stage is so loud, I'm sure every Jordanian on the other side of the Sea can hear them. Praise you, Jesus!

My only question so far is why they are doing this here. This is a show of sound, movement, and light that would perfectly fit any evangelical church in Tennessee.

"The spirit of the Lord is here, the power of the Lord is here," goes the next song.

A German pastor, by the name of Jürgen Bühler, who is the ICEJ's executive director, speaks in thick German English. He blesses the people arriving.

Next to him another person stands and says: "Holy Spirit, welcome!" And the crowd roars with approval.

This event, by the way, is broadcast on God Channel – yes, there is a TV station by this name. Strong winds blow sand into our faces as a black female singer sings *Hallelujah*. She has a voice and energy that are heavenly, and it makes me miss NY. Oh boy, she knows how to sing! And she knows how to get through to people. They get up, they raise their hands, they move with the wind blowing the sand and they chime in with her song with their eyes closed. I never knew Hong Kong people could be so loud.

A South African female pastor, a naturalized German by the name of Suzette Hattingh, who for years worked Reinhard Bonnke, a German evangelist, ascends the stage and with her heavily accented English she preaches to us. She seems to cherish the fact that this event is being broadcast on God Channel. "I'm on the way to Heaven," she shouts, though I don't know if she means it literally, or whether she's talking about the fact of being broadcast on TV. And then she orders us around: "I want you to stand, I want you to raise your hands."

All do. She goes on: "There's a woman watching us right now on God Channel who has only three more months to live. Go back to your doctor!" Yes. Right in front of our eyes, that woman gets healed. Like her mentor Bonnke, whom I saw in Germany the other day telling his followers that he resurrected the dead in Africa, this lady too believes, or pretends to believe, that she is God.

With one line out of the thousands she utters, she pays lip service to Israel, when she reminds us that Jesus was Jewish. In the other 99.9 percent of her many words she speaks of miracles, and then she speaks in tongues: "kuaka, chakaka, tugalka." None of this has anything to do with a Zionism of any kind. It's just missionary work, implicitly letting us know that we will all be sick unless we scream with her, "Jesus, kuaka, chakaka, tugalka."

This Christian Embassy does not shy away from the cheap use of the word "Jews" in order to get more and more converts, of whom the embassy now asks to donate generously to its coffers. They are not Christian Zionists, they are Christian Kuakas. The European lovers of Palestine build and renovate mansions for Palestinians; these Christian lovers of Israel are Kuakas who raise money for Jesus and resurrect the dead.

*   *   *

Once this is over, I turn my attention to more interesting events on my iPad. I find one quite a lovely event advertised by the BBC: "Diplomats from a number of European countries and the UN have reacted angrily after Israeli soldiers intervened to prevent them delivering aid to Bedouins in the West Bank." And it gets better: "One French diplomat said she was forced to the ground from her vehicle." The French diplomat, Marion Fesneau-Castaing, is quoted as saying: "This is how international law is being respected here."

In more detail the BBC goes on to say: "The aid was being delivered to Khirbet al-Makhul after homes there were demolished under a High Court order." An accompanying photo shows the head of a lady surrounded by booted soldiers with rifles pointed at her and fingers on or around the triggers. The image is not very clear, taken at a very strange angle, but all the visuals here easily remind you of Nazi Germany.

This BBC story strikes me as tailored for Tobi the German to pursue. I check more into it and find that it was the International Committee of the Red Cross (ICRC) that was one of the first to be involved in this issue, the Khirbet al-Makhul issue, and that earlier in the week they had tried to help the Bedouins in a similar manner.

I call them up.

Nadia Dibsy, a spokesperson for the ICRC, tells me that she was at the location at the time and saw Marion Fesneau-Castaing being beaten with her own eyes. I ask her a really stupid question: Why are diplomats taking on an activist role in a host country? Is this what diplomats are supposed to do? I live in New York, where the UN is headquartered, and naturally there are many, many diplomats in New York. Should I expect them to come to Harlem and stop any eviction notice against members of the black community by the New York courts?

Nadia didn't expect me to ask her stupid questions. I was supposed to react differently, obviously, and say what European journalists usually say in such cases: "Thank you very much, Ms. Dibsy, for taking the time to share this important piece of information with me."

But, idiot that I was, I came up with my stupid question.

Nadia, sensing a potential trouble, collects herself fast. She changes what she has said before and now tells me: "I was not there on Friday." She was there only earlier in the week and doesn't know what exactly happened when the diplomats were there. I ask her if it is normal for the ICRC to take action against Supreme Court rulings in other countries as well. She chooses not to answer directly and instead tells me that Israel is an occupying force and that there are international laws that Israel must observe.

Could it be that the Israeli Supreme Court doesn't know about this international law, or maybe simply decided to ignore the law? Nadia doesn't want to answer this question but tells me that according to international law Israel has no right to evict natives from the hills they share with their sheep.

I wish I could go and find out for myself what really transpired last Friday, only I have no clue as to how to find Khirbet al-Makhul on the map. Too bad Japan has not yet printed a map of Khirbet al-Makhul as well.

Between you and me, there's another thing I don't know: Why am I discussing international law with the ICRC? I know very little about them, true enough, but aren't they something like an international ambulance service? I don't know, but I guess they know better what they're doing and who they are. And so I ask ICRC if they would allow me to join them next time they're going somewhere, and I also inform them that I would be very pleased if I could see what they're doing from the moment of conception to the moment of completion.

They reply in the positive and now we are all happy.

The ICRC is one thing, diplomats are another. How do foreign diplomats, who are here for a short duration of service, even know where places like Khirbet al-Makhul are? I was born here, grew up here, and I never heard of Khirbet al-Makhul. How come they did?

Just out of curiosity, I ask an Israeli military officer for comments, and he tells me that there is an "old custom" of European diplomats who join up with leftist activists of all kinds on a regular basis and that they plan and plot their next moves together.

If this is true it sheds an interesting light on the world of European Mid East diplomacy.

* * *

I decide to try to discover the hidden world of diplomats.

The naïve man I am, I call the French Embassy and Consulate in Israel requesting an appointment with Marion, and could they please give me the French government's official comments on this story?

Did you ever try to squeeze a response out of French diplomats?

Ain't that easy.

Responding to my request, I'm told by the French authorities that I would be called back within an hour and be given a government-approved reaction.

Within one hour. As you might have guessed, in the diplomatic world of the French variety one hour means more than just one hour. It means, if you like in "German exact": not now, not ever.

And so, since the phone does not ring, I come up with a new scheme: Diplomats are a tough nut to crack, for they are trained in the ways of evading the truth, but if it's true that diplomats and left activists are working hand in hand, why not penetrate some human rights organization and find the answers to my questions on my own?

Which of the human rights organizations I should choose is a different question. There are so many anti-Israeli groups within Israel that it's not that simple to choose the best one. I go by the alphabet. B'Tselem, an Israeli-left NGO starts with B and is quite well known. I call them and share with them my most urgent personal need: I want to participate in one of their activities. A lady at the organization, named Sarit, soon contacts me and suggests that I join a man named Atef Abu a-Rub, a researcher for B'Tselem, on his next assignment: illegal home demolitions by the IDF.

Great. I call Atef and we make the arrangements to meet each other in Jenin, where he's located, in two days.

Jenin! Wow!

If I may say so, I feel really good about myself. I'm going to infiltrate the world of NGOs, none of them will know who I, Tobi the German, really am, and I'm going to find stuff nobody knows. I am, get a hold of this, a secret service man. When I'm done here, I'll teach the FBI, the CIA, the Shabak, and the Mossad what secret service really means!

I take a shot of Scotch whisky, those damn Scots know how to make good drinks, and feel in heaven.

Whisky goes well with – sorry for not being PC here – ladies of the night. I didn't find the dead Rahav, so let me go for a living whore.

Gate Thirty-Three

*Time to relax: pamper yourself with the ladies of the
night or watch faithful housewives in the zoo.*

KDOSHA IS THE HEBREW WORD FOR "FEMININE HOLINESS," WHILE KDESHA IS
the word for a "female prostitute." These two words are very close
and they share the same root. Rabbis don't like this but God, whose
mother tongue is Hebrew, seems to.

The holy whores, if you ever feel the need to spend some time in
their company, call the dirtiest and ugliest of Tel Aviv streets their
home, right by the African illegals.

The first two I see are fat white blondes, of Putin land, and they
communicate with each other in Russian. I stop by their "store" and
one of them asks me if I want to pee. I ask how much? She says: Free.
Pee is free.

I keep on walking, in search of holy local ladies. Sorry, blondes I
have enough of elsewhere.

Passing by a couple of expensive new vans, I see a lady who strikes
me as local and I say hi to her and wish her a great night ahead. She
ignores me, as if I were one of Jericho's dead. Sacred ladies are not
that easy.

I keep on walking. And walking. And walking.

I notice a sex shop that has very interesting operating hours: it's
closed on the Sabbath. Must be operated by some rabbi.

Yes. The ground I'm walking on is holy.

I make a U-turn and notice that the local sacred whore who wouldn't talk to me before is now schmoozing with another angel of the night. I see them looking at me, and I walk over to them.

The new lady asks: "What are you doing here?"

In search of the good life.

"This is good life? In this place?"

Is it the bad life here…?

"Whoever comes here most likely doesn't have a good life…"

And how's your life?

"Thanks be to the Lord, thanks be to the Lord!"

Blessed be the Lord?

"Yes."

This whore talks better than a rabbi!

Are you Israeli?

"Yes. And you? You look like a tourist."

No, I'm Israeli. How is work going?

"Well, those who take care of themselves are doing well."

How long have you been working here?

"We have been here a long – a very long – time!"

Is it frightening to spend the nights on the street?

"How about crossing the street, any street. Is that not frightening? We look after ourselves. We have knives, tear gas. We take good care of ourselves."

Where do you "perform"?

Pointing to a building nearby: "In the rooms inside there. There are rooms upstairs, downstairs, everywhere."

What's your rate?

"It depends. It starts at one-hundred shekel, if we stay in the client's car. After that it goes up."

The First Lady now intervenes: "It's like a meter in a taxi. The figure goes up and can reach as much as a thousand shekels."

Second lady: "It depends on the client. We look at him, at his face, and we make up the price depending on what we think we can get out of him."

You see a man, judge him on the spot, and come up with a price instantly?

"There's no other way!"

They should work in the jewelry business; that's how they decide on prices.

Are most of the clients Israeli? I ask.

"No. I prefer the Israelis, but most of them are tourists from overseas."

First Lady: "We are like food for the men. They need us, they must have us."

Do you have Haredi clients as well?

Second lady: "Many!"

First Lady: "Hasidic Jews, they are the best!"

Why?

Second lady: "They finish the fastest. They don't make problems. And whatever you tell them is holy for them! They accept what we say to them as if our words were written in the Holy Bible!"

Yep. Religious Jews know holiness when they see it!

Who is the largest segment of your clientele?

"The largest segment are Jews. The Jewish people (not just Israelis) are the majority of our clients. Hasidic Jews, criminal Jews – "

First Lady: "All of them, they come to us! We are their food!"

Do Palestinian men come here too?

Second Lady: "Of course."

Do you mind if the men are Jews or Arabs?

First Lady: "Look: I'm a Bedouin, how could I discriminate against Palestinians?"

Oh God in heaven! This holy lady of the night might be from Khirbet al-Makhul!

Second Lady: "The most important thing is that the man be a good human being."

First Lady: "When I see Russians, for example, I prefer not to go with them. They drink too much alcohol and they don't reach orgasmic climax. With Ethiopians there are also problems: they like to put their hands all over. The ones I like the most are Ashkenazi Jews. They are quiet, they are cute. I like them."

How many Jewish whores are there around?

Second lady: "A lot."

First Lady: "Sex has nothing to do with religion. Sex has no faith."

You are a Bedouin. Does your family know you're doing this?

"They don't have to know."

Second lady: "Do you tell your family everything?"

Do you live by yourself or do you have families of your own?

Second Lady: "I live with a man, my mate."

Does he mind what you're doing?

"He is a Haredi Jew."

Does he know what you are doing...?

"That's how we met!"

Wow!

"He lives a double life: outside he puts on those black clothes of the Haredi, with his *shtreimel* on, but inside the house he is normal. Really normal."

First Lady: "This country is a beautiful country. Everything you can think of, you'll find in this country. I was a special education teacher – "

How did you go from that to here...?

"How? On a bus!" (She giggles.)

How did you two start with prostitution?

Second lady: "Drugs. I started taking drugs, and then I had to do some prostitution. My family threw me out of the house and so I started working here. Thank the Lord, today I don't do any drugs. I'm a good girl now."

First Lady: "My family tried to force me to marry an old man, to be his third wife. I ran away!"

What is the worst part of working here?

Second Lady: "All kinds of crimes. Burglary, violence."

First Lady: "The other day I was thrown out of a car, after an hour inside it – "

Second Lady: "I was with a man in a car, and suddenly two other men came out of the trunk. They hit me so hard, I almost died. I was taken to the hospital."

First Lady: "Every day when I get out of the house I don't say, 'God, make me earn a lot of money.' I say: 'God, please help me come back home safely.'"

Second Lady: "Every day, before I leave the house I say the biblical verse: 'Hear O Israel, the Lord our God is One.'" (By tradition, this is uttered by people who face death.)

In case you didn't get it, my dear, these are the whores of Israel, praying whores!

Second Lady: "In the last few years, our lives have become much more dangerous."

How so?

First Lady: "Because of the Sudanese."

Second Lady: "The Sudanese, and the other blacks here."

First Lady to Second Lady: "Be careful that they don't hear you!"

Second Lady: "Bitches, all of them!"

What are the Sudanese doing to you, that you feel so strongly about them?

Second Lady: "They are not cultured people."

First Lady: "I don't blame them – "

Second Lady: "They use force against us – "

First Lady: "If you take Queen Victoria and put her here, under the same conditions, having no job, she would be behaving just like them! It has nothing to do with their race, or their color, but with their dire conditions."

Tell me, ladies: What are your dreams?

First Lady: "My dream is that all the Sudanese fly out of here."

Second Lady: "To have a home that's mine."

First Lady: "There is no path to happiness, unless you are happy with what you have."

You should join the Philosophy Department of Tel Aviv University. You'll be the best professor and you'll make tons of money…

First Lady: "I have enough money."

Second Lady: "If you want to study, believe me, the street is the best place to study. On the street you learn about life, about what really matters. Forget the prostitution element; leave it aside for a moment. If you want to learn about life, the best place to acquire knowledge is the street."

First Lady is now showing me what she has learned on the street that no professor would predict. She says: "If you come here, to this street, in a year and a half from now, you'll need a passport."

Why?

"It will be a different country. Soon, the Sudanese will demand independence – "

Second Lady: "Them, and with all that garbage they carry with them."

First Lady: "It is their right, isn't it? They live here and soon they will demand their human rights for self-recognition. Two or three years, tops, and these streets will be an independent state."

I guess that they also like women, right?

"Yes."

Do they have money to pay?

Second Lady: "The Sudanese have more money than the average Israeli."

What?

First Lady: "Go down the street and you will see for yourself. First thing you will notice: they control the drug market."

Second Lady: "Please write this down!"

What are your names?

Second lady: "Keren."

First Lady: "Nadine."

Across the street a Hasidic Jew is walking by, checking what's cooking. Nadine points at him.

Nadine: "You see? We just talked about them! This guy, can I tell you? he gets an orgasmic climax in one second!"

These ladies of the night are full of life, funny, creative, and it's a pleasure to talk with them. I don't know how much of what they have told me about themselves is true, but I have enjoyed every second of our talk.

I take a few photos with them: I face the camera, they face the opposite side. I hug Keren, perhaps a bit too tight, and she quips: "I think I'm going to charge you!"

Would be nice to go to Meah Shearim after this, to personally feel the difference between *kdesha* and *kdosha*.

On the way from here to there the ICRC office in Jerusalem contacts me. We talk and reach an agreement: I am to join them in a future operation, from conception to completion, in Palestine. Details to follow.

*   *   *

This week is the holiday of Sukkot and the religious love to celebrate it. In the time of the Holy Temple, every child knows, the Children of Israel would come to Jerusalem to celebrate this holiday. And today, the streets of Meah Shearim are packed with revelers. There are so many of them that the traffic is at a virtual standstill. They are dressed in their finest clothes, and as you walk amongst them you think you are in Europe, centuries ago.

Well, not exactly. It's more like Europe of old mixed with Afghanistan of today. There's a fenced sidewalk, designated for women, and no woman is to choose another path. From the street and from the sidewalk on the opposite side, where men walk or stand, the women look as if they were animals in a zoo protected by a wire fence.

God knows why, but I decide to cross into the women's area.

Let me tell you: one man surrounded by an untold number of women is a good feeling. Yes, I know, it's not nice to say, but as Keren and Nadine would define it, I'm surrounded by "food." On the wall of one of the houses I see this notice to women: "Women whose arms and legs were uncovered in this world, will be placed in a boiling pot of fire and burn [in the Hereafter]. They will cry in anguish and suffering. This is much worse than when a person is burnt while he is alive."

In Toldos Aharon, the institution I visited twice before, thousands of people dance and sing: "My soul is thirsty for You, Lord, and my flesh is longing for You."

I wonder if this is the same line they use when they visit the ladies of the night.

Gate Thirty-Four

Please help: European diplomats rush to help Bedouins who would like to have naked German women running between their goats.

I TAKE A TAXI TO JENIN, TO MEET ATEF OF B'TSELEM, AS PREVIOUSLY ARRANGED. The taxi driver takes me all over the West Bank – almost. He thinks he knows the way to Jenin, but the roads don't always obey him. It doesn't really matter, since this way I see more than I would otherwise see. And the West Bank, may I say it for the thousandth time, is splendidly gorgeous.

It is only with Allah's help, that we actually reach Jenin.

Atef, who is also a journalist for the Palestinian paper Al-Hayat Al-Jedida in addition to his activism, welcomes me in his office with my favorite Arabic coffee, and we walk to his car. We cross Cinema Jenin, which I've heard of many times before. Being a master agent, I stop to check it out. On its front wall it says, in stone, that it is supported by the "German Federal Foreign Office," the "Goethe Institut," the "Palestinian National Authority," and "Roger Waters." (In the year 2013, Pink Floyd's Roger affixed the Jewish Star of David on a floating pig during his summer concert.)

We walk a bit more until we reach Atef's car and I ask him where he's going to take me. "Khirbet al-Makhul." Yes, to the place where Marion the French made her great name as a savior of the people.

I thought we were going to see demolition of new houses, but I guess B'Tselem couldn't locate any real house demolition, and so they are sending me to a Tent in the News. This is not what I had bargained for, but better. Now I will be able to see what's on the mind of BBC et al, who are so busy with that Makhul. We drive for hours. The Jordan Valley has not only gorgeous mountains but it also has endless roads, and Atef talks unto me. The mountains, he says, used to be green.

Who turned them brown?

Well, the Israelis. There used to be waters under the mountains, he explains to me, but the Israelis stole them. It is possibly true, and it's also possibly true that Mecca used to look like Hamburg but then some Jews stole all the trees. I say nothing of the kind to Atef. I am German and I am polite.

As of this minute, until I leave Atef, I speak no Arabic. Other Do-Gooder Europeans walk here with translators, and so should Tobi the German. Period.

*   *   *

On the way Atef tells me that before we go to Khirbet al-Makhul, we are to first meet a Palestinian official in charge of Israeli crimes in the West Bank. I can't be any happier. He is the kind of guy, after all, I have always dreamt of dating.

We pass through an area called Tubas. I don't know if you have ever been there; I haven't. But now I am. There are buildings here so amazingly designed that you won't see the like of them even in the richest corners of Connecticut. I take out my iPhone and try to snap some photos, but Atef says I shouldn't, and he drives his car fast.

Yes, yes. I understand him. He is here to show me how miserable the Palestinians' life is because of the Israelis and he doesn't need any beautiful houses to cloud my vision. I feel for him. But the houses are too nice not to take a shot of them and I do. I guess I'm not the most polite German. Perhaps my great-grandparents were Austrians.

We reach a nice government building, officially known as State of Palestine, Governorate of Tubas and Northern Valleys. We get off the car and enter the building. I am to meet Moataz Bsharat, whose official title is Official of the Jordan Valley, Director of Security, and his job today, as I assume, is to tell me that the Israelis are forcing the Palestinians into destitution. It's a tough call, given his marvelous office, but he is probably a strong man and he will know how to handle it.

I am introduced to him by Atef and Atef says to me: "Moataz Bsharat is the official responsible for all the violence by the Israelis in the Jordan Valley." I'm not sure what Moataz's responsibilities really are, but I think this man could provide a great opportunity for me to find out what has really happened in Khirbet al-Makhul. This guy should know it all.

Can you tell me what happened there?

Moataz goes in circles with me, and only at the end he admits that Marion, the French diplomat, punched the Israeli soldiers when she got back up from the ground after having fallen down, and that she did this because the soldiers had punched her and the other diplomats first. Moataz, pointing at his computer, also tells me that he can show me all this right now, since he has it all on video.

Moataz thinks that now I should be happy because he answered my question and because he even told me that he got it all on video. The British journalist I met at Majdal Shams, who on his own decided that the Druze didn't get gas masks would, had he been here, be very happy to report that "it's all on video" without asking for any evidence of such. But I'm not British and so I ask Moataz: Could you please play the video for me? I'd like to see it.

Well, what a pity. "We are out of time," Moataz responds, and he must leave right now.

Moataz is seriously bewildered. He knows other Europeans, and they accept everything he tells them. What, in the name of Allah, is wrong with this Tobi the German?

* * *

Atef says that now we can go to Khirbet al-Makhul. As we get to the place I notice a van of the MSF (Médecins Sans Frontières, Doctors without borders) organization. Two people of this organization sit next to a couple of Bedouins and collect testimonies, which they write down.

How did the MSF get in here and why? I see no injured person around, only healthy Arabs, and I wonder what these doctors are up to. They introduce themselves to me: Federico, of Italy, who helps Arab victims of violence in settlers' areas and Eva, of the Czech Republic, a psychologist.

Both of these honorable doctors see the befuddled look on my face when seeing them and immediately make it clear to me that I had better not mention their presence. "We have to keep a low profile," the male doctor tells me. I respond by saying that they should be proud of their work here which leads them to change their minds. When I even ask if I can also take a photo of their beautiful faces they agree.

The short and sweet of what these two are doing here is this: making up diseases so they can stick it to the Israelis.

Long live Europe.

When the MSF doctors are done with the evicted people I, the

Master Agent, sit down with these Arabs to hear their story and measure their traumatic illnesses.

Mahmoud Bsharat, one of these and the main man of this place, tells me his life story. "Three years after the occupation," meaning 1967, he moved to Israel to work there. He came back to the desert in 1987. He has nine children and seven of them have university degrees.

Was he born here?

No. But he grew up here, or around here. People living in the desert, he tells me, move from one place to the other, all depending on the weather, on where they find better access to water, or whatever. Taking his combined statements it seems that he did not come to this place, Khirbet al-Makhul, before 1987. The assertion by the BBC, and other European media, that these Bedouins "have grazed sheep for generations" at this location is, as it turns out, a romantic fiction.

Whoever represents Mahmoud and the other Bedouins here must be smart people well able to manipulate facts. I ask Mahmoud who is the lawyer representing him in the Supreme Court and how much he costs. Well, Mahmoud never hired any lawyer and never paid anything to any lawyer. Who paid? Another Mahmoud, the Palestinian leader, Mahmoud Abbas.

Palestine is hiring a lawyer to fight Israel in Israel's courts. Interesting.

Where is Mahmoud the Bedouin planning to sleep tonight, now that he has been evicted from here? He is going to sleep here, he tells me.

The Israeli army demolished something, only the word *demolished* is too strong a word for what seems to have happened here. Before Israel demolished this place, I can see, it consisted of no more than corrugated iron shacks, tents, and plain wood beams, as the encampment next to where I sit can testify, and it would take approximately two hours to set the encampment up again. No evidence of any real housing here.

I ask Mahmoud to describe Israelis to me, since he has lived with them for so many years. "They are racists," he says. Why did he stay with them for twenty years? God knows.

He reminds me of the Ladies of the Night in Tel Aviv who are sure the Sudanese will soon demand a free country of their own inside Tel Aviv.

Other people around us, including Mahmoud's brother, join the conversation and I find out more details of the French diplomat Marion's story. She and other diplomats arranged for a truck, loaded with new tents and other goodies, and they came in with their own cars to help rebuild the encampment. After the soldiers had told everybody to leave the area, the truck driver left his truck and Marion charged onto the driver's seat in order to prevent the soldiers from driving the truck away. The soldiers, after repeatedly failing to convince her not to interfere, finally pulled her out of the driver's seat. During this process, Marion fell to the ground.

Again, the BBC is telling tales. Marion was not "dragged from her vehicle," but from the truck with the tents.

Did you see the soldiers punch Marion? I ask the eyewitness here.

"No. They only pulled her out of the truck."

What did the other diplomats do when this took place?

"They filmed."

Interesting work of European diplomats. They brought in the tents, and then they were busy filming. They knew in advance that the army wouldn't allow the encampment to be rebuilt, but they were in for a movie clip in order to shame Israel. I thought that a diplomat's job was to represent his or her country in the host country. Well, not European diplomats in Israel. Another interesting question: Who edited the video to exclude what Marion had been doing? Only the EU, and other honest brokers of truth and journalism, will know.

I take my time to check this on my iPad and find an Iranian news site showing a video of the event. In it I see Marion in the driver's seat, cut to Marion on the ground, and then cut to Marion punching a soldier. How Marion got to the ground is not shown, which suggests that she might have gotten there on her own for the sake of picture taking. In the image provided by the Iranian news site even the soldiers around her seem to be surprised to see her on the ground. Interestingly, in the BBC photo the faces of the soldiers were cut from the frame.

Great work of journalism.

* * *

Talking with the people around me, I learn even more: This encampment has been in and out of Israeli courts since 2008, and in all these years no demolition has taken place. Nobody has just come and brutally evicted people, tugging them out of their sleep. Khirbet al-Makhul, by the way, lies at the foot of a mountain where an army camp is based and it is likely that this is the reason why it was evacuated and not the others in the nearby mountains.

Mahmoud tells me another story: Israeli military aircraft used to fly above his goats and shoot at them, one after the other. I try to imagine MK Ayelet Shaked's husband chasing goats with his F-16 plane, dropping huge missiles on running goats.

I ask the people how they make a living in this place and they tell me that they make goat cheeses. Could they spare a sample? Yes, they could and they do. I try their cheese. What can I say? It was worth it coming here just for this salty cheese! I also get a large piece of pita bread to go with it; the best pita ever baked by human hands. Trust me on this.

Of course, no favor goes unanswered, and when I ask my hosts how they make love in this place, just in case they are married, they ask me for a favor: Could I hand them over two German ladies? "Give me two German ladies!" one of them asks of me. The ladies would not have to do any cooking or such, just lie naked and be fucked. We stand next to three big water tanks and I promise them three naked German ladies by twelve noon of the following day, a naked blonde on top of each water tank. We laugh really hard about the sex with the naked German ladies on top of the water tanks, but then Atef realizes that this isn't the right image of suffering Bedouins he is trying to convey, people laughing instead of suffering, and he asks me not to mention the part about the German ladies' nakedness. As for the Bedouins, they don't care a bit.

I ask Atef to take me to another encampment, one that has not been demolished by the Israelis.

As we are about to leave this place, I hear the story of Khirbet al-Makhul as it is to develop further: A lawyer, paid by the State of Palestine, is going to go to the Israeli Supreme Court again, trying to reopen the case. The Bedouins themselves don't really know what's going on around here since their case is handled by NGOs and the State of Palestine. And another thing I learn before I leave: They have never really lived here. They have their goats here, but they have other places as well. Where? They point at mountains ahead. This would explain why all I can see here are shacks of corrugated iron, beams, and folded tents.

*   *   *

Atef takes me to another encampment, this one of a farmer "living like a Bedouin," meaning a normal Palestinian.

Atef and the man who owns the place walk around with me to show me the property and, as we walk, I see the owner's wife sitting on the ground and fixing some pieces of clothes.

Just a little tour here is not enough for me. I want more. How do I get them, our host and Atef, to reveal themselves to me, to open up and share with me what they normally don't share with visitors like me? Well, this lady here can help me. I'll ask her intimate questions and get her, her husband and Atef as well, to treat me not just as another foreign journalist.

I ask the lady to tell me about her husband.

"He is very nice, very kind," she says.

Give me an example of his niceness and kindness.

"He is very good."

Give me an example of the good things he does to you.

She can't come up with any good things, except to mumble something about the Haj in Mecca.

Has he kissed you today? Has he given you, let's say, an ice cream?

Atef grabs me away. This is not what he wants me to see or ask.

We sit down with the man of the house. And I have a very important question to ask him: Have you kissed your wife today?

"I forget what I did."

When is the last time you kissed her?

Atef says I can't ask this question because, "There are kids here!"

I ignore Atef and ask our host again: When is the last time you kissed your wife?

He doesn't know what to say; he forgot the last kiss altogether. Atef comes to his help, telling the man: "You will not answer this."

In minutes' time, after more people from the area have assembled around us, the man declares me a Jew. Yep, just like that.

I tell him: You have to be careful; you don't say such a thing to a German!

And then I drop the big question to my host: Why do you think that I am Jewish?

Atef explains to me the obvious: "You want to know every detail. You try to create problems between the couple."

I protest. I tried to improve their marital relationship, I say.

Atef: "You tried to encourage the wife against him."

The host's daughter comes by. She tells me that she would like to study law abroad. I tell her that I wouldn't mind to make her dream come true, but that we must get married first.

Sadly, the marriage proposal of this non-Muslim is not accepted.

Maybe I have to come back later with a little Mercedes as my humble dowry.

But before I can plot my way to a shiny new Mercedes, my host drops a bomb. I, Tobi the German, "pay money to the Jews!" he accuses me, his future son-in-law.

When did I pay money to any Jew? Well, not me personally but my people, the Germans. And as this assembly views it, this is very wrong. I love to learn new things and this is what I learn today: We, Germans, allow the Jews to claim that we, Germans, killed them in Europe and that we even paid them compensations for something that has never happened.

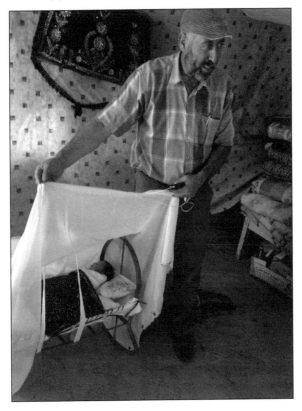

Do these people believe that the Jews were not killed in wwii? Atef, the man of B'Tselem, supplies the clearest answer: "This is a lie. I don't believe it." In short: the Holocaust is an invention of the Jews.

When we drive back to Jenin, Atef tells me that on occasion he works with Gideon Levy of *Haaretz*. He has been taking him around for about five times, serving as Gideon's guide and translator.

Good to discover Gideon Levy's guide and translator, good ole Atef, who is one of the leading B'Tselem's field researchers. And it's good to finally find out that the Holocaust has never really happened. Yep. There are just racist Jews all over, and B'Tselem will catch them all.

What transpires today is not so much about Arabs as it is about Jews and Europeans. *Haaretz* and B'Tselem are made of Jews who dedicate their lives to help those who hate them. As for the Europeans: Their diplomats behave in a manner that is the opposite of anything that diplomacy should be doing, with their journalists composing articles that are the opposite of what journalism should actually be doing. And to add insult to injury the Europeans generously fund Jews who don't like Jews.

*　*　*

I have Atef drop me off in central Jenin and I go to see a movie at Cinema Jenin. Today, I'm told by the man at the ticket office, they play a 3D movie that is very popular with the Jenin audiences. I pay for my ticket and I get those 3D goggles. Here in Cinema Jenin, they have the nicest 3D goggles I have ever seen. New York cinemas should learn from Cinema Jenin a little lesson. Well, the truth is: Cinema Jenin is generously funded by good-hearted people while New York cinemas are not.

I walk in.

Three people are inside. I am one of them. And this is a movie, lest we forget, that's "very popular with the Jenin audiences." At an earlier point Atef told me that usually about ten people attend shows here. He got the number wrong.

When I see how the Germans have thrown away their money on this cinema, I suddenly start believing the Palestinian narrative of Atef, and if I were a Palestinian living in Jenin I'd probably think the same. I would look at this "Cinema Jenin," an institution that the Germans have poured millions into, but in reality is a place where occasionally two people walk in, and ask myself why did they do it. The only logical explanation is this: Germans have nothing better to do with their money except to throw it on a deserted building that they call "Cinema." Why would they do such a thing? I have no clue. These are the Germans, they like to pour money on things that don't exist; they make up a story and then write the checks.

It is for this exact reason that they spend millions and billions on the "Holocaust" story. The Germans, for whatever reason, look for any excuse to download their money on people: A Cinema here, a Holocaust there. There was a Holocaust like there is a Cinema. Two people in each, and the Germans pay.

So simple.

The next day, B'Tselem issues the following statement: "The residents of Khallet Makhul petitioned the Israeli High Court of Justice, represented by their lawyer, Adv. Tawfiq Jabareen, requesting an interim injunction which will prevent their removal from the area. On the same day the High court issued the requested injunction, prohibiting the Civil Administration and the army from expelling the residents from their village and demolishing rebuilt homes."

I notice that B'Tselem has changed "Khirbet Makhul" to "Khallet Makhul." And this is really smart. "Khirbet" means ruins, or a "hole," which suggests a location that very few people, perhaps a man and his goat, live in. Not good for the cause. And so they came up with Khallet Makhul, which means Hill of Makhul. Brilliant.

How far a Jew will go – and how far European diplomats will go – to find fault with Jews is really remarkable.

Gate Thirty-Five

Peace and rape.

I'M BACK IN JERUSALEM WITH MY CATS. I FEED THEM MILK AND I GO FOR A walk.

I meet a very nice couple, both widely known, highly educated, highly intellectual, exemplary self-haters, optimal Arab lovers, and they touch me deeply. They are Israeli Jews and I won't identify them, what they do, or in what part of the town they reside.

They tell me three interesting stories. (1) They live in a beautiful home, which was renovated for them by an Arab contractor whom they knew and blindly trusted. When the contractor was about done with his work, for which he was handsomely paid, he presented them with a wonderful gift, for which he did not want to get paid: a big olive tree that he planted in their garden. They were very touched by his gesture and thanked him profusely. He listened to their thanks, looked them straight in the eye and said: "You don't have to thank me. I didn't do it for you, I did it for myself and my family." They did not understand what he was saying, and he explained: "Soon you will move out of this house." How so? "Because soon this land will be free of Jews." They were devastated. How could he say such a thing to them? (2) Years ago, many years ago, the lady was gang-raped by a bunch of Arab youth. (3) Years later, their granddaughter was sexually abused by an old Arab friend.

These three stories are the total sum of their personal experience with Palestinians, yet they won't allow themselves to be affected by any of these incidents.

The man explains to me: "I believe in humanism, I believe that the Palestinians are good people and that they want to live with us in peace. I believe that we have done them wrong and I believe that they have not done us wrong. It doesn't matter to me if what I believe in is factually right. I know it's not, but I don't care about facts! I want to believe, even if everything I believe in is false. Please don't make me see reality. I have fought it all my life. Please!"

At least he is honest.

His wife looks at me, but keeps quiet. I ask her what she feels, not her political views, but she just looks at me. Gently I push her to please share, and she gives me an intense look, yet keeps quiet. I ask her again to share her feelings; she moves her face away and up, looking for some magical intervention from somewhere above to help her. Finally, she opens up. She and her husband are fools, she tells me. She has come to this realization some time ago, but her husband cannot do the same. His worldview, the essence of his life, would collapse – and with it everything he has fought for in his life – if he allowed himself to see reality.

Before we separate, the husband tells me that I should read Gideon Levy's articles, so that I can see how unfair the Jews are to the Arabs. I tell him that Gideon's facts are questionable and that I can prove it to him. He tells me to please shut up. Reading Gideon's articles makes him feel good and he doesn't want me to disturb this strange happiness. Period.

As I walk away from this couple I think of the two peoples, the leftist Jew and the believing Muslim, both of whom you have to meet in person in order to recognize their unique characteristics. The leftist Jew, and forget now politics, is the most narcissistic of people that I've ever met. There's not a single moment, day or night, that he's not fully busy with himself or with other Jews. There's nothing on his agenda except his obsession to find fault with himself and his tribe. He just can't stop. No wonder Palestinians such as Professor Asma of Al-Quds University don't trust him, even though he is their intellectual mate and he spends his life defending them.

And then there's this religious Muslim who will fight to the death to preserve his al-Buraq Wall invention, a person who is extremely touchy about Muhammad and always feels the need to protect his prophet, as though Muhammad were made of thin glass. If you make a joke about Muhammad, you touch the most sensitive part in this believer's body, yes, and you had better run as fast as you can before he hurts you physically. Eye for an eye; your tooth for the Prophet's tooth. Strange.

The Sabbath is coming, Jerusalem is to close for business, and I take a bus out.

* * *

Rothschild Blvd., Tel Aviv. It is Friday night and the young secular people of Tel Aviv are out on the boulevard to show all passersby their young flesh. Rothschild Blvd. is the official name of this street but its real name is Legs, Ass, Breasts, and Muscles Galore Blvd. Here you have ice cream shops that sell yogurt with no sugar for three times the price of normal yogurt with sugar. Here you find bars that have more people in each of them than exist in the whole of China. Here the young, sipping imported water, discuss issues in lively Hebrew that no translator could ever properly repeat.

"Look, my brother," a young guy tells me, "you have to understand something here: 90 percent, you hear me, my brother, 90 percent of the Palestinians want peace. This is a fact, my brother."

How do you know this?

"Trust me, my brother, I know!"

But how do you know?

"I see, my brother! With my eyes, my brother! Bear with me, my brother, one minute. Do you know Palestinian literature, my brother?"

Here and there.

"I know it, my brother, and it is my favorite literature, my brother! It is a literature that preaches for peace. That's why I love it, my brother."

Do you read Arabic?

"Me? No, my brother."

Do you speak Arabic?

"No, my brother. Where are you from, my brother?"

Germany.

"Beautiful country. The best."

Have you been there?

"Not yet."

Quite a number of Israelis speak the "my brother" lingo. I try to avoid them as much as I can.

I sit down to sip something and read Gideon Levy's latest article, about his visit to Khirbet al-Makhul. He describes the place as if it were a death camp: A lonely starving kitten, the last to survive of all the cats. Emaciated, injured, thirsty, and hungry dogs living on pita crumbs that they get once every two or three days.

Gideon then goes on to describe the people, the saddest picture of misery you would be likely to encounter in any literature, and all I can think of is: at exactly what point in history were journalists given the permission to file thousand-word articles without a single word of truth?

Gate Thirty-Six

"We are very lucky that Hitler did not recruit German Jews to the SS." – Yehudah, a Polish Jew who survived Auschwitz

IT IS TIME THAT I, OBSERVER OF WEAK PEOPLE, FACE MY OWN WEAK SPOTS. I have been in Israel for a few months already and yet I have not set foot into the city of my childhood. It is time I do.

Bnei Brak, the most Haredi of cities in Israel, is a minutes-ride from Tel Aviv but worlds apart.

"No entry into Bnei Brak on Sabbath and Jewish Holidays," reads the official street sign at the entrance of my former hometown.

Uri, a cabbie from Lod having worked in Bnei Brak for two decades, shares with me his views of the town:

"Twenty years, and I had no problem with them. No drunks here. There are strange situations. When a couple comes together and they sit in the back. She asks for a phone but he doesn't give it to her directly, only puts it on the empty space between their seats and she picks it up from there. At certain periods they are not allowed to touch each other." He means when the woman is menstruating. "I think they shouldn't behave like this in front of strangers; that's the only criticism I have."

How's Lod?

"Lod is a mixed Arab-Jewish town."

How do you get along there?

"For twenty years I have spent the day time in Bnei Brak. That's my answer."

I get off two blocks from my childhood home. I expect to see the orange grove, the one that as a kid I would pass by every day. But there are no trees here anymore, no orange grove and no oranges. The only thing growing here now are big buildings and many people, all of them Haredi.

On another street corner, there used to be a newsstand; but no more. Papers are forbidden, and the newsstand is now a store selling wigs for married Haredi women.

I walk over to the house where I grew up.

Across the street from my house I see people standing in a line that hardly moves, at the entrance to my old neighbor's house, Haim Kanyevski's. I remember him, a man of no special attributes and little wisdom. Why are people standing in a line to see him?

"To get his blessing," tells me a woman watching what I watch.

She would like to get his blessing too, but Haim blesses only men.

With the years, it seems, Haim has gained admirers, people who are sure that if he prays for them they will be cured of their diseases, and that if he looks at them they will gain wisdom.

In the old days such an act would be considered idol worship, but not today. With the years, it seems, God has changed The Plan.

It is sad for me to witness how my childhood Judaism, a Judaism that worshipped scholarship, has now turned into a worship of a frail man. I watch in disbelief, regretting that I came here, and step back fast. The people here have changed, I have changed, and God seems to have changed too.

Next to my house a German Jew used to live, and he had chickens in the front yard. No chickens are there anymore, and he is gone too.

I take a taxi to Ramat Gan, the neighboring town, to see how other people view their childhood.

*   *   *

I enter a nursing home for the aged, mostly from Germany; a Yekkes' Old Home.

I meet Gertrud. Gertrud is of the family that owned the famed Kaufhaus Schocken in pre-War Germany. Her comfortable life ended when the Nazis came to power and the family started moving from one place to the other, ever running away from Hitler's messengers. She was born in Regensburg, then at the age of three her family moved to Nuremberg. In 1933 they moved to Hamburg, and then to another city yet again inside Germany and later to Amsterdam. In 1937 her family moved to what is now Israel. Her relative, Amos Schocken, is the owner of *Haaretz*.

Do you get a free subscription?

"No."

During WWII she was ordered into the British Army. The Brits promised her that she would stay in The Land [Israel] and put her and others on a train. "We drove and drove and drove until we woke up in the morning and we found ourselves in a desert. We were in Egypt. I looked around and I saw the desert, I saw tents, and I saw a cemetery. Among others, we buried there a friend, originally from Lübeck. She was alone in the world, no one of her family with her. She got a virus in her throat and they operated on her, but something went wrong and she died."

What did you do in Egypt?

"Hard work. I had to take parts of trucks apart, clean them in oil, then reconnect them. I became a sergeant."

Tell me: Did you know during those years what was happening in Europe?

"Don't you know? We got letters from Auschwitz, not written but printed. 'We are well, but we won't be able to write again.'"

When did you, Gertrud, first learn of the gas chambers?

"Hard for me to say. Hard for me to say."

Are you proud of being German, of your German culture?

"I hardly read Hebrew. I read only in German and in English."

So, you are proud of it?

"Proud? Listen: This is a culture!"

Gertrud has children, grandchildren, and great grandchildren. They are doctors, lawyers, musicians, and some other highly respected professionals.

"I never again went to Hamburg. In fact, I never again visited any of the cities in Germany that I stayed in." Some survivors, she tells me, go to visit the houses that belonged to their families before the war, but "I'll never do it."

Why not?

"What, to shame the people for what their parents did?"

What a *Yekke potz*.

Another lady, Riva, comes to talk with me.

Riva left Germany in 1938 with her physician father. When they came here, the Brits wouldn't let her father work as a doctor and so he opened a café. "It was called 'Doctor's Café.'"

Like Gertrud, she served in the British army in Egypt. Did she know the full extent of what was happening to Jews in Germany? No, she says.

What do you think of today's Germany?

"Merkel keeps them with a strong hand, but there are some Nazis who are still operating. Right?"

Not all in this nursing home are German. Yehudah, born in Krakow, is an example.

In 1942, as part of the underground movement in Poland, he threw Molotov cocktails at German soldiers in a café, then engaged in armed robbery, was caught and ended up in Auschwitz in the year 1943.

Primo Levi's book *Survival in Auschwitz*, he says, "is exact. Nobody else told the story as exactly as he did."

Did Yehudah know what was happening?

"In 1943 we knew that they were exterminating the Jews," though he didn't know how it was done.

When did you get out of Auschwitz?

"I escaped at the start of the death march, on 20 January 1945."

After Germany's defeat, and before leaving Europe for good, he took his revenge. "We made an operation inside a POW camp, where SS officers were held," he tells me, still enjoying the moment. Quentin Tarantino's *Inglourious Basterds* is fiction, but Yehudah is real.

Yehudah doesn't mince words when he talks about the Yekkes at this nursing home.

"We are very lucky that Hitler did not recruit German Jews to the SS," says this Polish Jew, meaning every word and syllable he pronounces.

At long last somebody's making me laugh.

I meet Amos Schocken later on, to ask him why he doesn't offer Gertrud a free subscription to his paper, *Haaretz*. I cannot believe his response: he doesn't even know that this woman is alive.

I am not Amos, and I like to know people and what they are about. I know, for example, Toby, my American lady who can't cook, and I know about her son, the man dedicated to an NGO called Adalah. It is time that this Master Agent finds out what Adalah is doing these days.

Gate Thirty-Seven

Alone among Bedouins: What will happen to you
if you walk into a Bedouin home and fondle the
most attractive hijab-covered lady you see?

ON THE TWO BUS SEATS NEXT TO MINE ARE MICHÈLE AND ALESSANDRA, OF France and Italy. They are going to the Negev on a fact-finding mission about Israel. They want to know how Israel treats its Bedouins and they are determined to find the truth.

They represent two NGOs in their respective countries, and they work with another NGO, EAPPI, the Ecumenical Accompaniment Programme in Palestine and Israel I have encountered before.

For the last two days Michèle has spent her time in Tel Aviv, working with Zokhrot (Women Remember), an Israeli NGO dedicated to bringing into Israel millions of Arabs worldwide who claim Palestine as their homeland and to remembering the "looting, massacres and incidents of rape of the Palestinian inhabitants" that the Jews have been afflicting on the Palestinians. What did Michèle do with the Zokhrot women? Well, great stuff: working to rename Tel Aviv streets according to their "original Palestinian names."

I guess Michèle doesn't like the fact that Jews live in Tel Aviv, a city founded by Jews.

Why are you interested in Israel?

"I don't want people speaking in my name," she says, and explains that she is Jewish and she is fed up with other Jews and Jewish organizations spreading lies all over the planet.

"The Israeli government is paying money to extreme-right Jewish organizations in France to manipulate the truth. They say that there's anti-Semitism in France but it's a total lie. There is anti-Islamism in France, not anti-Semitism."

Why is the Israeli government paying money to French organizations to say that France is anti-Semitic?

Michèle looks at me in total disbelief. She has never, ever met an idiot like me. Why don't I understand something so basic? Well, I don't. Could she please be patient with me and explain? Well, okay: Israel wants to make sure no one is criticizing it and that's why it accuses people ahead of any accusations from them and calls them racist before the others have a chance to charge Israel for its racism.

A bit complex, but brilliant!

These two ladies, as luck would have it, are going to Adalah's office in the city of Be'er Sheva, the queen city of the Negev region of Israel, which is where I'm heading, too. The office of Adalah is, of course, also good place for doing objective research on the Bedouin situation in Israel.

As I arrive in Be'er Sheva I see many women dressed in niqabs and burkas walking past me, and I ask myself if I'm not perchance walking backwards in time and am again in Istanbul Airport. But then I look at Michèle, the renamer of Tel Aviv streets, and I know I must be in a Jewish state. I proceed to Adalah's office, and so do the two European female research fellows.

Once we are there, Dr. Thabet Abu Rass, in charge of the office, speaks to us: "We are representing the rights of the Palestinian people. I have some papers to hand to you about the discrimination of Palestinians and the violations of their rights." He points to a map in his office. In Arabic it says the following: "Map of Palestine before *Nakbah* in 1948." (*Nakbah* means catastrophe, meaning the founding of Israel.)

When Dr. Thabet talks about Palestinians, he's not talking about the West Bank. What he's talking about are the Arabs who live in Israel proper and who are its citizens. And Adalah, Toby's son's favorite pro-Palestinian NGO, is deeply into these Bedouins.

I try to evaluate what I see and hear during Dr. Thabet's speech: Adalah, which, as I found out a while ago, would like to see Jews losing their homes, is working hard to make sure that Arabs keep theirs intact.

Dr. Thabet keeps plodding. The Negev, he says, "is 60 percent of the total geographic area of Israel." Dr. Thabet likes to talk about percentages: 95 percent of the Negev, and 93.5 percent of the land all over Israel, is "defined as state land. There's no country in the world which owns so much land, excluding North Korea."

Michèle jumps to protect North Korea. North Korea is not a racist state that excludes people due to racist ideology, but Israel is "discriminating on the basis of race, excluding Arabs from owning lands."

Fine.

"Israel moves in the direction of Judaization of Israel," says Dr. Thabet, and asserts that Israel "confiscates all the rights of the Bedouins."

Joining Dr. Thabet is Halil, who works in this office as well, and both accuse Israel of everything bad under the sun. Michèle, the researcher, doesn't ask questions but is constantly nodding in approval and frequently mumbling "Exactly!" and "Of course!" every time someone says something horrible about Israel.

"What Israel is doing is a creeping apartheid," Dr Thabet raises his voice in our ears. And Michèle says: "Of course."

Research.

I ask Dr. Thabet how many Bedouins are there altogether. "Two hundred seventy thousand," he answers, "of whom 210,000 live here and 60,000 in the Galilee." This afternoon, he tells us, he will take us to see some of them. But first, Halil will take us to a village, to see Bedouin life firsthand.

Introductory speech done, Halil takes us to his home. He drives a Mercedes.

We talk while he drives.

Halil says that Bedouins are not nomads, unlike the "myth propagated by the Israeli government and media." Bedouins, he says, were nomads "four hundred or five hundred years ago."

* * *

We reach his village. At the entrance there's a sign denoting the name of the area in green and white, a sign similar in shape and image to official road signs elsewhere in Israel. The sign reads: "Alsra" (the name of the village), and "Founded: Ottoman Era."

Underneath this sign is another sign, an image of a bulldozer, which means: this is a demolish-able area. Why so? Because the Jews are planning to demolish it. They actually "demolish a thousand Bedouin homes every year," Halil says to me.

I make a fast calculation: Israel is about sixty-five years old, which means that according to this statement, Israeli authorities have by now demolished sixty-five thousand Bedouin homes. I ask Halil if this is indeed the case and he says: Yes, that's true. I ask him how many Bedouins are there altogether, as sixty-five thousand homes, with Allah knows how many children per family, would add up to more Bedouins being evicted from their homes than actually exist.

Halil doesn't lose time and promptly corrects his figures: the figure of one thousand units is this year, but it didn't start like that. Every year the Israelis are demolishing more and more and more.

Figures, naturally, change with a stroke of the tongue.

This does not proceed well with our researcher, Michèle, and she's getting upset with me. I am of the "other side," she accuses me, and am just playing naïve by asking the questions I do.

At the entrance to Halil's home there is a sign on a sheet of paper: "Welcome in Alsira [sic]." His home is made of cement, looking like the average ugly shack you see in various TV reports featuring Bedouin lifestyle. Glued to the door of his house there is a paper he received from the Israeli authorities, "warning" him, he says, of their intention to demolish his house.

There's the figure 67 at the top of this warning, and Halil says that in the eyes of the Israelis the Bedouins are just figures, like in those "other places," Auschwitz, for example, where people were also no more than numbers.

The man drives a Mercedes and thinks he is in Auschwitz.

I look at the date of this warning notice: 2006.

The house is still standing.

The Jews obviously keep forgetting to visit Auschwitz.

What is the real name of this village, "Alsira," as he has at the entrance to his house, or "Alsra"? I ask Halil.

"Alsira," he says. The name in green and white, that official-looking sign at the entrance to his village, is actually wrong.

Well, those Ottomans!

By itself, the missing *i* is negligible, but it raises a red flag in my mind because it might indicate that this "Ottoman era" village is an invention, a "fast job" done by the people here. I might be wrong, but I decide to probe deeper into the Bedouin story.

* * *

We're sitting in the front yard of Halil's shack, and I ask him if he would mind me going inside. I'd like to see how a Mercedes-driving Auschwitz-prisoner lives, though I don't put it to him in these words. He says, sorry, I can't go in, because his wife is sleeping inside. These are not normal sleeping hours, but what can I say? He thinks he's done with me, but this Master Agent asks if I could see the inside of some other Bedouin homes, since it would be so enriching to see how the Bedouins live, but Halil says this is impossible at the moment because all the Bedouins are now at their jobs. No Bedouin is unemployed, and Halil's wife is asleep. Sounds very reasonable, but this Master Agent doesn't buy it. I know that I'll have to come up with a scheme to get my body into one or two shacks before the day is over.

Meantime, we go on talking. Halil has just finished studying law at an Israeli university, at one of the best law schools in the country, as he says.

This afternoon, he shares with us, fifteen to twenty young people are going to come here to serve as witness to the horrible life of Halil and his friends. They have just come into this land from Germany, he explains to me.

As Tobi the German, I'm very proud of my fellow Germans who in 2013 have flown all the way down here to see a computer printout of a 2006 sign announcing a forthcoming eviction of a Bedouin from his shack.

And now, after we have seen Halil's house from the outside, we drive back to Adalah's office. During the ride Halil speaks of the horrible economic situations of the Bedouins, only to be interrupted by a phone call. He takes his phone, an iPhone, and he answers the call.

A Mercedes and an iPhone, coupled with a law degree from an Israeli university, are the truest trademarks of the poor. This is theater of the absurd, I think to myself, and we're only in scene 1. It will be interesting to see how the plot of this play develops.

We talk, Halil and I.

I ask him to explain to me his real problems in life. If he views himself as an Israeli, he can indeed, I say, complain against the state and make demands for equal rights or for equal wrongs. But if he views himself as a Palestinian, I ask him, how come he demands that the state view him as its citizen when he is not viewing himself as a citizen of this state?

"I'm Palestinian, because I have Palestinian roots," says Halil. "I'm a proud Palestinian."

You should be proud. Palestine is a beautiful state.

Halil objects to the term "Palestine" since, he says, there is no state by that name.

I perfectly understand Halil: If Palestine exists, then the struggle is over, the NGO money well will dry up, and his biggest cause in life will die. But I don't say this to him, as this would make him jump at me and our conversation would end right there. And so, I ask him another question instead: Why is it that Palestinian government buildings everywhere have "State of Palestine" signs on their entrance doors? Are the Palestinians lying and cheating?

Halil doesn't like this. Obviously, he has not been to Palestine in ages.

Halil is not the only one objecting to my using the term "State of Palestine." The Peace and Love ladies in the back of the car object to the term as well. There's no Palestine, they assert, because Palestine has been occupied. And, as probably I should have seen it coming, Michèle is not going to let go, yapping and kvetching like an old Jewish lady from the Bronx. Slowly but surely, she starts getting on this Master Agent's nerves. And guess what? I tell her so.

* * *

You cannot – repeat: cannot – criticize Peace Lovers. They have a monopoly on compassion and truth, and they staunchly demand their basic human right to state their opinion without anybody uttering another word once they have spoken.

I don't like to accept orders and I insist on putting salt into what seems to be Michèle's really sensitive wound: her research methods, I tell her, are ridiculous.

Michèle, the educated and mannered French European, screams at me: "If you identify with the Shabak, this is your problem! I'm not a Palestinian and I won't lower my head for you!" Shabak is Israel's internal security service, also known as Shin Bet.

Who told you that I identify with the Shabak?

"You behave like Shabak. You interrogate like them. You are such an ugly man that I can't hold myself any longer. Me and my friend are Europeans and we won't tolerate your colonialist rule!"

You called me an ugly man...?

"Very ugly! You are a very ugly man. You are a terrible man."

I understand: no French lady can tolerate colonialism. The French, as history will testify, never, ever engaged in colonialism. No European nation ever did, to be more true to history.

Michèle can't stop. "You are a dominant colonialist person," she goes on. She also calls me a "disturbed" man.

European NGO activists are also great linguists. "You called me 'imbearable,'" she shouts at me. I ask her what "imbearable" means, since I don't even know this word, much less use it myself.

"I want you to be as far away from me as possible," she offers in response. "You are so ugly! You, Shabak!"

I think you've crossed all lines of proper human behavior–

"Then put me in jail, together with your friends!"

Halil doesn't know how to react to this comedy show in his car. He drives on, but soon enough loses control of the car and bumps head on into a car ahead of us.

That's all we needed here: a car accident.

The two cars stop, and the drivers examine the damage. Luckily, the impact was not too hard and the two sides decide to let go. We drive on.

Back in the office of Adalah I see something like a dart board on the wall, only what I see is not a dart board. I ask Halil what it is and he explains to me that this is a graph of the number of Bedouins and where they are from.

Total number is 800,000. "These are the figures for 2006," he explains, but today there's about a million Bedouins around.

We started with 270,000 and now we are at a million. This Bedouin issue starts looking to me like a copycat version of the Palestinian issue.

I notice that the name of the country these people come from is "Palestine." But since this is written in Arabic, it is assumed here that no outsider would get it. In short: they claim to be Israelis, demand equal treatment with every Israeli, but actually call this land Palestine, and themselves Palestinians.

It is time to go for a ride with Dr. Thabet, the man in charge of Adalah's office.

* * *

We are in Dr. Thabet's car, the European "researchers" and I, and we talk.

I ask Dr. Thabet: How many Bedouins are there? You told me earlier the figure was 270,000, but in your office I saw 800,000. Which figure is right?

"Two hundred seventy thousand. The 800,000 figure is the number of dunams (80,000 hectares)."

But Halil said the figure of 800,000 is that of the Bedouins in 2006 and that today we are talking about a million –

Dr. Thabet now goes in circles. He has something more important to tell me, about how "real democracy" works in Israel, meaning that there is none, at least when it comes to the Bedouins.

To prove his claim he points to an encampment, unrecognized by Israel, ahead of us that has no sign on the road pointing to it. Why a government would be forced to erect a sign to an encampment it does not recognize could make for an interesting PhD thesis for the lovely Dr. Eternity.

Dr. Thabet now takes us to a Bedouin village. We are seated at a simple table with plastic chairs in someone's backyard, are given water in plastic cups, and Dr. Thabet talks. The European researchers write down every word he says, how bad the Israelis are, how they discriminate against the Bedouins, and what miserable lives the Bedouins live.

The Europeans love these words. They vociferously note that the whole world knows about the plight of the Palestinians and is doing everything to make sure that the Israelis – meaning the Jews – don't kill them. It's time to repeat what has already been achieved with the Palestinians and start protecting the Bedouins from the Israeli claws as well.

Dr. Thabet likes the enlightening comment very much but remarks that the Bedouins do not stand a chance of succeeding. After all, there's a "creeping apartheid" going on here, he says, repeating a term he has already used before.

I ask Dr. Thabet to tell me where he lives.

Well, he lives in Beer Sheva, with the Jews.

Is this what you call apartheid?

He screams at me. "You, Jews!" he yells. Me? A Jew? This is totally unacceptable. But I let it go for the moment, as I want to know if my new friend is only busy with Adalah or whether there are other things he does with his time. What do you do for a living, Dr. Thabet? I ask him.

Well, this poor soul, please don't cry, is a professor at Ben-Gurion University.

How can you complain that the "Bedouins stand no chance of succeeding" when you are doing so well?

The Europeans keep their mouths shut, but their eyes spew hatred.

Dr. Thabet understands that his good life is not good for his cause, and so he moves on to the best defense known to man: attack. What

kind of a journalist am I? he wants to know. He has never met journalists like me. Why do I ask questions?

I patiently ask His Professorship to explain to me what is his problem with a journalist asking questions. He is smart, my professor friend, and he knows that the best way he can get out of this is to find fault with me. What are my faults? Well, says the professor, you have shown no sign of wanting to really find out the truth about the Bedouins. I beg him to explain himself and he does. You have never, he charges me, asked questions such as: How do the Bedouins live?

That's the height of chutzpah, and I say it to him. I asked his associate, Halil, to take me to visit Bedouins at their homes, but Halil wouldn't cooperate. Instead of visiting Bedouins at their homes I have been treated here to speeches. Do you really think, Dr. Thabet – and I raise my voice – that I came all the way here to listen to you and Halil? Couldn't I just have called you for that? Why the heck do you think I came all the way here? To see the life of the Bedouins, but you wouldn't let me! Instead, I have to sit here, like a stupid student of yours, and listen to you talking.

Do you really want to know the truth? I don't care what you say, zilch. I'm no human rights activist who came here to "find out" what he already believes is fact. I don't want your speeches, I don't want Halil's speeches. I want to be with the Bedouins, to visit them in their homes, sit at their tables, drink and eat with them – I don't mind paying for the food – and see everything for myself. Get it?

Master Agent has spoken.

As fast as his professorship allows it, Dr. Thabet realizes that the time for propaganda is over. The ball is in his court and if he doesn't act quickly he is going to turn into a laughingstock. He promptly tells a young activist by the name of Amir, a quiet guy who studied in Germany and is now back home, to take me around.

Dr. Thabet and the European researchers, the yapping Bronx Jewess with her Italian sidekick, exit; I stay with Amir.

I feel like being in Paradise. Finally.

*   *   *

I am at a Bedouin settlement by the name of Abu Kweider, which is made of a number of shacks in an indefinable order, but Amir helps me through the maze.

We walk toward a shack in front of us. Welcome to the shack of Hanan, an attractive Bedouin lady standing in front of the ugliest structure you can imagine to be called a home: a shack that is the mother of all shacks.

I am invited in. No more sitting on plastic chairs outside, like I experienced earlier today and with Atef of B'Tselem a few days back. Nope. I am invited in. I hope I won't vomit when I see the inside.

As I enter, I forget all proper German manners and I let out a huge "Wow!"

Wow. What a beautiful home, what a gorgeous house. How wonderfully decorated. How warm. How richly done. I wish it to be mine. Now.

Yeah. Now I know why Adalah people, and those of other NGOs, don't want me inside these houses, these shacks.

Hanan is not an activist, she is just human. She is religious, with hijab and all, the kind of human you would be told by any NGO personnel to respect and not to touch, God forbid, if you happen to be a man.

But I'm not an average man. I'm a Master Agent.

I put my hands around Hanan, caress her lovingly, and tell her that she is gorgeous, that her house is beautiful, and that I would love to have a photo of both of us together.

No journalist, certainly no white Peace and Love man, has ever done this with her and to her. It's the first time for her to feel the touch of a white man who shows her this basic human gesture of affection: a touch.

She asks me, laughingly, if I know what will happen when her husband comes in and sees us together like this. We laugh about it. And we connect.

No lecturer or activist, of any kind or sort, can make you feel one tenth of what I now feel by touching her, being with her, looking at her as a human being and not as an observer and defender of a political cause.

It is on this occasion that I grasp one basic reality: activists, on the Left or on the Right, by their very nature don't relate to people as humans.

I feel at home. Hanan asks me if I'd like some water, and I ask her if she has lost her mind. What water? Do I look to her like a white man, like all those cold idiots that she has seen before? She gets it. "Tea or coffee?" she asks. Coffee to drink, I tell her, and some food too, please. Have you got any food?

Lucky for Michèle that she isn't here; had she been here, she would have had a stroke.

I like Hanan. She possesses warmth that you'll be hard-pressed to find in modern Europe, warmth that you will find in New York only in tanning salons.

Hanan feeds me. What labneh, what olive oil, what bread, what coffee. This is a Seven-Star Shack Hotel.

I ask Amir, as my belly is about to explode from all the food in it, to take me to another shack.

* * *

Welcome to Najakh's shack: excessively ugly exterior, bewitchingly gorgeous inside.

Plain unbelievable.

As Najakh goes to bring tea and cake, after my belly has miraculously emptied and whispered in my ears that it has arranged room to accommodate sweets, Amir talks a bit about himself. He is one of thirty siblings, he shares with me. His father, you see, has three wives, and each gave him kids aplenty.

The tea and cake arrive safely. I ask Najakh how many wives her husband has.

Well, only two. Najakh is wife #1, and ten years after their marriage her husband married a second wife.

How did you feel when it happened?

"Very bad."

What did you say to him?

"Nothing."

Why not?

"I don't know. There was nothing to say. Honestly."

Did you cry? Did you scream?

"Of course I cried. I screamed. I was upset, I was sad. Everything."

And he saw it all and didn't care?

"Of course he cared. But in our culture, whatever the man feels like doing he does, even if he is going to get hurt from it. This is what he wanted and that's it."

How do you live with the second wife?

"She's in her home and I'm in mine."

You don't live in the same house?

"No. Of course not!"

And where does your husband live?

"One day here, one day there. One day honey, one day onion."

Does it still hurt you? Do you still feel the pain?

"Every day."

Do you talk to with the second wife?

"No."

How old is she?

"She is three years older than me."

Your husband likes older ladies?

Najakh laughs: "I married too, too young…"

Tell me, don't you want to just run away from it all?

"God forbid! I have children!"

Let me ask you another question: Did you at the time try talking with your father, asking him to intervene against your husband's second marriage?

"My father did this stupid thing!"

What do you mean? Did your father marry him off to the other woman?

"No, no."

She explains what she means: "My father also married two women. How could he tell him not to do the same?"

Did your husband talk to you about this before he got married?

"That he wanted to marry another one?"

Yes.

"Definitely. He didn't do it like: boom, here is another woman!"

How did he explain it to you?

"Just like that. For no special reason. He just wanted to marry. That was all."

Her own brother, she goes on to say, cooked the food for her husband's second wedding party.

She laughs as she says this, as if this was at all funny.

Do you have anybody here you can talk to about this, about what you feel?

"Hanan. She is my sister-in-law."

If Allah showed himself to you in the middle of the night and said: "Ask of me one thing and I'll grant it to you," what would it be?

"That my husband be healthy and good."

Wouldn't you ask Him to take that second wife and throw her into Satan's hands?

"No. I don't even think in these terms. She has a child now, what can I do?"

She says that "this is my fate," and that her husband "suffers now" because of what he did.

He suffers? From what?!

"He has two wives. It's not easy. I don't give up, she doesn't give up. He is living with a dilemma."

I assume that "giving up" means sex. I ask: Does he sleep in different beds every night, one night with you and the other night with her?

"Yes. He has got used to it already." She laughs again. "Three years like this. It's not simple."

She is sad. Her voice lowers. Her laughter is actually tears.

I'm probably the only stranger she has ever spoken to so freely about this.

Najakh's husband has built another house next door, a house that sticks in her eyes every waking moment, but Najakh never enters that house.

Amir and I exchange looks. It has never occurred to him, the human rights activist, that the women here lack basic human rights. Obviously it hasn't occurred to Adalah, neither has it occurred to the other NGOs working here or the various European diplomats working here as well. A note to Her Excellency Marion Fesneau-Castaing: Najakh's husband wouldn't mind having a third wife; I would gladly volunteer to take care of the wedding party.

* * *

My next stop is Lakia, a Bedouin town of eleven thousand residents that was built by Israel. No Jew is allowed to live there, says Ari of the pro-Israel NGO Regavim. There are fifty-three pro-Bedouin NGOs, says Ari, and there's Regavim. One against fifty-three.

Moving from Adalah to Regavim takes one phone call, but the distance between them is infinity. I hook up with Ari and with Amichai, a research fellow for Regavim, for a tour of Bedouinland as they know it. Amichai, like Ofir of Ashkelon, is formerly from Gaza and he, too, was evicted from his home in Gaza, demolished by the Israeli army.

Before the entrance to Lakia there is a water reservoir and we stop there. On the side of it I see a pile, one that looks like remnants of an older reservoir with graffiti on it, including a swastika.

Amichai explains to me that the old reservoir, made of thinner materials, used to be repeatedly damaged by Bedouin youngsters, who would poke holes into it over and over again.

Why would they damage their own source of water?

"They knew that the Israeli government would fix it back, since

Israel cannot afford to leave them without water. Now the government has built a new reservoir, made out of cement, and much thicker than the older one, and put a fence around it, plus security cameras."

He tells me more: two thousand new illegal structures are being built in Bedouinland every year, but Israel demolishes only about 10 percent of them because various NGOs take the government to court and it can take up to fifteen years for the courts to decide.

What is usually the result of these court cases?

"Those that finish the process, they usually end up in demolitions."

Why are the NGOs doing this, if they end up losing?

"Good PR against Israel."

Honestly, I start getting confused with the number games played here. Halil told me that Israel demolishes a thousand Bedouin units per year, and this guy now tells me that the Bedouins build two thousand illegal units per year. Both figures seem to me wildly exaggerated.

NGO people are more interesting to listen to when they don't mention figures.

Amichai, for example, tells me this: "Fifteen years ago if you called a Bedouin 'Arab,' he would hit you in the face. Today, with NGOs like Adalah working on their behalf, they see themselves as Arab and as Palestinian."

If my memory doesn't fail me, and speaking of the time I lived in Israel, I think he got this one totally right.

*　*　*

Regavim, being a lonely goat in the huge NGO farm, hardly has a chance of succeeding in its mission. There are simply too many NGOs working in the opposite direction. To make up for this discrepancy they spend more money than they would wish showing journalists what NGOs like Adalah would never show them.

Would you like, they ask Mr. Master Agent, to fly on a small plane? It's a plane of only one engine, and at times the flight is quite shaky, with turbulences here and there, but I can see what the birds see. If it's okay with the Master, Regavim would get the plane and foot the bill. Their idea is shockingly simple: If I agree to fly above the desert and see for myself what the Bedouins are doing down below, they wouldn't have to add another single word to convince me that they are right.

I'm a sucker for planes. To own a single engine, tiny plane that flies with the birds is one of my biggest dreams. I have never flown in such a beauty, didn't even know you could rent them, and I immediately accept.

They hope, they say, that I didn't eat beforehand, as my stomach might be jumping too much and react strangely. But, of course, I don't listen to them. I get myself something to eat – did I already mention the fantastic food in this land? – and a drink as well, and then I am ready to fly.

And fly I do. In a Piper Cherokee C.

What a sweetie! You would hardly get a pleasure like this, the immense greatness of flying in such a baby, almost anywhere else. You can fly First Class Plus on the most expensive airline there is, and you won't get one tenth of the pleasure I get by flying on this cutie. And sorry to say it, but this beats my Turkish Airlines hands down.

I fly on this Piper and in no time I transform from a fat man into a lovely bird. This is heaven!

Heaven is above, Bedouin is below: on this hill and on that, on this mountain and on that, in this valley and in that. Wherever I look I see the Bedouins. I don't count the numbers, but I get the picture: If Israel, or a real estate developer, would want to to build in the Negev their options would be limited. If they wanted to build on this mountain right below me, a huge mountain, they would have a problem: there are two Bedouins there who claim the whole mountain belongs to them. And if they try to build in this valley now under me as I fly, quite a big valley, they'd have the same problem. Every Bedouin wants a couple of wives and a couple of mountains. Try doing this in Stockholm or Washington, Paris or Berlin and you'd be taken to the nearest mental institution in an ambulance. And sorry, really sorry, but no NGO will get you out.

What I see down below is Bedouins all over, on huge swaths of lands. The Bedouins might have stopped wandering, but the mountains have not. Whenever a mountain sees a Bedouin, it invites him in. Don't believe me? Get your *zekel beiner* on a Piper.

It is on this lovely Piper that I make an oath: Once I land I will go to a tanning saloon, get darkish, put a keffiyeh over my head, catch me five brown ladies, and settle on the next available five virgin mountains. The Negev is huge, and there are quite enough mountains for me and my babes. Adalah will make sure I'm represented well, and European diplomats will build me my tents. A bright future is waiting for me once I'm on solid ground.

Back on mother earth, I check for Toby's telephone number. It is an urgent matter and I must talk to her son immediately: I need special funding for my tanning-salon sessions. Unfortunately, Ari and Amichai are waiting for me in their car next to my pretty Piper and they hijack me. We drive from one settlement to the other and then we get to al-Araqeeb, which I'm actually interested in. This is a settlement that Rabbi Arik, among many others of my future NGO funders, is working hard to support.

* * *

Al-Araqeeb is a village of twelve families that, according to a man named Aziz we meet while wandering around, has been demolished fifty-eight times. It was first demolished in 1948, and last in 2013. So Aziz. Ari, and Amichai listen, and I say nothing. Aziz continues to talk, giving us a short history of the place: all the residents here were employed, 573 of them, and the Israelis didn't like the fact that all of them were employed and so they destroyed the place.

Why would Israel want them unemployed?

"The Israelis want that all the Arabs be their slaves."

Not good news for me, a future five-ladies Bedouin.

Salim, another Bedouin, shows up and happily shares with me that foreigners come to visit them every day to offer help.

Aziz lives in a shack, which, he says, is actually a mosque, and others live in tents and corrugated structures by the cemetery. For a second there I ask myself if I'm in the Mount of Olives but no, I'm not. This place is geared to European NGOs, not to prayers by the grave of the Jew Menachem Begin. Salim asks me to join him a few feet away, at a "media center" inside a mobile home. A place kindly donated by the good souls of the NGO world. Here I see computers, a projector, printers, posters, and a variety of printed materials.

Most likely, this is the only press center in a cemetery.

A video is playing. In it we see a man in his beautiful house, walking in it room by room, followed by images of a woman passing by with a tray in her hands. Probably coffee, tea and sweets. Very cozy home. But minutes later we see a fire and many demonstrators who are trying to stop the coming demolition. We also see Israeli police cars, a helicopter, and then bulldozers. Houses are being destroyed. Foreign and local demonstrators are clashing with the police.

And then it's all gone. A village destroyed.

No human with a beating heart watching this clip can stay unmoved.

It is here that Aziz and Salim get me, and I move to their side. I totally identify with them.

Aziz raises his voice. He is angry. He says over and again that Israel, a racist entity, is out to destroy him because he's an Arab. I don't particularly like his broad accusation, but after having watched this clip I understand his pain.

Aziz recognizes that now I'm on his side and offers to show me to his home in the mosque. You can't tell that this is a mosque, but perhaps it used to be. And maybe it still is.

His wife is there, and he shows me to their bedroom. I like this Aziz and his culture. Can you imagine a New Yorker showing you to his bedroom on the first time you meet him? Nope. I love it!

Is this the place where you make love? I ask him. He laughs loudly. One time, he tells me, he did it very good.

How good? Did you make love ten times the same night, over and over again?

"We did it outside," he tells me. On the sand, by the hills and under the sky. It was wonderful!

Two horses are outside. Do you ride them? Yes, he does. He mounts a horse and he is happy, my Aziz. I'll die here, he tells me. "They [Israel] killed me fifty-eight times, but I'm still alive. I know one day I'll die, but I'll die with a smile."

He rides his horse, I walk by foot, and we meet by a well not far from either of us. Here he sings a song for me:

We shall not be moved. No, no, no.
No, no. We shall not be moved.
You can destroy my house, we shall not be moved.
You can uproot my trees, we shall not be moved.
No, no, we shall not be moved.

You can destroy our school, we shall not be moved.
You can uproot me from my place, but I shall not be moved.
This is Bedouin land, this is Bedouin land.

I sing with him: "No, no, we shall not be moved. No, no, we shall not be moved…"

And suddenly it hits me, like lightning: This song is not a Bedouin lyric, nor is the music. It is in English, not Arabic. The history of this place, Master Agent says to himself, is not written by Bedouins but by foreigners. No way in heaven could this man come up with this song in English on his own, as his English is not really good.

Who taught you this song?

"The Europeans!"

Salim: "Many foreigners come here to help us. Most and best are the Germans."

My identification with Aziz and Salim gets a blow. Yes, the clip that I saw was not nice, but I know already from my experience in Khirbet al-Makhul that NGOs know how to surgically edit a movie, and that what I see on a screen is a reflection of the image in the minds of those who make the movie rather than the reality on the ground. Who built the nice house before the bulldozers came? I ask myself. Fifty-eight times destroyed and fifty-nine rebuilt. Who was behind it? Did anybody really live in that house, or was it just a set? I'm in theater and I know how much it costs and how long it takes to build a set. A good set designer, well paid, can get it done in a day.

"You can uproot my trees"? What trees is he talking about? The only trees here in the last five thousand years are trees planted by Israelis after they had invented their special irrigation system.

I look at Ari and at Amichai, asking for their explanations. If I want, they tell me, they will give me pictures that they took. The people walking here, sometimes more than the ones I now see, don't really live here. They live in "recognized" towns such as Lakia, and come here to al-Araqeeb for a photo shoot with naïve foreigners or smart journalists. Regavim has some pictures of these Bedouins parking their Mercedes outside before they come by here.

The Master Agent that I am, I don't like to be handed photos that somebody else took. And so, I decide to judge for myself, and based on what I see. What do I see? Well, there's no infrastructure in this al-Araqeeb, and the beautiful home I saw in the movie doesn't really fit with this area. The water for the coffee would have had to have been taken from the well, like in the days of the biblical Abraham, but it was served in a living room that resembled a nice Texas villa. If that had indeed been a real house in al-Araqeeb, somebody with spare money would have had to build it first. Who could that be? Perhaps one of "the most and the best" who arrived here with Lufthansa or AirBerlin.

Let's stick it to the Jews. Why not?

* * *

As time passes I make it my duty to visit in a Bedouin school and speak with its most outstanding children in a recognized town. I want to see where a "Bedouin" starts. The brilliant students I meet are Israeli citizens, but they tell me that they are Palestinians, and they think the worst about Israel. The school is funded by Israel and by the German Konrad Adenauer Stiftung, my host for the trip to Jordan, among others. Then I try to get KAS to explain to me their side. The head of KAS just happens to be in Israel these days and I would love to meet him.

His office replies: "Due to Mr. Pöttering´s very tight schedule he won´t have enough time to give interviews during his visit in Israel."

If German men don't want to meet me, so be it. Maybe German ladies will. I try.

Kerstin Müller, a Green Party deputy, is about to assume the leadership role of her party's Heinrich Böll Foundation branch in Tel Aviv. Here's the lady's office response: "Unfortunately, her time schedule is very narrow in the coming weeks, therefore she won't be able to give an interview."

I put in a request to meet Prime Minister Benjamin Netanyahu. His press person, Mark Regev, tells me he'll be looking into it.

*   *   *

I drive around and around in the Negev desert, looking for Israel's rumored nuclear reactor in Dimona. I bump into some Black Hebrews, who live in a place called Village of Peace, and chat with youngsters who look very much like Barack Obama's children, but they know nothing about atoms. I keep on. On some roads I spot signs notifying drivers that these are military zones and that taking pictures, or merely stopping the car, is prohibited. At some point, on a road that I'm obviously not supposed to be on, I see a building that claims to be a place for atomic energy. There is a gate at the entrance but no human beings, neither black nor white.

The nuclear facility is not the Negev's only secret. Here you have what in English are called craters and in Hebrew *makhteshim*. Whatever their name, they are huge holes in the middle of the desert. There are a few craters here, and more than one explanation of how they have come into being. They are fascinating, they are frightening, they are enlightening, they are awesome, they are awe-inspiring, they are bewitching, they are gorgeous, and once you have seen them you can't forget them.

The roads in the Negev go on and on and on, apparently to infinity. Everywhere you look, every landscape, is a feast to the eye and soul. Look here: the colors of the sands change every few feet. Really.

And here, look, the Mizpe Ramon crater. What a beauty! You stand at the edge of a cliff, you take a look down under and around, and you realize how cruel and how inspiring nature can be. You must get out of your car to see and feel this huge hole in the earth. The formation on the edges, as well as their rough shapes, testify to something extraordinary that took shape here thousands of years ago. In one place I see a 'cut' in a mountain going down as deep as the Devil can reach. I put one foot on one part and another foot on the other part, and look down for Mr. Devil. It's a great moment.

I raise my head from the bottomless pit and stare at the ibexes walking leisurely by me. They won't run away when they see me, a human, for the desert is their place, their home, their kingdom and no human can hurt them.

In this miracle of nature called Negev, with its endless turns, roads, paths, and sands, almost no foreigner can be spotted. I am in the car for hours, driving endlessly, and for almost all the time, my car is the only car around. Over miles and miles and miles, I see no car behind, ahead, or to the side of me, only some army bases and Bedouin encampments.

"Israel will be tested in the Negev," David Ben-Gurion said many years ago, and today his words hang at the entrance to one of those IDF camps.

But I, Master Agent, will have to be tested in more places than this, and I leave this inspiring Negev and go to Jerusalem.

When you see stray cats drinking kosher milk it is also inspiring. In a closed session with my cats, now about six of them, we all agree that I have to dedicate a considerable amount of time to tying up some loose ends.

Who should be my first victim? The French, naturally.

Gate Thirty-Eight

Doctors without Borders and a dead rabbi with no trains.

MSF (MÉDECINS SANS FRONTIÈRES), WHICH IS BASED IN SWITZERLAND, HAS AN office in Jerusalem, and I go to visit them. I would like to know what it is they are doing in places such as Khirbet al-Makhul and why it is that they are there.

Their office is in Beit Hanina, an all-Arab neighborhood in east Jerusalem, and I excitedly wait to listen to the romantic sound of the French language. I meet some interesting people. Italians.

I join Christina, head of mission for the Spanish branch, and Tommaso, head of mission for the French branch. Both are Italian citizens. They have two offices and both their offices are in this same neighborhood. MSF needs two offices here because, I hear, they are very busy.

I ask Christina to tell me what they are doing.

First, she points at a map. There's a map on the wall of the MSF office and it has many "pockets," different sections in different places and different colors: here are Jews, there are Arabs. "It is a crazy situation," she says, and "if you look at the map it makes you sick." The main problem, I can see, is simple: too many Jews on the map. If you look at the map, seriously now, you'll get sick too. Christina, I think, is a cover name. The truth, I think, is this: she is Mother Theresa reincarnated. There's no other way of explaining why this sexy lady left healthy Italy and moved to sickening Israel.

Christina Theresa cares about the "situation," she tells me.

You are an Italian, why do you care about this place? What's the emotional gravity that makes you come here, that you wish so much to be here?

She wants to fix the problems here, she answers.

What are the problems?

"Lack of rights."

Whose side are you on?

"There are people here who suffer more."

What kind of suffering?

"There are people here who are not free to decide where they want to live."

Who are those people?

The Palestinians, of course.

This lady Saint knows her ways around Master Agents, extremely

talented in appearing like a pure lamb. I want to take a photo of her and send it to Minister Rula in Bethlehem, with my warm suggestion to appoint her the second Lady of Palestine.

Are the Jews free to live where they want?

"Yes. If they want to live in the West Bank they can."

Can Jews live, let's say, in Ramallah?

"Mmm. There are a few. There are journalists from *Haaretz* who live in Ramallah."

She is referring to Amira Hass, the feminine side of Gideon Levy.

Are other Jews living in Ramallah?

"As far as I know, that's all. Just Amira."

Saints often have a problem distinguishing between plural and singular, and I noticed it with other holy people in Rome. But what's interesting here is that our Lady of Palestine makes an issue of people's free choice to live in a place of their choosing, when her own office is in a neighborhood that accepts no Jews, a fact she readily admits to when questioned on this issue.

MSF is not a political organization, it is a medical organization; this, at least, is what they claim to be. "Doctors" is their name, and I'd like to know what, really, they are doing here. I ask my Saint this question. And then I ask another question, Question B: Does the MSF, a health organization, also treat sick Jews?

My questions are just too much for Tommaso. He and I know that no Jew is being treated by the MSF, but he can't admit to it for obvious reasons. I can see him getting really upset, making all kinds of faces in my direction. I ask him to be honest with me and tell me which side he is on. On the "weaker" side, he says, the Palestinians. I ask him what would happen – let's just imagine it – if this country united into one, in which case the Jews would be the minority. Does he think everything would be fine and dandy for the Jews, or does he think that the Jews would suffer?

"This is a possibility," he admits, that the Jews would become the weaker side and that the Palestinians would then take revenge.

Why, then, do you dedicate your time to help one weak people succeed in making the other people weak? What's the rationale for all of this?

He has no answer.

Beit Hanina, the all-Arab neighborhood in Jerusalem where this MSF office is located, has been cited to me by Palestinians as an example of an Arab neighborhood that is being neglected by the Israeli authorities due to their racist ideology. When I lived in Jerusalem years and years ago, I never visited this neighborhood, but now that I'm here I take my time to walk its streets. What can I say? If this is an example of a neighborhood being neglected, its residents should do their utmost to keep it neglected for eternity.

I wish I could stay longer in Beit Hanina but I have to go. I am to meet the editor in chief of *Haaretz* at his office in Tel Aviv and the clock refuses to stop.

* * *

Walking out of Beit Hanina I learn that sometimes the clock does stop. A loudspeaker outside the train station is being heard: No public transportation today due to the funeral procession of Rabbi Ovadia Yosef.

The Sephardi spiritual leader passed away earlier in the day and the authorities are estimating that many thousands will come to attend his funeral. How the thousands will come to Jerusalem if there is no public transportation is a logic I don't get.

In one of his books Ovadia Yosef, called Maran (something like "our teacher") by his admiring followers, suggested that thousands of Israeli soldiers died in the Yom Kippur war because they stared "at girls dressed in short skirts that show their thighs." Ovadia, born Abdallah, also accused Israeli Supreme Court judges for "having sex with menstruating women." And it is to this holy man's funeral that 200,000 people are scheduled to come, the Israeli media predict.

This Master Agent, as should be expected, is one of the early comers. I reach the epicenter of the funeral procession, standing across the place where his lifeless body lies. Within minutes, I feel like a sardine. People stream in my direction in the hundreds of thousands. Who said that only 200,000 people would come? This looks like a million or more. It's the same media, I remind myself, that reported that very few Israelis travel to Turkey these days.

Within a short time, the Israeli media change their earlier estimate, now reporting that 850,000 people are participating in the funeral, the highest number of funeral participants in the history of the Jewish state. This is over ten percent of Israel's Jewish population, and I feel the physical pressure of the people around me. People push, more and more, some standing on fences adjacent to nearby buildings, others standing on roofs of cars or on whatever object that would tolerate the weight of a human being. It is fascinating to watch, and disturbing at the same time. How come so many people have followed that man?

Next to where I am standing there is an advertisement by the Shas party, the party Ovadia helped to found and has controlled ever since. It says: "Follow the order of Maran and you'll be blessed with a good year." Too bad Maran couldn't bless himself. Another ad reads: "We love you, Maran."

A thought. If you take the followers of Maran, add the multiple thousands who follow the "Messiah," the late Lubavitch rabbi, plus the Nanakhs who go Na Nakh all day long, you will end up with about half of the Jewish population of Israel. Add to this mix all those people who believe in the heavenly animal, al-Buraq, you'll have more or less the total number of people who reside in this land. You can look at it differently: If you deduct from the total population of Israel those who believe in dead men or in flying horses or camels, the people you'll have left are the NGO activists and the editor in chief of *Haaretz*.

Ovadia Yosef had a long life. He was ninety-three when he died, but people want him alive forever. I watch a young lady in a women's section on the street crying uncontrollably, as if her beloved had just passed away.

I leave the scene and go to my cats. I think they have enough milk in their system and so I'll give them something else this evening, maybe tuna. Tuna with olive oil.

Gate Thirty-Nine

*Why do Europeans spend lavish sums of
money to watch a Jewish soldier pee?*

A RABBI OF ANOTHER KIND, RABBI ARIK OF RABBIS FOR HUMAN RIGHTS, IS ALIVE
and waiting for me at dawn the next day. Rabbi Arik gets enormous
funding from various organizations and he must deliver. Today he

does. Wearing a T-shirt that reads, "We are all al-Araqeeb," he stands by a van he has arranged to take me to an olive grove of a West Bank village called Burin, near Nablus. There I will join Palestinians who are scheduled to harvest their olives later today.

He is not joining me, as he was in Burin the day before, but he is paying for the van and a driver so that I can participate in his organization's holy mission to "serve and protect" Arab olive harvesters. Dan, an Israeli activist working for Arik, is coming along. Maurice, who is from Kenya and is another of Arik's activists, is also joining.

Maurice is studying International Peace and Conflict Resolution and is happy to take part in this trip, where Rabbis for Human Rights is protecting Arabs from Israeli soldiers and settlers out to hurt them.

*   *   *

Maurice, a man whose life mission is to achieve global peace, has checked around the world and found the one power that threatens international peace: Israel.

Just a few days ago, according to news reports, Muslim extremists entered a shopping mall and slaughtered the shoppers while cutting off their limbs one by one, in an attack that shocked the world in its gruesome brutality. This happened in Kenya, Maurice's homeland, and you'd assume that if Maurice wants to apply his Conflict Resolution techniques in a troubled spot, he would be doing so in Kenya. But no, he is here.

I ask him to explain this to me but, in reply, he gives me a nervous smile and stares at me as if I were the Devil Incarnate.

Abu Rami of Jerusalem is the van driver. He used to drive the former MK Uri Avnery, the oldest Israeli peace activist alive, and now he works with Rabbi Arik. As he drives, he points to places of interest. For example, to a house on top of a hill: "This is the house of Moshe Zar, the Chief Settler!" Don't ask me what this means; I don't know.

In due time we reach the village, and soon will be on our way to the olive grove, to protect the olive harvesting Arabs there from the brutal Jews.

A Palestinian farmer welcomes us. He has been shot by two settlers the other day, a year or so ago, and the marks on his body are still there, he says, for us to see. What's your name? I ask him.

"Bruce Lee."

Did he really say Bruce Lee, or was he trying to say something like "Brosely"? I'm not sure but I answer: Nice to meet you. My name is Kung Fu.

The sun is shining, the sky is blue, the wind is blowing nicely on our faces and the settlers are just near us, I'm told.

The mood is hot. A fight may be brewing soon with the settlers and I'm as excited as can be.

But first, we have to go up the hill to the olive trees. I almost fall ten times, as the way up is quite steep and some stones slide the moment I step on them, but what won't I do to help people from being killed by Jews? I would do everything.

We reach Bruce Lee's trees and we pick olives. I thought we would serve as guards against evil, not work like farmers, but I was wrong. Obviously, I neglected to pay attention to the word "serve" in "serve and protect."

Dan and Maurice, motivated servants, are hard at work with Bruce Lee on an olive tree, picking the little devils that fall into a sack lying on the ground.

"The settlers kill us," Bruce Lee says as the black man and the Jew are sweating to serve him.

How many of you have been killed by the settlers' fire so far? Dan, eavesdropping on my conversation with Bruce Lee, immediately interjects: "You can see it on the Internet." I don't respond to Dan and keep at Bruce Lee, asking again: How many have been killed by the settlers here so far?

"Two."

When?

"In 1999 or 2000."

That's quite a few years ago, and Bruce Lee looks at my face and realizes he didn't succeed in making me worry about the Jews. But Bruce Lee is smart and he knows that some white people might need a good story to get them scared of the Jews. Stories create emotions and Bruce Lee wants to touch Kung Fu.

The other day, he now tells me, a settler saw an Arab who was praying on the hills and asked the praying man to stop praying. The Arab didn't obey the Jew and continued to pray. The settler immediately got off his horse and shot the Arab in mid-prayer.

I never knew that settlers ride horses, but I don't know everything.

Did you see this with your own eyes, Bruce Lee?

"My neighbor told me."

Bruce Lee asks me who I am. A German journalist, I tell him.

"Thank you for reporting the Palestinian problems to the Europeans. We are happy with the European boycott" of settlement products.

You're welcome, Bruce Lee.

Bruce Lee is smart. Give a German like me compliments and I will fall for him head over heels.

Dan and Maurice, I notice, don't stop working. When watching them, it becomes clear that they are not professional olive harvesters, but their drive and motivation compensates for their lack of skill.

Hour follows hour and no murderous settlers show up, which is really not good news for Rabbi Arik. He must have prayed hard that God help the cause and that I see Jewish brutality first hand, but God got lazy lately and He has not sent the marauding Jewish settlers to kill us. Soon enough the rabbi decides to intervene in God's lack of reacting to his prayers. He calls me to offer his help: Would I like, he asks, to be taken around by a car, another car, to see the evidence of the horrible crimes that have been committed by the Jews in the past?

It is absurd that a rabbi would try so hard to prove that Jews are murderous creatures, but I love theater of the absurd – haven't I mentioned this already? – and I say that I'd be glad to be driven around places where Jews have killed the innocent.

A guy by the name of Zakaria, Rabbi Arik informs me, will soon come to pick me up.

But before Zakaria arrives, Bruce Lee invites all of us to eat with him, hummus with ful and pita.

As we eat, under a lovely olive tree, Bruce Lee tells me again that he was shot by the two settlers and adds two details: they are brothers, and he knows them.

What are their names?

He doesn't know their names, he says, only their faces.

Does anybody know?

Yes. There was an Israeli police inquiry into the case and charges have been filed in court.

In court, as far as I know, charges cannot be filed against faces; there must be names. Who has the names? I ask him. Yehudit from Yesh Din, an Israeli NGO that protects the legal rights of Palestinians, he says.

I write a note for myself to find this lady and get the details.

Meantime Zakaria arrives. He is a Palestinian from the village of Jit, and he has a business card that defines him as a "human rights coordinator."

*   *   *

I mount his impressive big van, with the latest technology inside, and he drives me around.

"What do you want to see?"

Everything.

He takes me to the village of Burin. We were in the olive grove of the village, and now we go to the village itself. In minutes we're there. It is a place, I think as I look at it, where the Angel of Misfortune dances every day. Wherever I look I see utter poverty that's really hard to look at.

Yes. This is what most news consumers of the world think Palestine is, and here I see it with my own eyes. International media, I'm confirmed, are honest brokers of the truth.

I need to inhale clean air and I go to buy cigarettes in a little shop, more like a hole in cement, and I stare at the smoke coming out of my mouth.

Beyond the smoke and across the street I see a bunch of kids and soon enough I start playing with them. They like it. And I like them. Sweet, happy – God knows why – they easily open up to me, a stranger. If anybody anywhere needed proof that kids can be happy on Angel Poverty Street, he or she should come here. I try to compare it with Great Neck, New York, where I lived quite many years ago. Great Neck is one of the richest suburbs of America, where kids get the best care the world knows of, best education, best toys, best food, best housing, best everything. Are they happier? Would you see them walking the streets together with so many smiles, and ever-sharing laughter? No way. The kids of Great Neck suffer from affluenza, but the kids of Burin don't even know that a disease like that exists.

I marvel at the sight of Burin's kids and play more with them.

Before long, more and more kids join me. I make up a song, "a o

e I a o o," and we all sing together, real loud: the best street theater Burin has ever witnessed.

To Zakaria, of Rabbis for Human Rights, the kids and I seem really crazy. He looks at me and the kids, and tells me this show reminds him of an Arab proverb: "If your friends are crazy and you are not, your mind will not help you." This means, of course, that now I'm free to do whatever I want and that he will have to play along with me. I like this.

A man on the other side of the street is trying to find out what kind of show this is, and he comes over. He introduces himself: Munir. And Munir, believe it or not, is also a human rights activist. Or, to be more exact, this man works for Yesh Din, an Israeli NGO that's generously funded by the German IFA (Institut für Auslandsbeziehungen), amongst others.

This developing scene – two Arabs paid by Jews to catch bad Jews, meeting on the same street corner – strikes me as a scene in a Franz Kafka novel. What happens here in front of my eyes is this: Israeli leftist NGOs are ever in search of their own people's wrongdoing and in competition with each other for recruiting local spies.

In any case, I ask Munir if he knows Yehudit.

Yes, of course he does. Why didn't I ask him before? She was just here!

Well, I didn't know Munir before. Can he call her?

He gives me her phone number.

Yehudit tells me she knows everything about Bruce Lee and the settler brothers, only there's a tiny problem: "I don't know the names" of the settlers. It's on my computer, she says, and it will take her ten minutes to find out.

Okay. I have ten minutes, ten hours, whatever she needs.

Some minutes later she calls. She has no name.

Wait a sec: Is there no court case, cases, or whatever?

"This you'll have to check with Muhammad."

Who is Muhammad?

"A lawyer."

Can you give me his telephone number?

"He is in Umm al-Fahm," she says, referring to an Arab town.

I say thank you and hang up. No point in chasing this any further.

*   *   *

Life moves on and Zakaria takes me to a house of which the Israeli army has burnt one room. Munir joins us. Zakaria parks his big black van by the side of a burned black room in a house. It's a beautiful image, I must admit. I enter the room, a small room, and indeed it seems to have had some fire visiting it.

Munir tells the story: "Last Saturday, 4:30 p.m., the army came to the village. Two soldiers got off a jeep, came close to the first house and threw a bomb inside the house. They started to say, 'You are not allowed to get outside any of the houses in the village,' and went to the second house and threw three bombs into the first floor. Then the kids and the people started throwing stones, and a lot of army soldiers came after this, ten jeeps. They threw three gas bombs into this house. Two small daughters and a baby were inside the house and the kids suffocated. People came in and took the kids out. I called the fire station and they extinguished the fire from the outside, the window."

Why did the army do this?

"It happens every day that the army comes here and throws bombs, and the children throw stones."

Every day?

"Every second day."

Were they here yesterday?

"No."

So they will come today. What time do they usually come?

"Around 4:00 p.m."

It's 2:00 p.m now. I'll wait here. Only two hours to go.

Now I have two hours to kill, and I think how best to use my time. An idea comes to me: since the Israeli army is coming here every second day throwing bombs into houses, I should be able to see many burnt houses. Can I see more burnt houses? I ask.

"No."

This doesn't look good. The German wants proofs of Jewish brutality and all they offer him are stories and no evidence. Germans, what can I do, are natural proof-seekers.

Well, this is the East and Allah is no dummy. Allah gave people brains, and so the lady of the house says that she took pictures of the event on her cellphone. It can all be proven!

Could I see the pictures, in case you have the phone with you?

Yes, she has the phone and I can see the pictures.

Please.

The lady goes out to bring the phone. And then she comes back, with the phone.

Great.

Can I see the pictures?

Well, not exactly. The pix are gone. The phone, how sad, has broken.

I realize that I'd rather wait for Prophet Mahdi than for the IDF to show up here, and so I walk with Zakaria back to the van and we drive on.

*   *   *

Rabbi Arik calls. The phone is on loudspeaker. Rabbi Arik and Zakaria speak in Hebrew, a language Tobi the German doesn't understand. I'm a German goy. Rabbi Arik tells Zakaria that if I'm willing to stay longer, for whatever period of time today, he should drive me around and show me places. Rabbis for Human Rights will pay the cost, Rabbi Arik says.

Good.

Zakaria tells me that this was Rabbi Arik on the phone and that he, Zakaria, will drive for an hour and then drop me back with Abu Rami, who will take me back to Jerusalem.

I protest. Rabbi Arik asked this German, me, to come here and I want to know what exactly my Jewish friend said to him. Zakaria has no choice, since the rabbi is my friend, and so he must be straight with me. He goes around and around, telling me that Rabbi Arik offered some different options but that he, Zakaria, thinks that one additional hour of driving around would be enough.

I tell Zakaria that I want to be driven around for as long as it takes. That's what I want and I think the rabbi would be very happy if this was to happen. I want to see more, I tell him. I want to see places, I want to see people, and I want to see houses. I'm a crazy man, I remind him, and I want to be driven around and see all the horrible things the Jews have been doing here. Let's go on this mountain, that hill, this and that road, I suggest.

Zakaria, realizing he's dealing with a really crazy man, a German friend of a Jew, drives on.

We see beautiful houses and I want to take pictures. Zakaria doesn't like the idea, just like Atef didn't want me to see the nice houses of the rich poor, but I insist. He must stop driving for a minute so that I can take pictures, I tell him.

Which village is this? I ask him.

"Burin."

Yep. The same Burin as before. Only Zakaria, before I told him where to drive, took me to the worst part of Burin. And only there. He and the rabbi wanted me to see poverty, and I almost believed their story.

I snap some photos on my iPhone and we keep driving.

As we drive on I see two flags on top of many electricity poles and other tall structures, and I ask Zakaria whose flags they are.

"The green flag is Hamas, the yellow flag is Fatah" (the PLO).

There seems to be a big contest here between the two.

We keep on driving, village in and village out. I notice one repeating sign in various villages and roads: USAID. I guess that America is spending in Palestine much more than I had ever imagined.

*   *   *

We keep on driving. Suddenly, on one of the roads we are driving on, we see an Israeli army jeep ahead of us. Arab youngsters will throw stones at it, Zakaria says, and the soldiers will then "respond with fire."

Let's follow the soldiers, I say to him, and see what happens. I want to see the fire! Naturally, of course, this German wants to see the Jews firing at Arab youngsters. We keep following the jeep, until it abruptly stops. Why did the Jews stop? I wonder.

"They make a checkpoint!"

Just like that. The Israeli army drives people crazy here. Israeli soldiers, when they are bored, amuse themselves by torturing the Arab people – suddenly putting up checkpoints, arresting people, and God knows what else.

We reach the jeep's position but it's not a quickie checkpoint as Zakaria said it would be. No cars are being stopped and we pass freely. I take a look at the jeep now behind me and I see one of the soldiers getting ready to pee. Zakaria's checkpoint jeep is in actuality a urinating-position jeep. Pee is free, as the Russian prostitute told me.

We keep on moving.

I drive Zakaria crazy, I know. I make him drive through many, many beautiful homes and neighborhoods in Palestine. If Rabbi Arik knew how I am spending his money he would have a heart attack.

And as we ride alongside the various gorgeous houses and rich landscapes of the Arab, Zakaria's phone rings. A North American man is on the line and he is very, very, very eager to help the Palestinian people and save them from the Israeli criminals. Where should he go, he asks Zakaria, in order to bear witness to the horrible crimes of the Israelis?

Zakaria is also very eager to help this poor North American caller.

The North American caller, for the record, is a member of the Christian human rights organization EAPPI, the Ecumenical Accompaniment Programme in Palestine and Israel I have run into already. He is a good Christian, and he wants to help the needy between prayers. EAPPI, I can see, is very busy in the Holy Land. Anna Maria, the Swiss beauty I met at Al-Quds, and Michèle, the ugly French woman I met on the bus, are also with EAPPI.

Zakaria tells him that it's really great that he has called. We are not working on Saturdays (Rabbis observe the Sabbath), he tells him, and Friday is only half a day (for the same reason), and so a good-news Christian would really be helpful. It would be great, Zakaria says to the lovely Christian, if he would also record what he sees.

Amazing how this system works! People land in this country with cameras in order to find bad Jews. If this guy had dedicated the amount of energy he's spending here to South Central LA, he would have found quite a number of horrible images to show to the world, but I guess he's too scared to walk around South Central's streets.

Zakaria drives on. We get to Qalqilya and I have no clue where else to ask Zakaria to take me. And so I tell my man that now I need a falafel. Grudgingly, Zakaria stops by a falafel stand. Master Agent is thinking hard where to go next, while munching his falafel, when he notices a road sign: Rawabi.

Rawabi. I remember the name. The other day I was given a brochure, I don't even remember by whom, about Rawabi, the "first Palestinian-planned city," a city built from scratch by the Palestinians of our time – not fourteen thousand years ago. The pictures in the brochure were splendid, and I remember that this new city has raised the biggest Palestinian flag in existence.

I would love to see it!

I tell Zakaria that I've just decided where to go next: Rawabi.

Rawabi? Why Rawabi? That's seventy kilometers from here, and seventy kilometers back. No way!

I insist. I must see Palestine.

Zakaria tries his best to dissuade me, but he fails. You don't argue logic with crazy Germans, I tell him. Period.

* * *

Rawabi. Have you ever been to Rawabi ("hills" in Arabic)? Rawabi is being built as we speak. Over one billion dollars have been spent on this city already. More to come, *inshallah*.

Rawabi. Have you ever seen Rawabi? When you enter Rawabi, you know that you have entered Paradise.

It stands on top of a mountain with a view that makes you feel as if you are on top of the world. And while Rawabi is still in the midst of construction, its first residents are to take possession of their units next year.

At Rawabi's entrance you will see the biggest flag your eyes have ever seen, a real giant, and it's overwhelming. Yes, it's just a flag, but what a flag! A flag surrounded by grass, ever more flags, statues, and music is playing to it from every corner of the earth.

I chat with one of the people around and ask him why such a big flag? He winks at me and says: To stick it to the Israelis. We laugh about it.

I walk a few steps away from the flag and enter Rawabi's sales office. What an office! This office is a top-of-the-line exhibition hall that shows the soon-to-be-completed city in miniature, including the buildings, the various city centers, the planned roads and anything you would want a city to have.

And much, much more.

Rawabi's architectural design is just outstanding: incorporating art, top technology, convenience, riches and beauty. When you see this, you will be hard pressed to match this city with any existing one, even in the richest of countries. Rawabi is shining in its awesomeness, it is spirited, it is captivating, it is magnificent.

Ramie, a well-dressed young man, shows me around. Using a laser pointer on the miniature model of Rawabi in front of us he explains to me some of the structures and contents of Rawabi: Convention center with an indoor theater, exhibition hall, a science museum, a cinema, retail stores, cafes, boutiques, a hyper market, a soccer stadium, a five-star hotel, an amphitheater, a mosque, a church, the municipality.

I stop this man who's talking too fast for my taste. I see no church and I ask him to repeat his last few words, as I have lost track, and he gladly obliges. His red ray laser pointer points to areas as he speaks: "Here's the mosque, here's the church, here's the municipality."

He points at the mosque when he says "mosque" and he points at the mosque again when he says "church."

I see no church. Where's the church?

Oh, he tells me, yes, they don't have the church in this model, but soon they'll update it.

Church or no church, I have spent enough of Rabbi Arik's resources by now and I tell Zakaria that I'm ready to go back.

As we drive back, Rabbi Arik calls. Zakaria is on another line and has no time for the Jew. He yells at him, as one would yell at a mad dog: "Get off the phone!"

Rabbi Arik, the ever-obeying Jew, does.

A beaten Jew, a disrespected Jew, a small Jew.

It is at this point that I feel really bad for Arik. He works so hard to please the Palestinians, at the expense of his own people and country, and in return he gets abused. I say nothing, as I'm not supposed to understand what was said in Hebrew.

Before my brain goes totally numb, perhaps it would be good if I talked to someone else, no Arab and no Jew. A European would be good. How about His Highness Lars Faaborg-Andersen, the EU ambassador to Israel?

Gate Forty

The EU ambassador would like to explain everything to you.

"THIS IS A VERY IMPORTANT, EXCITING TIME IN EU-ISRAEL RELATIONS," IS THE first thing His Highness, Head of the EU Delegation to Israel, says to me. Listening to these wise words, I know I have just met the smartest man in the region.

"What do you want to talk about?"

Why is the EU so interested in a regional conflict going on across the ocean between two peoples of totally different cultures from that of the EU, a conflict that is not about the day-to-day living of the average European? Why is the EU involved in this conflict, and why were you sent here to deal with it?

"I want to say that Israel is a very important partner for the EU. Israel plays a very important role in the region, a role that we of course want to have an influence on. The issue of the Israeli-Arab war, of the Israeli-Palestinian conflict, is a very central one in Europe. It is not a surprise. It receives a lot of media coverage. And if one spends just a couple of weeks in this country, one realizes the centrality of this issue."

I have no idea what this esteemed man is talking about. I've been here for months by now and the "centrality" that I see is that too many Europeans are taking center stage in it with cameras. But I choose not to confront him and instead ask His Highness the one-word question that Jews have asked for generations: Why?

"Because, I think, many Europeans realize that the Arab-Israeli conflict is a key fault line in the region, and intersects and interplays with all the other conflicts that are taking place and therefore solving this conflict is absolutely essential in trying to achieve overall stability in the region, because as long as you have the Israeli-Palestinian conflict you would have a central rallying point for the Arab states and also for Iran against Israel. Once you break that logic you'd be able to see new kinds of alliances developing in this region."

Take Syria, the neighbor of Israel. More people have died in the last few months in Syria than have died in the Arab-Israeli conflict in the last sixty-five years, or even one hundred years. The conflicts here, we see, are not just the little dot-on-the map called Israel but all over the area. The conflicts in Libya have nothing to do with Israel. The conflicts in Egypt have nothing to do with Israel. And the rallying cry in Syria, or Libya, is not Israel. And there are other conflicts in the world. Why do you think that the Arab-Israeli conflict is so important?

"Because we are also trying to work on the other conflicts. As you know, we are playing a role vis-à-vis Syria, we are also playing a role vis-à-vis Lebanon.... The reason why we are particularly keyed to trying to assist in solving the Israeli-Palestinian conflict is that, one of the reasons is, this is one of the conflicts that will lend itself to diplomatic solution, one where there's a fairly clear framework for negotiations and where the parties are not at war-footing with one another."

Did you invest as much money, resources, time, diplomatic efforts in solving the ages-old conflicts, for example, between Sunnis and Shiites, which is one of the main conflicts – unless you disagree with me – in the area, in the Middle East?

"The Sunni-Shi'a conflict has existed for centuries. The conflict between the Palestinians and the Israelis started, according to Prime

Minister Netanyahu, around 1921, with the expelling of Jews from Jaffa."

*   *   *

Expelling of Jews from Jaffa. What is this man talking about? Is he now buying everything Netanyahu is saying?

"And I think that our ambition is more realistic in terms of solving conflicts which have only raged for a more limited time than that of the Sunni-Shi'a conflict."

Are you saying to me that you are buying Benjamin Netanyahu's version of political realities, that the conflict started with the expelling of Jews from Jaffa? I have never heard of it, but I trust your –

"He said it at the Bar-Ilan [University] speech that he gave last Sunday. My point is that this is a conflict that has been going for a...maybe the last eighty, ninety years. The other conflict has raged for centuries. I mean, there is a fundamental – "

Do you think that solving the Israeli-Palestinian conflict will also help to solve the Sunni-Shi'a conflict, and all the other conflicts in the region?

"It will eliminate one of a number of conflicts in the region. It will not solve the other problems overnight."

But it will help?

"It will make it [the Sunni-Shi'a conflict] less complicated – "

To eventually solve –

"Yes. It will remove one stone in the shoe in trying to solve the others."

So, it will help to solve the other issues?

"Yes."

If I get this right, he's saying that the reasons why Europe is involved so deeply in this conflict are two: (1) The desire to erase the "central rallying point for the Arab states and also for Iran against Israel." (2) The desire to eventually solve the Sunni-Shi'a conflict.

Let me ask you another question. Some people say that the interest the EU takes in the regional conflict here, as opposed to other conflicts, is the age-old history between Christianity and Judaism that is spilling over even in the atheist philosophies of the Europeans, that the kind of animosity that had been going on for two thousand years is at least part of the reason for the EU and the European media's obsession, so to speak, in this conflict. Do you think this has anything to do with it?

"Not really. I think that if it has anything to do with history it is more a conflict that might remind Europeans of their own colonial past, because of certain traits, maybe, in the scenario, the situation, that could be likened to that."

Meaning that Israel is colonializing Palestinian lands, which reminds them of their history, but not the old Christian-Jewish history – is that what you mean?

"Yes. You have an Israeli administration of a…at least disputed…territory like you had during the colonial period of the European powers in countries outside the European continent."

So, do you say that from the European point of view the colonialist –

"I'm saying that this has more to do with it than with any kind of anti-Semitism."

If I get this right, there is a third reason why Europe is involved here: (3) Europe is trying to atone for its colonial past by issuing dictates to a non-European country.

That the same mouth utters these three reasons while not wearing a burka is a testimony to the genius of European diplomacy.

I go back home and tell the cats about the three reasons why the EU is sponsoring the ex-Jew Itamar. They are stray cats and they have seen the worst, but when they hear what I've just told them they meow so loud that I immediately conclude they would never be diplomats.

Maybe after I give them some kosher milk I should go to meet the EU's greatest evil: settlers.

Gate Forty-One

*If you see your neighbor's olive fields, do you leave
them alone or do you set them on fire?*

SETTLERS ARE VERY MUCH LIKE BEDOUINS: THEY LOVE MOUNTAINS, HILLS AND
fresh air, but there's one difference: their males can't have more than
one wife.

Life sucks.

Some assume that most people who live in the area captured by
Israel in the 1967 War, are "settlers" who have moved there because it
is much easier to afford a house in that area than in Israel proper. But
there is a core of settlers who didn't move behind the 1967 line due
to financial considerations but because they believe that Jews should
settle in all the land of biblical Israel, especially the West Bank and
Jerusalem, where most of the Bible was composed and where most
of its more important stories took place.

Out of the seven billion people now living on the earth, there are
about fifty thousands souls who agree with these settlers. Practically
everybody else is certain that they are the greatest obstacle to peace.
Personally, I have never understood why. Let's say that the land is
divided between Arabs and Jews, and let's say that the Arabs get the
whole of the West Bank. Why, I want to know, can't the Jews still live
there? There are millions of Arabs living in proper Israel, why can't a

few Jews with skullcaps live with the Arabs? In what book of law is it decreed that a land must be free of Jews?

Anyway, I go to meet the settlers, the real McCoy, the believers. Within this group there are sub-groups. There are believers who live in recognized settlements, and then there are the others, the Jewish Azizes and Salims who do not live in settlements but in "outposts," totally "unrecognized."

* * *

It is evening and I'm driven to the outpost of my desire, quite distant from a cluster of normal outposts, a one-family outpost alone in the wilderness, where the owner has asked for the assurance that I'm Jewish before he allowed me to visit his kingdom. "He doesn't want non-Jews in his property," my contact has told me. This means, sadly, that today I can't be Tobi or Abu Ali, instead I must be Rabbi Tuvia.

Getting to this man and his family is not easy, even if you're the most kosher of Jews. Where he lives is far away from everywhere and anywhere. There's no address and no mailbox, it's not registered

with anybody and no journalists can go there because Goyim and reporters are outlawed.

We drive on a path that would be fit for a tank. We have no tank, only a van, and we proceed cautiously. On the way to this Nowhere we are greeted by all sorts of animals, some that even zoologists have probably never heard of. One such animal, which is possibly owned by the American NSA, is running ahead of us as if to show us the way to our destination. It is a great help and a wonderful experience; I love to be guided by animals.

Once we get there, I see a couple of dogs, really big ones, then a couple of horses, then hundreds of sheep, and finally a couple and their children. They live in tents and in wooden structures, get electricity from generators, and their water supply comes from a source that only flying angels can identify.

I have just entered the property of Patriarch Abraham and Matriarch Sarah, I believe. The Arabs and the Jews might fight to the death for control of the holy tombs in Hebron, but the reality is that Abraham and family are alive and well and they're living here. Yes, there are computers around and cellphones as well, a testimony to a world in the future, but it's hard to spot them because they are overshadowed by rifles and pistols, without which this holy family would now reside in holy tombs.

They are Jewish shepherds, Jewish farmers, and Jewish warriors. The man of this house grows long hair, his kids as well, and his wife looks like a seductive nineteenth-century Mormon lady from Utah, centuries into the future.

The man, whom I'll call Moses, relates to me as if I were lower in rank than any of his animals and ignores my existence. His wife, on the other hand, warmly greets me with a boiling black coffee. With time, and once he has recognized that I'm a very charming man, Moses warms up to me and we chat.

Unlike most other settlements and outposts, there's no fence around Moses' huge property, no gate and no guards. Some of his neighbors on the other mountains and hills of this land are Jews, others are Arabs. The Arabs and he are bitter enemies and, if history is any proof, the Arabs will soon come to steal his sheep, shoot his hairy face, bury his little children, and inherit his lovely Mormon. On these mountains, you can safely assume, flying bullets are as much a part of nature as the flying angels and camels.

Are you not afraid to live here?

"God will protect me."

This is a dangerous place.

"Yes, it is dangerous to live here, but where is it not?"

His answer reminds me of a similar answer. "How about crossing the street, any street. Is that not frightening?" the Tel Aviv prostitute said to me. Yep: whores and patriarchs do think alike.

Why are you here?

"Why? It's mine!"

Since when?

"God has given this land to the Jews. Every centimeter of this land is holy and it is the will of God that Jews live here, and as long as the Jews keep God's will they will be protected."

There is not a minute, be it day or night, that various volunteers who are determined to protect this holy family do not guard this place. Of course, it is God who provides the volunteers, putting the will into their hearts to come here and stay up all night to watch the herd and the sleeping couple.

The landscape, sparkling stars over barren mountains and hundreds of animals, is supremely spectacular. The air is clear, and the winds play as do the finest instruments. Had Wagner or Mozart come here and listened to the music played so majestically by these winds, they would bury their faces in shame for their utter incapacity to write music that even remotely matches the pure sound of these winds and the low whisper of the goats. No wonder there's no TV in the tents or the wooden structure here, as the real-life images are a hundred-fold more captivating.

The bathroom is quite far, and the path to it uneven, but this outpost is not Beverly Hills. The furnishings are mostly made of wood, though there is a modern refrigerator in the kitchen, which is also a living room, study room, an office, and a prayer room. The rest of the house is the bare sands and the sky above. This is a Bedouin abode minus its sumptuous interior.

* * *

As night becomes ever more dark, the "Hummer" comes. This is an IDF armored vehicle, and four soldiers dismount from it. The soldiers are visiting to verify that the holy family is still alive.

They come from time to time, I'm told, show presence, and then leave. I look at them now. Mormon Sarah greets them with black coffee and cookies, and these Jewish soldiers sit with her for the drink. This is also the soldiers' time to play with their smartphones, which each of them does.

Once the soldiers are gone, the Holy Family leaves and I'm left to the mercy of fate.

And I think: These Jews are here not because Auschwitz forced them to be here. No. They are here because this earth is the expression of their souls. They and the mountains are one. The Christians believe in a Trinity, and these people too, only their Trinity is different: God, Earth, and Jews. This land for them is the breast of the Lord, from which they suck their milk. In Hebrew they frame it thusly: Torat Israel, Am Israel, and Eretz Israel, the Torah of Israel, the Nation of Israel, and the Land of Israel, are one.

When morning comes I see a little child milking the goats. The boy, with long sidelocks and a big skullcap, is a tough farmer. He is patient while milking one goat but jumps up and down before milking the next goat in an impressive sports showmanship.

I think of my little cats. They would love to be here. They would appreciate the fresh goat milk. Super kosher.

On the way out of Moses' property, the news comes in: a number of Arab men entered a settlement and approached a couple. They killed the husband with axes; his wife survived. This is the fourth murder of a Jew by an Arab in the last three weeks alone. B'Tselem, Rabbis for Human Rights, Yesh Din, and the various European NGOs have not issued statements condemning these losses of life.

*   *   *

I travel in God's mountains and hills, the biblical Judea and Samaria, until I reach Yitzhar, a settlement the residents of which fight both the Arabs and the IDF. "A Jewish soldier helps Jews," posters hanging on poles inside the Yitzhar settlement say. Whatever the meaning of this is, it seems clear that the Jews here and the IDF are not the best of friends.

To get a better understanding of what Yitzhar is made up of, I go to their yeshiva, their religious academy. Surprisingly, there is only one student in attendance. I try talking with him, but he behaves as though he is both deaf and mute.

I check the books on the shelves. This is not the kind of yeshiva I attended back then. This is a totally different animal. On the shelves here you can find books written by modern-day extremist rabbis who, in their spare time, discuss complex, brainy issues such as the permissibility of killing enemy children (Arabs) during war.

This is Yitzhar, arguably the most extreme settlement in the world, the residents of which are the biggest hotheads of the Right. I meet one of them, Benjamin, a man with a long beard, long sidelocks, and a big skullcap.

He says to me: "I'm not going to try to be 'nice' about it. I'm not interested in being PC or in giving you such an impression. I'm going to be straight with you. You see the olive field at the foot of the hill, down there? We set it on fire. Yes, we do such things. Not all of us, but some of us. Why? Because these are the laws of war. We are in a war with the Arabs for control of this land.

"This land is a war zone. If we don't show them that we are the lords, we will become their slaves. In other settlements, the Arabs plant olive trees right next to the border of Jewish settlements because they want to prevent the settlements from growing. With us, they know it's not going to work. We are the lords of this land."

Had I closed my eyes and exchanged "Arab" and "Jew," I would easily confuse this settler, Benjamin, for a Muhammad.

But he is Benjamin, not Muhammad.

I have met farmers before in my life, non-Jewish farmers in America and in Europe, and they talk more or less similarly and they will protect their lands the same way. But it is very strange, very uncommon, to listen to a Jew talking like this, like a normal "Goy." These Jews – like Moses, his goats, and his Mormon loveliness – are not the normal Jews.

Personally, I hardly get to meet conviction-driven Jews, say-what-I-think Jews, farming Jews, if-you-slap-me-on-one-cheek-I'll-slap-you-on-both-your-cheeks Jews. The Jews I know are neurotic Jews, weak Jews, self-hating Jews, hate-filled-narcissist Jews, accept-every-blame Jews, bowing to all non-Jews Jews, ever guilt-ridden Jews, ugly-looking Jews, big-nosed and hunch-backed Jews, cold Jews, brainy Jews, yapping Jews, and here-are-both-my-cheeks-and-you-can-slap-them-both Jews.

To me, the biggest proof that Jesus was Jewish is this: Who else, but a Jew, could come up with this statement: "If someone strikes you on the cheek, offer him the other one as well"?

I go back to Jerusalem, to my little herd of stray cats.

It is the end of the day on Friday, and the opening session of the Knesset is to take place on Monday. Should I go and mingle with the power brokers of Israel? What do you say, my cats?

Gate Forty-Two

An inaugural session of the Knesset.

BENJAMIN NETANYAHU AND SHIMON PERES SPEAK, AND IT IS BORING. OH, IS this boring! I would like to mingle with some MKs, one by one, but I can't see many of them in the main hall. Did they sneak out to have some tuna? I go to the MKs' dining room, and there I see a number of them. I order Coke Zero and join the legendary centrist MK Fuad Ben Eliezer at his table.

If you ask a rightist "What is Israel?" you are likely to hear the word "God" or the word "Treblinka" somewhere midway in his response. If you ask a leftist, you're likely to hear the word "occupation" at precisely the same spot. What will happen if you ask a centrist the same question? I try it on MK Ben Eliezer, and he replies.

"A homeland. For every Jew. This is the place where we can do anything we want. It's quite terrible to have eight million Jews living together, it's not that easy, but I think we're doing quite well."

I love this image of eight million Jewish *zekel beiner*s in one sack.

Fuad goes on: "All of our history, all our traditions, started here; don't forget. I'm too old to forget what happened to us sixty, seventy years ago. We have to learn our lesson and understand that we can only depend on ourselves. With all respect to the nations, European and other, the one nation responsible for ourselves, is us. We have to be."

Fuad, also known as Benjamin, tells me that he was the first Israeli official "who went to Arafat in Tunis, in 1993. Rabin sent me there to check one thing: Were they [the Palestinians] ready to take off the terrorist suit and put on a statesman's suit? I stayed forty-eight hours with Arafat, day and night, and I studied him. I came back and I gave Rabin a clear answer."

What did you tell him?

"I think that they are ready to switch suits."

This I never knew. What made Yitzhak Rabin change his outlook on the Palestinians was not a personal experience of the other side, but the result of Fuad's experience and recommendation.

Just in case, I ask MK Ben Eliezer if he knows my newest spiritual father, Jibril Rajoub.

"I got to know him in 1978, when he was in jail. He was busy translating [former Israeli prime minister] Menachem Begin's book *The Revolt* into Arabic. Later on I met him many times. He was my liaison for my 1993 trip to Tunis. He is a courageous man, he is a strong man, he is a good man; I respect him."

For my part, and since I have not heard from Jibril for some time, I shoot an e-mail to Jibril's office and tell him what Fuad thinks of him. He would like it.

I chat a bit more with Fuad and then I notice MK David Rotem, chairman of the Knesset's Constitution, Law, and Justice Committee, across the room and he is looking pretty bored. I go to him. It is my fate today, I think, that I fellowship with bored MKs.

"You ask me what you want, I will answer what I want!" he says to me.

What is Israel?

"Israel is the only country given to the Jewish nation. An empire of information (high tech), of science, of culture, and it is the only country from the countries around it that has succeeded in being democratic."

What does it mean a "country given to the Jewish people"? This doesn't mean much.

"If it doesn't mean much, this is very bad. In 1922 the League of Nations, which was later replaced by the UN, decided on a British Mandate for Palestine for the purpose of establishing a Jewish state. According to paragraph 80 of the UN's own mandate, all decisions made by the League of Nations have a legal validity and will stay legally binding to the UN. Europeans don't know history and don't know international law. They say that Israel occupies lands, but they don't know that according to international law this is not occupation."

So you don't believe in giving territories to the Palestinians?

"Of course not! Before the 1967 War, when Jordan and Egypt were holding the lands the Palestinians are now claiming, the Palestinians didn't want those lands. Why didn't they? They don't want to have a state!"

What, then, do the Palestinians want?

"If you ask me, I'll tell you: They want a war."

War forever?

"Forever. They feel good when they incite hatred against us, when they commit terror acts against us. The Palestinians' real nightmare is that one day a suicidal Israeli prime minister will tell them: Here, I'm willing to grant you a state!"

The Europeans, he tells me, support the Palestinians because the Europeans are anti-Semites, but this will not go on forever. One day "the Europeans will have enough of their anti-Semitism" and change. When? "I'm not an expert on anti-Semitism, but one day they'll understand that this hatred cannot go on."

MK David Rotem's party, the rightist Israel Beyteinu, is a coalition partner of Netanyahu, but if Netanyahu gives up territories, "we will leave the coalition."

Did you tell this to Netanyahu?

"Yes."

MK Yehiel Hilik Bar, Deputy Speaker of the Knesset and Secretary General of the Labor Party, is a centrist. He is the next bored MK that I save today. We chat a bit and he tells me that Israel is the only place for Jews, people who have been evicted from wherever they used to live.

What's special about Israel?

"We sell today, all over Europe and China, high tech and medicine. This is not normal for a country as small as Israel."

What about the political situation, the Israeli-Palestinian conflict? He's not worried. "By next decade," he tells me, there will be peace between the Arabs and the Jews.

Good to know.

*   *   *

I leave Jerusalem and go to Tel Aviv. I need a break. Sun and beach, coffee and beer can be good friends. But, sadly, I was not born to be a Tel Aviv guy. I get bored pretty quickly when doing nothing. I don't have my cats in Tel Aviv to pal around with, so I go to see Aluf Benn, editor in chief of *Haaretz* ("The Land"), a man I was supposed to meet just before Rabbi Ovadia Yosef passed away.

Haaretz, like most papers of the West that I'm familiar with, is more propaganda than news. It is in *Haaretz* that you'll read all the bad things that the Jews are doing, or even just thinking of doing, and very little of the bad stuff the Arabs are doing, not to mention what the Arabs are thinking of doing. It is also in *Haaretz* that you'll find all the doom and gloom that will happen to the Jews if they don't give the Arabs everything they ask for.

I ask Aluf to define "Israel" for me, and he does: "Israel is home."

Aluf has a home, and a home you can divide: half for your enemy, half for you. I wish I knew where my home was. My life started here, but I left long ago and have ever since lived in different places.

Aluf and I have one thing in common: media. And that's why we meet.

I ask Aluf a question that has been bothering me for a long time: Why are there so many foreign correspondents in Israel?

"Ask them," he says.

I love his short answers!

Haaretz is the one Israeli paper that serves as a "Bible" to herds of foreign journalists who keep quoting from it the way a Sephardi Jew would quote "Maran." I ask Aluf what's the newspaper's circulation. The answer is 70,000 copies. How many readers online? First he says 110,000, but then says he'd have to check it. Whatever the exact figure is, I now realize that almost nobody in this land reads *The Land*. This reminds me: Gideon Levy is still hiding from me.

The sad fate of *Haaretz* doesn't seem to bother Aluf. "I'm not a big dreamer," he tells me.

* * *

It is time now, after having asked people what Israel is, to meet people who are putting their lives on the line to protect Israel. I hope that my personal herd, the sweet stray cats, are doing well in Jerusalem, for I'm going to Haifa.

Gate Forty-Three

Experiencing war: inside an Israeli navy battleship in mid-sea.

ARMY: IDF. ARM: ISRAEL NAVY. UNIT: SAYERET PERES (RECONNAISSANCE PERES).
Number of ships in Unit: Four.

I am to join the battleship marked 816-TFD ("The Flying Dutchman").

Yes. Finally the IDF has woken up, recognizing the existence of
a Master Agent in their midst, and are willing to cater to my honor.
They have asked me where, within their various bases, I'd like to see
my *zekel beiner*, and the navy sounded appealing to me. I don't know
how to swim and if anything happens I will fly to Paradise, sit with
Maran in Heaven, and share a laugh about those who mourn our
passing away.

The IDF has agreed and I am here, at the gate of the Haifa base.
I pass the gate and I encounter a problem. The commander of the
unit that I'm scheduled to join is quite upset. "This is not what we've
agreed," he says to my accompanying twenty-something-year-old
female soldier. I don't know what he's talking about, except that he
wants me out. The soldier doesn't know what to say and she gets lost,
which means that I have to take command. In the Israeli navy, as you
might imagine, both Tobi the German and Abu Ali mean zilch. I need
another hat. Which hat should I put on my head? Well, how about the

Tough, Pissed Jew hat. I face the commander and tell him in perfect Pissing Hebrew: I'm not leaving!

The commander looks at me, Tough, Pissed Jew, and he knows that he has no choice but to succumb to His Toughness. Me.

I'm cleared to board the ship. A battleship. Yes, a battleship, but at first you don't notice that it's a battleship, for it's a really small baby ship.

I board the baby. It takes me less than a minute to realize that this is a little animal. Underneath the deck is a little house: a living room, a kitchen, a toilet, bedrooms, shells and bullets for decoration and an information room. People and explosives live here side by side, in total harmony, which makes for a really nice household for tough, pissed off people like me.

This ship has a name: *Dvorah* (bee). Cars have names, and ships too. There is a Mercedes and there's a Bee. Why bee? You figure this out on your own.

*   *   *

Engine on, we get ready to move. But the second the baby starts moving I register that this bee is really not a Mercedes. Nope. Mercedes is for humans, this bee is for anything but. For whatever reason, the *Dvorah* hates the words "shock absorbent" and it loves to shake your body mightily. As if this were not enough, the *Dvorah* also likes speed. Do you know what happens to your body when it is being shaken right and left, up and down, and that very very fast?

The waters are rough today, the waves are high, and this bee jolts accordingly plus more. Much more. If you don't hold tight either to a heavy machine gun welded to the body of this baby, or to some other equally impressive immovable part of the ship, you'll find yourself in Toronto in less than one second.

A soldier explains to me the secret of this ship. "It's called 'bee,' for a reason. It's small enough – twenty-one meters long – that it doesn't 'threaten' the enemy. It is fast, and it stings."

This is the kind of a baby you wouldn't want to mess with.

Today we are starting "dry," no live ammunition, and will end up with real fire. Duration: six to seven hours. Oh, Lordy Lord!

The soldiers on board ask me who I am and I tell them that I'm a European journalist. "What do they say about us?" a soldier asks me, speaking of the Europeans.

That you are a ruthless killer, that you are an animal, that you are a bitch.

"Is this what they really think?"

Sorry, but yes. Why are you serving in this army?

"This is my country, I was born here. This is where I live."

Second soldier, hearing this, remarks: "If serving in the army was not mandatory, I would be in the university now."

First soldier: "Don't listen to him, he's a half Romanian and a half Kurd."

What does this mean?

"He steals but he doesn't know what."

Would you serve in the IDF had it been a volunteer army?

"I would serve no matter what. None of us on this battleship have been forced to serve on it. You come to this Sayeret only if you choose to be here, and if you are found fit to be here."

You love this ship, ah?

"I live here, we live here, day and night. We sleep in this ship, we train on it, we fix it, we maintain it. This is home, our home."

Have you developed a personal relationship with this ship?

"Oh, yes!"

Today they're exercising one *grirah* (haul) after the other, each from a different angle and each to fit a certain circumstance. These exercises are physically demanding, since the cables alone weigh a ton or two. When they finish each *grirah* they form a circle and loudly yell: "816-TFD Hey!" As we know, 816-TFD is the number of this particular bee, which is also known as The Flying Dutchman. Hence 816-TFD. "Hey" just standing for "Hey."

From time to time, an alarm sounds. Tsemakh, their commander, turns the siren on and these soldiers must run up and down, hauling and carrying heavy objects. At one point, for example, a smaller ship comes by and a "wounded soldier" is being transferred to the bee.

Fun.

* * *

Occasionally there is a "cigarette and water" break. "A friend of mine," one of the smoking animals tells me, "is doing his service close to Palestinian cities. He tells me that he and the Palestinians drink coffee together, that they eat together, and that the Palestinians have very nice houses. Have you been to Palestinian cities?"

Yes.

"Is it true what my friend tells me?"

Yes, your friend is right. At least this is what I've seen.

"We never read this in the media. What are you going to write?"

I'll write what I see.

"Would you mind sending me what you have written once it's published?"

These ruthless animals are little babies who are scared of European journalists. I take a moment to look at these kids – yes, they're just kids. Yet the world refuses to see them for what they are, kids, preferring instead to view them as the epitome of evil.

An additional officer is with us today. He is the highest-ranking on board, doing his reserve duty, and his job is to check that the commander of this bee is performing well.

His sister, he tells me as he steers the ship, emigrated from Israel and is living in Munich. Their family roots are in Berlin, and she went back to her roots.

The waters are too rough today to "go wet," the Sayeret commander informs us, and we are to continue "dry."

About six hours into my bee ride, as we are about to reach the shore, I look at the dry land around me. Here is Haifa. Here is Kiryat Shmonah. Here is Akko. And there is Lebanon.

A few months ago, I had a meal at the American Colony Hotel in Jerusalem, and a receptionist said to me: "Our Palestine is small. Very small." He was talking about the "historic Palestine," from the River (Jordan) to the Sea (the Mediterranean). And as I stand on the bee in mid-waters looking out, I can vouch for it. Palestine, all of it, is indeed small, very small.

Gate Forty-Four

Jews are barbarians.

TO GET A BETTER PICTURE OF THE SIZE OF THIS LAND, I GO TO EILAT, ISRAEL'S southernmost city.

Welcome to Le Meridien Eilat, part of David Fattal's Fattal Hotels chain in Israel. David Fattal, who started his career in the hotel business as a reception clerk, today has thirty-one hotels in Israel, forty-five in Germany and a few others here and there.

I like this Le Meridien. It's not one of the most glorious hotels that I've been to, but it has a certain look that makes you think you're at a friend's home and not in a hotel. I have a big balcony, facing Jordan, right across the waters (Gulf of Aqaba/Gulf of Eilat), which obviously adds to the charm of the room. On the Jordanian side is an object that catches my eye: a giant Arab flag. I wonder why the Jordanians feel the need to fly such a huge flag. Is it for the same reason that the Palestinians fly their giant flag in Rawabi, to stick it the Jews? I don't know.

* * *

To get a better feel of my surroundings I leave the room and go down to the hotel's café. I order *caffe hafukh* (café latte), and the waitress, a young Israeli girl whose parents immigrated from Russia when she was a baby, takes the time to chat with me. I look like a classic European to her, and she would like to live where I live. "I'm not a

Zionist," she proudly explains to me, and she would rather not live here. Why she feels the need to tell this to me is beyond my capacity to understand.

I look at the tourists around me. I remember when I was a teenager, Eilat was packed with European tourists, all speaking foreign languages. The tourists I see here now are almost all Israelis. The international language here is Hebrew.

I go for a walk on the streets of Eilat. As in the hotel, the tourists outside are also Israelis.

When I was a teenager the Europeans I saw in Israel were lying naked on the beach sucking the sun into their pale skins. The Europeans I see these days in Israel, though not in Eilat, are fully dressed and they run around in an obsessive search for a bad Jew.

Has Europe changed? Have the Jews changed?

I meet some locals, Jews, and they explain Eilat to me: a city sandwiched between Jordan on the one side and Egypt on the other. It is just a few minutes' ride from each border, five minutes to Egypt driving this way and five minutes to Jordan driving the other way. On a clear day, when I look right across, they tell me, I will even see Saudi Arabia.

I don't see Saudi Arabia now, but I see Zoltan. Zoltan is a street comedian who makes his living by betting twenty shekels to a hundred that you will not be able to beat him and his bike. Zoltan rides his bike effortlessly in front of you and dares you to do the same. The deal is this: you hand Zoltan twenty shekels, you get the bike and you have to ride it for four meters the way he rides the bike. How does he ride it? Simple: he sits, he puts both his hands on the steering rod and both his feet on the pedals. Piece of cake, isn't it? Well, if you can do this he'll give you one hundred shekels; if you cannot, say goodbye to your twenty.

There's one little trick here, of course: Zoltan has built this bike with an opposite steering rod. If you turn the rod to the right the bike will go left, and if you turn it to the left the bike will go right. Passersby, especially machos walking with their girlfriends, are certain they can beat this Zoltan and make a quick buck. They mount the bike, sporting a big smile on their faces, only the moment they start riding they lose their balance and their smiles evaporate. Not one person avoids making the mistake of turning the rod in the wrong direction, even though all were told in advance how this bike works. It is an amazing experiment that proves beyond doubt the power of habit over logic.

For me, it took this Zoltan to make me understand why the Europeans are not coming to Israel for its beaches anymore. It's much more exciting to catch a Jew than to catch the sun. It's called habit. You can pause your hatred because of an uncomfortable Auschwitz moment, as the Europeans did a few decades ago, but to completely erase the habit of hatred is a much harder task.

Zoltan tells me that it has taken him months to get used to riding this bike, and that if he adds one tiny task to his newly acquired habit, such as holding a cigarette in his fingers while riding, he immediately loses control of the bike. Wow.

I go back to the hotel, sit by the pool, sip coffee, and smoke.

*   *   *

Yehudah, with his sixteen-year-old daughter, Leah, and his thirteen-year-old son, Avi, join me at my table. Leah tells me that she's moving to Germany soon, and Avi tells me that he would like to do the same.

Leah, who has recently acquired a German passport, is presently studying German at her high school in Eilat. She tells me: "Israelis don't respect other people. Israelis are also rude. Like, toward waiters. Israelis never say 'thank you.' When a waiter comes to serve them, they all say: 'This is not what I ordered!' They are never satisfied. But Germans are different. Germans always say 'please' and 'thank you,' they are always patient and they are always nice."

Yehudah: "Israelis are barbarians. After the summer, the hotels in Eilat have to fix broken doors, windows, and everything else because Israeli tourists break everything. In the old days, when the Europeans were the tourists, there were no problems, but now it's the Israelis who are the tourists and they have no respect."

I have a strong urge, right now, to divorce myself from these self-hating creatures. I go out, get into a cab and in minutes I'm in Aqaba, Jordan.

Welcome to Jordan, says a sign above my head. Welcome to Aqaba, says another.

I stand in Aqaba, facing Israel, and I stare at the landscape across from me on the other side of the Gulf. I feel my heart beating fast. There, on the other side, is Israel. I have, by now, spent months in Israel, spoken to hundreds if not thousands of its people, and all of them are now so far away.

From afar, looking at Israel, now just a tiny spot, I entertain the thought that I could fit the whole of Israel into the palm of my hand. What would I do, I ask myself, if Israel indeed landed in the palm of my right hand. Would I keep it close to my heart or would I throw it into the water in disgust?

So small, my Palestine, so small, my Israel!

I stare at the tiny country in my hand and I want to talk to it, but my lips don't move. Only my eyes speak to it, my wet eyes. I move away from the Gulf.

And after exactly two hours I'm back in Israel. There are loose ends I haven't tied up yet, pieces of a puzzle I haven't finished putting into place, and there are answers I haven't yet found.

My time in Israel is not over. Not yet.

Gate Forty-Five

A professor finds the real Jews: the Arabs.

PROFESSOR SHLOMO SAND OF TEL AVIV UNIVERSITY, WHOSE MOST RECENT book, *When and How I Stopped Being a Jew*, came out earlier this year, is facing me at a Tel Aviv café, the natural think tank of people like him.

Shlomo likes big statements.

"Chances are that the real descendants of the original Jews are the Palestinians living here today. A Palestinian living in Hebron is more likely to be a direct descendant of the ancient Jews than Tuvia."

Shlomo has harsh words up his sleeve with respect to Israel: "Israel will not finish before making a big Auschwitz in the Middle East."

What is it that makes Israel so cruel, so stupid?

"You, the Germans, are responsible for this."

I totally forgot that I'm German, especially since he knows me by the name of Tuvia. Good that he reminded me.

In any case: We, the Germans, introduced "Jewish" as a race, and then some strange people started calling themselves "Jews," and the real Jews, the Palestinians, are now getting killed by the "Jews."

I love Shlomo's one-liners. Here's one: Jews and Arabs live in Jerusalem, Israelis live in Tel Aviv.

A few feet away from us is the Zavta hall, where the former MK Uri Avnery is about to start celebrating his ninetieth birthday party. The theme of the evening, composed by Uri, is this: "Will Israel exist ninety years from now?"

Shlomo and I go to the party.

I walk over to Uri and wish him another ninety years, "to finish the job."

"I hope it will not take that long," he says.

I take my seat in the theater hall of Zavta, sitting in one of the front rows. On my left is Dr. Angelika Timm, the director of the Rosa Luxemburg Foundation, and in front of me is Gideon Levy. I ask Gideon what has happened to his promise to take me along me with him on one of his forays through the Palestinian world. "It hasn't been possible yet," he answers.

What's the big deal, I ask him? Just call me before you go and I'll come over. "I will do it," he says.

The stage is empty except for a slide with Uri and others lying on the ground in the Arab village of Bil'in, evidently protecting themselves against an IDF tear gas attack.

People here love this image: an image of Jewish brutality and cruelty.

Am I in a Jewish self-hating factory or is this a Palestinian cultural event starring two wayward Jews and three hundred self-loving Arabs?

I look around at the audience and see one Arab lady. Among the speakers tonight: no Arab. In other words: with one exception, everybody here is Jewish.

The evening proceeds slowly, as intellectual events usually do, and at one point Shlomo gets pissed off and screams that it is a shame that no Arab has been invited to speak. A person three rows behind me tries to calm Shlomo down: "We have invited them, but they didn't want to come."

But psychologically, Shlomo cannot allow himself to even entertain the idea that the Arabs have simply refused to show up for a Jew's birthday, and he totally ignores the caller.

The "Jewish" Professor Asma, from Al-Quds University, whom I met in my first week in Israel, was right: it is the Germans who are passionate about the Palestinians, not the Israelis. The intellectual Israeli leftists don't accept the Palestinians one bit, despite their lofty declarations of "I love the Palestinians." With the exception of the one Arab lady, no one here loves a Palestinian.

How could they? If you are a self-hater, if you have no capacity to love even yourself, how can you love anybody else? There ain't no room for love in your heart, man, and you had better start living with it.

As I sit here and watch these self-haters, I hear a voice within me asking: Is there anybody out there who is brainwashing these Jews to hate themselves?

Good question.

I leave the Jews of Zavta in search of the possible manipulators of the Jew.

Gate Forty-Six

*Take a guess: Which country invests the most
funds on anti-Israel campaigns?*

I STICK AROUND IN TEL AVIV AND GO TO MEET DAVID LIPKIND OF THE ISRAEL
Film Fund, an organization that is engaged primarily with feature
(fiction) films. David should be able to show me a graph of the money
flowing into the production of Israeli self-hate films, of which there are
many. Artists, sorry to say this, are a bunch of selfish, egocentric kids
who will sell their souls to the highest bidder. If a filmmaker knows
that you are a rich "anti-wood" person who will generously fund his
or her next project provided it delivers a strong anti-wood message,
he and she will be more than glad to turn your wish into a film.

I hope that today I will find the funders hiding behind the films.
The Israeli Film Fund, the largest of Israeli film sponsors with millions
and millions of shekels at its disposal, is often making Israeli films
happen with the help of generous foreign investors.

We talk, David and I. In the last ten years, David informs me, there
have been at least twenty-five coproductions between Germany and
Israel.

How many of the twenty-five have had to do with politics?

"I think something like 60 percent."

Are there any right-leaning coproduction movies?

"No."

In other words, Germany is working hard on influencing the minds of the Israelis, not to mention the minds of foreign viewers. Germany. Again.

There is still another missing link in my film puzzle: non-feature, documentary films. I'll have to find the organization in charge of them and its people.

But until I find them, I want to know who stands behind the non-film anti-Israel activities? In other words: Who is funding the various NGOs operating here?

*   *   *

I leave Tel Aviv and go to Herzeliya Pituakh, the high-tech capital of Israel. Nope, I don't plan to visit Google or Microsoft; I have them aplenty in the States. I have other plans. I'm going to have coffee with an Israeli army officer at a seaside café, who happens to be in Herzeliya Pituakh today. This meeting was arranged by the IDF Spokesman's office, at my request, and two soldiers from that office are attending.

Lieutenant Colonel S., whose area of expertise is "communication between the international community and Palestinian areas," shares this with me:

"The international community has 600 million euro investments in Area C (area under full Israeli control, where about 5 percent of Palestinians live)."

Are you speaking of all the money that has been invested here since 1967 till today?

"No. Right now, on the table."

How much money from 1967?

"Billions."

What countries have invested the most?

"The two of the greatest influence: the USA and Germany. And, of course, the UN, via various agencies."

Why are these two countries investing so much?

"This is a very sensitive question."

S. has a theory about this, but asks that it may be kept off record.

Once we're back on record, I ask him: How many NGOs are operating on the Israeli-Palestinian conflict?

"Three hundred. This estimate is for the West Bank only, excluding Gaza."

How many in Gaza?

"One hundred."

Talking about the effect of individual NGOs, he adds: "The Red Cross, in humanitarian issues, is the most influential of the NGOs."

How come they're the most influential?

"Because they are not running to the press."

The way it works is this: They don't "run to the press" because they use the press as a threat. They contact the Israelis and demand certain things, and if the Israelis don't do their bidding, the ICRC will go to the press and accuse Israel.

Which reminds me: ICRC and I have agreed that I join them in one of their operations. I write a reminder for myself and resume talking to the man facing me.

In terms of government investments it is the USA first and Germany second. Who are the biggest NGO players?

"In the NGO world it is also the USA first and Germany second."

Many of the American NGOs are citizen-funded, meaning rich citizens pour tons of money into their little pet projects. George Soros, a far-left Jewish billionaire, is an example, as is the far-right tycoon Irving Moskowitz. But in Germany it's a different story. For the most part, German NGOs are funded by political parties – don't ask me to explain this strange phenomenon – or by Church-related organizations that are funded by the government, which means that German NGOs are funded by the taxpayer, millions of taxpayers.

Why is it that the average German prefers to spend his own money on an endless chase of a Jew instead of on an enjoyable weekend in Florida or in Bad Gastein? Ask him. All I know is this: if he or she didn't want their money to be spent in this manner, they would be in the street demonstrating. Germans, after all, are famous for their love of demonstrating. And if they don't like to demonstrate – let's say it's too cold outside, or there are too many other demonstrations taking place at that very time – why don't they raise their resentment in huge Internet campaigns and online petitions?

Lieutenant Colonel S. shares with me a very interesting item: "Per capita, a Palestinian gets more financial support than any citizen of any country anywhere in the world."

What is the underlying reason for such help, is it anti-Semitism? Is it –

"I don't want to talk about this."

What is the number of Israeli NGOs operating in Palestinian areas?

"About a dozen."

Who is financing them?

"Mostly from abroad."

*   *   *

German involvement here has not started today. Various Germans have been interested in this part of the world long before there was a Palestinian issue. The German Templars (Tempelgesellschaft), for example, were around here in the nineteenth century. My present home in Jerusalem is a Templar house, which my cats are enjoying tremendously. Not far from here, in central Tel Aviv, those German Templars also founded a colony by the name of Sarona. They are no longer there, deported by the Brits as were other Templars in the land, and Sarona has since changed to HaKirya, where the brain and nerve center of the Israeli army and security is located.

History is more imaginative than fiction.

My next stop is old Sarona, which is probably the most secured real estate in the world. Under its military base, rumor goes, there is a huge city in the belly of the earth; floors above floors and roads above roads. Is it true? I ask a soldier, once I enter the base, "very few know what's under our feet," she replies.

When you walk here, a town within a city in the heart of Tel Aviv, you're impressed. A huge place, fascinating structures, various types of buildings, roads that look normal though one cannot take a step on them without being given specific permission to do so.

Again, the IDF Spokesperson's office has arranged this visit for me, at my request. I'm allowed to go to only one building, no photos please, in a specific room where Colonel D. of the Military Advocate General is waiting for me. D. is a legal adviser within the Israeli military in the West Bank, and I'm here to learn about the legality of everything concerning the "occupation."

I get a short introduction: in 1967 Israel imposed "belligerent occupation," legalese speaking. What does this mean? Well, it's not so simple, but the short and the sweet of it is this: Israel claims that the Geneva Convention is not applicable to the areas it captured in 1967, yet it operates within the convention's parameters as if it did accept their applicability.

Why? This is a political issue, outside the boundaries of this officer's responsibilities, he says.

Colonel D. supplies this additional information: In the West Bank, which Israel claims that its status is in question and does not admit nor deny that it's occupied, Israel applies the legal systems that existed there prior to 1967, going way back in the past. This means that the Ottomans', the British Mandate's, and the Jordanian legal systems are all part and parcel of the current legal system in the West Bank, while at the same time rules of International Law apply, as if this area were an occupied area. In the Golan Heights Israel annexed the territory, while within Jerusalem Israel imposed Israeli law, which legally is not the same as "annexation."

You must have an advanced law degree from Harvard Law School to understand this.

I like it clear and I ask the man: Is occupation by itself not illegal?

"It is legal, by international law. Otherwise there would be no laws regarding occupied lands."

This man acts as if he had been to Harvard.

What's the story with the settlements? Is it not illegal per Article 49 of the Fourth Geneva Convention? ("Individual or mass forcible transfers … are prohibited. … The Occupying Power shall not deport or transfer parts of its own civilian population into the territory it occupies.")

"Firstly, Israel claims that it did not move its residents into the disputed area, since the people moved themselves into it, as opposed to forced settlements. Second: Israel claims that it never defined the area as occupied. Third: Israel claims that as long as it is negotiating the status of the land with the other side, no court should get involved.

"In addition: Israel claims that the area in dispute, meaning the West Bank, never belonged to Jordan, Syria, or Egypt. There is a UN decision for dividing the land under British Mandate between Arabs and Jews, but this decision did not specify who the 'Arabs' are."

The above, I also learn, is being constantly challenged in Israeli courts, where most cases against the army are being filed by foreign-financed Israeli NGOs. But all in all, D. asserts, "Israel operates within the boundaries of International law."

What is international law?

"This is the million dollar question."

We go on to discuss this issue in minute detail, engaging in hair splitting arguments as if we were two Talmudic scholars, and end up with the magic formula: "Nobody Knows."

I am left to think about all this on my own.

Who decides what international law is? If you search deep and wide and walk where your eyes and your mind lead you, you will reach the seats in the UN Security Council in New York, on which four White people and one Chinese warm their asses. Sorry for being so graphic. Representing the victors of WWII, the folks who dropped bombs from fast-flying airplanes into the dark bedrooms of sleeping civilians, are the very same peoples who tell the rest of us what is and what is not legally permissible in conflict areas, and demand that we abide by their commands.

Yes, I know. The enemy they were facing then wasn't the sweetest of men. Would they act differently, though, today, when they are not facing a man like Wolfy, aka Adolf Hitler?

Or are they?

The figures for October 2013 in Iraq, the country which the law-abiding nations of the West have messed up big time, are just out: 979 dead in a mere thirty days. This figure does not include deaths from car accidents, diseases, or normal crime.

I get ready to leave the base, and as I step on its grounds one last time one word comes to my mind: Sarona. I wish I could meet the people of Sarona, ask them what made them come here. Sadly I can't, because the Brits expelled them long before I was born, but perhaps I could compensate for this impossibility by visiting Tabgha Monastery by the Sea of Galilee; there the Germans have outsmarted the Brits.

Gate Forty-Seven

Where Jesus Christ has fed the poor, a German monk is feeding visitors his deepest thoughts about the Jews.

I AM IN THE TABGHA MONASTERY AND BROTHER JOSEF, A LIVELY BROTHER WITH two wild eyes who was born in 1971 in Düsseldorf, Germany, greets me with a handshake and a smile.

Tabgha Monastery is owned by the Deutscher Verein vom Heiligen Land, which dates back to about 1890. German monks of a different order had been here even earlier but were put in jail by the Brits following the breakout of wwii. When they were in jail, the Verein, located in Köln, asked non-German monks to come over instead and look after the property. Father Jerome of Croatia, who was already here in 1933, took it upon himself to stay on and look after the property.

That was a smart move. Once the war was over, this German Verein still had the property, unlike the German Templars of Sarona.

Father Jerome, a really old man by now, is still around and when I ask him whether it would not have been better if he had stayed in Italy, where he was at the time, he doesn't answer.

I sit down with the younger monk, Brother Josef, whose real name is Tony, for a little heart-to-heart conversation.

Brother Josef, tell me something. What is a German like you doing here with the Jews?

It takes Brother Josef time to answer this question. In his youth, he tells me, he never thought of Israel. "I have to admit," he says, "that it took me years to allow Jerusalem and Israel, and the reality of this land, to enter my heart and my mind."

What happened?

He gives me a complex answer, which is more of a longwinded stream of consciousness than a reply, and then comes back and talks of the Israeli army's siege of Bethlehem, "in the fall of the year 2000, which made me think."

I ask him to tell me what happened, and what he thought at the time.

"A group of Palestinian militia stormed into the Nativity Church and took captive civilians who were inside and, in response, the IDF besieged the place."

So that's when the "reality of this land" reached your heart, as you said. What do you mean by "reality"?

"The reality of living under occupation."

Let me understand you, Brother: When the Muslims took your Christian brothers and sisters captive, endangering their lives in one of the holiest shrines of your faith, you changed your first allegiance, your allegiance to your Christian brothers, to those Muslims. Not just your allegiance, but you made an even greater decision in their favor by coming here. Does this make sense to you? To me, it's mind-boggling. Don't take this personally, but sometimes I think that whenever Germans talk about Jews, sense and logic mysteriously vanish. Am I wrong?

Brother Josef stares at me, then stares at some invisible point past me and, after a few moments of total silence, he blurts out: "Yes, it is mind-boggling."

I think I better drop the Jewish and German subject and talk to him about Tony under the cowl of Brother Josef. Remembering the monk I met at the Holy Sepulcher and his hot kisses, I ask this monk an intimate question.

Tell me, Brother, as a monk you have no intimate partner. What do you do when sexual desires come over you? How do you deal with them?

"Sometimes I cry."

Let me ask you this, and of course you don't have to answer, do you masturbate?

Brother Josef answers, in a low voice: "This is what monks do."

This ability of the German to give honest answers to even the most intimate questions, which I have witnessed many a time before, makes me love Germans. I might be very critical of them, but I also often admire them.

Brother Josef now takes me to the church, a place where between four and five thousand people visit daily, except on Sundays. When we go in, thank God it's Sunday. I notice a rock-like stone that seems totally out of place in this church. What is it? Well, you will never believe this! It is on this stone that Jesus Christ was sitting or standing

when sharing five loaves of bread and two fish with five thousand starving people and all were fully satisfied.

There is Jesus Christ, and there are the Christians. In Hebrew you don't say Christians but *Notzrim* (Muslim Arabs say *Nasraniyyin*), meaning Nazarenes, and Jesus Christ is called Jesus the Nazarene. Jesus lived not far from here, in Nazareth, and as I leave this place of his miracle making I go to visit his city.

Gate Forty-Eight

Here Jesus the Nazarene lived, but no other Jew is allowed to live here.

I GET A ROOM AT THE FAUZI AZAR INN, A FUNKY HOTEL WHICH IS A JEWEL IN the midst of Nazareth's Old City. The guests are free-spirit kind of creatures and you can have drinks and cakes, as many as you desire, all free of charge. The receptionists are two young Christian girls, one Finnish and one American, and both love the Arabs more than they love the not-really-nice Jews. As one of them says to me: "God chose the Jews not because they are nice."

What a nice welcome. I guess I had better be a Christian here. No Abu Ali, and no Tuvia. Just Tobi, Tobi the German Christian.

I go to take part in a Mass with the local people. Moments later, I find myself in a huge church with large pillars made of concrete. On the walls I see that the Arabs here refer to Jerusalem as Jerusalem and not as Al-Quds. Interesting. The service is done in Arabic, and only one Hebrew word is heard here: *Hallelujah.* (*Hallelujah* means "Praise the Lord" in Hebrew.)

After prayer I go to meet the priest, to see what's on his mind. "This is an occupied land. The Jews occupied it twice: in 1948 and in 1967."

Fine.

I mingle with the local people, to see what's on their mind, and I discover something quite interesting: No Jew lives in this city and no resident will sell his or her house to a Jew.

This is Nazareth, within the Israel of pre-1967.

I go back to the hotel and fall asleep, the only Jew in Jesus' town.

When morning comes, Lubna, whose main wish is to get married and very soon, *inshallah*, takes a group of us, Fauzi Azar guests, on a tour of Nazareth's Old City. As we walk I see big posters in support of deposed Egyptian president Mohamed Morsi, of the Muslim Brotherhood. During his short reign he was an unshakable supporter of Hamas, but now he is in jail. The people here, who are Israeli citizens, want him back in power. Hamas does not recognize Israel, wants nothing less than Israel's annihilation, and these people support Hamas.

Fine.

We stop at an old house, where no one lives, and we look at its architecture. Lubna explains to us that "no one lives here because the owners were forced out by the Occupiers." Lubna points at the ceiling, where we see burned beams of wood, and explains that "this is what people did centuries ago."

When was this house built?

"This house is from the first century and it belonged to the original Palestinian residents who lived in this city under the Ottoman rulers." The same Ottomans, I guess, who founded Alsra in the Negev, Halil's village so well protected by Adalah.

The Turks were here in the first century?

"Yes. They were the first occupiers of Palestine. Then the British occupied Palestine, and now it is Israel."

This is a very enlightening narrative. No Romans or Crusaders have ever been here, according to this narrative. The Turks, who in reality first showed up here in 1517, have their presence moved back by a millennium and a half according to this narrative.

I tell Lubna that no Ottoman even dreamt of being here in the first millennium, not to say century, since the Ottoman Empire started over twelve centuries later.

Members of our group, educated Westerners who have come to the Holy Land to show their sympathies with the "poor Palestinians," as one of them had told me before, wish that this strange German would stop talking. They ask no question of Lubna, and everything they hear they accept. They buy it all, wholesale, and they don't need me to disturb their peaceful morning "research."

Who are these people, Western people in whose midst I have lived for the past three decades? I make an appointment to meet the head of the German KAS in Jerusalem, Michael Mertes. Maybe he can explain to me a thing or two. His office is minutes away from my Jerusalem home, where I go next.

When my cats see me on the street outside, they run to the place where I usually leave the milk for them, looking at me with thankful eyes. Nadia, the famed singer, doesn't thank her providers, but my cats do.

Gate Forty-Nine

Who am I? Am I an offensive right-winger or a leftist troublemaker?

"WE SUPPORT THE STRENGTHENING OF DEMOCRACY AND THE RULE OF LAW IN Israel," KAS says in its literature. Personally I find it bizarre that a German foundation will come here to teach Jews what democracy is, but I don't think these words are the making of Michael Mertes, head of the KAS branch in Jerusalem.

I have met Michael before and he made me laugh. He told me a clever joke that I can't forget:

A man was sitting outside a Tel Aviv café writing when a passerby stopped by to ask him what he was writing about.

Writer: I am an author and I am writing a book about Israel.

Passerby: This is a huge job! How long are you planning to stay in the country?

Writer: I landed yesterday and I'm flying back tomorrow.

Passerby: You are going to write a book about a country after being in it for barely three days?

Writer: Yes.

Passerby: What is the title of your book, if I may ask?

Writer: "Israel: Yesterday, Today, and Tomorrow."

Before coming into Michael's office to meet him, I've made up my mind to be as honest as Brother Josef was with me and will say to

Michael what I think straight up. This is going to be a German-to-German conversation.

I share with Michael what I saw and witnessed while taking part in various KAS programs. I found, I tell him, that the Jews KAS is working with are people who believe that Israel is on the wrong side of history and justice, and that the Palestinians whom KAS is working with happen to totally agree with them. What's the point of KAS spending money on bringing these specific Arabs and Jews together?

And as for the Arabs sponsored by KAS, I have another question: I have spoken with some of them and found them not only to be strongly anti-Israel, but also classic anti-Semites. Why is it that a German foundation, especially given the delicate history between Germans and Jews, finds it necessary to support such people?

Michael doesn't like my questions and he tells me that he feels offended by me, that he is disappointed with me, and that I talk like a right-winger.

Incidentally, I am told by a confidential source that my request

for an interview with Benjamin Netanyahu and Avigdor Lieberman was rejected, as both their teams have concluded that I am a "leftist troublemaker."

Back at my Templar home with the cats I look up the dark sky and wonder: Why has this country, and especially this city, been such a magnet to so many people for so many years? Personally, I am conflicted about Israel. I grew up here, but I left. Naturally, as a country of my youth, especially this city of Jerusalem in which I spent many years, speaks to me. Strangely, it speaks to me more in the language of the Bible – though I'm not a religious person – than in the current sounds I hear in its streets.

Here in Jerusalem I feel the city's biblical characters walking, breathing, talking, dancing, and making love. Above the walls of this city and in the depth of its sands, I hear them and I see them. Yes, I do. I see its former kings and their courts, its scholars and its warriors, its tradesmen and its prophets; all of its people who once lived here but who to this very day stubbornly refuse to die.

Nir Barkat, the feisty mayor of Jerusalem, tells me that I should go for a walk in Jerusalem's City of David, take a Bible with me, and see for myself how point-by-point, page-by-page the two corroborate with one another. I like the idea of connecting with old Jerusalem and I go. I wish that Dr. Hanan Ashrawi would come along with me, but I have this strong feeling that she wouldn't.

Gate Fifty

A date with history: kings, professors, and a toilet.

I DON'T THINK THAT NIR BARKAT, WHO'S NOT RELIGIOUS, WALKS IN THE CITY of David with a Bible, but whatever he does, I choose to walk with a man named Assaf instead of a book named the Bible. I don't like maps that were not printed by the Japanese government, like that map of Jericho. Period.

He is Assaf Avraham of Israel Nature and Parks Authority, City of David, and he's an archeologist presently doing his PhD in the field. He speaks quietly into my ears: "The name of Jerusalem is Uru-shalem, the city of Shalem, a Canaanite god of the Middle Bronze Age period, around 2000 BCE. Jerusalem is the invention of King David, built around 1000 BCE. Earlier in the biblical text every person was allowed to build a shrine to God wherever he felt like, but King David decreed that there was only one place to worship God in. This was a political decision.

"In the year 722 BCE the Assyrians, the ancestors of today's Iranians, conquered Israel and destroyed the Kingdom of Israel. We assume that between 722 and 701 Jerusalem grew tremendously in terms of residents due to the Israelite refugees who moved south, to the Kingdom of Judah from the Kingdom of Israel which had now been destroyed. This is the assumption by Professor Israel Finkelstein of Tel Aviv University.

"Now for the City of David," he continues: "From 1000 to 586 BCE, this city was inhabited by the ancient Israelites, and we assume that most of the Bible was written in this place. Most of the archeological findings in the City of David are from the eighth to the sixth centuries BCE. But in some locations we have found evidence from the tenth to the eighth centuries BCE, which includes the Kingdom of David. Earlier findings were discovered in the Ophel Area, which is north of the City of David. Dr. Eilat Mazar of Hebrew Univeristy in Jerusalem, the granddaughter of Professor Benjamin Mazar, discovered fortifications from the tenth century BCE, which she calls the Wall of Solomon. She has also found the foundation of a huge building at the center of the City of David, which is from the tenth century BCE, and she theorizes that it is the palace of King David."

The City of David, near the Western Wall/al-Aqsa, is a treasure trove for the Jews and a pain in the neck for the Arabs. A walk in this area seems to indeed corroborate various passages in the Bible, and people like Hanan Ashrawi are not happy. But while the Arabs cannot do anything in the City of David, as it is governed by Israel, they can do much in the al-Aqsa/Western Wall area, Israel having given all authority over it to the Waqf, the Islamic Religious Trust.

Old discoveries there, such as a Temple Mount stone with the inscription "To the Trumpet Blowing," discovered by Benjamin Mazar decades earlier, are problematic for the Arabs, since they claim that al-Aqsa was not built over the ruins of a Jewish temple, and, Assaf tells me, whenever they can they destroy evidence of ancient Jewish life on the Holy Mountain.

He also cites the various maneuvers undertaken in the Western Wall/al-Aqsa area: in the late nineties, when the Waqf built an additional mosque in the al-Aqsa complex, they did excavations in the sensitive archeological area of the Temple Mount/al-Aqsa without any Israeli supervision. They then loaded tons of topsoil from the area on four-hundred trucks and dumped their contents in various locations. Some Israelis followed the trucks, to see where the soil was being dumped, and later Israel collected the dumped soil and deposited it in one location. Since then, and to this day, archeologists and their helpers are sifting the soil.

Dr. Eilat Mazar has made quite a number of discoveries not mentioned here, and which fellow archeologists from Tel Aviv University are partly disputing. The reason for their disagreement, as is often the case in science, is political and religious by nature: She is a Bible-inspired archeologist, which is not the case with the archeologists of Tel Aviv University.

During excavations at the foot of the Western Wall/al-Aqsa complex done earlier this year, she discovered thirty-six ancient coins, among them a gold medallion with the menorah (the Temple candelabrum) symbol on it, which archeologists date to the seventh century CE. A major discovery that, as far as I know, the Tel Aviv guys have not yet disputed.

Assaf offers to come with me on a tour of al-Aqsa, as he'd like to share with me some more archeological facts, and I accept. He asks that I show up before 7:30 a.m., when the "infidels" entrance to the complex opens. Assaf doesn't wish to recite the Fatiha, the way I tried to do some months ago.

*   *   *

At 7:10 a.m. the following day Assaf is already standing next to the entrance of al-Aqsa and he looks eager to enter. He starts by telling me that the Western Wall is five hundred meters long, which I've already heard months ago, and that it was built by King Herod as part of the Temple around 20 BCE. That temple is also known as the Second Temple, Assaf says, since the First Temple was built by King Solomon. "We don't know what this huge area was like before Herod's construction, as we can hardly do any archeological work here." As for the First Temple "it was built, according to biblical account, around 1000 BCE."

By 7:30 a.m., around fifteen hundred tourists, of whom only about five are Jews, are standing in line. "The area is very sensitive today," an Israeli policeman tells us before we enter.

Once we have entered I see Waqf guards all around. What's the story? When they spot Jews, Assaf explains to me, a guard will trail them to make sure that they don't pray here.

From I don't know where I hear a group shouting "Allahu Akbar!" I thought only infidels were here at this time of day, but obviously I was wrong.

I see Arab women in a few parts of al-Aqsa and of the Dome of the Rock, just sitting. As we pass by the Dome, Assaf gets passionate. "The diameter of the Dome is exactly the same as that of the Holy Sepulcher," he says, and immediately a Palestinian woman gets up from her seat and comes by to eavesdrop. In other places and under different circumstances this wouldn't mean a thing, but nothing is normal in this place. She could be a Waqf employee, and if she hears anything contradicting the Islamic faith an international crisis could immediately develop. These things have happened before. To calm her down, I greet her in Arabic. She softens up at once. Where you from? She asks. Germany, I say. Welcome to al-Aqsa, she replies with a loving smile and walks away.

The God of Islam loves the Germans.

Now safe, Assaf continues: "Architecture-wise, the Dome is of a Byzantine structure, and octagonal, and it seems that the structure was a church before. Another important fact is that each side of the octagon measures twenty meters, exactly as in other churches in the area. During the British Mandate, the British found a Byzantine mosaic underneath al-Aqsa, suggesting that a church existed in the area at some time." The Jewish Temple, he also tells me, "was exactly where the Dome is now, but there have been no scientific excavations done under the Dome at any period known to us."

He stops talking as another round of Allahu Akbar! shouts is heard. This time the yelling is louder and seems to involve many more people. Reason? Three old Jewish ladies and a bare footed man, who seems to be their guide, are passing by. Three steps behind them, and trailing them wherever they go, is an Israeli policeman and a Waqf guard. Reason? If any of these four opens a Jewish book and prays, riots will start. And this must be prevented at all cost.

A cleaning lady comes out of the Dome to clean its entrance. This is a rare opportunity for me to walk by and take a glimpse. As I approach the Dome the lady runs fast inside, closes and locks the door, so that I am not able to see anything. A tour guide passing by me tells his group that inside the Dome there are three strands of hair from Prophet Muhammad's beard.

A couple of steps from the Dome is a structure that Assaf calls a "baptismal font," complete with what seems to be the sign of the cross. "Why is this here," he asks, "if this was not a church?"

The truth is, the Crusaders who captured Jerusalem in 1099 CE, used this mosque as a church, and it could be that they also built the font. I don't know.

The atmosphere around me is very tense, as if everybody was

waiting for an explosion. You can sense the tension in the air. Frequent shouts of "Allahu Akbar" signify that a possible Jew is passing by.

That this is happening in Jerusalem, in the age of human rights, is frightening.

Assaf leaves and as I walk over to the public toilet, a few Waqf guards immediately get very busy. "Who is he?" one asks. "German," answers the other. I'm allowed to pee in the al-Aqsa toilet. Finally!

*   *   *

Freshly relieved, I go to the Temple Institute in the Jewish Quarter, an organization "dedicated to every aspect of the Holy Temple in Jerusalem." The Temple Institute arranges tours in its building where a model of the temple, plus many items therein, are shown to interested individuals. This could be my opportunity to finally see the cherubs that I was kvetching about when I just arrived in Israel. And so I join a tour to the Holy of Holies exhibition, and yes! I get to see the two all-gold cherubs! The cherubs, as I see here, are two creatures both of which have a human face, one male and the other female, and they face each other. The rest of their bodies look like a combination of small animals and birds, and each has huge wings.

I won two of two today: the use of the al-Aqsa toilet and seeing the cherubs. Took me almost half a year!

The cherubs, I hope I don't offend either Arab or Jew, are quite similar to al-Buraq: half of one creature, half of the other. Before there was al-Aqsa, Assaf claims, there was a church. Before there was al-Buraq, I claim, there was a cherub.

I'm the only Master Agent on the planet so happy to have found two golden cherubs!

I leave the institute and later on go to meet Assaf again, this time in the City of David. Assaf shows me a replica of the "Shiloah Inscription," the original of which was found in the City of David. The inscription, on a stone, was written in ancient Hebrew letters, dated 701 BCE. "Though Modern Hebrew and biblical Hebrew sound quite alike, the letters are very different. The Hebrew letters in use today,"

Assaf tells me, "are Assyrian, in accordance with the writing used in Assyria, which is the Iran of today."

The Shiloah Inscription describes the meeting point of two groups of tunnel diggers, each digging toward the other. One group was digging from the Gihon Spring and the other from the Shiloah in Jerusalem. King Hezekiah, who had anticipated an Assyrian siege of Jerusalem, built this tunnel in order to assure a flow of water into the city of Jerusalem. The Bible refers to this event in 2 Kings: "As for the other events of Hezekiah's reign, all his achievements and how he made the pool and the tunnel by which he brought water into the city, are they not written in the book of the annals of the Kings of Judah?"

This is a major discovery that substantiates the Jewish historical claim to this land as it confirms the existence of an ancient Jewish kingdom here. It is an extremely important text in the annals of Jewish history, which is rare because so very little was written in those days.

Are the Jews happy? Well, not completely: They don't possess the original stone.

Who does? Turkey. The Ottoman Empire, let's not forget, once ruled this place.

The original of this inscription, Assaf tells me, is at the Istanbul Archeology Museum. Years ago, Israel tried to get it from the Turks but did not succeed. It is Turkey, a land of many Muslims, which owns one of the biggest proofs for Jewish history in Israel.

Assaf is a dark-skinned, really dark, man. He looks like the cliché of a leftist but talks like the cliché of a rightist. At times, though, he surprises me.

"When I see the Arabs," he tells me, "sometimes I'm jealous. I see how they all say 'hello' to each other when they meet, how they hug each other, how they kiss each other. Sometimes you see them holding hands. They are one big family. This is the East. This is an Eastern culture. The West is different. The West is cold. Everyone to himself. There are very strong social differences between the two cultures and they don't mix. Had Israel been an Eastern country culturally, I believe we could live with each other as one. My parents were born in India, but I am a Westerner. I understand the differences."

As we speak, Arab kids play soccer and other games around us on the grounds of this archeological site. Assaf looks at them and says he'll have to call the police to get the kids away. I see a guard at the entrance and ask Assaf why the guard has allowed the kids in. "Because he is afraid of the Arab kids," he answers. Similar story, how strange, to the one in Hebron, where stone throwing kids scare the Israeli army.

Down the road is Silwan, an Arab neighborhood within Jerusalem. Silwan – its name derived from the Hebrew name Shiloah – is an interesting place. With the exception of two houses that are being protected by armed Israeli guards around the clock, no Jew steps a foot in there.

I go in. A big Palestinian flag hanging at Silwan's center, as if to say that this is not Israel, greets me. As I walk, and without any warning sign, a group of Arab youngsters approaches me and one of them takes off my baseball cap. He wants to know, I guess, if there's a skullcap under my hat.

He looks and he finds none, but still doesn't give me back my hat and walks away with it. He looks back to see if I run after him, but I don't. Running after him would be translated as fear. Not good here. Instead, I curse him and his group in Arabic.

This the kids did not expect. An Arab. Just like them. An older member of the group apologizes and I get back my hat.

Silwan, in the heart of Jerusalem, wants to be Judenfrei, like Nazareth, and various NGOs stand by their side. And as I keep on walking in Silwan, I think I finally understand why there are so many NGOs here. Where else could one practice his or her darkest wish for Judenfrei territories and still be considered liberal?

Does this my conclusion sound over-blown to you, too unreal, too judgmental? I wish that I were wrong. But if you come with me on a tour of this Silwan, and of this land, and walk with me in some of these places, where the NGOs rule and not even the Devil dares come, you will come to the same conclusion. Sorry.

Gate Fifty-One

A date with the Good Europeans: How good are they?

NES AMIM (MIRACLE OF NATIONS) IS A CHRISTIAN VILLAGE NEXT TO AKKO, A city on the sea near Haifa, founded a few decades ago for the explicit purpose of having Christians learn from Jews instead of criticizing them. I must find some good Europeans, I say to myself, and I go there.

It is Friday night, the beginning of the Jewish Sabbath and these Christians, mostly Dutch and German, are going to show off what they have learned from the Jews. First off, they bless the Sabbath in Hebrew. Well, kind of. Their Hebrew sounds like another language, a language that doesn't yet exist, but you must praise the attempt. Blessings done, food arrives. Food eaten, talk starts.

Nes Amim provides its facilities for "dialogue" groups, I learn. What kind of dialogues do they engage in? Arab-Jewish dialogues, for example. "The Israeli-Palestinian conflict is my business," a lady tells me.

How come?

"It is the UN that created Israel."

So?

"We created Israel and we are responsible for what it does."

The group agrees with this statement.

I guess that the "learn from Jews" statement of purpose of this village is just a statement.

I chat with a young German volunteer. He has been in Israel for three months and has learned a great deal. What have you learned so far? I ask him.

"That Israel implants mines next to Druze elementary schools."

How touching.

* * *

In neighboring Akko's Old City, also inside Israel proper, not one Jew lives. Road signs pointing to historical Jewish houses were taken away by the residents and replaced with signs containing Quranic verses. These residents and the people of Nes Amim are good, friendly neighbors.

It is on the streets of beautiful Akko that I meet a Swiss-German lady. "We have to remember what happened in wwii and we have to take responsibility. That is why I am here, to help the people," she tells me.

By the power of my stupidity I get sucked into a conversation with her. Which people do you help?

"I work mostly with Israeli Jews."

What do you do with them?

"We protect little Arab kids in Hebron from being stoned by Jewish settlers."

This lady is probably with EAPPI. If she's not, she should hook up with Michèle, they would make for a perfect couple.

Gate Fifty-Two

The legal system: Israeli parliament at work – the loudest mouths win.

AS AMERICAN SECRETARY OF STATE JOHN KERRY IS STEPPING UP HIS SHUTTLE diplomacy these days, landing in Israel every so often to pressure ministers, I choose to go to the Knesset repeatedly instead. No major policy change is going to take effect without the parliament's approval; why not meet the MKs?

There is a committee meeting today discussing the Bedouins that I want to attend. I saw the Bedouins; now it's time to see the parliamentarians decide about their fate.

A couple of years ago the so-called Prawer Commission, appointed by the Israeli government, issued its recommendations for various unrecognized Bedouin encampments in the Negev. The Prawer Plan suggested the relocation of some Bedouins to recognized settlements. The government appointed former minister Benny Begin, son of the late prime minister Menachem Begin, to look into it, and this resulted in some changes to the original Prawer Plan. The Prawer-Begin Plan, as it is now known, was issued earlier this year, and presently the Knesset is to decide whether to approve or disapprove of it.

In terms of people, this plan concerns the fate of about thirty thousand Bedouins who would be relocated. In terms of money, the government is offering to spend over two billion shekels in the process. In terms of living standards, this would solve the dire conditions some Bedouins are living under, as under this plan they will all from now on enjoy proper infrastructures in their communities. On the other hand, some encampments will have to be relocated and, even more importantly, if approved this plan will end the practice of building encampments in the Negev, which means that if anybody feels a special attachment to a mountain somewhere, he or she will no longer be able to just put up a shack or a tent and claim the mountain as their own.

How do I know all this? No, I'm not a Bedouin specialist, nor am I the legal adviser of any side to this dispute. The above is a compilation of literatures I got from both sides, mainly Adalah and Regavim. Truth be said, both sides assert in no uncertain terms that the Plan and its implications are hugely complex and complicated, but if you take the various lawyers and activists out of the equation and examine the story calmly, you'll find that the issue is actually quite simple.

What is not very simple are the politics that work mightily underneath both the pro and con of this issue. Namely, the Bedouin issue could well transform itself into the "Second Coming" of the "Palestinian Rights" religion. Various Israeli governments have known this and they have all acted erratically on this issue. If history is any guide, no final Knesset vote on it will take place before both Jesus and Muhammad have arrived on the same camel at the gates of Jerusalem. But don't tell this to anybody here, for they will be very offended.

The Committee now starts its session. MK Miri Regev chairs the committee and Benny Begin sits to her left. MKs sit in an inner circle of tables and non-MKs, NGO-looking faces, in the outer circle. Which of these circles have more power? Given that this is Israel, it's the NGO circle.

"The story of the Arabs after the Nakba attack in 1948," are the opening words, uttered by an Arab-Israeli MK. *Nakba*, as I have mentioned, means "catastrophe," which is what the Arabs call the establishment of the State of Israel. This MK accuses the Israeli government of destroying Arab villages while, at the same time, it keeps on building Jewish settlements. The method, as he sees it, by which the Jews operate is this: They have conquered the land in 1948 by the power of the gun and now they'll conquer additionally by the power of the law.

Once he's done, an Israeli NGO man takes his turn to speak. He demands that Israeli citizens be treated equally, including Arabs, and asserts that the Plan at hand does not do that. The third speaker says basically the same. So does the fourth speaker, an Israeli Jewish lady, member of one NGO or the other.

To my left an Amnesty International lady is sitting, busy with her smartphone, and she seems quite bored with the proceedings.

Personally I entertain the thought of taking a cigarette leave, but just when I start moving I see Rabbi Arik, the human rights rabbi, enter. I don't want to miss a blessing by a rabbi and I stay seated.

The fifth speaker gets his chance to talk and says more or less the same thing as the earlier speakers: Israel is racist, he says.

The sixth speaker: Ditto.

The seventh speaker: Ditto.

The eighth speaker, a Bedouin who says he's from al-Araqeeb, gets his chance to speak. It would have been nice if he had started with the "No, no, we shall not be moved" song but, sadly, he just screams.

The ninth speaker, a Jewish MK with a skullcap, Zvulun Kalfa of the far-right Jewish Home party, gets his turn. He says that he is surprised to see so many NGOs around and wonders why no NGO showed up when he was about to be expelled from his home in Gaza, prior to Israel's Gaza Withdrawal.

A barrage of shouts interrupts him.

When the shouts quiet down, he says that the law now being considered doesn't really matter because Israel is always afraid to enforce its laws on the Bedouin community, citing as an example the multiple women that Bedouin men marry. Polygamy is against Israeli law, he says, and another barrage of shouts interrupts him. Between you and me, it's really funny to watch feminists defend polygamy with so much passion.

The tenth person speaks, repeating what was said eight times before, more or less.

The eleventh speaker, a religious Jewish MK of the Right, speaks. She can hardly be heard. Shouts interrupt her, then more shouts and more shouts.

There is a pattern here that I can see: When a leftist speaks, he or she just does. When a rightist speaks, his or her words cannot be heard.

The shouting MKs here may remind you of the turbulent British MPs, but there are two glaring differences: (a) in Britain both sides shout; (b) the Brits have a sense of humor.

I go out to have a smoke. And then I need coffee and I go to the MKs' dining room, where I see MK Ahmad Tibi sitting lonely and in need of company.

Gate Fifty-Three

*The legal system 2: Is an MK allowed to respond to
your question by breaking your iPhone?*

MK AHMAD TIBI, A FORMER GYNECOLOGIST, IS ONE OF THE MOST FAMOUS OF
MKs. He is an Arab parliamentarian who is admired by the liberals
and deeply hated by the conservatives, and his name pops up every
so often. I love gynecologists and I sit next to him for a little chat, a
chat between a doctor and a German.

I ask MK Tibi to explain to me what I have just seen and heard:
right-wing people barraged by shouts from the Left. I want to know
why he and his friends acted so aggressively.

"We are on the side of the victims whose land has been stolen, and
they are on the side of the robbers who stole the land of the Palestinians and Arabs. Second: one of them called the Arab MKs 'animals.' It
is a very un-parliamentary word and he was to be deported from the
committee but he didn't even get any remark."

You could have responded to it, say, for example: "Hallo!" But why,
instead, the barrage of –

"This is parliament."

When you talk about the land that has been robbed, are you talking
about the land of 1948?

Instead of answering my question about the land that has been
robbed, in general, MK Tibi chooses to talk about the committee's

exchanges: "When I talked to MK Kalfa, I talked about Gaza. It was stolen and occupied in 1967."

In general, when you say, "We are on the side of the victims whose land had been stolen," are you talking about 1967 or about 1948?

"Here I talk about 1967 but as a victim inside Israel, yes, the Arab minority who are indigenous people suffer from confiscation of land from the very beginning of 1948, the construction of Israel, and these lands were confiscated from Arabs and delivered to Jews. It's racism."

Do you think the Jews robbed the Arabs of their land before 1967? Do you also call 1948 a robbery?

"It was confiscation of land from owners, original owners, from Arab owners. At least five hundred villages were destroyed and dismantled."

Do you think that the land of Israel before 1967 is legal, or do you view it as a confiscated land?

"If I am a member of the Israeli Knesset I recognize the State of Israel, but I totally object and oppose the occupation of 1967 and

the racist ways of dealing with non-Jews in Israel. Israel is a racist country!"

I try to get from MK Tibi a clear answer, which he is avoiding, and so I ask more specifically.

My question is this: Do you think that Israel should give the Arabs of Jaffa, Akko, and all those cities (from 1948) –

Tibi is now getting violent. He hits my iPhone, which I'm using to record this interview, as if he were about to throw it in the air, and angrily says: "You are asking the same question from the very beginning. I'm answering you but you are insisting – This is not journalism! You are asking for the fourth time the same question. Is it narrow-minding or what? You are trying to push me to say something that I don't want to say!"

The man has lost it. He is not used to being challenged by the media, and he was not prepared for a German like me to insist on getting answers from an Arab like him.

Well, somebody should have told him that not all Germans are the same.

Luckily for me, by the way, that ol' Steve Jobs made his phones sturdy enough to withstand angry Arabs.

*   *   *

A few steps from me I spot MK Moshe Feiglin, the flag bearer of the far right, and a man hated by most media.

These two MKs, MK Ahmad Tibi and MK Moshe Feiglin, are at the two extreme poles of the political map, and to be chatting with both of them on the same day may result in an emergency visit to the nearest psychiatrist. But, to me, having both of them back to back is a dream come true.

I pose the same question to Moshe I asked Ahmad. MK Moshe, Deputy Knesset Speaker and leader of the Jewish Leadership faction within the Likud, starts by schmoozing about Jews, the sort of Jews who won't let him talk.

"Jews have a problem."

What is it?

"They are told: We will burn you in Auschwitz if you get on the train, and they still get on the train. Jews run from the truth."

I hold tight to my iPhone, just in case MK Moshe is going to finish the job MK Ahmad started, but MK Moshe is not in the mood to break anything. He invites me to visit him at his office, and I accept the offer.

Welcome to Moshe Feiglin's kingdom.

Behind his throne is the flag of the State of Israel. To its right is a painting of Jerusalem's Old City, where al-Aqsa and the Dome of the Rock are replaced by the Jewish Temple. The Palestinians don't believe the Jews were ever here; Moshe doesn't believe they are here now.

I try to imagine Ahmad Tibi walking into here and seeing this. What he did to my iPhone is peanuts compared with what he would be doing to this room. It would be lovely if I could come up with a way to tempt him into this place, but nothing brilliant comes to my mind.

There are things better imagined than seen.

I look at MK Moshe. He looks like the average white intellectual, only with a skullcap over his head. He looks intently at me but speaks softly, though in a determined way. The man known to every Israeli news media consumer as disgusting, ugly, and repelling is in reality anything but that.

What does he stand for, and how come he has so many enemies? It is time to find out.

First, I ask him to explain to me what I saw earlier in the day at the Knesset Committee: the bunch of left-leaning NGOs all around and their shouts every time a right-leaning person opened his or her mouth. Is this normal?

"This is normal for the Israeli parliament. The leftists who speak loudly for democracy, a culture of discussion and fair debate, always prove themselves to act exactly the opposite. You could see it today, as it was very clear: whenever the Arabs and the Left talked, silence prevailed on the other side. It was very respectful. I did not find it easy to listen to what they were saying, but I respected their right to say what they thought. But when we started talking, when our turn came, you saw what happened. By the way, in comparison to other days, it was actually not so bad today."

Wait. How do you explain this? The liberal world, the intellectual world, is supposed to cherish debate –

"Come on. 'Liberalism' is just a camouflage. It is just a word that has no real meaning. The left doesn't represent either liberalism or communism. On the contrary: the Left, I discovered long ago, is an entity that justifies violence. They are open-minded only if you agree with them. If you want to see people who sit together and argue opposite views, where everybody has the same chance and freedom to speak, you have to go to a Haredi yeshiva."

Are you serious? Do you really think that you can discuss everything with the Haredi people? Don't you know that they –

"I'm talking about those Haredi people with a head on their

shoulders. Try it. You can discuss anything with them, even the question of whether God exists or not. On the other hand, try talking with a leftist about the idea that the Temple Mount should be given back to the Jews. Try arguing with him that the Oslo Accords have proved to have failed. Would you be able to even finish your sentence? No."

How come almost all NGOs today were of the Left? Where are the right-wing NGOs in this country?

"The reason is simple: money. For NGOs to exist you need money, and the ones who support and maintain the Israeli NGOs are foreigners, mostly Europeans, and they support only the Left. The rightist NGO that you saw, Regavim, is only being financed by Israelis, not Europeans. This is not what happens with leftist NGOs, who get their support not merely from foreigners but also from foreign governments, including Germany. This is a direct involvement of the foreign governments in the internal affairs of Israel. In the USA this kind of involvement is forbidden but, inappropriately, not forbidden here."

Why is the world interested in this tiny little place?

"You are getting into metaphysics here, and I don't know if you really want to get into it."

I do.

"Look: in Israel there are more foreign correspondents than in any other country by ratio to the number of people living in the country. There's an immense interest worldwide in what's happening here, which is not in proportion to the size of this land."

Why so?

"Humanity is breaking down morally and ethically and, as a result, it is waiting and wishing for direction from Israel, from the Jews."

I have no clue what he is talking about, but his is a different point of view and I want to hear it.

It is at this point that his assistant enters the room with two portions of yogurt. Moshe hasn't had anything to eat and he is starving.

* * *

MK Moshe Feiglin looks at me as he is eating. "You want me to give you intelligent answers, I assume, but no intelligent answers can come out of a man with an empty stomach."

He eats slowly, and as he joyfully licks his yogurt he talks about Ahmad Tibi, the love of his life, which I'll leave out of these pages. When he's done with his yogurt I ask him to explain to me why foreigners are interested in this land.

"You cannot understand what is happening in this land unless you view the landscape here with a lens of faith."

Talk to me.

"Look: you are not sitting here opposite a human being. The one you are facing is a dinosaur. Imagine yourself in the morning after having had breakfast, when you go to drop the trash outside. You are walking down the steps and suddenly you see a cute dinosaur, dressed with a nice tie. It would be strange, wouldn't it? This dinosaur is not supposed to exist anymore, but guess what? He exists, right in front of your eyes, and he's talking to you, the dinosaur is talking to you, a dinosaur who has lived with the Assyrians and the Philistines, and many others that you know only from the ancient history books. None of those tribes are here anymore but I, the Jew, am. Isn't it strange?"

I don't know if this MK Moshe has ever been to a museum and seen people looking at a dinosaur. If he had, he'd have seen them looking at the creature with love, not hatred. Is he suggesting that the West loves Israel?

"Talking about the West, take America for example. Many Americans, those who have built America, had a strong connection with Israel."

Forty, fifty years ago America was quite anti-Semitic and many a club had "No Blacks, No Jews" signs at their entrance doors.

"There are mixed feelings in the world about the Jews. Take England. Historically there existed what I call biblical romanticism. The Balfour Declaration, for example, could never have come out of Germany."

MK Moshe refers to British Foreign Secretary Arthur James

Balfour's letter to Lord Rothschild in November 1917, which in part reads as follows: "I have much pleasure in conveying to you, on behalf of His Majesty's Government, the following declaration of sympathy with Jewish Zionist aspirations which has been submitted to, and approved by, the Cabinet: His Majesty's Government view with favour the establishment in Palestine of a national home for the Jewish people." It is this declaration that eventually made for the establishment of Israel in 1948.

MK Moshe then goes on to tell me that the West, motivated by its Christian heritage, has helped create Israel in order to make "a balance between body and spirit" of the nations, in the hope that the "Holy Book would be written again," and that the very existence of Israel would serve to "redeem the rest of the world." The West, according to MK Moshe, thought that Israel would serve as a bridge between "Christianity that believed in refraining from the sexual and Islam that glorified sexuality, such as the Islamic heaven with its virgin brides." But Israel has disappointed them. "If we had responded positively to the hope the world had in us, the world would have supported us."

He reminds me of Arieh King, the real estate broker. Arieh claims that peace would come to this land if the Third Temple were to be built. MK Moshe has similar ideas, but he prefers to align himself with leftists, of all people. If Israel is just another Western state, he tells me, then populating this land with Jews at the expense of the Arabs is "colonization." If Israel chooses to deflect from its obligation toward this land, which are "grounded in the future and not in the past, Israel will lose its right to exist."

While almost any rightist would talk about the Jewish right to this land based on the Jewish history here, MK Moshe emphatically speaks of the future, not the past. To him, what gives the Jews the right to be in this land is rooted in the future, not in its history.

MK Moshe adds: "At some level I even understand the anti-Semites. Not that I am ready to give them any slack, especially not the Germans. And the truth is, it is not easy for me to give this interview for the German reader. I will never fly to Germany. I don't use, ever, any German product. Don't get me wrong. I will never go to Poland either. And no, I don't close my eyes to the anti-Semitism in the world.

"But I do say: humanity as a whole is not totally anti-Semitic. There is a love-hate relationship between Jews and non-Jews and it is our obligation to make love win. This is up to us to do. If we stand our ground, giving away no territory – and remember that most of the biblical stories took place in the West Bank – we will increase the love of the world for us. What is Israel without the Temple Mount, without Jerusalem, without Hebron?"

Asked to explain his feelings about Poland and Germany, he says: "The Pole sucks anti-Semitism from the breast of his mother, and his anti-Semitism is of the most vulgar kind, but with the German the story is different, and much more dangerous. The German's anti-Semitism is the essence of his culture. The German is of an extremely high spiritual level, and in this the German is very similar to the Jew – only the opposite."

If there's anti-Semitism in the world at large, it's the Jew's fault: "When Israel, in the 1967 War, kills tens of thousands of Egyptian soldiers and conquers the Golan Heights and the West Bank, what happens? Huge love for Israel in Europe! Check what I just said to you. It's amazing! When the Jews come back to their land and behave like the owners of the land, anti-Semitism goes away. But when the Jews are willing to give away the heart of their land to the Arabs, anti-Semitism rises. The Oslo Accords brought with them the Islamic suicide bombers. And if not for the handshake between Rabin and Arafat, the Twin Towers would still be standing today. Do you hear what I am saying to you?"

*   *   *

I do, and I drive to Tel Aviv to see Yitzhak Rabin's daughter, former MK Dalia Rabin, and hear what she has to say. I ask her a general question, to define "Israel" for me, and she gladly obliges.

"Same as other nations, where people get killed for a parking space,

only we have a small country, where the population is very condensed, geographically and socially, and everybody knows everybody. This, I think, is actually what makes us different, unique. Israel is not America, where a child in Atlanta shoots his classmates and we don't know who he is. Here in Israel it is everybody's business what you ate for breakfast.

"There's another thing here that makes us unique: We don't *mefar-ganim*. Now, this is a word so unique to us that you can't even translate it. [It's rooted in the Yiddish *farginen*, which in turn comes from the German.] If one of us succeeds in anything we immediately say bad words about him. Our thinking goes like this: If you're doing well, we're sure that you have done something horrible."

Why are you like this?

"I don't know. It's in our DNA."

Really. Explain to me why the Israelis are like this –

"I have to think about this. I really don't know. But the fact is, we love only the underdogs. If you fail, we think that you're a wonderful person."

Why?

"This is who we are. Another thing that's 'Israeli' is this: Whatever I do is everybody's business. You walk on the street and people say to you things like: Your hair doesn't look good. Your eyes look like this, your ass looks like that. Here people get inside your veins, as if that were their natural place to be. Israelis have this sense and feeling of togetherness; we are of one nation, one family, and it is my business if you date somebody. There is no distance here."

* * *

Being in Tel Aviv I take the opportunity of checking out an item I have on my list: finding out who is funding Israeli nonfiction films. The New Fund for Cinema and TV (NFCT), a fund that caters to documentary filmmakers, is having an event in the city today, and I go to meet them. The NFCT folks are the people who funded, together

with EU friends, *5 Broken Cameras*, which depicts a violent IDF in Bil'in, a film that went on to win an Oscar Nomination.

And this is what the person in charge tells me: "My estimation: 80 percent of Israeli-made documentary films that are political are coproduced with Europeans, and when I say 'European' I mean mainly the Germans, who on average fund 40 percent of the cost per film."

Germans again.

They just can't stop recruiting Jews who speak badly of themselves.

If German TV or film producers put on such films on their own there would be a huge outcry against them, blaming them – rightly – for anti-Semitism. To bypass this hurdle, German producers smartly finance Jews to do their dirty work. Sad.

Gate Fifty-Four

Show time: journalists join human rights activists in a staged demonstration involving firebombs and repeated calls to kill the Jews.

OUT OF THE BLUE SKY I GET AN E-MAIL FROM LINA, JIBRIL RAJOUB'S FAITHFUL assistant. She writes to me that Jibril would like me to join him the coming Friday, to celebrate with him the Palestinian Independence Day. It sounds strange to me that the Palestinians would invite foreigners to celebrate a Day of Independence with them, since they keep telling every foreigner that they have no state even if between themselves they say they have a state, but if Jibril invites me I go. People who know me tell me I shouldn't go. Jibril must know by now who you are, they argue, and his invitation to celebrate with him is a trap.

Logically they make sense, and so I decide not to follow their advice.

Come Friday, I go. I don't know what is the schedule of the festivities that are to take place soon, and neither does Lina. All I do know is this: Lina will pick me up at the Qalandiya checkpoint and from there we'll go to the Mövenpick Hotel in Ramallah.

When I arrive at Qalandiya checkpoint I see two young people, white people, who look like the classic European human rights types. Sorry to be saying this, which is so racist, but human rights folks have

this shine in their eyes that makes them look like brilliant idiots. No, really.

Anyway. Whatever. I approach them. I love young, white people. They are Hannah and Andy of Norway and England, respectively, and they are standing at this checkpoint to make sure the Arabs are not being treated badly by the Jews. They are members of the church-related EAPPI, they tell me, and they stand there four days a week, hours and hours per day. They have little mechanical counters, called clickers, and they click every time a person enters. Why do they have to know how many Arabs enter Israel is something the Virgin Mother may know, but not me.

How many people are actually crossing?

"'The average number of people entering Israel today is two-hundred per hour," they say.

They stand straight, like rulers, and they behave like lords of the manor. They make sure the Jews behave like humans, or else they will take action. Who anointed these kids to be guardians of justice is beyond me, but nobody is allowed to question Europeans, of whatever age, because they are the Lords.

It just occurs to me, don't laugh, that human rights activists are the biggest racists there are. Really, I'm not kidding. The normal racist fights within his own territory, wishing that his land be cleansed of those he hates. He is misguided, and his thoughts and deeds are deplorable, but at least he has a selfish motive: he wants his land and to be only his land. No KKK member, for example, is dedicating his life to clearing Turkey of Turks.

The European NGO folks are different. The Jew they are fighting does not reside in their territory, for he lives thousands of miles away, and yet, these Europeans travel thousands of miles to get the Jew – wherever they find him. I try to dig a bit deeper into these loveable kids.

What made you come to the Holy Land to start with? Was it some kind of a religious calling, a revelation?

The answer is, well, yes and no. Andy is a churchgoer and this is part of his religious service, he says with a sacred smile. Israel treats Bedouins badly and he is here to help them.

I don't see any Bedouin here, but why bother looking? We are all Bedouin.

This kid doesn't even know that he has mixed up the Bedouin issue with the Palestinian issue. As far as he is concerned, there is a Jew out there and he wants to catch him.

Fishermen love fish, Europeans love Jews, and both would like the object of their love well fried.

Hannah is an agnostic, she says, but she joined the church's human rights activities and that's how she got involved with EAPPI. She tells me that she used to have a Jewish boyfriend, but they broke up, and now she helps the Arabs.

It will be interesting to find out what happens with European girls who break up with their Palestinian boyfriends. Will they become Hasidic Jews?

To an extent, she reminds me of the German girl I met in Al-Quds University. That girl was helping the Palestinians because "I fell in love with the Jewish people."

In any case, four days a week in the life of our cute whites don't add up to seven days a week. Are they doing some other things with their precious time besides clicking their clickers?

Yes, they are. When they don't stand guard here, they go to Arab villages, distribute business cards, and tell the Arabs thusly: If you have any problem with the Israelis, please call us.

Wow.

I'd have spent the whole day with these kids, but Lina the "Bedouin" arrives and I have to bid them goodbye.

The Bedouin and the German drive to the Mövenpick.

We get there in time for breakfast. I'm not hungry but I treat myself to cake and coffee. The coffee is delicious. I can't wait for the festivities to start!

* * *

My good friend Jibril Rajoub is here. We hug. I really like this guy. I tell him again what I have told him before: You should be the Palestinian president!

"Had I wanted," he tells me, "I would have been. But I don't want. I chose Abu Mazen [Mahmoud Abbas] to be the president. For me it's enough to be the King Maker."

This Jibril is an interesting guy, and it is slowly dawning on me that he may be almost as good an agent as I am. Looking around me I notice that the guests at this Mövenpick, at least today, are not your average hotel guests. I look for the people with suitcases and maps, the usual marks of tourists, but I can't spot any. This Mövenpick, it strangely registers in my head, could be the place where Jibril has his headquarters. Everybody moving about here, how funny, is connected in one way or another to "Abu Rami," the other name of Jibril Rajoub.

I go to get myself a Diet Coke. The man behind the bar asks me for my room number, and I answer: Jibril Rajoub. The man runs to give me my Coke, as if "Jibril Rajoub" were the number of a suite.

I want to check this HQ of a hotel further, but Lina says we must leave the hotel now because we are going to Jericho. Jericho? Well, why not? Maybe I'll finally get to see Rahav. A whore is better than a hundred Cokes.

About one full minute later Lina is told that we are going to Ni'lin, not Jericho. God knows where that is, but I hope they have a Mövenpick there as well, or a whore.

We leave the Mövenpick and Lina says that the buses are waiting for us.

Buses? I can fit in a car, why do I need buses?

Well, there is no time for questions. In the hotel's parking area I see a few buses, each packed with people. I start talking with some of them. Jibril, it turns out, has invited foreign nationals in the name of his Olympic sports office to spend some great time in Palestine's posh hotels. He's got the budget.

Who are these people? With whom am I going to celebrate Palestinian Independence Day? Well, here is a German-educated African from Tanzania, who speaks good German. Is he a footballer? Not really. He works for the Foreign Ministry of Tanzania. And here's another guy from South Africa. What kind of sports is he into? Well, his father is a diplomat. Next to them is this lady from Mexico; her sport specialty is being a member of a leftist party in her homeland. And then there are others, the usual suspects: Europeans. None of the people here is an athlete, but so what?

Lina and I mount one of the buses and start moving, bus after bus.

"Abu Ali," Lina says about ten minutes into the ride, "we are not going to Ni'lin, we're going to Bil'in."

Bil'in. Is it the same Bil'in as in Yoav's movie, with that man Jonathan Shapira and the tear gas? The place that is featured in the film *5 Broken Cameras*? The place Uri Avnery had a picture of on the big screen at his birthday party?

Yes, it is.

I wanted to see the "Bil'in Protests," the weekly demonstrations against the separation wall in Bil'in, after having watched Yoav's movie. I checked for information about them and ways of how to get there, and then I found this article in the *New York Times*, dated June 2011, stating that the IDF had moved the wall away from its original location and that the weekly demonstrations had ceased.

What is in Bil'in? I ask Lina.

"Protest."

Protest? Aren't we all supposed to go to an Independence Day party?

It takes me seconds to understand. This *is* the party.

The *New York Times* may have decided well over two years ago that the demonstrations in Bil'in were over, only the demonstrators here obviously don't read the *New York Times*.

The mood in my bus is indeed celebratory. A Palestinian partygoer who has joined us asks me where I am from. I, Abu Ali, am from Germany, I tell him. And, as usual, he immediately loves me. "Hitler should have taught us what to do with the Jews, how to be thorough," he tells me passionately. I am used to Hitler references almost every time I tell a Palestinian that I'm German, but this is a new way of connecting the Hitler and Germany dots.

The landscapes revealing themselves to us as we are driving on are breathtaking: hills and roads intermingling, gorgeous white stone houses surrounded by greenish-brownish olive trees and impressively imaginative architecture. What richness of land, what beauty of hills, what gorgeousness of sands. I wish this ride would never end, but when each of us is given a Palestinian flag to carry, I know that soon it will. Why the flags? Well, we are to walk with a flag of Palestine on the barren hills of Bil'in for all to see.

I have never carried a flag, of any country, but it's good to start somewhere.

*   *   *

Our buses come to a stop and we dismount; more cars and more vans arrive in Bil'in and their passengers get off as well. I see many whites among them: "War Veterans" from the US of A, and French, Irish and, of course, Norwegian and German NGO angels. God bless the West. Some of these whites are wearing Hermes clothes mixed with Palestinian clothes, such as Keffiyehs, which they wear with extra love.

Will I ever live to see European human rights activists wearing Hasidic clothes, and be proud as hell for doing so? Would be real cool to see a Norwegian activist with a *shtreimel* and *tsitsis* and a German activist with the special Meah Shearim uniform of the Golden Chosen. Chances are, I believe, that I'll get to ride al-Buraq before my eyes see European activists with *shtreimel*s.

Slowly but surely a show gets into shape here, and the various actors take up their positions. First are the news people, journalists of European and Arab media. Carrying big cameras and small, microphones and other equipment, they move into their position on the "stage." One of the news media I recognize easily is the British Sky News. I used to think that news follows events, but I guess it's the other way around. As I can see here, journalists are actually the main players, and only after they have taken their position the rest of the people do as well. Funnily, "Made for TV" gets a fresh new meaning here.

Right next to me I see kids selling some interesting goods: nose covers.

What?

Yeah. The nose covers, one of the kids who is trying to convince me to get rid of my shekels in his behalf, explains to me will protect me from the gas canisters that the Jews will soon throw in our direction.

"Protest," I learn, is a business here. Around me I see various goods being sold by Bil'in villagers: Nose covers, keffiyehs, more flags, onions against tear gas, and other goodies.

Each person here, it slowly transpires, has a unique role to play in the show. In other words: everybody here is an actor. And everything works in stages: Journalists take positions, kids sell goods, and the choir – praying elders – is now moving into place. This last group is taking their position on prayer mats, which were laid under a tree in the hill before we arrived.

The acting stage is the bare ground, a huge stage.

Quite interesting.

And these are the locations: Journalists are positioned in front with big "Press" costumes on their bodies, next to them are the 'shabab,' Arab youth, and behind them are the tourists and the choir. The praying choir, all Arab, are under the tree, tourists are to their right.

The Prologue of this play starts right now. Tourists taking photos of themselves and of each other, complete with flags and keffiyehs, as the Arabs are listening to a Friday sermon by an imam. The imam holds a microphone, which is connected to huge loudspeakers mounted on a nearby van, and he shouts: "This is our land, a holy land that belongs only to Arab Muslims. No others are to be here. This is Arab land. This is Muslim land. This is the land of the Prophet!"

It is good to have this sound effect, because a show should have good sound instruments.

Lefty whites on the right hold big banners against Jewish racism, at the same exact moment the imam shouts juicy racist treasures in Arabic. The two groups, praying Arabs and keffiyeh-dressed foreigners, make for a very interesting combo.

Prologue continues. The Arab prayer-choir men stay in place while the foreigners start moving. Most of the foreigners are young, but some are quite old and they can hardly walk on the uneven paths of the hills. One of them, in a wheelchair, is maneuvering his way between stones in a heart-rending show of defiance against the horrible Jews down one of the hills nearby.

Yes, there are Jews there. Soldiers. About ten altogether.

Journalists do the last sound and light check, and will soon be ready for Curtain.

*   *   *

Time to start scene one.

Carrying a Palestinian flag, I walk closer to the soldiers, to get a good view of the situation.

Curtain.

The youngsters, Shabab, start their sling shot show, throwing as many stones as they can at the soldiers.

Nothing happens.

Heavier stones are then hurled at the soldiers, this time in the oldest and simplest way of throwing stones: the Shabab pick stones from the ground, as heavy as they can, and throw them.

No response yet from the Jews

Act 1, scene 2:

The Shabab throw firebombs at the soldiers.

A soldier responds with a tear gas canister into the air. I guess this is a warning shot.

Scene 2 is over; scene 3 is about to start.

TV cameras shoot pictures. Shabab continue with more shots and IDF soldiers respond with a barrage of tear gas canisters.

Stupid me, how didn't I think of it, I get the first portion. I move away fast, but I'm in the midst of the barrage. I breathe harder and harder and my eyes get quite tearful. I never thought of it, stupid me, but there's a reason why this is called tear gas.

Right ahead of me is a Palestinian ambulance, donated to Palestine by the Swiss people, the famous neutral people of the planet. I get myself inside it, and I feel like vomiting. I spit all over the Swiss ambulance. Thank God this is not Al-Quds here, or the Waqf would have shot me for blasphemy.

I think of the ambulance I saw in Zfat, donated by American Jews, which aids in saving wounded Syrians, as compared with this ambulance, gift of the Swiss, which aids in shooting Israelis.

In any case, I get a little piece of cloth that was before soaked in alcohol and am told to put it close to my nose. What a miraclemaker this alcohol is! In seconds the effects of the gas are gone. The team of this ambulance is very dedicated to European naïve idiots like me and I'm sincerely thankful to the paramedics for helping me out and I soon get off the ambulance.

I pass by the praying actors, who are staying away from the action, and realize how smart they are. Why should they get hurt? Let the foreigners get hurt, it is the best thing for the Cause! And indeed, this formula works like magic. The German-educated Tanzanian Foreign Office official says: "When you criticize Jews they say you are anti-Semite, but now I see that it's true what they say about the Jews!"

I'm not sure what act or scene is now playing, I lost count inside the ambulance, but the exchange between stones plus firebombs and gas canisters involves greater quantities of flying objects on both sides and I assume that we might have reached the climax point of the show. We are probably in Act II somewhere.

I go to sit with the Arabs, away from the tourists and the Shabab, and I speak a bit with Jibril. "Hitler could learn from them," he says, speaking of the Jews. I have heard this line before from him, but here it has extra weight.

Happy music is now playing from the moving loudspeakers, ever higher in volume, and this fire show now turns into a musical.

Lina's daughter calls her. "Why didn't you tell me you were going to Bil'in?" she asks her mom. "I'd like so much to be there!" It's funny to listen to this. On the one hand the Palestinians complain about the IDF throwing tear gas at them, and on the other hand they're so sad when they miss the tear gas.

Music stops for a few seconds. We are probably at the end of Act II.

"Allah is with you. Kill them!" a command from the loudspeakers is now being heard, at a volume that could potentially waken Rahav of back to life, had this demonstration taken place in Jericho. The loudspeakers, directed at the Shabab, repeat over and again as loud as can be: "Allah is with you. Kill them! Allah is with you. Kill them! Allah is with you. Kill them! Allah is with you. Kill them!"

"You" means Arabs, "them" means Jews.

Allahu Akbar.

I light up a cigarette. Then another. And another.

One of the Praying Arabs, sitting pretty under a tree, urges me to run to the foreigners and throw stones at the Jews. I tell him what I've learned long ago from the Haredi of Israel: prayer is stronger than missiles. I'm no fool. I am Abu Ali.

Act III, scene 4.

Sky News is leaving the arena.

Act III, scene 5.

Slowly, the other journalists and video teams start making their way out.

5 Broken Cameras, the Oscar-nominated film about the Bil'in protests, "shows life in one Palestinian village," the *New York Times* writes in a glorifying review of this film. If you sit in New York and watch a docu-film you may believe that what you see is real. When you are here in Bil'in, and if you understand Arabic, you know better. "The Bil'in protests" is a show, a show of "Allah is with you. Kill them!" Personally,

I don't believe in "Death to the Arabs" and I don't believe in "Death to the Jews," even if the latter has been nominated for an Oscar.

It's time to go home and leave the praying Jews, Shlomo Sand's Jews, behind.

What a wonderful Independence Day.

Our bus takes us back to the Mövenpick, and I bid goodbye to Jibril. I know that this is probably our last time together. He is bound to find out one day or another that I'm not the Aryan he has come to believe me to be, and on that day our short friendship will be completely over. Still, I like him and it's hard for me to know that I won't hug this man again. I'll miss him, a man made of pride and charisma. He orders a car to take me back to Jerusalem and we part ways. On the way to Jerusalem I stop at a Palestinian grocery store to pick some good Palestinian olive oil. I look at my new bottle and notice this line: This product was not made by the occupiers.

* * *

Back in Jerusalem I mount the light rail, the tramway that travels through the heart of Jerusalem, from the Jewish neighborhoods in the west to the Arab neighborhoods in the east. At every stop, announcements are made in three languages: Hebrew, Arabic, and English. These three languages, what a sweet miracle, live in complete harmony inside this train. It touches me deeply.

There's another miracle that I suddenly pay attention to, so many months into my journey: Hebrew. Millions speak of the resurrection of Jesus but almost nobody is paying attention to the other resurrection, the resurrection of the Hebrew language. So many here speak Hebrew, Jews and non-Jews, a language that practically died two thousand years ago.

The train is packed with Arabs, Jews, and tourists who are on top of one another. I like this density. When we push one another, however soft or hard, we notice and we feel that all of us are of the same material: flesh, blood, and nerves.

This light rail should be the dream, the symbol of any person honestly caring for human rights, as this little miracle on iron tracks brings people together in the most imaginable way humanly possible. But no, human-righters are dead set against this train. The UN Human Rights Council, in a resolution approved by 46 to 1 (the USA being the 1), states: "Mindful that Israel is a party to the Fourth Geneva Convention... [the UN] expresses its grave concern [about] the Israeli decision to establish and operate a tramway between West Jerusalem and the Israeli settlement of Pisgat Zeev, which is in clear violation of international law and relevant United Nations resolutions."

How exactly is the Fourth Geneva Convention in conflict with a light rail? The ICRC, the International Committee of the Red Cross, which states that it "acts as the guardian of International Humanitarian Law," being the author of all of the Geneva Conventions, is an organization I should get to know better. It is "the most influential of the NGOs," Lieutenant Colonel S. said to me at the time, and I like the word *influential*.

I get off the light rail and walk over to my stray cats.

Gate Fifty-Five

The end: the Red Cross vs. the Jewish state. How white vans with little red crosses roam this land on a crusade to get all its Jews out.

MORNING COMES AND I SHOW UP AT THE ICRC OFFICES IN SHEIKH JARRAH, Jerusalem. The ICRC has an office in Tel Aviv as well, but that office

is "only for political reasons to show that we don't recognize Israeli sovereignty in Jerusalem," an official tells me.

Sheikh Jarrah. I know this place from the time I lived in Jerusalem, a neighborhood that I also kept hearing about long after I had left as well. Sheikh Jarrah is right by the 1967 border that divided Jerusalem at the time. For years, even after Israel took over east Jerusalem in the 1967 War, Sheikh Jarrah remained an Arab-only neighborhood. But quite a lot of years ago an Israeli Sephardic Community organization claimed ownership to seventeen properties in the neighborhood and presented documents of ownership dating back to Ottoman time. Their claim was contested in various Israeli courts, a process that took years, and in 2009, following a Supreme Court decision that recognized their right, Jews moved into three houses.

The presence of Jews in the neighborhood was followed by international condemnations and weekly demonstrations by Arabs and leftist Jews. The international community and the demonstrators demanded that Jews should not be allowed to live anywhere in Sheikh Jarrah. Why would the international community get busy with three little houses is an issue that Franz Kafka should have dealt with, not me.

An officer with the organization shows up to greet me, and together we go to the van that will take us to Jenin, where the ICRC has been active since 1975.

While we're driving, the man talks. "When they demolish houses we come together with the PRC [Palestinian Red Crescent] and offer hygiene kits and tents to the people who have just lost their homes. All the buildings in Sheikh Jarrah (other than the three houses mentioned above) have 'vacate' orders and Israel will put settlers there."

I don't know this man but by the tone of his voice I can tell that he really doesn't like the Jews. Thank God I'm German.

"They [Israel] will demolish your house if you cannot prove ownership, but to prove ownership is very hard because the original papers might have been filed with the Ottomans, with the British or even with the Israelis, but the papers are somewhere in some safe. If you cannot prove ownership for the past thirty years, they will force you out. This is not all: if you add a balcony to your house they will evict you and demolish your house."

This is really bad. How many homes have been demolished in Sheikh Jarrah so far?

He tries to add them all up in his mind and by the end of the process he comes up with the exact sum: zero.

One of us must have had one shot of brandy too many. I hope it's not him, because he's at the wheel.

* * *

We drive through gorgeous landscapes, which fill my heart with joy, and my new friend feeds me with more info: "To be a full member of the ICRC, Israel must remove all of its ambulance bases from disputed areas."

What happens if a person gets sick in the disputed areas?

"In cases of emergency, Israel would have to coordinate entry with us to those areas."

In other words, if a Jewish settler on some West Bank mountain has a heart attack, he'll have to wait until the ICRC approves an Israeli ambulance to come over from, let's say, Tel Aviv.

Swiss neutrality.

My new friend continues to talk: "Israel is also not allowed to use its emblem, the Star of David, outside its own country, because this symbol is a religious symbol, it's a Jewish sign."

Isn't the Half Moon emblem, used by the PRC, an Islamic symbol?

"Yes, it is."

Isn't the PRC using this emblem?

"Yes."

But the Half Moon can be used anywhere?

"Yes."

Let me understand, isn't the ICRC against the use of religious symbols?

"No, this is different."

Why?

He can't explain this to me, but I think it's very simple: Islam starts with an "I" and Judaism starts with a "J."

Quite a number of years ago in New York, I attended an event with New York Jewish leaders and then-Senator Hillary Rodham Clinton, in which she expressed her satisfaction with the Red Star of David's acceptance as a full member by the ICRC. (The Red Star of David is called the MDA – *Magen David Adom* in Hebrew.) At the time it struck me as just another attempt by a New York politician to endear herself to the Jews living in her state, but now that I'm riding this ICRC van I become more curious about the ICRC membership issue. I write a note to myself to further investigate this matter.

As the ride continues, we talk about the Fourth Geneva Convention and other delicate, happy issues.

The Fourth Geneva Convention, created in 1949, was like the other Geneva Conventions the brainchild and creation of the ICRC, and it has become part of International Law. Here, in this part of the world, it dictates what Israel can, and cannot, do in the areas it captured in 1967. The ICRC, the man tells me, is the "guardian of International Humanitarian Law." The ICRC's decisions, though not legally binding, still end up being part and parcel of what is known as "International Law."

Interestingly, my new friend tells me that the ICRC also declared that Gaza, from which Israel withdrew in 2005, is still an Occupied Territory. This means, of course, that Israel is responsible for it and its citizens. If you live in Gaza and want to spend five years studying music, like Nadia, Israel will have to foot the bill.

Israel withdrew from Gaza; why is it still occupied?

"Because Israel closes its border to Gaza."

Syria closes the border to Israel. Is Syria, legally speaking, occupying Israel?

"That's different."

Why?

"Israel is blocking access to Gaza through international waters."

What's the difference between waters and dry land?

My man gets a headache from me and has no idea how to handle me.

Did the ICRC also declare Tibet and Cyprus, to cite two examples, as "occupied territories"?

"I'll have to come back to you on this. Contact me tomorrow."

Will do.

It just so happens, and this is happening with every new mountain we approach during this ride, that a new fact about the ICRC is being revealed to me. For example: if you want to be on the board of the ICRC you must be Swiss, otherwise forget it. In addition: the ICRC board meetings, where major issues are being decided, are private affairs of the board members, and the minutes of these meetings are not made public.

"I may be wrong on this. Put this on the list of questions," he tells me.

Will do.

Is there a supervising body that checks and examines the board's decisions?

Well, not really. In the lands of democracy and international laws, where checks and balances must be part and parcel of the game, there are exceptions. At the highest levels of decision-making bodies at the heart of democratic societies, dictators rule supreme.

We drive further and further, through ever-more-gorgeous landscapes with not one Jew in sight anywhere until we reach Jenin Refugee Camp, which is within the bigger city of Jenin. The camp is assisted primarily by the UNRWA (United Nations Relief and Works Agency for Palestine Refugees in the Near East), I'm told, and the ICRC has joined UNRWA's effort.

* * *

Israel left Jenin long ago, with all its soldiers. Why keep a refugee camp, now that the Palestinian government is the one controlling the area?

An old man, resident of the camp, answers: "Because we want to go back to where we came from!"

Where is that?

"Haifa."

Were you born in Haifa?

"No, I was born here. But my home is Haifa, which has been taken over by the Zionist terrorists."

Haifa is within the Israel of 1948. And without Haifa we can say goodbye to Israel. Is this what this man wants?

Of course.

I should have brought MK Ahmad Tibi along with us. It would be interesting to see if he would try to do something to this man's cellphone.

Instead of MK Tibi, a child comes by.

"Where are you from?" the older man asks him.

"Jenin."

"No! Where are you *from*?"

"Haifa!"

This is a show, generously financed by the UN. The UN and the ICRC employees here, Palestinian or European, nod in agreement at every "Haifa" mention, which goes against the grain of everything and anything these organizations say in public, but I prefer not to raise this issue. Instead, I ask the old man: Do you believe that you'll get back there, to Haifa?

"As much as I believe in Allah!"

More people come, including local ICRC employees, and we all chat. A bunch of Jenin men, young and old, tell me that they are all "refugees from Haifa." Good to know.

Sitting outside an UNRWA building in the camp, a local ICRC woman explains to me what the ICRC is doing in Jenin: "We support the UNRWA activities at their community center in the Jenin Refugee Camp. Today we are painting the center and its walls outside and we are going to provide the youngsters with soccer uniforms, with balls, and with various football-related needs. In general, we tell the people here who we are and what we do, such as our protection of the civilian population against violations of international laws by the Israelis. We tell them, to give you an example, that if any of them has been beaten at a checkpoint, he should come to us and report the incident. We also tell them to come to us in case anyone is violated by the Israeli forces."

Lieutenant Colonel S., who told me that the ICRC doesn't run to the press, is right, but only to an extent. The ICRC runs to the Haifa Refugees and incites them against the "Israeli forces." The ICRC doesn't tell them that according to "International Law" Haifa belongs to the "Israeli forces."

No. What they learn here is that they should keep guard against the forces, like the video-carrying couple in the Jewish part of Hebron, where kids throw stones at Jewish girls. If the "forces" try to stop them throwing stones, they take pictures and go to the good souls of the ICRC. In addition: yes, the ICRC doesn't run to the press. What they do instead is organize events for the press, as they are organizing this "event" for me just now.

As usual, the Jews prove themselves to be pretty naïve creatures.

Press or no press, I ask myself this question: Does the ICRC protect Palestinians or does it instigate them? And what exactly are the "UNRWA activities" that the ICRC is supporting? As far as I can see here, by the way the two interact, UNRWA and ICRC are Siamese twins.

UNRWA. They run schools for these Haifa Refugees, but what do they teach in these schools?

The UNRWA Community Center could provide a clue or two.

*　*　*

I enter the UNRWA Center's main hall, freshly painted by the ICRC. At the entrance there is a plaque with the name of this place: Hall of the Martyrs. I walk a few steps and then I see another hall, of the martyrs again. "Martyrs" in Palestinian culture means those who die in clashes with Israeli soldiers, or those who die while killing Jewish civilians, such as during suicide missions. I proceed to the library – yes, they have one here – and I see on the shelves a book I bought in Amman quite some time ago, a book I know to be anti-Semitic.

UNRWA, which claims to "provide assistance and protection for some five million Palestine refugees," is one of the cutest animals in the human rights zoo. It extends the definition of "refugee" to grand- and great-grandchildren of Arabs who once lived here.

To understand this process better, I interview a top UNRWA official to explain the process to me, and he tells me that the UN is extending refugee status to other international refugees as well, not only Palestinians, only he is short on details and instead sends me to "Google" on my own. When I ask him if Germans and Hungarians who fled certain geographical areas during WWII, or those who were ordered to leave their homes by the end of the war, are also refugees, including their great-grandchildren, he looks at me as if I have just lost my mind. When asked to tell me how many Palestinian refugees there are, not just those registered with UNRWA, he estimates that there are eleven million Palestinian refugees alive today.

And then I ask him the most important question one could ask this man: How many Arab refugees were there in 1948? In other words: How many "original" refugees – from which the UNRWA folks get the figure of five or eleven million today – actually existed at the time? Well, not that easy for UNRWA to answer. I'm immediately asked that our conversation be off the record, meaning that I can't name the official I'm interviewing and that I can't quote him directly.

And so, without directly quoting, here's the answer: UNRWA did not exist in 1948 and therefore UNRWA does not have the figures. Yep. Just like that. Very interesting, and very illuminating. The fact that one can ascertain that there are five (or eleven) million great-grandchildren without having the faintest idea how to prove it – in addition to this being a mathematical impossibility since original numbers are unknown – shows that UNRWA employs mathematical geniuses far smarter than Albert Einstein. Of course, if UNRWA keeps granting refugee status to every grandchild of every Palestinian it assumes to have lived – and all indications show that UNRWA folks will – we will soon have more Palestinian refugees in the world than Americans and Europeans combined.

But enough about UNRWA, at least for the moment.

An ICRC man approaches me to tell me that later on there will be a group session and that the ICRC people expect me to join the session. I say that I'd gladly do that.

Before the group session is to start, I meet a bunch of people, all locals. All, it soon becomes clear, have been to or have a family member living in one certain country: Germany. Yeah. In fact, there's even a neighborhood in east Jenin called "Germany," a proud Haifa Refugee tells me. One of the ladies here excitedly also tells me that "there is a monument, in central Jenin, for a fallen German plane from the World War. You should go and see it!"

Over and again, as in so many other instances in Palestine, these Haifa Refugees tell me how much they like Germany, the only country that knew how to deal with its Jews. Here in Jenin, in case I didn't know, refugee males share with me that they like German women very much.

A bunch of teenagers play soccer, wearing sports gear given them by the ICRC, and once the game is over, in just minutes, the ICRC people say that they would like me to talk with these teenagers. Why such a short soccer game? Well, it was just a show, for me to see and enjoy.

Do you have a girlfriend? I ask one of the teenagers.

"No," he says.

Would you like to have one?

"Yes."

Would you like your girlfriend to be from Jenin?

"No. I'd like to have a girl from Germany."

As I sit with the teenagers, ICRC folks come in to see and hear what I do with their kids. I just keep on. I ask the rest of the teenagers:

Would you also like to have German girlfriends? Anybody who does, raise your hands!

They all do.

"German women went through two world wars but still took good care of their children," an older man sitting nearby tells me.

And I, Abu Ali, have nothing left to say except: Yes, we Germans are the best.

*   *   *

As this goes on, some ICRC folks talk to each other on the side, I don't know what about, and then one of them comes to me and says: "The group session has been postponed to next month. Sorry." One of them, I can tell, has smartened up and has told the others that they were making fools of themselves. Haifa. Germany. Nazis. Is this what the ICRC would like to be made public? It would be better for them, much better, if they stop this show at once.

The UNRWA is in charge of education here. The ICRC is in charge of telling the UNRWA-educated kids of their rights. Soon these kids, and their families, will live in Haifa and in Jaffa, in Jerusalem and in Tel Aviv.

Fourth Geneva Convention.

International Law.

I take my time, sitting alone with my iPad, to learn more about the ICRC, but it's not that easy. The way the ICRC operates is more in line with the way you'd expect dark regimes to operate than an organization claiming to be a champion of human rights and democracy. Going over the materials they provide on their website, I realize that this organization, aided by top lawyers and sophisticated linguists on its payroll, uses language designed to hide rather than reveal. Yet, miraculously, the ICRC is held in highest esteem and its decisions are blindly accepted.

Examples:

- In 1990, the UN General Assembly awarded the ICRC an "observer status" in the UN.
- Security Council Resolution 446 states in part: "Affirming once more the Fourth Geneva Convention . . . is applicable to the Arab territories occupied by Israel since 1967, including Jerusalem." This interpretation of the convention can come from only one source: the ICRC, the people who created the convention ages ago and the ones who keep interpreting its various articles as time moves along and as they see fit.

Powerful Cross.

These guys are major players, not just drivers of cute vans, and they flex their muscles. If I'm not mistaken the ICRC, which defines itself (Article 2 on legal status) as a "legal personality," was the first to define the West Bank, Gaza, and east Jerusalem as "Occupied Territories."

I write a note to myself to ask for clarification about this issue in my e-mail tomorrow.

As I'm driven back to Jerusalem in the same Red Cross van that brought me here, I feel the muscles it flexes on the road: Every Jew is afraid of us. Every Arab honors us. God is dead, ICRC is alive.

I shouldn't be proud of it but I, too, start getting into this power thing. When you drive a Red Cross car in Israel, you feel powerful. Nobody stops a Red Cross car. This is no ambulance, dear; this is a Swiss machine that turns you into a King Herod. When you are inside a Red Cross car, you look at Israeli soldiers with spite, like one would look at a slave. You're the ruler here, not them.

What can I tell you? If you happen to be an egotistical maniac or a ruthless operator, and you want to see your dream of countries with no Jews come alive, come here to Israel and join the Red Cross. If for some reason you don't like little red crosses but still have a yearning for power, you can fulfill all your most sadistic heart's desires by becoming an EAPPI human rights activist with a clicker. Whichever of them you end up joining, Red Cross or EAPPI, you will be viewed by all nations and by all nationals as the kindest, loveliest, and most humane of all living people.

* * *

Following my excursion with the ICRC, I sit down to chat with Israel's Deputy Foreign Minister, Zev Elkin. During our conversation he tells me that the Red Star of David, which is a private organization, is a full member of the ICRC, following an agreement the MDA reached with the PRC (Palestine Red Crescent Society) years ago not to operate in the West Bank and in east Jerusalem.

Zev tells me that many east Jerusalem Arabs are very upset about this, since PRC ambulances transfer patients only to Arab hospitals and not to Jewish ones, which are known to be far superior. Zev also tells me, by the way, that the American Secretary of State John Kerry, who keeps popping into Israel every few days, is a man influenced by European thinking and that this is why he is bent on solving the Arab-Israeli conflict by hook or by crook. Interesting.

* * *

From my abode in Jerusalem with the cats I submit questions to the

ICRC in writing, as I said I would. Initially they try to avoid responding in detail, but following an intense face-to-face conversation with the ICRC's Head of Delegation in "Israel and the Occupied Territories," Juan Pedro Schaerer, and with the ICRC's head of Legal Department, Anton Camen, I'm promised that the ICRC will be specific and direct and that they will answer all my questions. Not surprisingly, their promise is only partially honored. Following are excerpts from my correspondence with the ICRC:

Can non-Swiss be on the board of ICRC?

"No."

According to ICRC, are Cyprus or Tibet, to cite two examples, occupied territory?

"In principle the ICRC will first and foremost share its legal reading bilaterally and confidentially with the parties in a conflict.... The ICRC could later communicate its classification publicly."

Would it be correct to say that the ICRC publicly declared the 1967 areas captured by Israel as "occupied" while it did not do the same with Cyprus and Tibet?

"I do not have anything to add."

Was the ICRC the first to determine that territories captured by Israel in 1967 are "occupied territories"?

"No. The first to consider these territories occupied territories was probably the IDF."

In conversations with the Israeli army, the IDF has disputed this assertion. Yet, leaving this aside for the moment, was the ICRC second in declaring the areas in question as "occupied"?

"Unfortunately for your continuing requests, I have to put main priority on other issues now."

Not including emergency expenditures (such as floods, earthquakes etc), could you please supply a list of the top-ten countries where ICRC is operating for the past ten years, in terms of moneys spent?

In response, I'm advised to find out on my own.

In one of the e-mails from the ICRC I'm also told that the ICRC shares its analysis "with state parties to the Geneva Convention and they follow our reading of the law, with the exception of Israel."

You don't need to be a lawyer to understand what this means. China and the ICRC see eye to eye on Tibet. Russia and the ICRC see eye to eye on the war in Chechnya. The ICRC and all the nations, in fact, see eye to eye no matter what the issue, "with the exception of Israel."

Damn Jews.

I don't know why a bunch of Swiss-only nationals, individuals who were never elected in any democratic process and whose meetings are secretive, have so much power. This is so absurd that it's not funny anymore. The fact that anything a country has signed with the ICRC should not be treated in the same manner as when a country signs a document with Google or Apple, and that an agreement signed with the ICRC should be subjected to various UN resolutions or actions is, I think, absurd.

Yet, no matter what I say, the ICRC has unparalleled power. And what does the ICRC do with its power? The ICRC invests great sums of money and effort in finding fault with the Israelis, the Jews. Its agents traverse and scour the width and the breadth of this land in endless search of stories that would paint Israel as a warmonger and war criminal, its "ambulances" roam the mountains and the hills of this land in protection of Haifa Refugees lusting after young German women, and its scholars warm their office seats dreaming of Juden-frei lands and composing sophisticated tales masked as reports that brilliantly hide their hatred.

By itself, the story of ICRC is not extremely important. After all, why should we waste time on a few Swiss chocolate bankers? But nothing is more symbolic of our Zeitgeist than our culture's image of both the ICRC and Israel. It is in this Internet age, when people believe that all information is accessible to them, that they choose to see the Red Cross as a society of human angels and Israel as a bunch animalistic devils.

We, the human race, have a perfect record of lying to ourselves, with the Internet as without it.

The ICRC, of course, is not alone.

UNRWA and the various European NGOs operating here are their natural allies. The age-old story of Europe's hatred of the Jew is continuing to this very day with just one minor adjustment: In the days of old, Europeans didn't have to get on a plane to fight Jews, who were then living as guests in their countries and at their mercy, but today they must travel the extra mile to satisfy their thirst to hurt the Jews. One would hope that in our "enlightened" era Europeans would no longer have so much hatred and that Germany, with its history as a leader of Jewish annihilation, would not be heading this European herd of Jew haters – but the inexplicable hatred of the Jew refuses to die.

Add to this pot of senseless hatred the self-hating Jews in this land and you'll know why Michel, the Catholic architect married to a Jewish Israeli lady, wants a plane ticket out. My only question of him, in case he plans to take his Jewish wife along for the ride, is this: Where are you planning to hide her?

Israelis rarely admit that they have fears, especially a fear for their very existence. To know what they really feel deep inside their hearts, at their subconscious level, you will have to catch them in their nakedness. Ran Rahav, the PR guru of the rich, provides for just such an opportunity days before I leave Israel. Kindly, he secures a seat for me to a sold-out concert by Israeli superstar Eyal Golan at Israel's prime concert hall, the Palace of Culture in central Tel Aviv.

Eyal has recently been entangled in various police investigations, but the well-to-do Israelis, those who can afford the astronomically high ticket prices of his concerts, have a need to be with him, no matter what. This is clearly evident during one of his songs, his last for the evening, when the thousands rise to stand as one person, joining him to sing with him these words: "The most important thing is to not be afraid... The King of the Universe will guard us from all others... The nation of Israel will never give up; we will stay on the map. Always!"

What is going on with these people? I ask myself. This year marks sixty-six years from the establishment of the State of Israel, why is it that they find the need to jointly declare that they will "stay on the map"? It is in this moment, the moment when the richer of society practically vow not to be erased from the map, that the Israeli's subconscious fear is being exposed in all its nakedness. Concertgoers in New York and Berlin, Moscow and Tokyo don't vow that they won't be erased from the map; the Jews in Tel Aviv do.

Epilogue

LEDERHOSEN BACK IN THE SUITCASE – THEY WEREN'T MUCH HELP – I'M READY
to leave. I started my journey in the most gorgeous of architectures
in Jerusalem, and I end it in the most ravished of places, in Jenin. I
started with Kings, David and Herod, and I end with Haifa Refugees.
When I started the journey I was awed, when I end it I'm dismayed;
when I started my journey laughter was my companion, when I end
it a tear joins me; when I started this journey hope was my neighbor,
when I end it despair stares me in the face.

Witnessing the tremendous investments and endless attempts of
the Europeans, not to mention the Germans, all geared to undermine
the Jews in this land, in Israel, was an extremely unsettling experience.
Being showered with love by the Arabs, just because they thought I
was an Aryan, a German, was very discomforting. Watching the Jews
and seeing how powerless they are, even now that they have their own
state, was distressing.

If logic is any guide, Israel will not survive. Besieged by hate from
without and from within, no land can survive for very long.

Miraculously, the Jews have built one of the most sophisticated,
intense, beautiful countries of our time, but what are they doing to
keep it? They hate themselves, they belie themselves, they are full of
fears and many of them rush to get another passport; they want to go

back to Poland, to Austria, to Germany – lands where their forefathers were hunted down and killed.

And what am I doing? Just the same: I am going back to Germany.

Am I a Jew just like them? Am I not Tobi the German? Am I not Abu Ali? My name is, sorry, Tuvia. Goodness of God. What a joke. A joke, I fear, only the Chosen People will truly comprehend.

Adios, my sweet cats. You, of all creatures of this land, have a clear and sensible direction: milk and tuna. I am thankful that we met, for you have provided me with companionship in a land I felt so alone in. I am leaving this land, and I am leaving you. You will fare better here. You are Jewish cats, stay with your kind. Enjoy this land, my stray cats, as long as it lasts. I'll miss you terribly. Shalom.

Tuvia Tenenbom
Israel, 2014

Author's Note

THIS BOOK IS NOT A WORK OF FICTION; THE PEOPLE MENTIONED HERE AND THE stories told herein are real. Unless otherwise stated, all names of people and locations are real.

The various stories mentioned on these pages, historical or otherwise, are as told to me by the people I met and do not always reflect my opinion. But the findings in this book, such as the likelihood of Israel's eventual demise or the various NGOs' brutal campaigns against Israel inside the country's borders, are mine. The main findings in this book, none of which I even thought of before starting my journey, are based on countless encounters in every possible location, at times taken at serious risk to my life.

I am well aware that these findings differ greatly from many other findings, done by other people, on this very subject matter – and rightly so. The findings in these pages, let me remind you, are not based on abstract theories and fancy stories concocted in the comfort of remote labs or refreshments-heavy lecture halls.

The journey recorded here took many months to complete, starting in 2013 and ending in 2014.

My deep thanks to all interviewees, those who tried to help me and those who tried to manipulate me, those who were honest with me and those who lied to me, those who knew me by my real name and those who knew me by my other names: "Tobi the German" and "Abu Ali."

Tuvia Tenenbom